S0-BZU-754

JOURNAL FOR THE STUDY OF THE NEW TESTAMENT SUPPLEMENT SERIES
120

Executive Editor
Stanley E. Porter

Editorial Board
Richard Bauckham, David Catchpole, R. Alan Culpepper,
Margaret Davies, James D.G. Dunn, Craig A. Evans, Stephen Fowl,
Robert Fowler, Robert Jewett, Elizabeth Struthers Malbon

Sheffield Academic Press
Sheffield

Approaches to New Testament Study

edited by
Stanley E. Porter
and David Tombs

Journal for the Study of the New Testament
Supplement Series 120

BS
2393
. A67
1995

Copyright © 1995 Sheffield Academic Press

Published by Sheffield Academic Press Ltd
Mansion House
19 Kingfield Road
Sheffield, S11 9AS
England

Printed on acid-free paper in Great Britain
by Bookcraft
Midsomer Norton, Somerset

British Library Cataloguing in Publication Data

A catalogue record for this book is available
from the British Library

ISBN 1-85075-567-1

CONTENTS

ACKNOWLEDGMENTS

We wish to thank the many different people who have contributed to the writing of this book. In particular we wish to acknowledge: the readiness of our contributors to combine insight and scholarship with accessibility and relevance; the energy and enthusiasm of colleagues, partners and friends who have assisted in what is presented here; the practical help and support of our respective institutions; and ever helpful cooperation of Sheffield Academic Press, especially for their speedy and expeditious publishing of the manuscript.

The Editors

ABBREVIATIONS

AB	Anchor Bible
ABR	*Australian Biblical Review*
AnBib	Analecta biblica
ANRW	*Aufstieg und Niedergang der römischen Welt*
ASR	*American Sociological Review*
ATR	*Anglican Theological Review*
BA	*Biblical Archaeologist*
BBR	*Bulletin for Biblical Research*
BETL	Bibliotheca ephemeridum theologicarum lovaniensium
BI	*Biblical Interpretation*
Bib	*Biblica*
BibRev	*Biblical Review*
BIS	Biblical Interpretation Series
BJRL	*Bulletin of the John Rylands University Library of Manchester*
BJS	Brown Judaic Studies
BNTC	Black's New Testament Commentaries
BT	*The Bible Translator*
BTB	*Biblical Theology Bulletin*
CBQ	*Catholic Biblical Quarterly*
CBQMS	*Catholic Biblical Quarterly*, Monograph Series
ConBNT	Coniectanea biblica, New Testament
CRINT	Compendia rerum iudaicarum ad Novum Testamentum
CSR	*Christian Scholar's Review*
DJD	Discoveries in the Judaean Desert
ETL	*Ephemerides theologicae lovanienses*
EvQ	*Evangelical Quarterly*
ExpTim	*Expository Times*
FFNT	Foundations and Facets: New Testament
FN	*Filología Neotestamentaria*
FRLANT	Forschungen zur Religion und Literatur des Alten und Neuen Testaments
HBT	*Horizons in Biblical Theology*
HNTC	Harper's New Testament Commentaries
HTR	*Harvard Theological Review*
HUCA	*Hebrew Union College Annual*
ICC	International Critical Commentary

IDBSup	*Interpreter's Dictionary of the Bible*, Supplementary Volume
IEJ	*Israel Exploration Journal*
Int	*Interpretation*
JAAR	*Journal of the American Academy of Religion*
JANES	*Journal of the Ancient Near Eastern Society*
JBL	*Journal of Biblical Literature*
JETS	*Journal of the Evangelical Theological Society*
JJS	*Journal of Jewish Studies*
JSJ	*Journal for the Study of Judaism*
JSNT	*Journal for the Study of the New Testament*
JSNTSup	*Journal for the Study of the New Testament*, Supplement Series
JSOT	*Journal for the Study of the Old Testament*
JSOTSup	*Journal for the Study of the Old Testament*, Supplement Series
JSPSup	*Journal for the Study of the Pseudepigrapha*, Supplement Series
JTS	*Journal of Theological Studies*
KEK	H.A.W. Meyer (ed.), Kritisch-exegetischer Kommentar über das Neue Testament
LADOC	Latin America Documentation
LCL	Loeb Classical Library
LT	*Literature and Theology*
MeyerK	H.A.W. Meyer (ed.), Kritisch-exegetischer Kommentar über das Neue Testament
Neot	*Neotestamentica*
NGS	New Gospel Studies
NICNT	New International Commentary on the New Testament
NIDNTT	C. Brown (ed.), *The New International Dictionary of New Testament Theology*
NovT	*Novum Testamentum*
NovTSup	*Novum Testamentum*, Supplements
NRSV	New Revised Standard Version
NTL	New Testament Library
NTS	*New Testament Studies*
NTTS	New Testament Tools and Studies
OBO	Orbis biblicus et orientalis
Rel	*Religion*
ResQ	*Restoration Quarterly*
RSV	Revised Standard Version
SANT	Studien zum Alten und Neuen Testament
SBL	Society of Biblical Literature
SBLDS	SBL Dissertation Series
SBLMS	SBL Monograph Series
SBLSBS	SBL Sources for Biblical Study
SBLSP	SBL Seminar Papers
SBS	Stuttgarter Bibelstudien

SBT	Studies in Biblical Theology
SJLA	Studies in Judaism in Late Antiquity
SJT	*Scottish Journal of Theology*
SNTSMS	Society for New Testament Studies Monograph Series
SocQuart	*Sociological Quarterly*
SPB	Studia postbiblica
STDJ	Studies on the Texts of the Desert of Judah
THES	*Times Higher Education Supplement*
THKNT	Theologischer Handkommentar zum Neuen Testament
TLS	Theology and Liberation Series
TLZ	*Theologische Literaturzeitung*
TRev	*Theologische Revue*
TS	*Theological Studies*
TSK	*Theologische Studien und Kritiken*
TU	Texte und Untersuchungen
UBS	United Bible Societies
UBSGNT	United Bible Societys' *Greek New Testament*
VTSup	*Vetas Testamentum*, Supplements
WBC	Word Biblical Commentary
WMANT	Wissenschaftliche Monographien zum Alten und Neuen Testament
WUNT	Wissenschaftliche Untersuchungen zum Neuen Testament
ZTK	*Zeitschrift für Theologie und Kirche*

LIST OF CONTRIBUTORS

Beverley Clack
Roehampton Institute London, England

Kent D. Clarke
Roehampton Institute London, England

Craig A. Evans
Trinity Western University, Langley, B.C., Canada

Thomas R. Hatina
Roehampton Institute London, England

Stanley E. Porter
Roehampton Institute London, England

Jeffrey T. Reed
Roehampton Institute London, England

Philip Richter
Roehampton Institute London, England

Dennis L. Stamps
University of Birmingham, England

David Tombs
Roehampton Institute London, England

INTRODUCTION

Stanley E. Porter and David Tombs

This collection attempts to display through theoretical discussion and practical application a number of the most prominent approaches to New Testament study being practised in the guild today. There have been a number of recent books on method, and although this one may superficially look like the others, it has several important distinctives that set it apart.

First, this volume combines what might be called traditional approaches with more recent approaches, treating them all on the same level of discussion and presentation. We recognize that there are a number of approaches to interpretation of the New Testament. Although many now eschew the traditional forms of criticism, we believe that these still have value and we present them on an equal footing with the others. On the other hand, we recognize that even for those trained in the traditional areas of historical criticism there is growing interest in other methods, not necessarily as replacements for historical criticism but as supplemental. Several of these newer methods are presented as well.

Secondly, this volume is designed for a wide range of audiences. Unlike many of the other volumes that introduce various interpretative methods, which are apparently designed with students in mind, this volume attempts to address both students and scholars alike. This has been a difficult task, but it is one that we have taken seriously from the start. Each of the essays (although each in its own way) presents some history of the discipline involved, discusses questions of method and practice, and to varying degrees presents the results of practice of such criticism, occasionally in distinction to other methods. Consequently, this book should have appeal on several levels. It should function well as a textbook, especially for an exegesis course, or one that surveys various hermeneutical or interpretative issues currently being discussed in New

Testament studies. For students, this may well serve as a first introduction to the various disciplines involved. But in the way that the volume is constructed in terms of discussion and scholarly documentation, each essay provides plenty of material for students to pursue in terms of their own research and writing, as well as critical reflection on the discipline. The students that we have in mind may well be advanced undergraduates, although this volume will probably serve usefully as a set text for various graduate or post-graduate courses, especially for students at master's level who have an advanced seminar in approaches to study of the New Testament or those at doctoral level who wish to expand their range of interests. However, we are convinced that this volume will also fill an important void for scholars as well. Since most of the volumes that deal with approaches to critical study are written for students, scholars it seems have been neglected. There have been many occasions when we have noted that fellow members of the guild have desired to know more about another approach to the New Testament. It is not that they do not want to read the best primary literature on the subject; it is that they may not even know where to begin finding the best materials. This volume is designed to remedy that situation by providing knowledgeable and informed synopses by those working in these fields to guide further reading, as well as presenting a solid theoretical basis for initial evaluation and critical reflection.

Thirdly, a distinctive feature of this volume is that it presents essays written only by those who are proponents (to varying degrees) of the disciplines and have expertise in the respective fields, either through earned degrees and/or research and publications. One of our frustrations in assessing material written regarding some of the newer areas of critical study of the New Testament has been that at the end of reading a treatment from a particular perspective, the question has been: what would someone who is actually trained in that field say? Consequently, for example, the essay on the sociological approach to the study of the New Testament is written by a trained sociologist who is also a trained New Testament scholar, and one who has written in both fields. Similar statements can be made of all of the subject areas. This is not to say that each of the authors speaks for the entire discipline, but that each essay represents an opinion from within that particular field of study, not an opinion of someone who has simply read a few books in the area or who has an outsider's interest in it. We believe that this brings several benefits to the volume. The first is commitment to the approach being studied. Each of the authors may well have criticism of how the respective field is being developed, but each is also a part of the ongoing discussion and has a vested interest in how it progresses. The second is the mindset that is brought to the discussion. As will become evident in reading the essays, the way one approaches a given discipline may well vary from the way one approaches another discipline. This volume attempts to display each discipline in its best light, or at least in the best light that one who knows the inner workings of that discipline can cast upon it.

The nine essays included here can be divided into four categories. The first is concerned with historical-critical issues, and includes the essays on source, form and redaction criticism of the Gospels and on the use of historical backgrounds for the study of the New Testament. These two chapters are similar in orientation in that they cover methods familiar to most New Testament scholars. However, each also presents material that will be of worth both to those wanting to know more about historical criticism and to those who already are convinced by it. For example, in the chapter on criticism of the Gospels, Craig Evans acknowledges the role that recent literary criticism has played, and offers an extended critique of a recent literary reading of Luke's Gospel in the light of contemporary redaction criticism. In the essay on the use of background material, Thomas Hatina re-opens the question of how much we know about various Jewish groups, utilizing the most recent Qumran findings.

The second set of essays is concerned with more literary topics, and includes the essays on literary criticism proper, rhetorical criticism, and canonical criticism. The essay on literary criticism attempts to take a wide-ranging and constantly changing field and place it into a larger historical and critical context. It reflects the view of one who sees much merit in some of the earlier literary-critical methods, but attempts to illustrate how they can be profitably wedded to historical criticism. Although some would place rhetorical criticism under the category of literary criticism, especially modern rhetoric, here it is given a separate chapter. Dennis Stamps draws on recent work on 1 Corinthians to show how attention to the rhetorical situation helps to formulate an approach to the Pauline material. The chapter on canonical criticism introduces a field of study that often is discussed without full knowledge of the subject. One of the problems is the diversity in what is called canonical criticism and another is the fact that examples of exegesis using canonical criticism are still hard to find. Kent Clarke attempts to define the discipline and show how it works when discussing the New Testament.

The third group of essays is concerned with social-scientific methods of study of the New Testament, and includes the essays on linguistics and social-science criticism proper. Jeffrey Reed focuses on four of the most important areas of linguistic study of the New Testament: semantics, pragmatics, sociolinguistics and discourse analysis. For many, it may come as a mild surprise to find that the field of linguistics is itself so diverse. In the essay on social-scientific study of the New Testament, Philip Richter gives a brief survey of the strengths and weaknesses of the subject before devoting considerable attention to exemplifying social-science criticism in action. He utilizes a model little used in New Testament study, destigmatization theory, to explore examples of responses to Jesus in Luke–Acts and Paul.

The fourth and final group of essays is concerned with what might be called liberation criticisms, and includes the essay on Latin American liberation hermeneutics and feminist interpretation. The essay on liberation hermeneutics approaches the area from its theological perspective, recognizing that this method is not so much an exegetical approach but a theoretical orientation that utilizes the work of the other exegetical models. What is important for liberation hermeneutics is the prior commitment to issues regarding the poor. This is one of the more thorough treatments of this subject written with New Testament scholars in mind. In the essay on feminist interpretation, Beverley Clack surveys the field of recent feminist interpretation and discusses how it has been concerned to establish its own exegetical position in the light of the traditional orientation of the guild of New Testament scholars.

Although there are other topics that might well have been included in this collection, including dividing several of the essays above into other essays, each one warranting an essay in its own right, we have resisted the temptation to expand too far and have included these statements, thinking that they capture much of the current state of play in the study of the New Testament. The goal of the volume is to provide workable models for those interested in expanding or deepening their knowledge of the various approaches to New Testament study.

SOURCE, FORM AND REDACTION CRITICISM:
THE 'TRADITIONAL' METHODS OF SYNOPTIC INTERPRETATION

Craig A. Evans

1. *Introduction*

In recent years a plethora of studies have appeared developing and
promoting new methods of biblical interpretation, particularly with
respect to the Gospels. These methods fall under the general rubric of
'literary criticism' because of their emphasis on the text in its final form,
in contrast to the older methods of criticism which tended to emphasize
the sources, redaction, and pre-publication history of the text.
Structuralism, post-structuralism, deconstructionism, and reader-response
criticism constitute distinct aspects of literary criticism's emphasis on a
'close reading' of the text.[1] These critical methods ask questions
pertaining to genre, form, structure, plot development, characters,
rhetoric, the narrative world, and implied authors and readers.[2] The
function of the Old Testament in the New, usually spoken of as

---

1. For introductory discussions, see J.P. Tompkins (ed.), *Reader-Response
Criticism: From Formalism to Post-Structuralism* (Baltimore: Johns Hopkins
University Press, 1980); J.L. Resseguie, 'Reader-Response Criticism and the
Synoptic Gospels', *JAAR* 52 (1984), pp. 307-24; R.M. Fowler, 'Who is "the
Reader" in Reader Response Criticism?', *Semeia* 31 (1985), pp. 5-23;
E.V. McKnight, *The Bible and the Reader: An Introduction to Literary Criticism*
(Philadelphia: Fortress Press, 1985); M. Sternberg, *The Poetics of Biblical Narrative:
Ideological Literature and the Drama of Reading* (Indiana Literary Biblical Series;
Bloomington: Indiana University Press, 1985); E. Freund, *The Return of the Reader:
Reader-Response Criticism* (London: Methuen, 1987).

2. For a discussion of the history and assumptions of this development, see
N.R. Petersen, *Literary Criticism for New Testament Critics* (Philadelphia: Fortress
Press, 1978); R.A. Spencer (ed.), *Orientation by Disorientation: Studies in Literary
Criticism and Biblical Literary Criticism* (Pittsburgh: Pickwick Press, 1980);
E.V. McKnight, *Postmodern Use of the Bible: The Emergence of Reader-Oriented
Criticism* (Nashville: Abingdon Press, 1988).

intertextuality, has also been taken up as part of the agenda of the literary criticism of today.

These methods have made useful contributions to the task of exegesis. It has been the perceived shortcomings of the older, conventional modes of interpretation that have in large measure prompted the turn to the new methods. Redaction criticism offers an instructive illustration, for in its classic form this method struggles with the Gospel of Mark (much more than it does with the Gospels of Matthew and Luke). This is the case because interpreters do not possess this Gospel's sources. How is one able to distinguish source from redaction? Apart from a few places where there is general agreement, opinion diverges widely as to what constitutes received tradition and what the Markan evangelist and his community added. And now that doubt has been cast on Markan priority (which will be taken up shortly), the same problem is felt with respect to the Gospels of Matthew and Luke. For these reasons and for others, many interpreters of the Gospels have been attracted to methods that analyze a given Gospel on its own terms, as a whole, without attempting to disentangle putative sources from redaction. It is now assumed that the evangelists were in basic agreement with what they chose to put down on paper and that what they wrote conveys their perspective, whatever the origin of the traditions.[3]

Much of this reasoning is sound.[4] Classic redaction criticism tended to exaggerate the differences of perspective between source and redaction. Major hypotheses rested on what was, in some instances, slight and ambiguous evidence. Worse still, because there was a tendency to view the evangelists much as they had been viewed earlier by the form critics (i.e. as scissors-and-paste editors), interpretation was sometimes fragmented and isolated. Today's redaction criticism, which has evolved into something more akin to composition criticism,[5] is more contextually

3.   For illustrative contrasts to the assumptions and methods of Marxsen, Bornkamm, and Conzelmann, see analyses offered by D. Rhoads and D. Michie, *Mark as Story: An Introduction to the Narrative of a Gospel* (Philadelphia: Fortress Press, 1982); J.D. Kingsbury, *Matthew as Story* (Philadelphia: Fortress Press, 1986); R.C. Tannehill, *The Narrative Unity of Luke–Acts: A Literary Interpretation* (Philadelphia: Fortress Press, 1986).

4.   I am, however, skeptical of certain facets of 'reader-response' criticism. For an evaluation of the new literary criticisms, see S. McKnight, *Interpreting the Synoptic Gospels* (Grand Rapids: Baker, 1988), pp. 121-37.

5.   Understanding the discipline as *Kompositionsgeschichte* was in fact recommended by E. Haenchen, *Der Weg Jesu* (Berlin: Töpelmann, 1966), p. 24.

sensitive. This is a welcome development. But there is a danger inherent in the employment of these new methods, if conventional modes of exegesis are neglected. An exegesis that cares little about history and sources is in danger of misunderstanding the text and distorting the distinctive motifs the respective evangelists may have wished to convey.[6]

In my judgment, the traditional methods of Synoptic criticism remain essentially valid, while the newer forms of literary criticism are vulnerable to oversights and/or subjective misreadings, to the extent that they ignore the gains and insights of the traditional methods. The balance of this paper is divided into two parts. The first part will review the 'traditional' methods of Synoptic interpretation, briefly treating their potential, as well as their limitations. The second part will illustrate the weakness of the new literary criticism, when it is pursued without regard to the traditional methods of interpretation.[7]

2. The 'Traditional' Methods of Synoptic Interpretation

The traditional methods of Synoptic interpretation (or criticism) are source criticism, form criticism, and redaction criticism.[8] Source criticism preoccupied scholars for most of the nineteenth century and had its

6.   Some of the recent works are open to criticism. For example, P.L. Danove's *The End of Mark's Story: A Methodological Study* (BIS, 3; Leiden: Brill, 1993) interprets Mark as though there is nothing else to study. A similar approach is found in J.P. Heil's *The Death and Resurrection of Jesus: A Narrative-Critical Study of Matthew 26–28* (Minneapolis: Fortress Press, 1991). Many narrative and literary insights are offered, but Matthew's relationship to sources and history is neglected. The same can be said of Heil's *The Gospel of Mark as a Model for Action: A Reader-Response Commentary* (New York: Paulist Press, 1992).

7.   In this chapter it is assumed that both literary and historical aspects of exegesis are important. For a helpful statement from this perspective, which emphasizes Old Testament interpretation, see J. Barton, 'Historical Criticism and Literary Interpretation: Is There Any Common Ground?', in S.E. Porter *et al.* (eds.), *Crossing the Boundaries: Essays in Biblical Interpretation in Honour of Michael D. Goulder* (BIS, 8; Leiden: Brill, 1994), pp. 3-15.

8.   Other criticisms, such as textual criticism, tradition criticism, and historical criticism, apply more broadly to biblical literature as a whole. The first seeks to establish the oldest, perhaps even original, wording of the text, while the second attempts to trace the origin and development of various traditions, in whatever biblical writings they may appear. The last attempts to determine the presence of historical material and how it should be understood in the *Sitz im Leben Jesu*. Historical criticism is the principal preoccupation of scholars concerned with Jesus research.

roots in the eighteenth century and achieved in the early twentieth century a near-consensus (that Mark and Q were the principal sources of Matthew and Luke). About the time this near-consensus began to emerge, form criticism appeared and occupied scholars' attention for much of the second quarter of the twentieth century. Before interest in form criticism had waned, redaction criticism arose, claiming scholarly attention for much of the third quarter of the twentieth century. If we reach back to J.J. Griesbach of the late eighteenth century, it is fair to say that these three traditional critical approaches have dominated Synoptic scholarship for some two hundred years.

These three closely-related methods laid the foundation for modern interpretation of the Gospels. No serious commentary fails to interact with all three; every commentary has benefited from the discoveries made through the application of these methods. We may review them in the order of their development.[9]

Source Criticism
Source criticism of the Synoptic Gospels has been almost exclusively concerned with the resolution of the Synoptic Problem, that is, how to account for the literary relationship that the Gospels of Matthew, Mark,

---

9. For helpful (English) descriptions and assessments, see I.H. Marshall (ed.), *New Testament Interpretation: Essays on Principles and Methods* (Exeter: Paternoster Press; Grand Rapids: Eerdmans, 1977); R.N. Soulen, *Handbook of Biblical Criticism* (Atlanta: John Knox, 2nd edn, 1981); R.H. Stein, *The Synoptic Problem: An Introduction* (Grand Rapids: Baker, 1987); S. McKnight, *Interpreting the Synoptic Gospels*; *idem* (ed.), *Introducing New Testament Interpretation* (Guides to New Testament Exegesis, 1; Grand Rapids: Baker, 1989); E.P. Sanders and M. Davies, *Studying the Synoptic Gospels* (London: SCM Press; Philadelphia: Trinity Press International, 1989); D.A. Black and D.S. Dockery (eds.), *New Testament Criticism and Interpretation* (Grand Rapids: Zondervan, 1991); D.A. Carson, D.J. Moo, and L. Morris, *An Introduction to the New Testament* (Grand Rapids: Zondervan, 1991), pp. 19-60; W. Stenger, *Introduction to New Testament Exegesis* (Grand Rapids: Eerdmans, 1993).

I have chosen to treat the traditional criticisms in their historical order of development. They could also be treated in a functional order, in which form criticism is treated first (because of its concern with the development of the oral tradition), source criticism second (because of its concern with the relationship of written sources), and redaction criticism last (because of its concern with the final composition of the Gospels themselves). I have chosen the historical order of development principally because form criticism and redaction have presupposed the results of source criticism.

and Luke clearly evince.[10] That there is some sort of literary relationship can scarcely be doubted, but how to account for it is open to many interpretations. One of the earliest explanations was offered by Augustine who thought Mark was an abbreviation of Matthew (cf. *De consensu evangelistarum* 1.2.4). Matthean priority was in all probability the assumption of the early Church, from the second century on.[11] Augustine's was an attempt to explain the literary relationship of Matthew and Mark, the two Synoptics with the largest amount of overlap.

In the eighteenth century J.J. Griesbach defended Matthean priority, but contended that Luke had made use of Matthew and that Mark had combined and abridged both Matthew and Luke.[12] The Griesbach hypothesis held sway for about a century, eventually giving way to the views of H.J. Holtzmann and B.H. Streeter, in which Mark (or *Ur-Marcus*) and a source of sayings (i.e. 'Q') were understood to be the principal sources of Matthew and Luke.[13] In the wake of Streeter's

10. D. Wenham, 'Source Criticism', in Marshall (ed.), *New Testament Interpretation*, pp. 139-52; S. McKnight, 'Source Criticism', in Black and Dockery (eds.), *New Testament Criticism*, pp. 137-72; Stein, *The Synoptic Problem*, pp. 139-57; *idem*, 'Synoptic Problem', in J.B. Green, S. McKnight and I.H. Marshall (eds.), *Dictionary of Jesus and the Gospels* (Leicester and Downers Grove: InterVarsity Press, 1992), pp. 784-92; Sanders and Davies, *Studying the Synoptic Gospels*, pp. 51-119; C. Focant (ed.), *The Synoptic Gospels: Source Criticism and the New Literary Criticism* (BETL, 110; Leuven: Leuven University Press, 1993).

11. The evidence assembled by E. Massaux (*The Influence of the Gospel of Saint Matthew on Christian Literature before Saint Irenaeus* [3 vols.; NGS, 5.1–3; Macon, GA: Mercer University Press, 1990–93) would seem to lead to this conclusion.

12. J.J. Griesbach, *Synopsis Evangeliorum Matthei, Marci et Lucae una cum iis Joannis pericopis: Quae historiam passionis et resurrectionis Jesu Christi complectuntur* (Halle Saxonum: J.J. Curtii Haeredes, 2nd edn, 1797).

13. H.J. Holtzmann, *Die synoptischen Evangelien: Ihr Ursprung und geschichtlicher Charakter* (Leipzig: Engelmann, 1863); B.F. Streeter, *The Four Gospels: A Study of Origins* (London: Macmillan, 2nd edn, 1930). Holtzmann (*Lehrbuch der historisch-kritischen Einleitung in das Neue Testament* [Freiburg: Mohr [Siebeck], 3rd edn, 1892], pp. 342-61) later abandoned the *Ur-Marcus* hypothesis. An important antecedent to Holtzmann's work was the observation that Mark's contents and order constituted the common ground among the three Synoptic Gospels; cf. K.F.W. Lachmann, 'De ordine narrationum in Evangeliis synopticis', *TSK* 8 (1835), pp. 570-90; C.H. Weisse, *Die evangelische Geschichte, kritisch und philosophisch bearbeitet* (2 vols.; Leipzig: Breitkopf und Hartel, 1838); C.G. Wilke, *Der Urevangelist, oder, exegetisch kritisch Untersuchung über das Verwandtschaftsverhältnis der drei ersten Evangelien* (Dresden and Leipzig: Gerhard Fleischer, 1838).

work the Two-Document (or Two-Source, as most today seem to prefer) Hypothesis came to dominate Synoptic scholarship and came close to becoming a consensus (a rare phenomenon in biblical scholarship).[14] Today most New Testament scholars accept the priority of Mark.[15]

In 1964 W.R. Farmer challenged the dominant thinking. He and others have argued for a return to Griesbach's Two-Gospel Hypothesis.[16] But their assault on the Two-Source Hypothesis has been unsuccessful.[17] It has been unsuccessful, in my estimation, for the following six reasons:

14. The Oxford Seminar in the early years of this century also gave impetus to scholarly support for the Two-Document Hypothesis; cf. W. Sanday (ed.), *Oxford Studies in the Synoptic Problem* (Oxford: Clarendon Press, 1911).

15. See H.G. Wood, 'The Priority of Mark', *ExpTim* 65 (1953–54), pp. 17-19; J.A. Fitzmyer, 'The Priority of Mark and the "Q" Source in Luke', in D.G. Buttrick and J.M. Bald (eds.), *Jesus and Man's Hope* (Pittsburgh: Pittsburgh Theological Seminary, 1970), pp. 131-70; G.M. Styler, 'The Priority of Mark', in C.F.D. Moule, *The Birth of the New Testament* (London: A. & C. Black, 3rd edn, 1981; San Franciso: Harper & Row, 1982), pp. 285-316; C.M. Tuckett, *The Revival of the Griesbach Hypothesis: An Analysis and Appraisal* (SNTSMS, 44; Cambridge: Cambridge University Press, 1983); J.S. Kloppenborg, *The Formation of Q* (Philadelphia: Fortress Press, 1987); S.E. Johnson, *The Griesbach Hypothesis and Redaction Criticism* (SBLMS, 41; Atlanta: Scholars Press, 1991); J.D.G. Dunn, 'Matthew's Awareness of Markan Redaction', in F. Van Segbroeck *et al.* (eds.), *The Four Gospels 1992* (3 vols.; BETL, 100; Leuven: Leuven University Press, 1992), II, pp. 1349-59; R.H. Stein, 'The Matthew–Luke Agreements against Mark: Insight from John', *CBQ* 54 (1992), pp. 482-502.

16. B.C. Butler, *The Originality of St Matthew: A Critique of the Two-Document Hypothesis* (Cambridge: Cambridge University Press, 1951); W.R. Farmer, *The Synoptic Problem: A Critical Analysis* (New York: Macmillan, 1964); T.R.W. Longstaff, *Evidence of Conflation in Mark? A Study of the Synoptic Problem* (SBLDS, 28; Missoula, MT: Scholars Press, 1977); H.-H. Stoldt, *History and Criticism of the Marcan Hypothesis* (Macon, GA: Mercer University Press, 1980); D.B. Peabody, *Mark as Composer* (NGS, 1; Macon, GA: Mercer University Press, 1987).

17. Tuckett, *The Revival of the Griesbach Hypothesis*; Stein, *The Synoptic Problem*; Johnson, *The Griesbach Hypothesis*. Recent major commentaries either defend or presuppose the Two-Source Hypothesis; cf. D.C. Allison and W.D. Davies, *The Gospel according to Saint Matthew* (ICC; Edinburgh: T. & T. Clark, 1988); J.A. Fitzmyer, *The Gospel according to Luke* (AB, 28 and 28A; Garden City, NY: Doubleday, 1981, 1985); R.H. Gundry, *Mark: A Commentary on his Apology for the Cross* (Grand Rapids: Eerdmans, 1993); and M.D. Hooker, *The Gospel according to Saint Mark* (BNTC; London: A. & C. Black, 1991).

1. Mark's *literary style* lacks the polish and sophistication that one regularly encounters in Matthew and Luke. Indeed, Markan style is Semitic, non-literary, and sometimes may even be described as primitive. One must wonder, if Farmer is right, why the Markan evangelist would have chosen time after time to rewrite Matthew and Luke in a cruder and less polished form. Why not simply reproduce one version or the other? Why introduce Semitic words (which are often not found in the Matthean and Lukan parallels) only to have to translate them? It is more probable that Matthew and Luke represent improvements upon Mark. Mark's writing style, when compared to Matthew and Luke, supports Markan priority not posteriority.

2. In comparing the Synoptics one observes that sometimes Mark's version of a story is *potentially embarrassing*. Jesus and the disciples are sometimes portrayed in a manner that either appears undignified or possibly at variance with Christian beliefs. For example, during the storm on the Sea of Galilee the disciples cry out, according to the Markan version, 'Teacher, do you not care if we perish?' (4.38). One could infer from Mark's version a lack of respect for Jesus, especially from the perspective of a Christian who revered Jesus as the Son of God. How could the disciples have questioned Jesus' concern for them? The question of the frightened disciples is put much more politely and innocuously in Matthew: 'Save, Lord, we are perishing' (8.25) and in Luke: 'Master, Master, we are perishing!' (8.24). Mark's version of Jesus' reply, 'Have you no faith?' (4.40), could imply that the disciples are faithless. Matthew's version: 'O men of little faith' (8.26) and Luke's version: 'Where is your faith?' (8.25) soften the rebuke. The disciples do indeed have faith; their lack of faith is temporary and is due to their fear. Other examples like this one are not hard to find (e.g. Mk 6.49-52 = Mt. 14.26-33; Mk 14.37-41 = Lk. 22.45). Has Mark rewritten the essentially positive portraits of the disciples, as he finds them in Matthew and Luke, or have Matthew and Luke improved upon the negative portrait that they found in Mark?

More importantly, it should be pointed out that in Mark there is often a lack of propriety with respect to Jesus himself. Almost always Matthew and/or Luke attempts to dignify or at least in some sense qualify these passages. For example, according to Mark, 'the Spirit drove [Jesus] out into the wilderness' (1.12). Not only is this picture somewhat undignified, but the verb that is used is ἐκβάλλειν, the verb that is customarily used in describing the exorcism of demons (Mk 1.34,

39; 3.15, 22, 23; 6.13; 7.26; 9.18, 28, 38). According to Matthew, 'Jesus was led up [ἀνάγειν] by the Spirit into the wilderness' (4.1). According to Luke, 'Jesus, full of the Holy Spirit, returned from the Jordan, and was led [ἄγειν] by the Spirit' (4.1). It is hard to understand why Mark would transform these statements into the one that we find in his Gospel. Potentially embarrassing expressions of emotion on the part of Jesus are also omitted by Matthew and Luke. For example, the reference to Jesus' anger (Mk 3.5) and the reference to Jesus being 'beside himself' (Mk 3.21) are omitted by Matthew and Luke. If he did not find these descriptions in his Matthean and Lukan sources, why would the Markan evangelist insert such material? Again, many other examples can be offered (e.g. Mk 3.31-35 = Mt. 12.46-50 = Lk. 8.19-21).

3. Where there is no Markan parallel, *Matthean and Lukan divergence* is greatest. This phenomenon is explained best in reference to Markan priority, rather than Matthean. There is significant divergence in two areas involving material not found in Mark. We see this in the distribution of the double tradition (i.e. Q) throughout Matthew and Luke. With a few easily explainable exceptions (such as placing John the Baptist's 'Brood of vipers' speech and the story of the three temptations at the same point in the narrative), the double tradition is found in different contexts. This has not been convincingly explained by advocates of the Griesbach hypothesis. Why would Luke follow Matthew's narrative sequence, but break up his collections of Jesus' sayings (such as the Sermon on the Mount) and scatter them throughout his Gospel? We also see such divergence in the material special to Matthew (M) and Luke (L). Although a small and important common core of material can be detected in the Matthean and Lukan versions of Jesus' birth and resurrection, we have here a remarkable amount of divergence. In short, what we observe is that where there is no Mark to follow, this is where Matthew and Luke go their separate ways. This observation is very difficult to explain assuming Matthean priority, but it is exactly what one should expect assuming Markan priority.

4. Another indication of Markan priority lies in the observation that in some instances, due to omission of Markan details, *Matthew and Luke have created difficulties*. R.H. Stein has provided several examples that illustrate this feature well.[18] (a) Because he has omitted Mark's description of the removal of the roof and the lowering of the paralytic

18. Stein, *The Synoptic Problem*, pp. 70-76.

(Mk 2.4), Matthew has removed the immediate reason for the editorial comment regarding the faith of the (four) men (Mt. 9.2b). Matthew's readers, if unfamiliar with Mark, are left to wonder why Jesus is said to have 'seen their faith'. (b) Omitting Mark's explanation of the Passover pardon (Mk 15.6-11), Luke nevertheless goes on to narrate that the people cried out for the release of Barabbas (Lk. 23.18). However, the evangelist does not explain on what basis the crowd could have expected Pilate to release anyone, whether it be Jesus or Barabbas or anyone else. (c) According to Mk 10.18 Jesus asks the man, 'Why do you call me good?' In Mt. 19.17 the question is slightly (but significantly) different: 'Why do you ask me about what is good?' It is not hard to see why Matthew would have changed Mark's form of the question (is Jesus implying that he is not good?). But it is not clear why Mark would have changed Matthew's form of the question. Although he changed the question, Matthew did not change the answer: 'One there is who is good'. This form of the answer fits better the question as it is found in Mark, in that it is in reference to the goodness of beings (such as God or Jesus), not to the subject of goodness. Accordingly, Matthew betrays his knowledge of the Markan form of the story. (d) According to Mk 10.35-37 James and John make a request of Jesus to sit at his right and left in his glory. The question arouses the indignation of the other disciples, so we should not be surprised that the scene is mitigated in Matthew. According to Mt. 20.20-21 it is the *mother* of James and John who makes the request. But Matthew again betrays his knowledge of Mark's version, when he has Jesus reply: 'You [pl.] do not know what what you [pl.] are asking' (Mt. 20.22 = Mk 10.38). The plural clearly indicates that Jesus was addressing James and John, not their mother. Consequently, Mk 10.35-38 is surely what underlies Mt. 20.20-22, and not the reverse.

5. The small amount of material that is *unique* to the Gospel of Mark also supports Markan priority. This material consists of 1.1; 2.27; 3.20-21; 4.26-29; 7.2-4, 32-37; 8.22-26; 9.29, 48-49; 13.33-37; 14.51-52. In reviewing this material one should ask which explanation seems the more probable, that Mark added it or that Matthew and Luke found it in Mark and chose to omit it. The nature of the material supports the latter alternative, for it seems more likely that Matthew and Luke chose to omit the flight of the naked youth (14.51-52), the odd saying about being 'salted with fire' (9.48-49), the strange miracle where Jesus effects healing in two stages (8.22-26), the even stranger miracle where Jesus

puts his fingers in a man's ears, spits, and touches his tongue (7.32-37), and the episode where Jesus is regarded as mad and his family attempts to restrain him (3.20-22). If we accept the Griesbach-Farmer Hypothesis, we would then have to explain why Mark would choose to add these odd, potentially embarrassing materials, only to omit the Sermon on the Mount/Plain, the Lord's Prayer, and numerous other teachings and parables found in the larger Gospels. It seems much more likely that Matthew and Luke represent *improvements* upon Mark.

All of the points that have been considered point in this direction. Matthew and Luke have improved upon Mark's style. They have heightened its christology. They have improved upon the image and authority of the apostles. They have considerably augmented Jesus' teaching, but in a way that does not suggest dependence of one upon another. And they have omitted potentially confusing and embarrassing material.

6. The final consideration that adds weight to the probability of Markan priority has to do with the *results* of the respective hypotheses. The true test of any hypothesis is its effectiveness. In biblical studies a theory should aid the exegetical task. The theory of Markan priority has provided just this kind of aid. Not only has Synoptic interpretation been materially advanced because of the conclusion, and now widespread assumption, of Markan priority, but the development of critical methods oriented to Gospel research, such as form criticism and redaction criticism, which have enjoyed success, has also presupposed Markan priority. In countless studies, whether dealing with this pericope or that, or treating one of the Synoptic Gospels in its entirety, it has been recognized over and over again that Matthew and Luke make the greatest sense as *interpretations of Mark*.[19] If the Griesbach-Farmer Hypothesis were correct, one would expect major breakthroughs in Markan research. After all, we would now know what Mark's sources were. But Farmer's following have not cast significant light on Mark. C.S. Mann's commentary on Mark, which does presuppose the Griesbach-Farmer Hypothesis, has not been successful, illustrating instead the problem encountered when attempting a verse-by-verse analysis of Mark based on Matthean priority.[20]

19. See Tuckett, *Revival of the Griesbach Hypothesis*, pp. 186-87.

20. Although Mann has followed Farmer and so believes that Mark is dependent upon Matthew and Luke (C.S. Mann, *Mark* [AB, 27; Garden City, NY: Doubleday, 1986], pp. 51-66), he frequently finds examples where Mark has preserved the most

The discussion of form criticism and redaction criticism that follows will presuppose Markan priority and the essential elements of the Two-Source Hypothesis. The example that will be treated in the second part of the paper will likewise presuppose this critical orientation.

Form Criticism

Form criticism attempts to identify specific literary or sub-literary forms and infer from these forms the function or setting in the life of the early Christian community (i.e. *Sitz im Leben*).[21] It is assumed that the tradition of the life of Jesus was 'minted by the faith of the primitive Christian community in its various stages'.[22] Of the three traditional

---

primitive form of the tradition and is not dependent upon Matthew or Luke (e.g. p. 202: 'not derived from Matthew and Luke'; p. 214: 'a Petrine reminiscence'; p. 217: 'not derived from Matthew...certainly far more vivid in style than Luke's stereotypical account...a traditional piece, and the style suggests reminiscence by one of the participants'; pp. 218-19: 'Mark's version, with its vivid detail, may owe far more to an original oral reminiscence than to the other evangelists'; *et passim*). But according to the Griesbach Hypothesis, Mark is supposed to be a conflation *of Matthew and Luke*, not of primitive materials, some of which derive from eyewitnesses (which is more consistent with theories of Markan priority). Mann does not appear to be aware of the extent to which the results of his analysis conflict with his view of the Synoptic Problem. His exegetical conclusions tend to undermine the very theory upon which he has based his commentary.

21. For basic bibliography, see W.G. Doty, 'The Discipline and Literature of New Testament Form Criticism', *ATR* 51 (1969), pp. 257-321; E.V. McKnight, *What is Form Criticism?* (Philadelphia: Fortress Press, 1969); E.E. Ellis, 'New Directions in Form Criticism', in G. Strecker (ed.), *Jesus Christus in Historie und Theologie* (Tübingen: Mohr [Siebeck], 1975), pp. 299-315; S.H. Travis, 'Form Criticism', in Marshall (ed.), *New Testament Interpretation*, pp. 153-64; G. Lohfink, *The Bible: Now I Get It! A Form Criticism Handbook* (Garden City, NY: Doubleday, 1979); W. Kelber, *The Oral and Written Gospel* (Philadelphia: Fortress Press, 1983); K. Berger, *Formgeschichte des Neuen Testaments* (Heidelberg: Quelle & Meyer, 1984); *idem, Einführung in die Formgeschichte* (UTB, 144; Tübingen: Franke, 1987); Stein, *Synoptic Problem*, pp. 161-228; McKnight, *Interpreting the Synoptic Gospels*, pp. 71-82; Sanders and Davies, *Studying the Synoptic Gospels*, pp. 123-97; D.L. Bock, 'Form Criticism', in Black and Dockery (eds.), *New Testament Criticism*, pp. 175-96; C.L. Blomberg, 'Form Criticism', in *Dictionary of Jesus and the Gospels*, pp. 243-50; G. Strecker, 'Schriftlichkeit oder Mündlichkeit der synoptischen Tradition? Anmerkungen zur formgeschichtlichen Problematik', in Van Segbroeck *et al.* (eds.), *The Four Gospels 1992*, I, pp. 159-72.

22. E. Käsemann, *Essays on New Testament Themes* (SBT, 41; London: SCM Press; Naperville: Allenson, 1964), p. 15.

criticisms, form criticism is the most problematic. It is problematic because by its very nature a great deal of subjectivity comes into play. We really do not know what the practices were of first-century Christians who told and retold the sayings of and stories about Jesus.[23] Therefore, we can never be sure of precisely what setting a piece of tradition may reflect.

The German scholars who applied form criticism to the Gospels assigned a great deal of the traditions to the early Church, rather than to Jesus himself.[24] English form critics were less skeptical.[25] Recent discussion has been quite diverse. Harald Riesenfeld and Birger Gerhardsson, taking a different tack, have argued that the tradition is reliable, since Jesus, like the rabbis of old, taught his disciples to memorize his teachings.[26] Rainer Riesner has argued for even greater confidence in the general reliability of the Synoptic Gospels.[27] But their

23. This point has been convincingly made by E.P. Sanders, *The Tendencies of the Synoptic Tradition* (SNTSMS, 9; Cambridge: Cambridge University Press, 1969).

24. K.L. Schmidt, *Der Rahmen der Geschichte Jesu: Literarkritische Untersuchungen zur ältesten Jesusüberlieferung* (Berlin: Trowitzsch & Sohn, 1919); M. Dibelius, *Die Formgeschichte des Evangeliums* (Tübingen: Mohr [Siebeck], 1919; 2nd edn, 1933; 3rd edn, 1959); ET: *From Tradition to Gospel* (Cambridge: James Clarke; New York: Charles Scribner's Sons, 1934); R. Bultmann, *Die Geschichte der synoptischen Tradition* (FRLANT, 12; Göttingen: Vandenhoeck & Ruprecht, 1921; 2nd edn, 1931; 3rd edn, 1957 [= FRLANT, 29]); ET: *The History of the Synoptic Tradition* (Oxford: Basil Blackwell; New York: Harper & Row, 1963); *idem, Die Erforschung der synoptischen Tradition* (Giessen: Töpelmann, 1925; 2nd edn, 1930); ET: 'The Study of the Synoptic Gospels', in R. Bultmann and K. Kundsin, *Form Criticism: Two Essays on New Testament Research* (New York: Willett, Clark, 1934), pp. 11-76.

25. V. Taylor, *The Formation of the Gospel Tradition* (London: Macmillan, 1933; 2nd edn, 1935); C.H. Dodd, *The Parables of the Kingdom* (London: Nisbet, 1935); *idem,* 'The Appearances of the Risen Christ: A Study in Form-Criticism of the Gospels', in D.E. Nineham (ed.), *Studies in the Gospels: Essays in Memory of R.H. Lightfoot* (Oxford: Basil Blackwell, 1955), pp. 9-35.

26. H. Riesenfeld, *The Gospel Tradition and its Beginnings: A Study in the Limits of 'Formgeschichte'* (London: Mowbray, 1957); B. Gerhardsson, *Memory and Manuscript: Oral Tradition and Written Transmission in Rabbinic Judaism and Early Christianity* (Lund: Gleerup, 1961). Gerhardsson supposes that the words of Jesus may have been carefully preserved as rabbis carefully preserved the words of Scripture.

27. R. Riesner, *Jesus als Lehrer: Eine Untersuchung zum Ursprung der Evangelien-Überlieferung* (WUNT, 2.7; Tübingen: Mohr [Siebeck], 1981; 4th edn, 1994).

work has been criticized for importing rabbinic principles of discipleship.[28] It is argued that we cannot assume that Jesus' followers and the generation that followed them emphasized memorization to the degree that it would appear that many rabbis of later generations did. In any event, comparison of the Synoptic Gospels reveals to what extent the sayings of Jesus have been edited, paraphrased, and diversely contextualized. The very phenomena of the Gospels tell against Gerhardsson and company. Accordingly, the difficult question of how extensive were early Christian editing and expansion of the dominical tradition still remains open.

In general, we can agree with the classic form critics that the sayings and stories of Jesus functioned in various ways in the life of the early Church. Certain traditions served liturgical functions, others served evangelistic and apologetic purposes. But this should remain a general observation. The greater the specificity, the greater the subjectivity.[29]

Some form critics have emphasized the role of prophecy in early Christianity in shaping dominical tradition and in generating it altogether. In my judgment Eugene Boring's thesis, to the effect that much of dominical tradition arose through early Christian prophecy, is no longer persuasive or widely held.[30] Boring is certainly right in finding that much of the dominical tradition has been reinterpreted, largely through recontextualization, but there is little objective evidence of wholesale creation through prophetic utterance or otherwise.[31]

28. See M. Smith, 'A Comparison of Early Christianity and Early Rabbinic Traditions', *JBL* 82 (1963), pp. 169-76; Sanders, *The Tendencies of the Synoptic Tradition*, pp. 294-96.

29. E.P. Sanders (*Jesus and Judaism* [London: SCM Press; Philadelphia: Fortress Press, 1985], p. 16) appropriately comments: 'The form critics were right in thinking that the material changed; they were wrong in thinking that they knew how it changed'. The early Christian community sometimes left behind obvious traces, as seen for example in the parenthetic comment, 'Thus he declared all foods clean' (Mk 7.19). But rarely are such traces this obvious.

30. M.E. Boring, *Sayings of the Risen Jesus: Christian Prophecy in the Synoptic Tradition* (SNTSMS, 46; Cambridge: Cambridge University Press, 1982); *idem, The Continuing Voice of Jesus* (Louisville: Westminster/John Knox, 1991).

31. For criticisms of Boring's conclusions, see D.E. Aune, *Prophecy in Early Christianity and the Ancient Mediterranean World* (Grand Rapids: Eerdmans, 1983), pp. 240-42 (on Jesus tradition, see pp. 153-88); D. Hill, *New Testament Prophecy* (Atlanta: John Knox, 1979), pp. 5-9 (on Jesus tradition, pp. 48-69). Aune and Hill are responding to Boring's dissertation and to earlier studies presented in the *SBLSP* (1973, 1974, 1976, 1977) and *JBL* (1972). For an earlier statement that is compatible

In my judgment, the most prudent position to take is that on principle most material ultimately derives from Jesus, but that most material has been edited and recontextualized. Here the assumptions and conclusions of the Jesus Seminar are particularly problematic. The Seminar's color scheme ('red'—Jesus said it; 'pink'—something close to what Jesus said; 'gray'—doubtful that Jesus said it; and 'black'—Jesus definitely did not say it) is unrealistic and misleading.[32]

In a certain sense, most of the material should be rated pink, if we are speaking of the sayings as approximating the utterances of Jesus. But in another sense, most of the material should be gray, or even black, if we are speaking of what the material precisely meant and in what setting(s) it was spoken. It is this latter dimension that vexes Jesus research. But in the case of the historical Jesus, we at least have a pretty good idea of the environment, situation, and principal events of Jesus' life during and at the end of his ministry. In contrast, we know comparatively little about the early Palestinian Church and not a great deal more about the Church of Asia Minor and Greece. Yet Bultmann and Dibelius (and now the Jesus Seminar) exhibit a remarkable degree of confidence about what early Christians were saying and thinking. In many places these scholars are able, so they tell us, to penetrate behind obscure utterances and find out with what the Church of the mid-first century was dealing.

The difficulties that form criticism faces should not deter us from engaging in its task. Proper identification of the form of a given pericope plays an important role in exegesis. Understanding the nature of a form that commonly occurs in the Gospels (such as parables) is also very helpful in exegesis and in the complicated task of distinguishing (where it in fact needs to be distinguished) the meaning in the life of Jesus from later meanings invested in the tradition as it was passed on and put to use in Christian circles.

As an example of how form criticism aids in the exegetical and historical task, let us consider the troublesome Parable of the Pounds

with Boring's conclusions, see F.W. Beare, 'Sayings of the Risen Jesus in the Synoptic Tradition', in W.R. Farmer *et al.* (eds.), *Christian History and Interpretation* (Festschrift J. Knox; London: Cambridge University Press, 1967), pp. 161-81.

32. See now R.W. Funk and R.W. Hoover (eds.), *The Five Gospels: The Search for the Authentic Words of Jesus* (New York: Macmillan, 1993). This book is dedicated to Galileo, Thomas Jefferson, and David Strauss. One reviewer thinks it would have been better to have dedicated it to P.T. Barnum, the great American showman.

(Lk. 19.11-27). Comparison with the parallel version in Mt. 25.14-30 suggests that what we have in Luke is in all probability the combination of two parables, a Parable of the Pounds (vv. 13, 15b-24) and a Parable of the Throne Claimant (vv. 12, 14-15a, 27).[33] Most of the components of these parables have been preserved and can be reconstructed. The Parable of the Throne Claimant probably ran as follows:

> A nobleman went into a far country to receive a kingdom and then return. But his citizens hated him and sent an embassy after him, saying, 'We do not want this man to reign over us'. When he returned, having received the kingdom, he commanded: 'Bring these enemies of mine, who did not want me to reign over them, and slay them before me'.

The original Parable of the Pounds probably read something like this:

> (When a man went on a journey,) he called ten of his servants, gave them ten pounds, and said to them: 'Trade with these till I come'. (When he returned, he commanded his) servants, to whom he had given the money, to be called to him, that he might know what they had gained by trading. The first came before him, saying: 'Lord, your pound has made ten pounds more'. And he said to him: 'Well done, good servant! Because you have been faithful in a very little, you shall have authority over ten cities.' And the second came, saying: 'Lord, your pound has made five pounds'. And he said to him: 'And you are to be over five cities'. Then another came, saying: 'Lord, here is your pound, which I kept laid away in a napkin; for I was afraid of you, because you are a severe man. You take up what you did not lay down, and reap what you did not sow.' He said to him: 'I will condemn you out of your own mouth, you wicked servant! You knew that I was a severe man, taking up what I did not lay down and reaping what I did not sow? Why then did you not put my money into the bank, and at my coming I should have collected it with interest?' And he said to those who stood by: 'Take the pound from him and give it to him who has the ten pounds'.

The traditional interpretation of this parable (whether understood as one complex parable or as a combination of two simpler parables) would have us see Jesus as the nobleman, who commissions his servants and departs for heaven, someday to return. When he does return, he will settle accounts. His servants will be rewarded according to their faithfulness and his enemies will be punished. The Lukan introduction

33. See Taylor, *The Formation of the Gospel Tradition*, p. 105; M. Zerwick, 'Die Parabel vom Thronanwärter', *Bib* 40 (1959), pp. 654-74; F.D. Weinert, 'The Parable of the Throne Claimant (Luke 19:12, 14-15a, 27) Reconsidered', *CBQ* 39 (1977), pp. 505-14.

(v. 11) underscores the theme of the delay of the kingdom's appearance.

A form-critical assessment of Lk. 19.11-27 creates problems for this traditional interpretation. Form-critical work on the parables, since the days of Adolf Jülicher, has raised doubts about parables as christological allegories. But these problems do not derive from form-criticism alone. Historical and sociological considerations make it highly improbable that the meaning that the Lukan evangelist has apparently assigned to the parable(s) could have been the meaning in the *Sitz im Leben Jesu*. The 'severe man' of the Parable of the Pounds is a thief and gouger and evidently a non-Torah observant Jew who thinks nothing of violating the Law's commands against usury (cf. Exod. 22.25; Lev. 6.2; Ps. 15.5). Jesus' agrarian, marginalized following could not possibly have looked upon such a figure with respect and admiration. He would have been viewed with loathing and contempt. The 'nobleman' of the Parable of the Throne Claimant scarcely paints a better picture. He is hated by his citizens and when he returns he has them executed in his very presence. What is more, the experience of the nobleman is probably based on the actual experience of Archelaus, son of Herod the Great. It is hard to believe that Jesus would have expected his hearers to view this man as a model for the awaited Messiah.

Other form-critical observations support the findings of history and sociology. Luke's introduction steers the parable toward the theme of the appearance of the kingdom. The insertion of v. 26 ('To every one who has, more will be given...') heightens the idea of reward in a spiritual or moral sense (cf. Mk 4.24-25; *Ab.* 1.13 ; *b. Ber.* 40a), and probably accounts for the presence of v. 25, which acts as a bridge between the parable proper and the inserted proverb.

Two parables that in the *Sitz im Leben Jesu* were probably directed against the political and social establishment (i.e. kings are unforgiving and ruthless in their treatment of political enemies; profit-hungry landowners reward servants who gouge and exploit and punish those who do not) have been given new applications in the life of the early Christian community. The combined parables taught Christians that faithful service will be rewarded and that those who have rejected Jesus will be judged. The Lukan evangelist, perhaps reflecting the theological interests of his community, finds in the parable's departure motif anticipation of a delay before Jesus returns and the kingdom is established.

Redaction Criticism

Redaction criticism is concerned with the manner in which the respective evangelists and their communities edited the written traditions. It is assumed that much can be learned about the evangelists and their communities by carefully observing what traditions were retained, how they were supplemented, how they were reworded, and how they were recontextualized. The evangelists' literary work is assumed to provide important insights into their respective theologies.[34]

In its earliest presentation redaction criticism presupposed the results of source criticism (i.e. the Two-Source Hypothesis) and of form criticism (i.e. that the early Church freely shaped, even created, the dominical tradition to serve its needs). Willi Marxsen's pioneering work on the earliest Gospel, the Gospel of Mark, ran into difficulties, because the distinction between tradition and redaction was not always clear.[35]

34. J. Rohde, *Die redaktionsgeschichtliche Methode: Einführung und Sichtung des Forschungstandes* (Hamburg: Furche, 1966); R.H. Stein, 'What is *Redaktionsgeschichte*?', *JBL* 88 (1969), pp. 45-56; *idem*, *Synoptic Problem*, pp. 231-72; N. Perrin, *What is Redaction Criticism?* (Philadelphia: Fortress Press, 1974); R.T. Fortna, 'Redaction Criticism, NT', *IDBSup*, pp. 733-35; S.S. Smalley, 'Redaction Criticism', in Marshall (ed.), *New Testament Interpretation*, pp. 181-95; W. Kelber, 'Redaction Criticism: On the Nature and Exposition of the Gospels', *PRS* 6 (1979), pp. 4-16; McKnight, *Interpreting the Synoptic Gospels*, pp. 83-95; E.V. McKnight, 'Form and Redaction Criticism', in E.J. Epp and G.W. MacRae (eds.), *The New Testament and its Modern Interpreters* (Atlanta: Scholars Press, 1989), pp. 149-74; Sanders and Davies, *Studying the Synoptic Gospels*, pp. 201-98; Johnson, *The Griesbach Hypothesis and Redaction Criticism*; G.R. Osborne, 'Redaction Criticism', in Black and Dockery (eds.), *New Testament Criticism*, pp. 199-224; *idem*, 'Redaction Criticism', in *Dictionary of Jesus and the Gospels*, pp. 662-69; J.R. Donahue, 'Redaction Criticism: Has the *Hauptstrasse* Become a *Sackgasse*?', in E.S. Malbon and E.V. McKnight (eds.), *The New Literary Criticism and the New Testament* (JSNTSup, 109; Sheffield: Sheffield Academic Press, 1994), pp. 27-57. Donahue's essay traces the development of redaction criticism and explores in what ways the method has contributed to the newer forms of literary criticism and sociological readings of the Gospels. He concludes that redaction criticism has not reached a dead end (*Sackgasse*) but a crossroad (*Querstrasse*), 'where different methods continue to intersect' (p. 48).

35. W. Marxsen, 'Redaktionsgeschichtliche Erklärung der sogenannten Parabeltheorie des Markus', *ZTK* 52 (1955), pp. 255-71; repr. in *idem*, *Der Exeget als Theologe: Vorträge zum Neuen Testament* (Gütersloh: Gerd Mohn, 1968), pp. 13-28; *idem*, *Der Evangelist Markus: Studien zur Redaktionsgeschichte des Evangeliums* (FRLANT, 67; Göttingen: Vandenhoeck & Ruprecht, 1956; 2nd edn, 1959); ET: *Mark the Evangelist: Studies on the Redaction History of the Gospel*

His objectives more than his conclusions proved to be of enduring worth. Günther Bornkamm and Hans Conzelmann, who practiced the new method on Matthew and Luke, were able to achieve more convincing and longer lasting results.[36]

In the case of Matthew we observe a tendency to group Jesus'

(Nashville and New York: Abingdon Press, 1969). For criticism of the subjectivity in scholarly attempts to distinguish source and redaction in Mark, see reviews by R. Pesch in *TRev* 72 (1976), pp. 101-102, and *TRev* 73 (1977), pp. 459-60.

For attempts to distinguish Mark's sources from his redaction and to establish criteria for doing so, see R. Pesch, *Naherwartungen: Tradition und Redaktion in Mk 13* (Düsseldorf: Patmos, 1968); J.D. Kingsbury, *The Parables of Jesus in Matthew 13* (Richmond: John Knox, 1969); P.J. Achtemeier, 'Toward the Isolation of Pre-Markan Miracle Catenae', *JBL* 89 (1970), pp. 265-91; *idem*, 'The Origin and Function of Pre-Markan Miracle Catenae', *JBL* 91 (1972), pp. 198-221; K. Kertelge, *Die Wunder Jesu im Markusevangelium: Eine redaktionsgeschichtliche Untersuchung* (SANT, 23; Munich: Kösel, 1970); R.H. Stein, 'The Proper Methodology for Ascertaining a Markan Redaction History', *NovT* 13 (1971), pp. 181-98; T.J. Weeden, *Mark—Traditions in Conflict* (Philadelphia: Fortress Press, 1971); J.R. Donahue, *Are You the Christ? The Trial Narrative in the Gospel of Mark* (SBLDS, 10; Missoula, MT: Scholars Press, 1973); F. Neirynck, *Duality in Mark: Contributions to the Study of Markan Redaction* (BETL, 31; Leuven: Leuven University Press, 1973; 2nd edn, 1988); E. Best, 'Mark's Preservation of the Tradition', in M. Sabbe (ed.), *L'évangile selon Marc* (BETL, 34; Leuven: Leuven University Press, 1974), pp. 21-34; W. Schenk, *Der Passionsbericht nach Markus: Untersuchungen zur Überlieferungsgeschichte der Passionstraditionen* (Gütersloh: Gerd Mohn, 1974); D. Juel, *Messiah and Temple: The Trial of Jesus in the Gospel of Mark* (SBLDS, 31; Missoula, MT: Scholars Press, 1977); E.J. Pryke, *Redactional Style in the Marcan Gospel: A Study of Syntax and Vocabulary as Guides to Redaction in Mark* (SNTSMS, 33; Cambridge: Cambridge University Press, 1978); U. Luz, 'Markusforschung in der Sackgasse?', *TLZ* 105 (1980), pp. 653-54; F. Neirynck, 'The Redactional Text of Mark', *ETL* 57 (1981), pp. 144-62; C.C. Black, 'The Quest of Mark the Redactor: Why Has it Been Pursued, and What Has it Taught Us?', *JSNT* 33 (1988), pp. 19-39; *idem, The Disciples according to Mark: Markan Redaction in Current Debate* (JSNTSup, 27: Sheffield: JSOT Press, 1989); Donahue, 'Redaction Criticism', pp. 29-34.

36. G. Bornkamm, 'Enderwartung und Kirche im Matthäusevangelium', in Bornkamm, G. Barth, and H.-J. Held, *Überlieferung und Auslegung im Matthäusevangelium* (WMANT, 1; Neukirchen-Vluyn: Neukirchener Verlag, 1960), pp. 13-53; ET: 'End-Expectation and Church in Matthew', in Bornkamm *et al.*, *Tradition and Interpretation in Matthew* (NTL; London: SCM Press; Philadelphia: Westminster Press, 1963), pp. 15-51; H. Conzelmann, *Die Mitte der Zeit: Studien zur Theologie des Lukas* (Tübingen: Mohr [Siebeck], 1954); ET: *The Theology of St Luke* (New York: Harper & Row, 1960).

teachings into five major discourses (chs. 5–7, 10, 13, 18, 24–25), often placing Jesus on a mountain. There is interest in citing Scripture as 'fulfilled'. The word 'righteous' appears to be part of a theme revolving around what it means to believe in Jesus and be a Torah-observant Jew. The infancy story is told in such a way as to be reminiscent of Moses' brush with death as an infant. The Pharisees are singled out for especially harsh criticism (chs. 15, 23). All of this led Bornkamm and his many successors to the various conclusions that the author was in all probability Jewish, that he was fending off charges that Christians did not keep the Law and that Jesus lacked the necessary credentials to be Israel's awaited Messiah.[37]

In the case of Luke we encounter a dramatically different treatment of traditional materials and distinctive features in the material found only in Luke. Luke does not often cite Scripture as fulfilled, but he does weave the language and themes of Scripture into the narratives and speeches of his characters. His version of the infancy narrative is particularly instructive in this regard. Whereas five times Matthew claims that this or that event related to Jesus' birth was in fulfillment of something one

37. Besides the work of Bornkamm and his pupils, see R.H. Gundry, *The Use of the Old Testament in St Matthew's Gospel* (NovTSup, 18; Leiden: Brill, 1967); D.R.A. Hare, *The Theme of Jewish Persecution of Christians in the Gospel according to St Matthew* (SNTSMS, 6; Cambridge: Cambridge University Press, 1967); M.J. Suggs, *Wisdom, Law and Christology in Matthew's Gospel* (Cambridge, MA: Harvard University Press, 1970); W.G. Thompson, *Matthew's Advice to a Divided Community: Mt. 17,22–18,35* (AnBib, 44; Rome: Biblical Institute Press, 1970); O.L. Cope, *Matthew: A Scribe Trained for the Kingdom of Heaven* (CBQMS, 5; Washington: Catholic Biblical Association, 1976); J.P. Meier, *Law and History in Matthew's Gospel* (AnBib, 71; Rome: Biblical Institute Press, 1976); B. Przybylski, *Righteousness in Matthew and his World of Thought* (SNTSMS, 41; Cambridge: Cambridge University Press, 1980); T.L. Donaldson, *Jesus on the Mountain: A Study in Matthean Theology* (JSNTSup, 8; Sheffield: JSOT Press, 1985); S.H. Brooks, *Matthew's Community: The Evidence of his Special Sayings Material* (JSNTSup, 16; Sheffield: JSOT Press, 1987); D.E. Orton, *The Understanding Scribe: Matthew and the Apocalyptic Ideal* (JSNTSup, 25; Sheffield: JSOT Press, 1989); G.N. Stanton, *A Gospel for a New People: Studies in Matthew* (Edinburgh: T. & T. Clark, 1992); M.P. Knowles, *Jeremiah in Matthew's Gospel: The Rejected-Prophet Motif in Matthaean Redaction* (JSNTSup, 68; Sheffield: JSOT Press, 1993). For commentaries on Matthew that blend traditional redaction criticism with the more recent holistic approach of literary criticism, see R.H. Gundry, *Matthew—A Commentary on his Literary and Theological Art* (Grand Rapids: Eerdmans, 1982; 2nd edn, 1994); D.A. Hagner, *Matthew* (WBC, 33A, 33B; Dallas: Word, 1993, 1994).

prophet or another said, Luke claims no fulfillment but records several canticles (such as the Magnificat and the Nunc Dimittis) which are laced throughout with important scriptural traditions. Luke's interesting and much disputed Central Section (chs. 10–18 or 19) challenges assumptions held about election, that is, who is saved and who is not, and why. When we take Luke's second volume into account, Acts, we find a pronounced interest in stewardship and the early Church's success in breaking down the barriers between Jews and Gentiles. All of this has led Lukan interpreters to conclude that this evangelist was probably a Gentile with some personal knowledge of the synagogue, who knew portions of the Greek Old Testament, and who was interested in showing how the Gentile mission stood in continuity with biblical history.[38]

38. Besides the work of Conzelmann, see H.-W. Bartsch, *Wachet aber zu jeder Zeit! Entwurf einer Auslegung des Lukas-Evangeliums* (Hamburg and Bergstedt: Reich, 1963); H. Flender, *St Luke: Theologian of Redemptive History* (London: SPCK; Philadelphia: Fortress Press, 1967); T. Holtz, *Untersuchungen über die alttestamentlichen Zitate bei Lukas* (TU, 104: Berlin: Akademie, 1968); S. Brown, *Apostasy and Perseverance in the Theology of Luke* (AnBib, 36; Rome: Biblical Institute Press, 1969); T. Schramm, *Der Markus-Stoff bei Lukas: Eine literarkritische und redaktionsgeschichtliche Untersuchung* (SNTSMS, 14; Cambridge: Cambridge University Press, 1971); S.G. Wilson, *The Gentiles and the Gentile Mission in Luke–Acts* (SNTSMS, 23; Cambridge: Cambridge University Press, 1973); G. Braumann, *Das Lukas-Evangelium: Die redaktions- und kompositionsgeschichtliche Forschung* (WF, 280; Darmstadt: Wissenschaftliche Buchgesellschaft, 1974); P. Zingg, *Das Wachsen der Kirche: Beiträge zur Frage der lukanischen Redaktion und Theologie* (OBO, 3; Fribourg: Universitätsverlag; Göttingen: Vandenhoeck & Ruprecht, 1974); L.T. Johnson, *The Literary Function of Possessions in Luke–Acts* (SBLDS, 39; Missoula, MT: Scholars Press, 1977); J. Ernst, *Herr der Geschichte: Perspektiven der lukanischen Eschatologie* (SBS, 88; Stuttgart: Katholische Bibelwerk, 1978); J. Jeremias, *Die Sprache des Lukasevangeliums: Redaktion und Tradition im Nicht-Markusstoff des dritten Evangeliums* (KEK, Sonderband; Göttingen: Vandenhoeck & Ruprecht, 1980); C.H. Giblin, *The Destruction of Jerusalem according to Luke's Gospel: A Historical-Typological Moral* (AnBib, 107; Rome: Biblical Institute Press, 1985); D.L. Bock, *Proclamation from Prophecy and Pattern: Lucan Old Testament Christology* (JSNTSup, 12; Sheffield: JSOT Press, 1987); R.L. Brawley, *Luke–Acts and the Jews: Conflict, Apology, and Conciliation* (SBLMS, 33; Atlanta: Scholars Press, 1987); P.F. Esler, *Community and Gospel in Luke–Acts: The Social and Political Motivations in Lucan Theology* (SNTSMS, 57; Cambridge: Cambridge Unversity Press, 1987). For commentaries on Luke that blend traditional redaction criticism with the more recent holistic approach of composition criticism, see Fitzmyer, *The Gospel according to Luke*; J. Nolland, *Luke* (WBC, 35A, 35B, 35C; Dallas: Word Books, 1989-93).

Redaction criticism's single greatest vulnerability lies, of course, in whether or not source critics have found the solution to the Synoptic Problem. I have argued above that Markan priority, which is held by most New Testament scholars today, is the most probable solution. If I am wrong, then my redaction-critical judgments are inaccurate and misleading. But it is redaction criticism itself that lends support to Markan priority, in that time after time Matthew and Luke make better sense as revisions and interpretations of Mark rather than Mark as conflation and interpretation of Matthew and Luke.

To many interpreters the fecundity of the traditional methods of Gospel criticism is plainly evident. But whether out of doubts as to their certainty (say, in the case of source criticism, Markan priority; or, in case of redaction criticism, how to understand Mark, whose sources we do not have) or out of a desire to press forward for more nuanced appreciation of the evangelists' sensitivities or out of a deconstructionist's skepticism that original meaning is unattainable and pointless, there has been of late a remarkable surge in interest in new literary methods. As was admitted at the beginning of this essay, some of these new methods have offered some useful insights. But I worry that in their pursuit some of the gains of the traditional methods may be forgotten. The problem can be illustrated in a thoughtful essay treating a feature of Lukan theology.

3. *Luke's Portrait of Jesus in the Wilderness: Context, Intertextuality, and Close Reading*

A recent paper by Robert Brawley illustrates well the potential strengths and weaknesses inherent in the new literary criticism.[39] Although he is primarily concerned with intertextuality[40]—in this case the presence and function of the Old Testament in Luke's portrait of Jesus in the wilderness (Lk. 4.1-13)—Brawley's overall approach to Luke–Acts exemplifies a 'close reading' of the text, with special interest in Luke's

39. R.L. Brawley, 'Canon and Community: Intertextuality, Canon, Interpretation, Christology, Theology, and Persuasive Rhetoric in Luke 4.1-13', in E.H. Lovering (ed.), *Society of Biblical Literature 1992 Seminar Papers* (SBLSP, 31; Atlanta: Scholars Press, 1992), pp. 419-34.

40. See R.B. Hays, *Echoes of Scripture in the Letters of Paul* (New Haven: Yale University Press, 1989).

implied reader.[41] It is fully contextual so far as Luke–Acts is concerned. For the most part his observations are nuanced and insightful.[42] He observes the presence of the quotations from Deuteronomy 6 and 8 and shows how important they are to the meaning of the pericope. Each of the three temptations is skillfully unpacked and its relationship to important Old Testament themes explored.

Although Brawley's treatment of intertextuality has much to commend it—both in terms of method and in terms of the specific details relating to the wilderness tradition—I cannot help but wonder if Brawley's literary approach (which his paper assumes, but does not argue at length) is in danger of confusing themes inherent in the temptation tradition with themes developed by the Lukan evangelist. Brawley's close reading of Luke apparently operates on the assumption that Luke was fully conscious of the Old Testament allusions and interpretative traditions found within and presupposed by the temptation narrative. From this assumption it is concluded that since these allusions and traditions appear to revolve around Israel's experience in the wilderness, the evangelist must have intended his audience to understand Jesus as reliving and in an important sense overcoming the wilderness temptations and failings of Israel of old. The temptation narrative is understood in this light and is interpreted in the Lukan context accordingly.

There is a potential problem with this approach, however, and it derives not from Brawley's understanding of intertextuality, but from his application of literary criticism. Had Luke been the creator of the temptation narrative, the assumption that the wilderness motif was paramount for understanding Jesus would probably be justified. But the temptation narrative—complete with Old Testament quotations and allusions—is traditional, not Lukan. Luke has edited this material, to be sure, but he did not create it. If one holds to Markan priority, then the narrative came from Q or something like it; if one holds to Matthean priority, then the narrative came from Matthew itself. Either way, the narrative did not originate with the Lukan evangelist. What this means is that we cannot assume that the evangelist was aware of or cared to

---

41. For discussion of Luke's implied reader and 'counter reader', see Brawley, 'Canon and Community', pp. 433-34.

42. For an excellent assessment of the Lukan perspective over all, see Brawley's *The Jews in Luke–Acts*.

exploit the wilderness motif in all of its facets.[43] It was the original writer (or speaker) who was concerned to develop this theme and so drew upon specific texts of Scripture, not Luke the later user of the narrative. Of course, it is probable that the evangelist knew that Jesus' replies were quotations taken from Deuteronomy. It is probable as well that the evangelist perceived the presence of the wilderness theme. Deuteronomistic traditions appear to underly Luke 9.[44] And, of course, in Acts 3 and 7 Jesus is specifically identified as the prophet like Moses, promised in Deut. 18.15-19. That the evangelist viewed the material favorably should probably be assumed, since, after all, he chose to include it. But this does not mean that the Old Testament quotations in the temptation narrative clearly reveal what was the Lukan evangelist's primary or only concern, something we might conclude if Luke were our only Gospel.

What the Lukan evangelist created was the *context* and *setting* of the temptation narrative, not the narrative itself. This contextualization will likely tell us more about his understanding of the narrative than its Old Testament allusions and interpretative traditions. Assuming Markan priority, we observe that Luke has inserted his version of Jesus' genealogy (Lk. 3.23-38) between the baptism (Lk. 3.21-22 = Mk 1.9-11) and the Temptation (Lk. 4.1-13 = Mk 1.12-13). On the other hand, assuming Matthean priority, Luke's placement of the genealogy is all the more startling, in that the evangelist has deliberately removed it from the beginning of the infancy narrative (cf. Mt. 1–2 and Lk. 1–2). Other peculiarities of the Lukan form of the genealogy should also be noted. First, the genealogy begins with Joseph and moves back in time to ancient ancestors. This stands in contrast to the Matthean version of the genealogy (and Old Testament and Jewish convention), which begins with the ancient ancestors and moves forward to Joseph. Secondly, the Lukan genealogy reaches back to Adam, indeed, back to God himself. This again contrasts with the Matthean genealogy, which traces Joseph's lineage to Abraham. In short, the Lukan evangelist has deliberately placed his genealogy outside the infancy narrative and between the

43. In the same collection of SBL Seminar Papers, J.A. Fitzmyer ('The Use of the Old Testament in Luke–Acts', in Lovering [ed.], *Society of Biblical Literature 1992 Seminar Papers*, p. 531) correctly comments that although 'the story of Jesus' temptation is a dialogue in which the conversation is wholly that of OT quotations', it 'is derived from 'Q' and so is not necessarily a Lucan feature'.

44. See D.P. Moessner, 'Luke 9.1-50: Luke's Preview of the Journey of the Prophet like Moses of Deuteronomy', *JBL* 102 (1983), pp. 575-605.

baptism and temptation narratives, has evidently reversed the conventional genealogical sequence, and has extended it to the first human being.

Is the Lukan placement of the genealogy relevant for our understanding of the temptation narrative? It probably is. The genealogy concludes with '...the son of Adam, the son of God' (3.38). It is very likely that Luke himself added τοῦ θεοῦ.[45] Three verses later the devil tempts Jesus: 'If you are the son of God [τοῦ θεοῦ]...' (4.3). The juxtaposition of these designations is intentional and meaningful. Apparently the Lukan evangelist has invited his readers to compare Adam, the first son of God and only person in the genealogy to be qualified in this manner, with Jesus, the second son of God. On the basis of a 'close reading' of the Lukan narrative (a close reading mindful of source-critical and redaction-critical findings), the Old Testament figure of Adam seems to be primarily in view, not the figure of Moses.

With Adam in mind, we should take another look at the temptation narrative in the Lukan context. Jesus' temptation to eat bread parallels Adam's temptation to eat of the fruit of the forbidden tree.[46] But Jesus refuses this and all succeeding temptations. Frustrated, the devil departs from Jesus 'until an opportune time [ἄχρι καιροῦ]' (4.13). This opportune time comes during the passion. According to the Lukan narrative, Satan entered Judas, who then began 'seeking an opportunity [εὐκαιρίαν] to betray him' (22.3-6). The betrayal is described as the 'hour' of the 'power of darkness', when Jesus is betrayed into the hands of his enemies (22.53). Although sorely tested during his passion, Jesus resolves to do the will of his Father (22.39-46) and so remains God's faithful son. By dying on the cross, Jesus regains Paradise, which Adam the first son of God had lost. According to LXX Gen. 3.24-25:

> And the Lord God sent him out of the paradise [ἐκ τοῦ παραδείσου] of luxury to cultivate the ground out of which he was taken. And he cast out Adam and caused him to dwell opposite the paradise [τοῦ παραδείσου] of luxury, and he positioned the cherubim and the fiery sword [ῥομφαίαν] that turns about to guard the way of the tree of life.

The human catastrophe brought on by Adam's sin is remedied by the death of Jesus. Humanity may now re-enter Paradise. This is seen when

---

45. So Fitzmyer, *The Gospel according to Luke I–IX*, p. 491.
46. So J. Neyrey, *The Passion according to Luke* (New York: Paulist Press, 1985), pp. 165-84.

Jesus tells the repentant criminal: 'Today you will be with me in Paradise [ἐν τῷ παραδείσῳ]' (23.43). But the parallels with Adam and Satan traditions appear elsewhere in material unique to Luke. Lk. 10.17-20 is instructive:

> The seventy returned with joy, saying: 'Lord, even the demons are subject to us in your name!' And he said to them: 'I saw Satan fall like lightning from heaven. Behold, I have given [δέδωκα] you authority [ἐξουσίαν] to tread [πατεῖν] upon serpents [ὄφεων] and scorpions, and over all the power of the enemy; and nothing shall hurt you. Nevertheless, do not rejoice in this, that the spirits [πνεύματα] are subject to you; but rejoice that your names are written in heaven.'

This dominical tradition seems to reflect the language found in *T. Levi* 18.10-12:

> And he will open the gates of Paradise [τοῦ παραδείσου] and will remove the threatening sword [ῥομφαίαν] against Adam and will give [δώσει] to the saints to eat from the Tree of Life, and the spirit of holiness will be upon them, and Beliar will be bound by him. And he will give [δώσει] authority [ἐξουσία] to his children to tread [πατεῖν] upon evil spirits [πνεύματα].

Another text says that a savior will come who 'will make war against Beliar...and will take from Beliar the captives, the souls of the saints... and the saints will refresh themselves in Eden' (*T. Dan* 5.9-12). In Jesus, this hope has finally been realized. The prophetic oracles promised the coming of a deliverer who 'will give authority to [God's] children to tread' (δώσει ἐξουσίαν τοῖς τέκνοις αὐτοῦ πατεῖν) upon evil spirits. When the disciples report that the demons are subject to Jesus' name, Jesus is able to say, 'I have given to you authority to tread' (δέδωκα ὑμῖν τὴν ἐξουσίαν τοῦ πατεῖν) upon 'snakes' (i.e. demons and evil spirits). Jesus' statement may very well have been intended to be understood as a fulfillment of the promise of *T. Levi* 18. Because the second son of God (in contrast to the first son of God) was obedient, humanity now has the opportunity to re-enter Paradise.

The references to 'temptation' during the passion add further support to the Adam typology that has been suggested for the temptation story, for they recall the earlier encounter between Jesus and Satan: 'Having completed every temptation [πάντα πειρασμόν] the devil departed from him' (Lk. 4.13). Because of his own success in overcoming temptation, Jesus, the evening that he will be betrayed and arrested, is able to encourage his frightened disciples: 'You are those who have continued with me in my temptations [πειρασμοῖς]. And I assign to you, just as the Father assigned to me, a kingdom, that you may eat and drink at the table in my kingdom' (Lk. 22.28-30). Shortly before his arrest Jesus exhorts his disciples: 'Pray that you do not enter into temptation [πειρασμόν]' (22.40). Luke has taken this saying from his Markan source where it occurs only once (Mk 14.38), but for emphasis he repeats it at the close of the scene (Lk. 22.46).

Apparently the Lukan evangelist wished the passion temptations to remind his readers of Jesus' wilderness temptation. As 'son of God' Jesus was tempted. Because he did not succumb to temptation, he was able to regain 'Paradise'. Since the epithet, 'son of God', appears to have been deliberately qualified by an association with Adam, and since it is 'paradise' that Jesus regains through his obedience, the possibility of a Lukan Adam-Jesus typology should be seriously taken into consideration.

What Brawley has said about the temptation narrative applies better to the Matthean context.[47] In that context Jesus is the exemplary Israelite, the true son of Abraham and son of David (cf. Mt. 1.1). As a faithful Israelite, he has not succumbed to the temptations that robbed the wilderness generation of the marvelous things that could have been. But in Luke's context, Jesus is the second son of God, who, when tempted, does not fail, as did Adam the first son of God.

Questions, of course, remain. First, on what basis can the Lukan evangelist describe Adam as 'son of God'? Secondly, how was Jesus, the second son of God, able to resist the very temptation that defeated Adam, the first son of God? A close reading of the Lukan narrative leading up to and just beyond the temptation narrative will find the answer to these questions in observing the important role played by the Holy Spirit. According to Lk. 1.35, because Jesus is conceived by the Holy Spirit, he can be called 'holy' and 'son of God'. This is the only place where the evangelist explains on what basis Jesus can be so identified. Jesus is son of God by virtue of his generation by the Holy Spirit. It is probable that this observation provides the answer to our first question. Adam also can be called son of God, because like Jesus, he too had been generated by the Spirit of God: 'And God breathed into (Adam's) nostrils the breath (or Spirit) of life; and Adam became a

---

47. To a certain extent this is borne out in the study by B. Gerhardsson, *The Testing of God's Son (Matt 4.1-11 & Par.): An Analysis of an Early Christian Midrash* (ConBNT, 2.1; Lund: Gleerup, 1966).

living being' (Gen. 2.7). If Jesus and Adam had parallel inceptions, then why did the latter succumb and the former withstand the devil's temptation? For Luke, the answer again lies with the Holy Spirit. At Jesus' baptism the 'Holy Spirit descended upon him in bodily form, as a dove' (3.22). σωματικός ('in bodily form'), which Luke has added, intensifies his Markan (or Matthean) source. This adverb is probably to be understood in the metaphysical sense current in popular philosophies and religions of the time. That is, the Holy Spirit has not merely descended upon Jesus in some sort of visionary or symbolic sense, as the parallel accounts in the other Gospels could be understood. It has descended upon Jesus in fullness, substance, and power. Following the genealogy, the Lukan evangelist again takes up his source. According to Mark, the Spirit drives Jesus out (ἐκβάλλειν) into the wilderness (Mk 1.12). In contrast, Luke says that Jesus was 'full of the Holy Spirit' and 'was led by the Spirit' (Lk. 4.1). After the temptation, Luke affirms that 'Jesus returned in the power of the Spirit into Galilee' (4.15). Shortly thereafter, Jesus reads from the scroll of Isaiah ('The Spirit of the Lord is upon me, because he has anointed me to preach good news...') and declares that 'Today this scripture has been fulfilled' (4.18, 22). In short, it would appear that it was by virtue of his Spirit-filling and empowerment that Jesus, the second son of God, was able to withstand the temptations of the devil and regain Paradise for humanity.

Luke's Adam/Jesus typology is closely bound up with the evangelist's concern for the Gentiles. Adam was created by being given God's Spirit. But because of his sin and fall, he was not able to impart the Spirit to his posterity. As the first son of God, Adam failed. But Jesus, the second son of God, succeeded and can now impart the Spirit of God to his disciples, thus generating more 'sons of God'. Those who follow and obey Jesus will be 'sons of the Most High' (Lk. 6.35). Since this passage is apparently drawn from Q (cf. Mt. 5.44-45), it may not represent a distinctive Lukan idea. But in the passage concerned with marriage and the afterlife (Lk. 20.27-40 = Mk 12.18-27) the Lukan Jesus says, 'they cannot die any more, because they are equal to angels and are sons of God, being sons of the resurrection' (Lk. 20.36). The parallel in Mark reads only, 'they are like angels in heaven' (Mk 12.25). Luke declares that they can no longer die, because they are 'sons of God'. Luke's redaction coheres with his Adam/Jesus typology. Adam, the first son of God, sinned and died. Jesus, the second son of God, obeyed and lived (as seen in his resurrection). Those who believe in

Jesus will follow in his steps, no longer subject to death, being sons of God and sons of the resurrection.[48]

In my judgment, the Lukan evangelist has tempered the temptation narrative by its association with 'Adam the son of God'. In the Lukan context, Jesus is not simply a new and better Moses or a perfect role model for Israelites; he is the perfect role model for all people, Jews and Gentiles alike. The evangelist has widened the temptation narrative's frame of reference, in keeping with his universalism.

Brawley's conclusion, which is on target, coheres better with the son of God typology proposed above than it does with the wilderness typology that he has emphasized. According to Brawley:

> It is possible to locate Luke–Acts in the midst of a community that valued the LXX, read and studied sufficiently that it was a part of the cultural repertoire from which to draw allusions. The implied author anticipates an authorial audience that will catch allusions to the LXX. But the communal nature of the use and recognition of allusions may imply the expectation that the authorial audience will experience a suasive summons to repent of its exclusivism.[49]

I think that this is precisely the point of Luke's typology. As the second son of God, Jesus succeeds in regaining paradise, something that Adam the first son of God lost and the Sinai generation failed to regain. Because Jesus the second son of God recovered Paradise, Luke is able appropriately and meaningfully to extend the Markan quotation of Isa. 40.3 to include Isa. 40.5: 'All flesh will see the salvation of God' (cf. Lk. 3.4-6). All flesh will see it, because the second son of God has resisted temptation and defeated Satan.

The point of the second part of this essay is to illustrate the potential danger in neglecting questions of source and tradition.[50] My discussion has not offered a full exegesis of certain passages from the Gospel of

---

48. For more on this line of interpretation, see my essay, 'Jesus and the Spirit: On the Origin and Ministry of the Second Son of God', in C.A. Evans and J.A. Sanders, *Luke and Scripture: The Function of Sacred Tradition in Luke–Acts* (Minneapolis: Fortress Press, 1993), pp. 26-45, esp. pp. 36-45.

49. Brawley, 'Canon and Community', p. 434.

50. For a similar discussion, with a focus on tradition criticism, see S.E. Porter, 'Can Traditional Exegesis Enlighten Literary Analysis of the Fourth Gospel? An Examination of the Old Testament Fulfilment Motif and the Passover Theme', in C.A. Evans and W.R. Stegner (eds.), *The Gospels and the Scriptures of Israel* (JSNTSup, 104; Studies in Scripture in Early Judaism and Christianity, 3; Sheffield: Sheffield Academic Press, 1994), pp. 396-428.

Luke. The point that it hopes to make is much more modest. Close readings of biblical texts are important; apart from them exegeses will be incomplete. But equally important are source criticism and redaction criticism, when they can be undertaken with a fair degree of objectivity. Knowing how an evangelist has contextualized his materials is as important as considering the contents of the materials themselves.

JEWISH RELIGIOUS BACKGROUNDS OF THE NEW TESTAMENT: PHARISEES AND SADDUCEES AS CASE STUDIES

Thomas R. Hatina

1. *Introduction*

First-century CE Judaism as a religious background must be respected and analyzed in its own right as a rich and vibrant socio-religious environment within which Jesus, his disciples, and most of the New Testament writers were immersed. Like most religions in late antiquity, Judaism was inseparable from politics. It played an integral part in the bureaucratic, cultural, economic, and military components which composed first-century Palestine. The Temple, for example, was not only a place of worship, but it functioned as the national treasury. Jewish society in the first century was marked by complexity, given its subordination to Rome, the Hellenistic milieu wherein private and voluntary associations were common, and the absence of a tenacious Jewish authority. Judaism was characterized by pluralism which formulated a variety of differing experiences, expressions, and interpretations.[1] The traditions of the various Jewish sects, such as Essenes, Samaritans, Pharisees, Sadducees, and Christians, in the Hellenistic pre-70 period have recently come to be identified as components of the greater com-

---

1. C. Rowland, *Christian Origins: From Messianic Movement to Christian Religion* (Minneapolis: Augsburg; London: SPCK, 1985), p. 80; A.J. Saldarini, *Pharisees, Scribes and Sadducees in Palestinian Society: A Sociological Approach* (Wilmington, DE: Michael Glazier, 1988), p. 60. Post-biblical Jewish groups cherished their Bible as a living text, essential for the theocentric life. It was a source from which ongoing traditions were developed: motifs were typologized, laws were amplified and reapplied, nonhistorical texts were historicized, and prophecies were deciphered, reapplied, or revitalized. This period produced some radical interpretative strategies which resulted in extremely innovative results. See M. Fishbane, 'Torah and Tradition', in D.A. Knight (ed.), *Tradition and Theology in the Old Testament* (Philadelphia: Fortress Press, 1977), pp. 275-300 (295).

plex of early Judaism.[2] Each sect shared a common, perhaps arrogant, presupposition of being the true community of God in practice and belief. The Samaritans, for example, considered themselves to be the true descendants from the ancient tribes of Ephraim, Manasseh, and Levi; thus, accordingly they regarded themselves as genuine Hebrews and Israelites even though they rejected the traditions associated with Jerusalem and the Judean branch of the religion. The Samaritan claim was essentially identical to that of other Jewish sects, namely that they possessed the authentic interpretation of the Mosaic faith, that they participated in correct religious practice, and that they were the true Israel of God.[3] These notions are particularly evident among the religious reformers of both the Essenes and the early Christians—such as the Teacher of Righteousness, Jesus, and Paul—who presented themselves as the authoritative interpreters of Torah and the Prophets, and in turn became spokesmen for their respective forms of Judaism.[4] Often in these matters social factors are inseparable from theological ones. Minority groups which are dissatisfied with society and its leadership utilize an apologetic strategy to serve their agenda for change. This sometimes results in a protest group labelling a dominant sect as deviant, while at other times it causes the protest group to accept their own deviant status and separate from mainstream society.[5]

The essential element in the reconstruction of any religious environment in history is the critical use of primary sources. Data from these sources must be utilized in a cautious manner by giving due attention to a variety of critical issues associated with them, such as provenance, author's purpose, and social setting. While serious students of Christian

2.   I use 'sect' in an encompassing manner to refer to any minor religious group or movement within the confines of Judaism. On the diverse use of this term in religious studies, see B.R. Wilson, *Magic and the Millennium: A Sociological Study of Religious Movements of Protest among Tribal and Third-World Peoples* (London: Heinemann, 1973), pp. 16-26.

3.   J.D. Purvis, 'The Samaritan Problem: A Case Study in Jewish Sectarianism in the Roman Era', in B. Halpern and J.D. Levenson (eds.), *Traditions in Transformation: Turning Points in Biblical Faith* (Winona Lake, IN: Eisenbrauns, 1981), pp. 323-50 (323-24).

4.   M. Fishbane, *Biblical Interpretation in Ancient Israel* (Oxford: Clarendon Press, 1985), p. 1; Rowland, *Christian Origins*, pp. 75-80; L.H. Schiffman, 'Qumran and Rabbinic Halakhah', in S. Talmon (ed.), *Jewish Civilization in the Hellenistic-Roman Period* (Philadelphia: Trinity Press International, 1991), pp. 138-46 (142).

5.   Saldarini, *Pharisees, Scribes and Sadducees in Palestinian Society*, p. 70.

origins are familiar with the critical aspects of the New Testament, they sometimes lack the same awareness in their use of non-canonical sources when doing comparative analyses. New interdisciplinary methods are increasingly being applied to these sources to illuminate our understanding of first-century Palestine. In particular, there is an increased interest in viewing first-century groups and individuals within the social fabric of their world, which is radically different from our own. Specific questions raised in sociology, social anthropology, and political studies are incorporated in order to view the data from the vantage point of the contemporary context. Social frameworks are being constructed wherein texts can be interpreted. This approach should not come as a surprise, for in the last thirty years there has been a massive shift by historians away from traditional history (e.g. narrative of the actions and policies of prominent figures) and towards social history. What was once at the periphery of the discipline is now at the centre.[6] It is important to stress, however, that although modern sociological concepts are useful, they should never replace or obscure the actual socio-historical context in the effort to organize and present the data. This is precisely R. Horsley's criticism of G. Theissen who divides the historical material into various 'factors' in order to highlight certain material.[7] The data in this kind of approach are used as an illustration of modern sociological categories and concepts.

The study of Jewish religious groups as background for the New Testament is significant for at least three reasons. First, most obviously it illuminates the socio-historical setting so that we can better understand the New Testament documents and the essence of Christianity in its early days. When the New Testament is read within its own socio-religious framework, the polemical and apologetic character of the documents is illuminated. Comparing early Christian thought with other forms of Judaism helps to disclose the various influential factors that shaped the emergence of the new religion. Secondly, it is essential for historical-Jesus research. One cannot properly understand or authenticate the social and religious agenda of Jesus unless one has some prior

---

6. P. Burke, *History and Social Theory* (Ithaca, NY: Cornell University Press, 1993), p. 19.

7. R.A. Horsley, 'High Priests and the Politics of Roman Palestine: A Contextual Analysis of the Evidence in Josephus', *JSJ* 17 (1986), pp. 23-55 (26-27); G. Theissen, *Sociology of Early Palestinian Christianity* (Philadelphia: Fortress Press, 1978).

understanding of the social and religious dynamics of his contemporaries. And thirdly, when the portrayal of the religious setting from non-canonical sources is compared with the portrayal by New Testament writers, certain valuable inconsistencies arise. I regard these inconsistencies as valuable because they raise important questions about sources, the audience, and the purpose of a given work. For example, when a Gospel account disagrees with a variety of different sources on the description of a particular group like the Pharisees, it should not be viewed negatively as if the purpose of highlighting the inconsistency is to undermine the reliability of the New Testament writer. Legitimate inconsistencies should be viewed as being extremely beneficial because they serve to intensify research and thus lead to an enhancement of our understanding of the nature of a given primary source.

In the following case studies on the Pharisees and Sadducees, my aim is not a reconstruction, but a survey and assessment of some main issues concerning the current critical appraisal of sources which are often appealed to in the reconstruction of Jewish groups in late antiquity. Both case studies include an examination of the pertinent texts in Josephus, Qumran (often disregarded in studies on Pharisees and Sadducees), and rabbinic literature. There is some degree of overlap since both groups often appear in the same texts. I conclude each case study by comparing the data obtained from non-canonical sources with selected accounts from the New Testament, and draw attention to the threefold significance offered above.

2. The Pharisees

Since the Pharisees appear in the New Testament and Josephus as a prominent group, their identity and role in first-century Palestinian society have preoccupied scholars for over a century. Pharisees have been described in a number of ways such as a leading political group, an influential religious party, an academic group, and a lay movement seeking the priesthood. In the past, the method of historical reconstruction has often suffered from harmonization whereby independent references to the Pharisees from Josephus, the New Testament, and rabbinic literature were uncritically treated as definitive propositions. Sources were uncritically accepted primarily by apologetically-minded Jewish and Christian scholars who were determined to defend the historical reliability of either the Gospels or the early tannaitic literature. Since the texts referring to the Pharisees are fragmentary, sometimes too much liberty was taken in the filling-in of the gaps.

Josephus

Although there are about fourteen different passages in the works of Josephus that make mention of the Pharisees, two are particularly relevant and most often considered as background material for the New Testament, partly because they are set within the same historical period—the Herodian period and the war with Rome. The first account is *War* 2.8.14 §§162-163, 166 (cf. *Ant.* 13.5.9 §172) where the Pharisees are described as having the reputation of being the most accurate inter-preters of the laws and holding the position of the leading sect alongside the other two philosophies, those of the Sadducees and the Essenes (cf. §119). They are further described as believing in fate and the re-embodiment of the soul of a good person. Their relationship with one another and with the community is marked by affection and harmony, in contrast to the Sadducees who are rude to one another and to outsiders.

The second account, which is written approximately fifteen years later (93-94 CE), is *Ant.* 18.1.3 §§12-15. This passage presents the Pharisees as an influential group among the townsfolk on the basis of their beliefs and character. The beliefs outlined in this passage include the re-embodiment of the soul of a good person, punishment for evil souls and reward for good souls, and the combination of fate and free will. Their character is marked by integrity and tolerance—as displayed through their simple lifestyle, faithful observation of their own commandments, and respect and deference for their elders. Josephus describes the Pharisees as being so popular and influential that 'all prayers and sacred rites of divine worship are performed according to their exposition'.[8] The influential status also extends into the political arena in *War* 2.17.3 §411 where Josephus aligns the principal citizens and the chief priest with the 'notable Pharisees' as a kind of task force that publicly expresses an opposition towards the revolutionaries at Massada who persuaded the Temple officials not to extend services to the Romans.[9]

Recently, S. Mason has referred to Josephus as being the most histori-cally conscious of all our primary sources since he is the only author

---

8. See also *Ant.* 13.10.5 §288.
9. This account agrees with *Life* 5 §21 where Josephus claims to have consorted with the chief priests and the 'leading Pharisees' outside the Temple.

who had direct contact with the group prior to 70 CE.[10] Despite this consciousness, several difficulties can be raised on the value of Josephus's description of the Pharisees during the time of Jesus.[11] First, while the Pharisees appear during Herod's reign (37–4 BCE) and then prior to the war with Rome (66 CE), there is no mention of them between these periods. However, given the nature of the study of late antiquity, wherein the lack of specific data is expected during a relatively quiet period, it is justifiable to draw lines of continuity from one period to another provided that no significant event which may have altered the continuity has occurred between them.

Secondly, the descriptions of Pharisaic belief and conduct may be intended to satisfy the questions raised by a Greco-Roman audience—such as the question of fate and the immortality of the soul.[12] Several scholars have also argued that the *Antiquities*, in particular, possesses an apologetic dimension aimed at defending the Jewish rights (or 'ancestral laws') in a Greco-Roman world.[13] But this may not distort the picture of the historical Pharisees; it may merely highlight those aspects which Greeks and Romans would appreciate. Mason suggests that the beliefs of the Pharisees (i.e. resurrection and fate) are included in the accounts simply because they reflect mainstream Jewish faith, while the position of the Sadducees, which denies them, is 'un-Jewish'.[14] Nevertheless, the concern brings attention to important questions which must be asked in determining the value of Josephus's description, such as: Why did Josephus include certain Pharisaic beliefs and exclude others? What

---

10.   S. Mason, *Flavius Josephus on the Pharisees: A Composition-Critical Study* (SPB, 39; Leiden: Brill, 1991), p. 17. Although Mason gives the most detailed text-critical and composition-critical treatment of Josephus's Pharisees, he rarely considers social-scientific questions. Unfortunately, he does not interact with Saldarini's *Pharisees, Scribes and Sadducees in Palestinian Society*.

11.   For a survey of scholarly interpretations of Josephus's Pharisees, see Mason, *Flavius Josephus on the Pharisees*, pp. 18-39.

12.   L.L. Grabbe, *Judaism from Cyrus to Hadrian*. II. *The Roman Period* (Minneapolis: Fortress Press, 1992), p. 473.

13.   See, for example, H.W. Attridge, 'Josephus and His Works', in M.E. Stone (ed.), *Jewish Writings of the Second Temple Period: Apocrypha, Pseudepigrapha, Qumran Sectarian Writings, Philo, Josephus* (CRINT; Assen: Van Gorcum; Philadelphia: Fortress Press, 1984), pp. 185-232 (225-26).

14.   Mason, *Flavius Josephus on the Pharisees*, p. 174. Mason is quick to point out that while Josephus may be in agreement with the Pharisees on several matters, he does not endorse their position *per se*.

purpose does the mention of Pharisaic conduct serve in the narrative?

And thirdly, a number of scholars have suggested that *Antiquities*, unlike *War*, tends to exaggerate the influence of the Pharisees in the pre-war setting. Neusner, for example, claims that Josephus favours the Pharisees by assigning to them an important political role in the *Antiquities* because they became the dominant group in post-war Palestine. On the basis of the Gospels and his critical examination of the Mishnah, Neusner argues that in reality the Pharisees refrained from all political involvement during the Herodian period.[15] Some scholars who have also noticed a pro-Pharisee bias maintain that it does not distort or misrepresent the group's political involvement after Herod's death.[16] A. Saldarini has responded to this supposed pro-Pharisee agenda in the *Antiquities* by arguing that (1) Josephus's treatment of the Pharisees does not differ from his description of other groups, including several anti-Pharisaic statements; (2) Josephus's relatively infrequent mention of the Pharisees does not favour an apologetic agenda; (3) the *Antiquities* describes their involvement in the revolution more fully than in the *War*; and (4) rabbinic heirs to the Pharisees were probably not well established as a dominant group when the *Antiquities* was written.[17] Saldarini argues that Josephus was neither pro- nor anti-Pharisaic in his overall portrayal; rather his assessment of all the groups 'is guided by larger political principles, especially the desire for orderly government and keeping the peace'.[18] According to Saldarini certain Pharisees are regarded favourably only when they participate in acts of moderation and tolerance, such as in the attempt by some to avert the war with Rome. Mason, for different reasons, also concludes that Josephus does not have a pro-Pharisaic agenda. Although Josephus agrees with the Pharisees on major philosophical issues, they do not hold the place of prominence among Jewish sects for him as do the Essenes.[19] Sometimes they do not even appear in a good light, as in the example where

---

15.   J. Neusner, *From Politics to Piety: The Emergence of Pharisaic Judaism* (Englewood Cliffs, NJ: Prentice-Hall, 1973), pp. 45-66. For a summary of his views, see *idem*, *Formative Judaism: Religious, Historical and Literary Studies. Third Series: Torah, Pharisees, and Rabbis* (BJS, 46; Chico, CA: Scholars Press, 1983), pp. 61-82; *idem*, 'Mr. Sanders's Pharisees and Mine', *BBR* 2 (1992), pp. 143-69.

16.   D.R. Schwartz, 'Josephus and Nicolaus on the Pharisees', *JSJ* 14 (1983), pp. 157-71 (166).

17.   Saldarini, *Pharisees, Scribes and Sadducees in Palestinian Society*, p. 128.

18.   Saldarini, *Pharisees, Scribes and Sadducees in Palestinian Society*, p. 131.

19.   Mason, *Flavius Josephus on the Pharisees*, p. 175.

Josephus connects the Pharisees with the school of Judas, which he abhors.[20]

In response to Neusner's claim that the Pharisees were not politically involved after Herod's death, Saldarini argues that a division between political and religious influence is too radical because it does not incorporate the complexity of their society where politics and religion were intermingled, nor does it seriously consider their political participation immediately prior to the war with Rome. Saldarini concludes that while the Pharisees were politically and religiously based, they were not, as a group, part of the governing class; rather they should be viewed as 'one of a large number of forces which made up Jewish society', for it was only the 'notable' few within the group that gained prominence.[21] In short, they should be viewed as a minor social force that competed for popularity.[22]

Josephus's presentation of the Pharisees during Herod's reign and then during the war with Rome allows for a certain degree of speculation about their status and religious influence between these periods. The Pharisees can be described as a largely literate and organized group that sought influence with the ruling class in order to achieve their ideals of how society was to function. They are best situated within the retainer class which is subordinate to and dependent upon the ruling class.[23] Individual Pharisees, however, became important leaders due to their prominence within the group or on the basis of family status.[24] On the whole, they were well known for their social concerns and respected for their extra-biblical traditions and interpretative abilities, perhaps because

20. *Ant.* 18.1.6 §23. For a detailed analysis, see Mason, *Flavius Josephus on the Pharisees*, pp. 282-85, 306-308.

21. Saldarini, *Pharisees, Scribes and Sadducees in Palestinian Society*, pp. 106, 132-33. See also Grabbe, *Judaism from Cyrus to Hadrian*, II, p. 473.

22. For a survey of discussion on the impact of the Pharisees in first-century Palestine, see D. Goodblatt, 'The Place of the Pharisees in First Century Judaism: The State of the Debate', *JSJ* 20 (1989), pp. 12-30.

23. Saldarini, *Pharisees, Scribes and Sadducees in Palestinian Society*, p. 114. The 'retainer class' is a category used by G. Lenski (*Power and Privilege: A Theory of Social Stratification* [New York: McGraw-Hill, 1966], pp. 243-48) to describe a people who do not possess wealth or power, yet do not engage in the vocations of the lower class. They serve the ruling class through a variety of bureaucratic, educational, military, and religious functions. They often possess specialized skills, like literacy, record keeping, and legal knowledge.

24. Saldarini, *Pharisees, Scribes and Sadducees in Palestinian Society*, p. 120.

these traditions were already popular.[25] There is no indication that the teaching of extra-biblical traditions (those not recorded in the law of Moses), from the time of their restoration during the reign of Alexandra Salome (*Ant.* 13.6.2 §408), were ever discontinued.[26] In relation to the lower classes, Josephus describes the group as being tolerant, moderate, and well liked. Since most of the Pharisees did not have hereditary ties to powerful positions, unlike the Sadducees, they stressed social relations in order to win favour and influence.[27]

Qumran

While the Pharisees are not specifically mentioned by name in Qumran literature, some scholars have suggested that they are metaphorically alluded to by the derogatory appellation דורשי החלקות ('seekers after smooth things'). One important document where this phrase appears several times is 4QpNah (= 4Q169).[28] Y. Yadin suggests that if this pesher refers to the exchange between Demetrius III and Alexander Janneus, as recorded in *War* 1.4.4-6 §§92-97 and *Ant.* 13.14.2 §§379-383, then דורשי החלקות in 4QpNah 1.7, 2.2, 4, 3.3, 6-7 refers to those Jews who invited Demetrius to assist them in their battle against Janneus. Yadin argues that the writer of the pesher condemns the דורשי החלקות for betraying their country when they requested Demetrius's help and thus justifies their execution by claiming that it is in accordance with the mosaic law. According to Yadin and others, the דורשי החלקות are most likely to be identified with the Pharisees.[29] The references to

25.   Mason, *Flavius Josephus on the Pharisees*, pp. 174-75. M. Goodman (*The Ruling Class of Judaea: The Origins of the Jewish Revolt against Rome AD 66–70* [Cambridge: Cambridge University Press, 1987], p. 84) suggests that the Pharisees' reputation of being the most accurate interpreters of the law enabled them to develop harmonious relations with the community.

26.   A.I. Baumgarten, 'The Pharisaic *Paradosis*', *HTR* 80 (1987), pp. 63-77 (64-65). See also *idem*, '*Korban* and the Pharisaic *Paradosis*', *JANES* 16-17 (1984–85), pp. 5-17 (16-17).

27.   Saldarini, *Pharisees, Scribes and Sadducees in Palestinian Society*, p. 122.

28.   For text and translation, see J.M. Allegro (with the collaboration of A.A. Anderson), *Qumrân Cave 4.I (4Q158-4Q186)* (DJD, 5; Oxford: Clarendon Press, 1968), pp. 37-41.

29.   Y. Yadin, 'Pesher Nahum (4Q pNahum) Reconsidered', *IEJ* 21 (1971), pp. 1-12 (2, 12); D. Flusser, 'Pharisäer, Sadduzäer und Essener im Pescher Nahum', in K.E. Grözinger *et al.* (eds.), *Qumran* (Darmstadt: Wissenschaftliche Buchgesellschaft, 1981), pp. 121-66; D. Dimant, 'Qumran Sectarian Literature',

דורשי החלקות as an established group have been dated to the final days of Hasmonean rule, during the conquest of Pompey (76-63 BCE).[30]

This appellation is also found in CD and 1QH. In CD 1.18-19, for example, the דורשי החלקות are condemned for wrongly lightening the yoke of the Torah by means of incorrect interpretation. A. Baumgarten argues—against the views of F. Cross and G. Jeremias who associate the designation with a group of Hellenizing Jews—that the designation points to the Pharisees because (1) the root דרש can be understood in the technical sense it had at Qumran for 'exposition', 'interpretation', or the 'searching' of Scripture which is consistent with Pharisaic reputation gathered from other sources; and (2) by a process of elimination, the description of the דורשי החלקות in 4QpNah suits the Pharisees better than any other group.[31] In 1QH, an example of the appellation is recorded in Col. 2, lines 15 and 32. In both of these references, דורשי החלקות appears in parallel to the denounced 'interpreters of error/lies' from whom the writer of the psalm was delivered. It is argued that the parallel description of this condemned party best suits the Pharisees.[32] In this setting of hermeneutical competition, the appellation seems particularly appropriate for a group whose interpretation is denounced. H. Stegemann suggests that this kind of derogatory name is not uncommon, for the Qumran community used a variety of polemical designations for the

in Stone (ed.), *Jewish Writings of the Second Temple Period*, pp. 483-550 (511); M.A. Knibb, *The Qumran Community* (Cambridge Commentaries on Writings of the Jewish and Christian World 200 BC to AD 200; Cambridge: Cambridge University Press, 1987), pp. 24, 209-19.

30.   Dimant, 'Qumran Sectarian Literature', p. 512.

31.   A.I. Baumgarten, 'The Name of the Pharisees', *JBL* 102 (1983), pp. 411-28 (421 n. 42). Cf. F.M. Cross, *The Ancient Library of Qumran* (Garden City, NY: Doubleday, 1958), p. 91 n. 25; G. Jeremias, *Die Person der Lehrer der Gerechtigkeit* (Göttingen: Vandenhoeck & Ruprecht, 1963), pp. 130-31. L.H. Schiffman ('New Light on the Pharisees', *BibRev* 8 [1992], pp. 30-33, 54 [32-33]) has also argued for the relevance of CD in reconstructing the Pharisees by pointing to the phrase 'builders of the wall' (4.19; 8.12-13) which refers to the opponents of the Qumran sect who supposedly transgressed certain laws. The key to identifying the 'builders of the wall' with the Pharisees, according to Schiffman, is the content of laws condemned by the Qumran sect. These laws reflect Pharisaic laws in the tannaitic material. The phrase 'builders of the wall' is probably an earlier adaptation of the Mishnaic concept 'build a fence around the Torah' (*m. Ab.* 1.1).

32.   See Flusser, 'Pharisäer, Sadduzäer und Essener im Pescher Nahum', pp. 157-62; M. Mansoor, *The Thanksgiving Hymns* (STDJ, 3; Leiden: Brill, 1961), pp. 106 n. 16, 110 n. 6.

Pharisees—such as אפרים ('Ephraim', e.g. 4QpNah 2.2; CD 7.12), אבשלום בית ('house of Absalom', e.g. 1QpHab 5.9), or בית פלג ('house of Peleg', e.g. 4QpNah 4.1; CD 20.22)—all of which were intended to portray the supposed apostasy and dissension of the group.[33]

Saldarini is skeptical in attributing דורשי החלקות to the Pharisees. In his surprisingly brief review of Qumran as a possible source, he argues that neither the Nahum pesher, nor the supposed Josephus parallels (*War* 1.4.4-6 §§92-97; *Ant.* 13.14.2 §§379-383) specifically mention the Pharisees. Although Saldarini's cautious remarks need to be considered, I suggest that the association of דורשי החלקות with the Pharisees is more than conjecture even if it is less than established fact. It is at this point the best option.

One of the most important documents that sheds light on the halakhic orientation of the Pharisees prior to the destruction of the Temple is the recently published 4QMMT (= 4Q394-398).[34] This document, which appears to be in the form of a letter, outlines more than twenty halakhot peculiar to the sect of the author. Disagreement over the halakhot, which are primarily concerned with Temple rituals, is what caused the sect to separate from Jerusalem. The author, known as 'we', attempts to persuade another group, known as 'they', to adopt the halakhot. Although the identity of the groups in the letter is not known for certain, it is commonly argued that the 'they' group is the Pharisees who had influence in the Temple establishment. This identity is made on the basis of exact agreements between the condemned halakhot of the 'they' group in MMT and the halakhot attributed to the Pharisees in rabbinic literature.[35] One example is *m. Yad.* 4.7 which reads: 'The Sadducees

33.   H. Stegemann, 'The Qumran Essenes—Local Members of the Main Jewish Union in Late Second Temple Times', in J.T. Barrera and L.V. Montaner (eds.), *The Madrid Qumran Congress: Proceedings of the International Congress on the Dead Sea Scrolls, Madrid 18-21 March 1991* (2 vols.; STDJ, 11; Leiden: Brill, 1992), I, pp. 83-166 (159).

34.   See E. Qimron and J. Strugnell, *Qumran Cave 4.V: Miqṣat Maʿaśe Ha-Torah* (DJD, 10; Oxford: Clarendon Press, 1994); R. Eisenman and M. Wise, *The Dead Sea Scrolls Uncovered* (Shaftesbury: Element, 1992), pp. 182-200.

35.   Qimron and Strugnell, *Qumran Cave 4.V*, pp. 143, 175. While there are only a few exact parallels in the rabbinic texts where halakhah is a matter of dispute between the Pharisees and Sadducees, there are more parallels between the denounced halakhot in the Qumran scrolls and rabbinic halakhot where the two groups are not mentioned. See Y. Sussmann, 'The History of the Halakha and the Dead Sea Scrolls: Preliminary Talmudic Observations on (4QMMT)', in Qimron and Strugnell,

say: "We complain against you, Pharisees, for you declare unbroken columns of liquid incapable of transmitting ritual impurity'". The same objection is raised by the sect of the author in 4Q394 8 iv 5-8 which reads: 'And concerning liquid streams: we are of the opinion that they are not pure, and that these streams do not act as a separative between impure and pure (liquids). For the liquid of streams and (that) of (the vessels) which receives them are alike, (being) a single liquid.'[36] The point of the debate is whether a connection caused by an unbroken column of liquid makes the clean upper vessel unclean.[37]

The Qumran literature provides some data on the Pharisees that are consistent with Josephus. Despite the fact that the perspective is rather hostile, the Pharisees appear as a group that is passionate about interpreting the law, forming and enforcing extra-biblical traditions, and being politically involved. As I will show in the example of Jesus' dispute with the Pharisees in Mk 7.5-8, certain accounts of the Pharisees in the Gospels are also consistent with this portrayal.

Rabbinic Literature
Focus on the use of rabbinic literature in the interpretation of pre-70 Pharisees came about as a reaction to Christian reconstructions at the turn of this century which argued that the Pharisees in first-century Palestine represented a marred legalistic Judaism that was soon to be replaced by Christianity.[38] Reconstructing the historical Pharisees in light

Qumran Cave 4.V, pp. 179-200 (186-91); translated by L. Moscovitz from *Tarbiz* 59 (1989–90), pp. 11-76.

36.   Translation is from the composite text (B 55-58) in Qimron and Strugnell, *Qumran Cave 4.V*, p. 53. For an alternate translation, see Eisenman and Wise, *The Dead Sea Scrolls Uncovered*, p. 195.

37.   Sussmann, 'The History of the Halakha and the Dead Sea Scrolls', pp. 188-89.

38.   E.g. E. Schürer, *The History of the Jewish People in the Time of Jesus Christ* (trans. J. Macpherson, S. Taylor, and P. Christie; 5 vols.; Edinburgh: T. & T. Clark, 1886–90); W. Bousset, *Die Religion des Judentums im neutestamentlichen Zeitalter* (Berlin: Reuther und Reichard, 1903); E. Meyer, *Ursprung und Anfänge des Christentums* (3 vols.; Stuttgart and Berlin: J.G. Cotta'sche Buchhandlung Nachfolger, 1921–23). Jewish scholars responded to the legalistic perception of the group by arguing that the Pharisees were primarily a lay movement that was empathic to the concerns of the common people. E.g. J. Lauterbach, *Rabbinic Essays* (Cincinnati: Hebrew Union College, 1951); L. Finkelstein, *The Pharisees: The Sociological Background of their Faith* (2 vols.; Philadelphia: Jewish Publication Society, 1938).

of rabbinic literature has consequently been enthusiastically welcomed and adopted by scholars from differing religious perspectives. Most of these scholars conclude that the Pharisees served as an important religious group whose intellectual bias and oral instruction made them the forerunners of rabbinic Judaism.[39] While these conclusions are certainly more sympathetic in contrast to earlier assessments, they unfortunately suffer from a lack of critical judgment in the collection of data by treating all texts as historically reliable. Furthermore, texts from Josephus and the rabbinic corpus, which span several centuries, are often blended together into a single narrative without proper critical appraisal.[40]

The critical examination of rabbinic sources by J. Neusner has revolutionized the way Pharisees are studied. Neusner's approach has challenged the general historical reliability of the rabbinic sources like the Mishnah and Tosefta by drawing attention to their redactional processes. He argues that the theological views of pre-70 Pharisees are difficult to access since the rabbinic material has been heavily edited, revised and re-applied to new settings. Only a handful of laws in the Mishnah appear to antedate 70 CE.[41] Neusner suggests that the Pharisees, once a dominant political group under the Hasmonean dynasty, became less significant politically and religiously during Herod's reign. Although they were a dominant force neither in the Temple establishment, nor in the political arena, their drive for obtaining socio-religious influence and prominence in the first century BCE continued after the destruction of the Temple.[42] The focus within the sketchy rabbinic accounts about the Pharisees is on

---

39. Some of the most influential works include R.T. Herford, *The Pharisees* (New York: Macmillan, 1924); G.F. Moore, *Judaism in the First Centuries of the Christian Era* (3 vols.; Cambridge, MA: Harvard University Press, 1927–30), I, pp. 56-92; S. Zeitlin, *Studies in the Early History of Judaism* (4 vols.; New York: Ktav, 1974), II, pp. 259-91; E. Rivkin, *A Hidden Revolution* (Nashville: Abingdon Press, 1978); J. Bowker, *Jesus and the Pharisees* (Cambridge: Cambridge University Press, 1973).

40. For a polemical survey of past scholarship, see J. Neusner, *The Rabbinic Traditions about the Pharisees before 70* (3 vols.; Leiden: Brill, 1971), III, pp. 320-68.

41. For a discussion on pre-70 Mishnaic laws, see J. Neusner, *Judaism: The Evidence of the Mishnah* (Chicago: University of Chicago Press, 1981), pp. 45-75; idem, *The Mishnah before 70* (BJS, 51; Atlanta: Scholars Press, 1987). For a criticism of Neusner's position on the validity of the Mishnah for reconstructing pre-70 Pharisees, see G. Stemberger, *Pharisäer, Sadduzäer, Essener* (SBS, 144; Stuttgart: Katholisches Bibelwerk, 1991), pp. 40-41.

42. Neusner, 'Mr. Sanders's Pharisees and Mine', pp. 143-69.

the internal affairs of the group, with primary interest given to the relationship between the House of Shammai and the House of Hillel.[43] Much of the debate within the party, according to rabbinic material, centres upon ritual purity, agricultural taboos, Sabbath and festival behaviour, and how in the end all of these affect table-fellowship.[44] Neusner claims that the rabbinic stories of Pharisaic conflicts do not include Pharisees opposing other groups, such as Sadducees.[45] If by 'conflict' Neusner means disagreement or debate, I find this description limiting in light of passages like *m. Yad.* 4.6-7 and *ARN* A 5 where disagreements between Pharisees and Sadducees are recorded.

When Neusner compares the sources which refer to pre-70 Pharisees, he notices discontinuity between Josephus on the one hand and the rabbinic record and the Gospels on the other. Josephus is criticized for omitting important features such as the two Pharisaic Houses and table-fellowship, and for including certain doctrines which appear nowhere in the rabbinic or Gospel accounts.[46] Omission, however, does not necessarily indicate discontinuity. All we can say is that those aspects which Josephus deems important do not coincide with other sources. Josephus's description of Pharisaic political influence immediately prior to the war with Rome is not invalidated by rabbinic and Gospel accounts which focus on legal issues. As Saldarini has pointed out, religion and politics in first-century Palestine were closely connected.[47] Moreover, the few similarities that do exist should not be dismissed or minimized, such as the importance of extra-biblical tradition and the focus on their reputation as biblical interpreters.

The legal agenda of the Pharisees in the Roman period, as described in rabbinic literature and the Gospels, can be extended back into the Hasmonean dynasty via texts like 4QMMT, hence allowing a broader base for historical reconstruction.[48] In light of this new evidence from Qumran, some scholars are now arguing that certain tannaitic texts which mention the Pharisees can be considered as generally accurate and thus relevant for New Testament study. An example which is commonly used to demonstrate the historical reliability of Pharisaic

43. Neusner, 'Mr. Sanders's Pharisees and Mine', p. 153.
44. Neusner, 'Mr. Sanders's Pharisees and Mine', pp. 155, 157.
45. Neusner, 'Mr. Sanders's Pharisees and Mine', p. 150.
46. Neusner, 'Mr. Sanders's Pharisees and Mine', pp. 154-55.
47. Saldarini, *Pharisees, Scribes and Sadducees in Palestinian Society*, p. 214.
48. Schiffman, 'New Light on the Pharisees', pp. 31-32.

accounts in tannaitic material is the ritual of the red cow. In *m. Par.* 3.7 the 'elders of Israel' (apparently Pharisees) claim that a priest who has bathed does not need to wait for the sun to set on the last day of the purificatory period in order to be ritually clean before the burning of the cow. This view is explicitly condemned by the Qumran sect (4Q394 3-7 i 16-19) which claims that the purification process in the red cow ritual includes waiting until sunset.[49] The Pharisaic view in the Mishnah agrees with the view of the condemned party in the Qumran text. This kind of agreement invalidates form-critical claims that the Mishnaic account is an anachronistic myth developed by second-century rabbis.[50]

The Significance for New Testament Study

The numerous references to the Pharisees in the New Testament do not include much detailed information about their role and beliefs despite their interactions with Jesus on a host of topics like ritual purity, the Sabbath, marriage and divorce, and religious and political authority. Most of the information about the Pharisees in the New Testament appears in contexts of debate with Jesus. That Jesus had dealings with the Pharisees should not be categorically dismissed. Since Jesus was not a prominent figure during his lifetime, he would not have been noticed by the ruling class of Jerusalem, but he would have been confronted by local leaders of Galilee who were equally vying for influence among the people. Saldarini suggests that the Pharisees were most like part of the local Galilean leadership, though not coterminous with any part of it.[51] The problem of using the New Testament accounts is that the Pharisees are often portrayed in a negative light as opponents or inquisitors of Jesus. The bias of the evangelists is particularly noticeable when the Pharisees—some of whom were well educated—are portrayed as being rhetorically and hermeneutically inferior to Jesus. They often lack a comeback. Although on this point the Gospels' picture does not square with the data that have been presented from other sources—for the

---

49. Qimron and Strugnell, *Qumran Cave 4.V*, pp. 152-53; Schiffman, 'New Light on the Pharisees', p. 54. See also J. Baumgarten, 'The Pharisaic–Sadducean Controversies about Purity and the Qumran Texts', *JJS* 31 (1980), pp. 157-70, who argues that the *Temple Scroll* directs the same halakhah against the Pharisees.

50. E.g. J. Neusner, *History of the Mishnaic Law of Purities, Part 22* (Leiden: Brill, 1977), pp. 224-50.

51. A.J. Saldarini, 'The Social Class of the Pharisees in Mark', in J. Neusner *et al.* (eds.), *The Social World of Formative Christianity and Judaism: Essays in Tribute to Howard Clark Kee* (Philadelphia: Fortress Press, 1988), pp. 69-77 (71).

Pharisees were well known for their abilities to provide responses, given their reputation as interpreters of the law—it does not invalidate the historical reliability of all the conflict accounts. The claim that the evangelists lacked knowledge of Jewish society in the time of Jesus is probably an overstatement.

Instead of focusing on the problematic aspects associated with the portrait of the Pharisees painted in the Gospels as is commonly discussed, I examine Mk 7.5-8 as an example of a debate between Jesus and the Pharisees which can be considered historically reliable. In this context, the Pharisees and scribes notice that some of Jesus' disciples are eating with unwashed hands and ask in v. 5: 'Why do your disciples not walk according to the tradition of the elders, but eat their bread with impure hands?' Omitting the quotation from Isa. 29.13 in vv. 6-7, Jesus answers in v. 8: 'Neglecting the commandment of God, you hold to the traditions of men'. Both the question posed by the Pharisees and the response by Jesus have been the centre of vigorous form-critical and redactional assessment. The question is often scrutinized for its supposed lack of correspondence to Jesus' reply (vv. 6-23),[52] or its incoherence with the historical milieu.[53] The response is generally considered a

52.   E.P. Sanders, *Jesus and Judaism* (Philadelphia: Fortress Press, 1985), p. 266; H. Räisänen, 'Jesus and the Food Laws: Reflections on Mark 7.15', *JSNT* 16 (1982), pp. 79-100 (81-82); M. Dibelius, *From Tradition to Gospel* (New York: Charles Scribner's Sons, 1971), p. 220.

53.   E.J. Pyrke (*Redactional Style in the Marcan Gospel: A Study of Syntax and Vocabulary as Guides to Redaction in Mark* [Cambridge: Cambridge University Press, 1970], p. 161) has argued that the reference to Pharisees and scribes is a Markan redaction, since words like Φαρισαῖος and γραμματεύς are often used redactionally. W. Grundmann (*Das Evangelium nach Marcus* [THKNT, 2; Berlin: Evangelische Verlagsanstalt, 1971], p. 46) and R.P. Booth (*Jesus and the Laws of Purity: Tradition History and Legal History in Mark 7* [JSNTSup, 13; Sheffield: JSOT Press, 1986], p. 34) only deny the presence of the Pharisees and not the scribes, for it is more probable that only a scribal commission would have been sent from Jerusalem to question Jesus' position on tradition. J. Lambrecht ('Jesus and the Law: An Investigation of Mark 7,1-23', *ETL* 53 [1977], pp. 24-83 [48]) argues that the entire question is redactional. Mark supposedly has utilized a source which discusses a particular incident such as handwashing or the purity of utensils and expanded it in this question to include the spectrum of Pharisaic tradition. K. Berger (*Die Gesetzesauslegung Jesu: Ihr historischer Hintergrund im Judentum und im Alten Testament. I. Markus und Parallelen* [WMANT, 40; Neukirchen-Vluyn: Neukirchener Verlag, 1972], pp. 461-62) argues that v. 5 was constructed to suit the *Sitz im Leben* for the purity logion.

Markan creation simply because it has the characteristic of 'driving home the point',[54] or because it 'serves to exaggerate the controversial aspects of the debate'.[55] While I agree with R. Booth that the question in v. 5 may be a conflation of two separate questions which ask 'Why do your disciples (1) not live in accordance with the tradition of the elders, and (2) eat with unclean hands?', I do not concur that the second question alone constitutes the earliest form and that the first question should be relegated to Markan redaction. Booth objects to the traditional quality of the first question (against Hübner)[56] on the basis of the supposed improbability that Jesus would have argued against the whole tradition by pointing to particulars such as Corban which did infringe on the commands of God.[57] But is it really that unlikely that Jesus should object to Pharisaic tradition as a whole, especially if it appeared to him that there was a negligence of loving God in the process? The challenge against Pharisaic tradition may in fact be the kernel of the debate[58] and not, as Booth suggests, a later addition used to weld together the entire discourse (7.1-23).[59]

Since it can be shown historically that Pharisaic traditions were occasionally challenged within Judaism, then the authenticity of the exchange between Jesus and the Pharisees becomes a reasonable option. In contrast, if there existed no record of opposition to Pharisaic tradition within Judaism, there would indeed be a high degree of suspicion about the historical reliability of this interaction, especially within a setting

54.   Booth, *Jesus and the Laws of Purity*, p. 42.

55.   R.W. Funk *et al.*, *The Five Gospels: The Search for the Authentic Words of Jesus* (New York: Macmillan, 1993), pp. 67-68.

56.   H. Hübner, *Das Gesetz in der synoptischen Tradition* (Witten: Luther, 1973), p. 146. See also W.G. Kümmel, 'Jesus und der Traditionsgedanke', in E. Grässer *et al.* (eds.), *Heilsgeschehen und Geschichte* (Marburg: Elwert, 1965), p. 29. Hübner and Kümmel both support the traditional quality of the question because they see its unity with the subsequent Corban reply. They differ, however, in stressing the force of the 'tradition of the elders'. Hübner places more emphasis on Jesus' opposition to general tradition of which handwashing is only a subsidiary, whereas Kümmel seems to indicate that the handwashing part of the question is prominent.

57.   Booth, *Jesus and the Laws of Purity*, p. 64.

58.   See also R. Bultmann, *The History of the Synoptic Tradition* (trans. J. Marsh; Oxford: Basil Blackwell, 2nd edn, 1968), pp. 17-18; V. Taylor, *The Gospel according to Mark* (London: Macmillan, 1952), p. 334.

59.   Booth, *Jesus and the Laws of Purity*, p. 65.

where the Church was experiencing conflict with Jewish religious leadership. Methodologically, I do not begin with the primacy of Jesus' words. Instead I begin by viewing Jesus typologically as a religious figure who seeks to transform the shape and direction of his social world.[60] When Jesus' interaction with the Pharisees is approached from this perspective, a credible portrait emerges on the basis of other examples of antagonism toward Pharisaic tradition which chronologically precede and follow Mark's account. First, Josephus describes the Pharisees as observers and teachers of tradition (παράδοσις) which is not recorded in the Torah.[61] For this reason, they are denounced by the Sadducees who supposedly adhered only to the laws in the written word.[62] As a result of this tension between the groups (within the context of Hyrcanus) Josephus writes that 'the two parties came to have controversies and serious differences'.[63]

Secondly, as I have shown above, the Qumran community also responded negatively to Pharisaic tradition. Baumgarten has pointed to 1QH 4.14-15 as one example of such opposition. The text reads:

60.   See M.J. Borg, *Jesus in Contemporary Scholarship* (Valley Forge, PA: Trinity Press International, 1994), pp. 12-13.

61.   After surveying the material in which Pharisaic *paradosis* is attacked, Baumgarten ('The Pharisaic *Paradosis*', p. 66) concludes that 'The use of *paradosis* across independent sources indicates that we are dealing with a technical term that refers to the regulations observed by the Pharisees but not written in the law of Moses'. In Mk 7.3, 5 these traditions are called τὴν παράδοσιν τῶν πρεσβυτέρων, the same distinction that appears in *Ant.* 10.4.1 §51. Baumgarten (pp. 73-74) suggests that if τῶν πρεσβυτέρων is different than τῶν πατέρων, then it may be an implicit claim of prestige by the Pharisees whereby their own traditions are aligned with the elders of antiquity in the biblical era, starting from Moses. The first part of the question in Mk 7.5 would thus accurately represent a self-description by the Pharisees.

62.   *Ant.* 13.10.6 §297. The interpretation of this passage has generated a debate. Some scholars, such as Rivkin (*A Hidden Revolution*, p. 41) and J.M. Baumgarten ('The Unwritten Law in the Pre-Rabbinic Period', *JSJ* 3 [1972], pp. 7-19 [12-14]) argue that the Sadducees rejected the Pharisaic regulations because they were not written down. In other words, they rejected the oral form of the regulations. In contrast to this view, others such as Neusner (*The Rabbinic Traditions about the Pharisees before 70*, II, p. 163) and Mason (*Flavius Josephus on the Pharisees*, p. 242) argue that the rejection was content (not form) oriented. That is, the Sadducees objected to the Pharisaic traditions because they were not present in the written laws of Moses.

63.   *Ant.* 13.10.6 §298.

> They seek Thee with a double heart
> > and are not confirmed in Thy truth.
> A root bearing poisoned and bitter fruit
> > is in their designs;
> they walk in stubbornness of heart
> > and seek Thee among idols,
> and they set before them
> > the stumbling-block of their sin.[64]

According to M. Mansoor, the expression in line 14, 'They seek Thee with a double heart' (וידרשוכה בלב ולב), is a reference to hypocrisy and comparable to Ps. 12.3-4[65] where certain descendants of the faithful are characterized by 'flattering lips' and a 'double heart' because of their hypocrisy. Baumgarten observes that the description of the group under attack by the psalmist in this context (1QH 4.7, 11) resembles the derogatory appellation for the Pharisees, דורשי החלקות.[66] The phrase 'stubbornness of heart' (שרירות לבם) in line 15 commonly appears in Qumran literature as a description of those who pursue human inclinations rather than divine law.[67] The context here concerns the hypocrisy of those who have turned from true revelation (i.e. God's word) to their own teaching, which is considered idolatry by the psalmist.

Thirdly, some early tannaitic rabbis also record Sadducean opposition to Pharisaic tradition. Historical reliability does not concern me at this point, for if the following examples merely reflect post-70 controversies, it indicates that a certain degree of animosity toward Pharisaic traditions still continued, thus chronologically bracketing the Markan account. In the fifth chapter of *ARN* A, an attack on a Pharisaic tradition is attributed to the Sadducees: 'The Pharisees have a tradition that they inflict suffering on themselves in this world, but in the world to come, they will have nothing [while we, at least, enjoy this world]'.[68] Though this objection by the Sadducees is not intended to be universal, it does suggest that at least some aspect of the Pharisaic tradition was being

---

64. Translation is taken from G. Vermes, *The Dead Sea Scrolls in English* (London: Penguin Books, 3rd edn, 1987), p. 175.

65. Mansoor, *The Thanksgiving Hymns*, p. 125 n. 7.

66. Baumgarten, 'The Pharisaic *Paradosis*', p. 71; *idem*, 'The Name of the Pharisees', pp. 421-22.

67. Baumgarten, 'The Pharisaic *Paradosis*', p. 71.

68. Translation is from J. Neusner, *The Fathers according to Rabbi Nathan: An Analytical Translation and Explanation* (BJS, 114; Atlanta: Scholars Press, 1986), p. 48.

challenged. J. Bowker cites a more general dispute over tradition from
sepher Yosippon which reads,

> The *prushim* [Pharisees] used to say: 'We keep the Torah which our
> fathers entrusted into our hands, interpreting (*mprshth*) it according to the
> Hakamim who interpreted (*prshu*) Torah traditionally (*lqblah*)'. The
> Sadducees used to say: 'We do not adhere or listen to every tradition
> (*mswreth*) and every interpretation (*peyrush*), but to the Torah of Moses
> alone'.[69]

Finally, opposition to another Pharisaic tradition is recorded in Acts
23.6-7 where Paul causes a dissension between the Sadducees and
Pharisees over the issue of resurrection. Here is another example of anti-
Pharisaic sentiment which post-dates Jesus' ministry. Since there is
evidence for the continuity of antagonism by other Jews towards
Pharisaic tradition from the reign of John Hyrcanus to the early tannaitic
era, Jesus' dispute in Mk 7.5, 8 appears as nothing out of the ordinary.
While Mark probably added the quotation of Isa. 29.13 in vv. 6-7, there
is no reason to deny the historical reliability of vv. 5 and 8.

3. *The Sadducees*

In comparison to the Pharisees, the Sadducees have received very little
attention by scholars. Two of the best studies on the Sadducees are
composed by J. Le Moyne[70] and A. Saldarini.[71] Although Le Moyne is
more thorough in reviewing previous literature and virtually exhaustive
in his use of primary sources, I find Saldarini more critical in the use of
rabbinic material and more cautious in identifying the Sadducees' social
status.[72] Most descriptions of Sadducees are said to come from

69.   Bowker, *Jesus and the Pharisees*, p. 168. A similar dispute, in principle,
seems to be occurring in the following examples where 'scribes' may refer to the
heirs of the Pharisees. *b.'Erub.* 21b states, 'My son, be more careful in [the
observance of] the words of the Scribes than in the words of the Torah, for in the laws
of the Torah there are positive and negative precepts; but as to the laws of the Scribes,
whoever transgresses any of the enactments of the Scribes incurs the penalty of
death'. Likewise, *m. Sanh.* 11.3 reads, 'Greater stringency applies to [the observance
of] the words of the Scribes than to [the observance of] the words of the [written]
Law'.

70.   J. Le Moyne, *Les Sadducéens* (Paris: Gabalda, 1972).

71.   Saldarini, *Pharisees, Scribes and Sadducees in Palestinian Society*.

72.   See also the overview and bibliography in G. Baumbach, 'Der sadduzäische
Konservativismus', in J. Maier and J. Schreiner (eds.), *Literatur und Religion des*

66

Approaches to New Testament Study

Josephus, the New Testament, and rabbinic literature. A portrayal based solely on these sources is often said to be of limited value since these sources represent an antagonistic perspective toward the Sadducees—either by contrasting them with the Pharisees in Josephus and rabbinic literature or with Jesus in the Gospels. But recent studies in Qumran literature reveal that the Sadducees are most likely responsible for the authorship of some of these documents. If this is the case, it incorporates a category of sources which represent a pro-Sadducean bias.

The derivation of the name 'Sadducee' is difficult to establish and has generated at least three possibilities. Some suggest that the name derived from the Hebrew word for 'righteous' or 'just' (צדק). Others propose that the name derived from Zadok, a disciple of Antigonus of Soco in the second century BCE (*ARN* A 5). Still others attribute the name to Zadok who was high priest during the reign of David (2 Sam. 8.17) and Solomon (1 Kgs 1.34). These last two suggestions, however, are not mutually exclusive. According to Le Moyne's detailed study, there seems to be no firm conclusion on the name's etymology.[73]

Josephus

When Josephus's portrayal of the Pharisees is compared with that of the Sadducees, a marked difference is immediately observed. The Sadducees appear to have no redeeming qualities or beliefs. The stark contrast between these groups, however, does not necessarily indicate a pro-Pharisaic bias or an anti-Sadducean bias if Josephus is read as a proponent of order and the anti-revolutionary cause.[74] Although Josephus does not mention the Sadducees as often as the Pharisees or the Essenes, he does include three references which can be beneficial in reconstructing the group as part of the religious background of the New Testament. First, in *War* 2.8.14 §§164-166 Josephus contrasts certain beliefs and behavioural qualities of the Sadducees with those of the

Frühjudentums (Würzburg: Echter Verlag, 1973), pp. 201-13.

73. Le Moyne, *Les Sadducéens*, pp. 155-63. On the origin of the group, see also the following which are not discussed by Le Moyne: G. Baumbach, 'Das Sadduzäerverstandnis bei Josephus Flavius und im Neuen Testament', *Kairos* 13 (1971), pp. 17-37; E. Bammel, 'Sadducäer und Sadokiden', *ETL* 55 (1979), pp. 107-15.

74. Saldarini, *Pharisees, Scribes and Sadducees in Palestinian Society*, p. 105. In contrast, Mason (*Flavius Josephus on the Pharisees*, p. 175) interprets Josephus as being anti-Sadducean. When the Sadducees are compared with the Pharisees and Essenes, Mason claims that they appear almost irreligious.

Pharisees. In the context of describing the Jewish philosophical schools, the Sadducees (called the second school) are described as rejecting fate and endorsing free will. The implication is that God is in no way responsible for evil. Also, unlike the Pharisees, they deny the immortality of the soul and the supposed punishments and rewards after death. Behaviourally, they are identified as being boorish (τὸ ἦθος ἀγριώτερον) among themselves and rude (ἀπηνεῖς) in their inter-actions with their peers from other sects. The Pharisees, in contrast, are described as being affectionate and relationally oriented within the community.

Secondly, a similar contrast of certain beliefs is recorded in *Ant.* 18.1.4 §§16-17 (cf. 13.5.9 §§171-172). After describing certain Pharisaic beliefs and practices that win favour with the townspeople, Josephus launches into a brief description of the Sadducees' beliefs and practices which, by vivid contrast, appear inferior. Unlike the Pharisees, the Sadducees are described as (1) believing in the more traditional view of the mortality of the soul and body, (2) accepting no observances apart from the laws, and (3) encouraging disputes with their teachers. Josephus closes this pericope by claiming that when the Sadducees assume some kind of office they submit, though unwillingly, to 'the formulas of the Pharisees' due to public pressure.

Finally, in *Ant.* 20.9.1 §199 Josephus describes how Ananus the Sadducean high priest had James the brother of Jesus along with several others executed just prior to the war with Rome. This is the only place where a high priest is described as a Sadducee. A brief general statement describes the Sadducees as being 'more heartless than any of the other Jews...when they sit in judgement'. Josephus takes his stand with the opponents of Ananus who seek to avoid discord.[75] The condemnation of Ananus is not necessarily indicative of an anti-Sadducean bias. It may instead be indicative of Josephus's disapproval of any action or group that incites conflict.

The Sadducean rejection of 'observances apart from the laws' has been interpreted in two ways. Some argue that the Sadducees simply denied the legal authority of all non-Torah traditions.[76] Others argue that Josephus does not say that the Sadducees only observed biblical laws,

75.   Le Moyne, *Les Sadducéens*, pp. 239-40.

76.   Lauterbach, *Rabbinic Essays*, pp. 31-39; E. Schürer, *The History of the Jewish People in the Age of Jesus Christ (175 BC–AD 135)* (rev. and ed. G. Vermes, F. Millar and M. Black; 3 vols.; Edinburgh: T. & T. Clark, 1973–87), II, pp. 407-12.

nor does he say that the Pharisees followed oral laws. The passage simply points to the diversity of traditions. The Sadducees had a different interpretation of biblical laws than the Pharisees.[77] On the basis of these interpretations the Sadducees, like any other Jewish group in the Second Temple period, adhered to certain traditions that were not explicitly mentioned in the Torah, but were derived from it.[78] Their willingness to dispute with their own teachers also indicates the presence of controversial traditions and interpretations within their own group. J. Blenkinsopp observes that no Jewish group formulated their religious distinctives according to a *sola scriptura* principle.[79]

Josephus describes the Sadducees as being politically oriented and often associated with the ruling class; some held important offices, at least one was a high priest, and a certain Jonathan was a close friend of John Hyrcanus.[80] Their social status is further supported by several other observations. First, their reputation of favouring harsher punishments is indicative of a group that is responsible for restraining social disobedience. Secondly, the preference for Pharisaic traditions by the common people implies that Pharisaic customs and legal interpretations met the needs of the lower classes, while the Sadducean interpretations were economically and politically advantageous for the ruling class.[81] And thirdly, the Sadducean belief in the traditional biblical view of the mortality of the soul and body is representative of a ruling class which tends to be conservative in a traditional society.[82] The association with the ruling class certainly indicates that some Sadducees were in powerful positions, but it does not follow that all Sadducees were in the ruling

77.   Saldarini, *Pharisees, Scribes and Sadducees in Palestinian Society*, pp. 113, 303.

78.   J.M. Baumgarten, 'The Unwritten Law in the Pre-Rabbinic Period', pp. 7-19; A.I. Baumgarten, 'The Pharisaic *Paradosis*', p. 65; Le Moyne, *Les Sadducéens*, pp. 372-79; Schiffman, 'Qumran and Rabbinic Halakhah', pp. 142-43.

79.   J. Blenkinsopp, 'Interpretation and the Tendency to Sectarianism: An Aspect of Second Temple History', in E.P. Sanders, A.I. Baumgarten and A. Mendelson (eds.), *Jewish and Christian Self-Definition*. II. *Aspects of Judaism in the Greco-Roman Period* (Philadelphia: Fortress Press, 1981), pp. 1-26.

80.   *Ant*. 13.10.6 §293.

81.   Saldarini, *Pharisees, Scribes and Sadducees in Palestinian Society*, p. 114. It is, however, possible that the Pharisees taught traditions which were already popular among the lower classes (see Mason, *Flavius Josephus on the Pharisees*, pp. 174-75).

82.   Saldarini, *Pharisees, Scribes and Sadducees in Palestinian Society*, p. 304.

class, or even that the ruling class was only comprised of Sadducees. Although many may have belonged to the aristocratic class as Le Moyne maintains,[83] it should be noted that the group's membership was not excessive.[84] Politically and religiously, the Pharisees appear to have been their primary rivals. The animosity goes back to the reign of John Hyrcanus who deserted the Pharisees and joined the Sadducees because he believed that the Pharisees sanctioned a slanderous statement about him. Hyrcanus abrogated Pharisaic regulations and punished those who observed them. Josephus describes the Pharisees as having the confidence of the masses, while the Sadducees were supported only by the wealthy.[85]

Qumran

It is often claimed that the picture of the Sadducees painted by Josephus, the New Testament, and rabbinic literature is of limited value since these sources are written from an anti-Sadducean bias.[86] If a reconstruction is solely dependent on these sources, then methodologically this is a correct assessment. The problem with several recent reconstructions of the Sadducees, however, is that they ignore the relevant data in the Qumran literature. An attempt to relate the Sadducees with the Qumran group is not new. Several years ago some scholars argued that the priestly hierarchy within the community, known as 'Sons of Zadok' in CD (e.g. 3.20–4.10), should be related to the Sadducees rather than the Essenes.[87] The hypothesis, however, was quickly abandoned. It was argued that the Qumran group, which is not specifically named, corresponded to the descriptions of the Essenes by Josephus, Philo and Pliny the Elder, rather than the Sadducees who, in comparison, lacked a concrete description in the Second Temple sources. There has been, however, a resurgence of the Sadducean hypothesis by several scholars, most notably L. Schiffman and J. Baumgarten, who have noticed parallels between Qumran and tannaitic halakhot.[88] It is observed that

83. Le Moyne, *Les Sadducéens*, pp. 349-50.

84. Saldarini, *Pharisees, Scribes and Sadducees in Palestinian Society*, p. 300.

85. *Ant.* 13.10.6 §§293-298.

86. E.g. Grabbe, *Judaism from Cyrus to Hadrian*, II, p. 484; Saldarini, *Pharisees, Scribes and Sadducees in Palestinian Society*, p. 299.

87. E.g. R. North, 'The Qumran Sadducees', *CBQ* 17 (1955), pp. 164-88.

88. Some of the pioneering studies include L.H. Schiffman, *The Halakhah at Qumran* (SJLA, 16; Leiden: Brill, 1975); *idem, Sectarian Law in the Dead Sea Scrolls: Courts, Testimony and the Penal Code* (BJS, 33; Chico, CA: Scholars Press,

certain halakhot postulated by the Qumran group coincide with the position of the Sadducees in the tannaitic records of the disputes about ritual purity with the Pharisees. The Temple Scroll (11QT) is commonly presented as evidence not only for parallels between Qumran and rabbinic halakhot, but also for a Sadducean connection with the author(s) of the document.[89] More evidence for the Sadducean hypothesis has been presented with the announcement of 4QMMT in the mid-1980s. Sussmann is convinced that the importance of this new scroll cannot be underestimated, for its halakhot, which he believes are Sadducean, will prove decisive in resolving the long debate over the identity of the group that influenced the authorship of other Qumran scrolls.[90] There is no doubt among many scholars that MMT contains certain halakhot that correspond exactly to Pharisaic–Sadducean conflicts preserved in tannaitic texts. In particular, the views espoused by the author(s) of the letter correspond to the views of the tannaitic Sadducees.[91] The parallels presented above in the analysis of the Pharisees between *m. Par.* 3.7 and *m. Yad.* 4.6-7 on the one hand and MMT on the other, can suffice as examples here.

While H. Stegemann agrees that much of the halakhot in the Qumran literature is Sadducean, he isolates three basic problems which, he claims, have already been partly resolved. First, there is the possibility that given the time span between the Hasmonean period and the tannaitic period, certain Essenic halakhot may have been included in the rabbinic texts within the Sadducean rubric, especially since Essenic halakhot were more familiar to the rabbis. Secondly, most of the Second Temple halakhot which did not conform with the Pharisaic-rabbinic traditions may have been practiced by both the Essenes and the Sadducees. Many Essenes and Sadducees may have shared a common

1983); Baumgarten, 'The Pharisaic–Sadducean Controversies about Purity and the Qumran Texts', pp. 157-70.

89.   Schiffman, 'Qumran and Rabbinic Halakhah', pp. 138-46. See also *idem*, 'The Temple Scroll and the Systems of Jewish Law of the Second Temple Period', in G.J. Brooke (ed.), *Temple Scroll Studies* (JSPSup, 7; Sheffield: JSOT Press, 1989), pp. 239-55.

90.   Sussmann, 'The History of the Halakha and the Dead Sea Scrolls', p. 192.

91.   L.H. Schiffman, 'The New Halakhic Letter (4QMMT) and the Origins of the Dead Sea Sect', *BA* 53 (1990), pp. 64-73 (69); Sussmann, 'The History of the Halakha and the Dead Sea Scrolls', pp. 179-200 (192); J.M. Baumgarten, 'Recent Qumran Discoveries and Halakhah in the Hellenistic Roman Period', in Talmon (ed.), *Jewish Civilization in the Hellenistic-Roman Period*, pp. 147-58 (152).

halakhot before the Jewish priests split into antagonistic groups during the middle of the second century BCE. And thirdly, aside from the disputed laws, many of the halakhot in the Qumran literature may have been common to all three groups—Pharisees, Sadducees, and Essenes.[92]

Without moving into the details of the debate over the identity and the origin of the Qumran group, I merely wish to give attention to the strong probability of Sadducean self-identity in some of the Qumran scrolls and hence endorse the potential value of these texts for reconstructing the historical Sadducees. The agreements between Qumran and tannaitic halakhot suggests that at least some of the rabbinic accounts of pre-70 Sadducees should be deemed as historically reliable. Furthermore, since the Sadducees are most likely responsible for 4QMMT and perhaps other Qumran texts, a more balanced presentation of them is possible. The pro-Sadducean Qumran texts provide a comparative framework against which anti-Sadducean texts can be evaluated.

Rabbinic Literature

In the rabbinic corpus there are relatively few appearances of the Sadducees. Most of the examples appear in contexts of disagreement between the Pharisees or sages.[93] The historical reliability is often considered highly suspect since the Sadducees are always painted in a poor light for not conforming to the traditions of the Pharisees. The Sadducees do not receive a fair hearing since they are used by the rabbinic authors as a group to be refuted and denounced for the purpose of defending the legitimacy of rabbinic teaching. In the Talmudic literature, they are sometimes considered as heretics or illegitimate Jews. The issue which is most commonly disputed between the two groups is the appropriation of purity laws.[94] Some, however, claim that the essence of the disagreements is the Sadducean rejection of oral law and

92. Stegemann, 'The Qumran Essenes', pp. 106-107.

93. There are only seven pericopae where Pharisees are juxtaposed with Sadducees, according to J. Lightstone, 'Sadducees versus Pharisees: The Tannaitic Sources', in J. Neusner (ed.), *Christianity, Judaism and Other Greco-Roman Cults: Studies for Morton Smith at Sixty. Part Three: Judaism before 70* (SJLA, 12; Leiden: Brill, 1975), pp. 206-17 (207).

94. Examples from the Mishnah include *Yad.* 3.6-7; *Nid.* 4.2; *Par.* 3.7. For an overview of the rabbinic texts, see Le Moyne, *Les Sadducéens*, pp. 176-317; E. Rivkin, 'Defining the Pharisees: The Tannaitic Sources', *HUCA* 40-41 (1969–70), pp. 205-49; Lightstone, 'Sadducees versus Pharisees', pp. 206-17.

the acceptance of a literal hermeneutic.[95] Although the hermeneutical differences between the groups are an important point of departure, I doubt that the Sadducees can be distinguished from the Pharisees on the grounds of a literal interpretation of the Scriptures. Every group in Judaism understood their respective interpretations to be correct, while at the same time rejecting the interpretations of rival groups. It is highly improbable that any group in the first century would have denied that their own interpretation was 'literal'.[96] Furthermore, the rabbinic corpus is silent on disagreements over hermeneutical principles for interpreting Scripture and on the criteria that distinguish oral law from written law.[97]

The same cautious remarks that were voiced above about the use of rabbinic literature in reconstructing the pre-70 Pharisees obviously apply here. The relevant material in the tannaitic and amoraic writings cannot simply be collected uncritically into a single narrative and considered as historically accurate.[98] The Mishnah is often considered unreliable because of its hostility toward the Sadducees. Saldarini notices that the Tosefta can also be misleading since it repeatedly replaces earlier accounts of Sadducees with the Boethusians, who were most likely also a first-century group. The opponents of the Sadducees also differ in parallel accounts. Sometimes they appear as Pharisees, sometimes as sages, and at other times simply as an anonymous 'they'.[99] Le Moyne cautions about using the Babylonian Talmud where, on several occasions, 'Sadducees' is inserted into the text to replace earlier references to 'heretics' (*mînîm*).[100] The confusion and interchange of these groups along with the anti-Sadducean bias casts a shadow of doubt on the general reliability of these texts. Saldarini concludes his assessment of the value of the rabbinic sources by stating that 'these variations indicate

95. Le Moyne, *Les Sadducéens*, pp. 378-79; S. Sandmel, *The First Christian Century in Judaism and Christianity: Certainties and Uncertainties* (New York: Oxford University Press, 1969), p. 70; Rivkin, 'Defining the Pharisees: The Tannaitic Sources', pp. 40-41.

96. Blenkinsopp, 'Interpretation and the Tendency to Sectarianism', pp. 1-26.

97. Lightstone, 'Sadducees versus Pharisees: The Tannaitic Sources', p. 216; Saldarini, *Pharisees, Scribes and Sadducees in Palestinian Society*, p. 301.

98. An example of an uncritical use of rabbinic literature is V. Eppstein, 'When and How the Sadducees Were Excommunicated', *JBL* (1966), pp. 213-24.

99. Saldarini, *Pharisees, Scribes and Sadducees in Palestinian Society*, pp. 226-27. See also Stemberger, *Pharisäer, Sadduzäer, Essener*, pp. 41-46.

100. Le Moyne, *Les Sadducéens*, pp. 97-98.

that the Sadducees became stereotyped in later rabbinic literature as the "opponents" of rabbinic Judaism, rather than treated as a real first century group with its own identity and understanding of Judaism'.[101] Likewise, Lightstone warns that any attempt to reconstruct the Sadducees of the first century on the basis of rabbinic literature is historically flawed,[102] but when the sources are compared with earlier accounts from Josephus, the New Testament, and particularly the Qumran literature, they take on a new significance. In the sphere of halakhah, the tannaitic rabbis can be considered generally trustworthy in their preservation of tradition from the Second Temple period. At the same time one should not refrain from reading them critically—keeping in mind their selectivity, tendentiousness, and particular interests.[103]

The Significance for New Testament Study
The New Testament agrees with Josephus and *ARN* A 5 on at least two points: the denial of resurrection, and the group's association with the religious and political leadership. The denial of resurrection is of particular interest for obvious reasons. In the synoptic accounts, the only appearance of the Sadducees where they are not accompanied by another group is found in the story of the debate with Jesus over the validity of resurrection (Mk 12.18-27; Mt. 22.23-33; Lk. 20.27-40). In the book of Acts, the Sadducees are associated with the Jerusalem leadership—either with the Temple authorities (4.1), the high priest (5.17), or the Sanhedrin/Council (23.1-7). It must be stressed, however, that the New Testament (along with Josephus) does not indicate that all or even most of the key religious or political positions were occupied by Sadducees in the first century, despite the common assumption to the contrary by many scholars.[104] In fact, none of our sources even equate

101. Saldarini, *Pharisees, Scribes and Sadducees in Palestinian Society*, p. 227.

102. Lightstone, 'Sadducees versus Pharisees', p. 217.

103. Baumgarten, 'Recent Qumran Discoveries and Halakhah in the Hellenistic Roman Period', pp. 155-56.

104. E.g. N.T. Wright, *The New Testament and the People of God* (Minneapolis: Fortress Press, 1992), pp. 210-11; W.D. Davies and D.C. Allison, Jr, *A Critical and Exegetical Commentary on the Gospel according to Saint Matthew* (3 vols.; ICC; Edinburgh: T. & T. Clark, 1988–), I, p. 302; F.F. Bruce, *The Book of the Acts* (NICNT; Grand Rapids: Eerdmans, rev. edn 1988), p. 89 n. 5; J. Jeremias, *Jerusalem in the Time of Jesus: An Investigation into Economic and Social Conditions during the New Testament Period* (Philadelphia: Fortress Press, 1969), p. 230.

the Sadducees with the priestly party; they only claim that certain priests were Sadducees.[105]

There is also an apparent disagreement between the New Testament and the other sources. The New Testament does not consistently represent the same rivalry between the Pharisees and Sadducees, aside from one dispute about the issue of resurrection (Acts 23.7-8). In Matthew, the groups are often placed alongside one another as if they were somehow similar. On several occasions Matthew unites them as common opponents of Jesus by using phrases like 'Pharisees and Sadducees coming for baptism' (Mt. 3.7), 'leaven of the Pharisees and Sadducees' (Mt. 16.6), and most surprisingly, 'teaching of the Pharisees and Sadducees' (Mt. 16.12). One gains the impression that Matthew is simply not concerned with the distinctives of the Sadducees' views aside from the relevant issue of resurrection. The evangelist is either uninformed about the distinctions and naively portrays them as two leading Jewish groups who represent the mainstream of opposition to the early Church,[106] or he presumes a knowledge of the groups by his audience and combines them because they shared some common interests—especially their opposition towards Jesus and the Baptist.[107] G. Stanton observes that Matthew does not combine the two groups whenever the opportunity arises, but appears to be selective for the purpose of developing a broader pattern which places a gulf between Jesus and his followers on the one side, and a variety of Jewish groups and leaders on the other.[108] Whatever the case may be, noting the apparent inconsistency is an important observation because it raises overarching questions about Matthew's agenda. In general terms, inconsistencies between the New Testament and other sources should not be feared nor minimized as if they somehow disparage the New Testament accounts; rather, they should be welcomed as incentives to further research in the introductory matters of New Testament studies, such as genre, aim and theological character, sources, audience, and authorship.

---

105. G.G. Porton, 'Diversity in Postbiblical Judaism', in R.A. Kraft and G.W.E. Nickelsburg (eds.), *Early Judaism and its Modern Interpreters* (Philadelphia: Fortress Press; Atlanta: Scholars Press, 1986), pp. 57-80 (66).

106. E.g. J.P. Meier, *Law and History in Matthew's Gospel* (AnBib, 71; Rome: Biblical Institute Press, 1976), p. 19.

107. Saldarini, *Pharisees, Scribes and Sadducees in Palestinian Society*, p. 167.

108. G.N. Stanton, *A Gospel for a New People: Studies in Matthew* (Louisville: Westminster/John Knox Press, 1993), pp. 136-37.

Comparative analysis can also aid in clarifying the meaning of a text. One example is Acts 23.8 where Paul, in the midst of his hearing before the Council, instigates a fierce debate between the Pharisees and Sadducees about resurrection and angels. The text reads, 'For the Sadducees say that there is no resurrection, nor angel, nor spirit; but the Pharisees acknowledge both (τὰ ἀμφότερα)'. But what is meant by 'both'? In light of the picture that emerges regarding Sadducean beliefs from other sources, the denial of resurrection is consistent; but the denial of angels appears inconsistent with the Sadducean belief in the Torah which on occasion makes mention of angels. D. Daube has challenged the universal assumption that 'both' refers to (1) resurrection, and (2) the existence of angels, by arguing that, while resurrection is correct, angel and spirit as a synonymous construction refers to the interim state between death and resurrection.[109] Daube observes that popular Jewish belief understood the interim state of a good person as being in the mode of angel or spirit. This understanding of the text is consistent with the Sadducean denial of an afterlife (e.g. *Ant.* 18.1.4 §16). My point is that a historical reading of the New Testament must be comparative. The question of inconsistency in Sadducean belief would have never been raised if other sources were omitted. And as a result, it is doubtful that Daube's analysis of Acts 23.8 would have ever been proposed. It simply will not suffice to deem Luke's description of Sadducean belief as self-sufficient, as some tend to do; nor is it adequate to claim that Luke is committing an error, as others often suggest.[110] Both positions are at fault for not considering the religious background against which the text is placed.

4. *Conclusion*

The study of Jewish religious groups as background for the New Testament must begin with a critical assessment of all the sources. Past approaches which were marked by illegitimate harmonization have been replaced by methods that are sensitive to each document's provenance, redaction, and purpose. Interpretations of sources are increasingly being offered from interdisciplinary perspectives, particularly the social sciences. This results in viewing the various Jewish groups in relation to

109. D. Daube, 'On Acts 23: Sadducees and Angels', *JBL* 109 (1990), pp. 493-97 (493).
110. Daube, 'On Acts 23: Sadducees and Angels', p. 493.

each other, the stratification of classes, the political and religious environment, and the economic climate. As in the study of first-century Judaism, the various groups should not be viewed as being in the shadows of a nascent Christianity. The perspective should be the reverse, for Christianity emerged from the cradle of Judaism. Whether one begins a reconstruction of first-century religious groups with the New Testament or non-canonical literature is not important, as long as all the sources are equally evaluated. I have suggested at least three reasons why the study of religious groups as background is significant for New Testament study: (1) it helps to clarify the meaning of texts; (2) it is essential for historical-Jesus research; and (3) apparent inconsistencies serve as a catalyst for further research.

Future studies of the Pharisees and Sadducees cannot be restricted to data found in Josephus, the New Testament, and rabbinic literature as is often the case. With the recent announcement of 4QMMT, Qumran literature has once again been shown to be a viable source. The addition of Qumran literature to the corpus of established sources is highly significant for two reasons. First, if 4QMMT is a condemnation of the Pharisees by the Sadducees, as most scholars think, it provides a perspective on both groups not found in other sources. For example, with the addition of 4QMMT, it can no longer be said that all our sources pertinent to Sadducean research are antagonistic. Secondly, several explicit agreements between the halakhot in 4QMMT (and other Qumran texts) and the halakhot in tannaitic literature have supported the historical reliability of a number of tannaitic texts that refer to the Pharisees and Sadducees.

LITERARY APPROACHES TO THE NEW TESTAMENT: FROM FORMALISM TO DECONSTRUCTION AND BACK

Stanley E. Porter

1. *Introduction*

Despite the fact that literary-critical exegesis of the New Testament is of only fairly recent provenance, the New Testament itself suggests that literary sensitivity has been necessary from the start. For example, in Jn 2.21, the author tells his readers that when Jesus mentioned the temple 'he spoke of the temple of his body', an example of Jesus using metaphor. In Mt. 13.1-9 with 18-23 and 13.24-30 with 36-43, the parables of the sower and the wheat and tares are interpreted by Jesus using allegory.[1] In Gal. 4.22-25, Paul uses allegory regarding the sons of Abraham; and in 2 Cor. 3.6, Paul's distinction between the 'written code' that kills and the 'spirit' that gives life became the justification for medieval allegorizing, besides illustrating personification.

Throughout the last nearly two millennia there has been much pre-critical literary reading of the Bible.[2] For example, Pseudo-Longinus, in *On the Sublime* 9.10, says of Moses: 'So, too, the lawgiver of the Jews, no ordinary man, having formed a worthy conception of divine power, gave expression to it at the very threshold of his *Laws* where he says: "God said"—what? "Let there be light", and there was light. "Let there be earth", and there was earth' (LCL). After early diversity regarding interpretative stances—between the Antiochian and Alexandrian schools—in the Western Church New Testament interpretation was dominated for centuries by the allegorical method. Although not a part

---

1. It is immaterial for this chapter whether Jesus actually gave this interpretation, the item that has been of most concern to interpreters.

2. See R. Grant with D. Tracy, *A Short History of the Interpretation of the Bible* (London: SCM Press, 1963; 2nd edn, 1984) for a history of interpretation of the Bible; cf. J.L. Kugel and R.A. Greer, *Early Biblical Interpretation* (Philadelphia: Westminster Press, 1986).

of literary-critical exegesis today, the allegorical method is a literary method. Allegorical interpretation, whether implicitly or explicitly, posits an extended metaphor in a written work, in which various persons, actions or even objects are equated with meanings at various levels.[3] Despite attention to matters of context in much Reformation exegesis, it was not until Jülicher's work on the parables that allegory's stranglehold on parable interpretation was loosened (though not completely eliminated, as recent work has shown).[4]

Thus literary issues have had a place in interpretation of the Bible, including the New Testament, from earliest days. This continued with the rise of modern criticism.[5] Lowth in his *Praelectiones de sacra poesi Hebraeorum* (1753; ET *Lectures on the Sacred Poetry of the Hebrews*, 1815) developed his well-known scheme of Hebrew parallelism (synonymous, antithetic, step) as an attempt to establish suitable criteria for the analysis of Semitic poetry.[6] His interest grew out of the concern to show that Hebrew poetry was not inferior to classical poetry, to which it bore very little (if any) resemblance. A similar concern was found in the form-critical work of Gunkel,[7] and the generic approach of R. Moulton.[8] Many of these were attempts to show that the biblical writings were not inferior to their classical counterparts, by illustrating that the Bible had many of the same classical forms. This generic or form-oriented approach has had a recent resurgence, although not apparently for the same apologetic reasons.[9]

3.   See C.H. Holman, *A Handbook to Literature* (Indianapolis: Bobbs-Merrill, 3rd edn, 1972), p. 13.

4.   See A. Jülicher, *Die Gleichnisreden Jesu* (2 vols.; Tübingen: Mohr–Siebeck, 1899). Among the few who have tried to revive the allegorical interpretation of parables is C.L. Blomberg, *Interpreting the Parables* (Downers Grove, IL: InterVarsity Press, 1990).

5.   An interesting summary of this history is found in R. Morgan with J. Barton, *Biblical Interpretation* (Oxford: Oxford University Press, 1988), pp. 205-10.

6.   Since disputed, especially by J.L. Kugel, *The Idea of Biblical Poetry: Parallelism and its History* (New Haven: Yale University Press, 1981), and R. Alter, *The Art of Biblical Poetry* (New York: Basic Books, 1985), although they have differing views on the literary character of the Old Testament. See also A. Berlin, *The Dynamics of Biblical Parallelism* (Bloomington: Indiana University Press, 1985).

7.   E.g. H. Gunkel, *What Remains of the Old Testament and Other Essays* (London: Allen & Unwin, 1928).

8.   R. Moulton, *The Literary Study of the Bible* (Boston: Heath, 1899).

9.   See D.E. Aune, *The New Testament in its Literary Environment* (Philadelphia: Westminster Press, 1987); *idem* (ed.), *Greco-Roman Literature and*

With the growing dominance of the higher-critical method, however, interest by biblical scholars in the aesthetic literary dimension of the biblical text diminished,[10] so that the major literary interpretation of the Bible was by those outside the guild of biblical scholars.[11] The height of this was perhaps reached in 1946 when Auerbach wrote his *Mimesis*. In this classic work (not least because it is a scholarly work written without footnotes), Auerbach draws a contrast between his characterization of the flat characters and events found in the classical epic (e.g. the failure of the suitors to recognize Odysseus until Eurycleia, the nurse, sees the scar on his leg) and the depth and layers of background in the biblical account (e.g. Abraham's sacrifice of Isaac in Genesis 22).[12] In 1952, Chase published her *The Bible and the Common Reader*, representing the Bible as literature movement, which has continued in many ways, although outside the mainstream of most biblical exegesis.[13] She takes a

the New Testament (SBLSBS, 21; Atlanta: Scholars Press, 1988); G.D. Fee and D. Stuart, *How to Read the Bible for all its Worth: A Guide to Understanding the Bible* (Grand Rapids: Zondervan, 2nd edn, 1993 [1981]); J.L. Bailey and L.D. Vander Broek, *Literary Forms in the New Testament* (London: SPCK, 1992). For a literary discussion of the topic, see H. Dubrow, *Genre* (Critical Idiom; London: Methuen, 1982).

10. An apparent exception to this might be treatments of chiasm, which are by my estimation not to be considered particularly literary by either ancient or modern standards. See J. Welch (ed.), *Chiasmus in Antiquity* (Hildesheim: Gerstenberg, 1981).

11. Important to note here are, among others, R. Alter, *The Art of Biblical Narrative* (New York: Basic Books, 1981); *idem*, *The World of Biblical Literature* (New York: Basic Books, 1992); N. Frye, *The Great Code: The Bible and Literature* (New York: Harcourt Brace Jovanovich, 1982); and F. Kermode, *The Genesis of Secrecy: On the Interpretation of Narrative* (Cambridge, MA: Harvard University Press, 1979).

12. E. Auerbach, *Mimesis: The Representation of Reality in Western Literature* (trans. W.R. Trask; Princeton: Princeton University Press, 1953), esp. pp. 3-23. However, this has been questioned by K.R.R. Gros Louis, 'Abraham: II', in K.R.R. Gros Louis with J.S. Ackerman (eds.), *Literary Interpretations of Biblical Narratives, Volume II* (Nashville: Abingdon Press, 1982), pp. 71-74.

13. M.E. Chase, *The Bible and the Common Reader* (London: Macmillan, 1952). This area covers a range of works. See, for example, R. Henn, 'The Bible as Literature', in M. Black and H.H. Rowley (eds.), *Peake's Commentary on the Bible* (London: Nelson, 1962), pp. 8-23; L. Ryken, *The Literature of the Bible* (Grand Rapids: Zondervan, 1974); *idem*, *Words of Delight: A Literary Introduction to the Bible* (Grand Rapids: Baker, 1987); *idem*, *Words of Life: A Literary Introduction to the New Testament* (Grand Rapids: Baker, 1987); L. Ryken and T. Longman, III

common-sensical approach to literary criticism, often equated with those who are suspicious of professional literary or biblical interpreters.

Thus, despite long-standing interest in the literary nature of the Bible, it is only within the last twenty years, or so, that New Testament scholars have begun exploring what it means to offer a literary-critical reading of the New Testament. Much of the current interest in biblical literary criticism stems from the 1969 SBL presidential lecture of Muilenburg.[14] His essay programmatically called for scholars to move beyond form criticism and consider literary issues, such as structure and aesthetics. Muilenburg's literary criticism essentially amounted to what he called and in many ways has developed into rhetorical criticism, although Muilenburg invoked the language of the New Criticism, which at the time was anything but new, having been first developed in the 1920's (see below). Nevertheless, it was new to the vast majority of biblical scholars, and found a welcome reception, not least because of a sense of frustration with higher criticism. Despite the fact that so far as the New Testament was concerned Muilenburg never did much substantive literary analysis,[15] many people have looked to Muilenburg's essay as the start of a new era in literary criticism that took firm root first in Old Testament studies.[16]

(eds.), *A Complete Literary Guide to the Bible* (Grand Rapids: Zondervan, 1993); R. Alter and F. Kermode (eds.), *The Literary Guide to the Bible* (Cambridge, MA: Harvard University Press, 1987); M.N. Ralph, *'And God Said What?': An Introduction to Biblical Literary Forms for Bible Lovers* (New York: Paulist, 1986); W.A. Kort, *Story, Text, and Scripture: Literary Interests in Biblical Narrative* (University Park: Pennsylvania State University Press, 1988); S. Prickett and R. Barnes, *The Bible* (Cambridge: Cambridge University Press, 1991); S. Prickett (ed.), *Reading the Text: Biblical Criticism and Literary Theory* (Oxford: Basil Blackwell, 1991).

14. J. Muilenburg, 'Form Criticism and Beyond', *JBL* 88 (1969), pp. 1-18; followed, for example, by J. Dewey, *Markan Public Debate* (SBLDS, 48; Chico, CA: Scholars Press, 1980).

15. An exception is his early 'Literary Form in the Fourth Gospel', *JBL* 51 (1932), pp. 40-53.

16. See D.M. Gunn, 'Narrative Criticism', in S.L. McKenzie and S.R. Haynes (eds.), *To Each its Own Meaning: An Introduction to Biblical Criticisms and their Application* (Louisville: Westminster/John Knox, 1993), p. 174. This kind of criticism has continued to develop, in large part aided by the fact that several of the major figures in the interpretation of the Old Testament from a literary perspective were also literary critics in their own rights, such as Robert Alter and Meir Sternberg (*The Poetics of Biblical Narrative: Ideological Literature and the Drama of Reading*

Before discussing the rise of literary criticism of the New Testament, however, the place of redaction criticism in relation to literary-critical exegesis must be considered.[17] As mentioned above, form criticism began as a type of literary criticism, concerned with generic or form-critical questions. However, form criticism did not reach its literary potential. Content to examine forms only in so far as they were part of a larger historical-critical investigation, form criticism never fully developed a sense for the relationships among the forms within a given work. In the light of these limitations redaction criticism offered great promise, since at least in some versions of redaction criticism the Gospel writers were seen to be authors, not just compilers, and the changes to their sources were seen to be meaningful literary features. Among redaction critics there have been at least two reactions to literary criticism. The majority of rigorous redaction critics seem to hold that, while there may be some merits to literary criticism of the New Testament, they need to distance what they see as responsible criticism from literary criticism. Common points of critique are that literary-criticism is too subjective, without the kinds of rigorous methodological controls that supposedly exist in higher criticism, that literary criticism is a-historical and hence without appropriate contextual basis, and that literary criticism has been a method that has enabled some critics to dodge difficult historical and theological questions. As seen below, there is much truth in these points of criticism. At least one commentator on the relation between literary and redaction criticism, however, has argued that many redaction critics have been more faithful to the literary-critical agenda than have many of the literary critics themselves, with the result that often redaction critics have produced more insightful and well-argued readings than have some of the literary critics, who methodologically naively perpetuate a common-sensical phenomenological criticism with little substantive argumentative support.[18] Despite the latter view, and in the light of continuing assessment of redaction criticism and its place within critical enquiry, it seems that redaction criticism will never be seen to answer

[Bloomington: Indiana University Press, 1985]); cf. also S. Bar-Efrat, *Narrative Art in the Bible* (JSOTSup, 70; Sheffield: Almond Press, 1989).

17. See ch. 1 of this volume, and the literature surveyed in E.V. McKnight, 'Form and Redaction Criticism', in E.J. Epp and G.W. MacRae (eds.), *The New Testament and its Modern Interpreters* (Atlanta: Scholars Press, 1989), pp. 149-74.

18. See S.D. Moore, *Literary Criticism and the Gospels: The Theoretical Challenge* (New Haven: Yale University Press, 1989), pp. 56-68.

the kinds of questions that many literary critics believe need to be answered. Redaction criticism, especially in its earlier forms (before having been influenced by literary criticism?), is often thought to have failed to see the whole text, concentrated more on seams or changes in the text rather than on what the text retains from its source, argued too much on the basis of word statistics, been wed to a particular kind of historical agenda, and been only concerned with a narrow range of 'theological' questions, often equated with reconstructions of early Christian communities. In the light of the growth of literary criticism, however, and as the essay on historical criticism of the Gospels indicates, redaction criticism has been and probably will continue to be influenced by literary methods.[19]

Having surveyed several background issues, I now turn to recent literary criticism of the New Testament. My discussion takes three major parts: theory, practice and assessment. In the first, I discuss the slow growth of New Testament literary interpretation, especially in relation to Old Testament study, and then mention the crucial issue of interpretative authority. In the second, I trace the several literary-critical trends as they have developed in New Testament study, citing a few representative works and offering a brief critique. I begin with the naive and then move to the more critically aware New Critical (or phenomenological) analyses (including so-called narrative criticism), turn to reader-response criticism, and conclude with postmodernism and deconstruction. In the third part, I offer a brief conspectus of strengths and limitations of literary-critical exegesis and what I perceive to be the future prospects of it. My survey of the field differs significantly from several other treatments,[20] the most noticeable being the way in which I define literary criticism. I do not

19. See J.R. Donahue, 'Redaction Criticism: Has the *Hauptstrasse* Become a *Sackgasse*?', in E.S. Malbon and E.V. McKnight (eds.), *The New Literary Criticism and the New Testament* (JSNTSup, 109; Sheffield: Sheffield Academic Press, 1994), pp. 27-57.

20. For enlightening treatments of New Testament literary criticism, among many see the following: E.S. Malbon and E.V. McKnight, 'Introduction', in Malbon and McKnight (eds.) *New Literary Criticism*, pp. 15-26 and examples in the rest of the volume; Morgan, *Biblical Interpretation*, pp. 211-68; N. Petersen, *Literary Criticism for New Testament Critics* (Philadelphia: Fortress Press, 1978); T. Longman, III, *Literary Approaches to Biblical Interpretation* (Grand Rapids: Zondervan, 1987); and J.C. Anderson and S.D. Moore (eds.), *Mark and Method: New Approaches in Biblical Studies* (Minneapolis: Fortress Press, 1992), esp. chs. 2–4.

attempt to confine it to a single movement or a single thing, and I treat it here as it applies virtually entirely to the New Testament.[21]

2. Theoretical Questions in New Testament Literary Criticism

a. The Late Arrival of New Testament Literary Criticism

Literary interpretation of the New Testament took longer to catch on than Old Testament literary study,[22] and it has still not included substantial treatments of all types of New Testament literature. The first reason for this slow development may have been the belief that quantifiable examples of recognizable literature (such as psalms and poetry of various types, proverbs, epic narratives such as Exodus, etc., found in the Old Testament), such that recognized authorities in literary study would devote books and articles to their interpretation (as noted above), were not to be found as easily in New Testament studies. The vast majority of earlier discussion of 'literary questions' was in terms of how the New Testament writings were to be positioned in relation to other Hellenistic literature.

Although there was discussion in the early part of this century of the literary character of the Gospels as ancient biography, the form-critical

21. I do not treat here structuralism, which I consider to be a moribund subdiscipline of New Testament studies (and only tangentially related to literary criticism), nor do I treat rhetorical criticism, which is treated elsewhere in this volume. For an essay that confuses these two with literary criticism, see R.R. Melick, Jr, 'Literary Criticism of the New Testament', in D.S. Dockery, K.A. Mathews and R.B. Sloan (eds.), *Foundations for Biblical Interpretation: A Complete Library of Tools and Resources* (Nashville: Broadman & Holman, 1994), pp. 434-53. Those wanting material on structuralism and biblical studies should consult D. Patte, *What is Structural Exegesis?* (Philadelphia: Fortress Press, 1976); *idem, The Gospel according to Matthew: A Structural Commentary on Matthew's Gospel* (Philadelphia: Fortress Press, 1987); and *idem, Paul's Faith and the Power of the Gospel: A Structural Introduction to the Pauline Letters* (Philadelphia: Fortress Press, 1983). For a general introduction, see J. Culler, *Structuralist Poetics: Structuralism, Linguistics, and the Study of Literature* (Ithaca, NY: Cornell University Press, 1975). Neither do I equate literary criticism with stylistics, as does A.B. Spencer, 'Literary Criticism', in D.A. Black and D.S. Dockery (eds.), *New Testament Criticism and Interpretation* (Grand Rapids: Zondervan, 1991), pp. 227-51.

22. For a treatment of Old Testament literary criticism, see Gunn, 'Narrative Criticism', pp. 172-78; J.C. Exum and D.J.A. Clines (eds.), *The New Literary Criticism and the Hebrew Bible* (JSOTSup, 143; Sheffield: Sheffield Academic Press, 1993).

conclusion was that they were unique, neither the *Hoch-* nor *Kleinliteratur* of the ancient world. This viewpoint has predominated until recent times. Although there have been occasional arguments for the literary nature of the Gospels, the argument is not one that many literary critics are used to making. Rather than assessing internal features of the text, such as character, plot, setting or something similar, the arguments have been almost entirely related to whether the Gospels are examples of ancient biography.[23] It is significant that the parables have since World War II solicited a number of literary interpretations, but this has probably been encouraged by the fact that the parable has been seen to be one of the proven form-critical types.[24] Most recent discussion of Acts has been about Acts as a theological or historical book, with opinions varying according to theological orientation. In recent years, literary questions have been raised regarding Acts, but they are of a generic type, whether Acts utilizes one of the set forms of ancient writing, either a sea-voyage or some form of ancient fiction. Although these theories have convinced many, they have not convinced all;[25] the level of literary analysis of Acts is still quite jejune. Readings of the Gospel of John have moved ahead of the Synoptics,[26] recognizing its more literarily sensitive language. The Gospel opens with what many have argued is a highly literary and allusive introduction,[27] Jesus' language is recognizably literary, and the plot has commended itself to analysis.[28]

23. For a good recent discussion, see R.A. Burridge, *What are the Gospels?: A Comparison with Graeco-Roman Biography* (SNTSMS, 70; Cambridge: Cambridge University Press, 1992).

24. For a survey of interpretation, see Blomberg, *Interpreting the Parables*, pp. 133-63; cf. C.W. Hedrick, *Parables as Poetic Fictions: The Creative Voice of Jesus* (Peabody, MA: Hendrickson, 1994), esp. pp. 39-89.

25. See S.E. Porter, 'The "We" Passages', in D.W.J. Gill and C. Gempf (eds.), *The Book of Acts in its First Century Setting.* II. *Graeco-Roman Setting* (Grand Rapids: Eerdmans, 1994), esp. pp. 548-58.

26. See the collection of essays in M.W.G. Stibbe (ed.), *The Gospel of John as Literature: An Anthology of Twentieth-Century Perspectives* (NTTS, 17; Leiden: Brill, 1993).

27. See F. Kermode, 'St John as Poet', *JSNT* 28 (1986), pp. 3-16.

28. See M.W.G. Stibbe, *John as Storyteller: Narrative Criticism of the Fourth Gospel* (SNTSMS, 73; Cambridge: Cambridge University Press, 1992); *idem, John* (Readings; Sheffield: JSOT Press, 1993); *idem, John's Gospel* (London: Routledge, 1994); T.L. Brodie, *The Gospel according to John: A Literary and Theological Commentary* (New York: Oxford University Press, 1993).

Study of the epistles has been overly dominated in this century by Deissmann's disjunction between the literary epistle and non-literary letter.[29] The New Testament letters, including Paul's, so far as Deissmann was concerned, were non-literary, and hence not subject to examination the way epistles, such as Plato's, were. Study of epistolary form has progressed since Deissmann, primarily in two directions. The first is New Testament epistolary structure, especially as it favourably compares with the non-literary papyrus letters.[30] Interpreters of letters now appreciate more the structure of the letter, the function of its various parts, the various formulas used in the letter form and the like. The second direction is rhetorical analysis. Rhetorical analysis is itself a complex field of exploration, with debate regarding whether an ancient or modern rhetorical model should be used, and how a writer such as Paul is to be seen in relation to these models (see ch. 4 of this volume). Neither of these models is a literary model as discussed here, however. Apart from some very rudimentary attempts, serious literary investigation of the epistles is only beginning.[31] One of the major factors to include is being able to see epistolary arrangement of material as in some way creating a literary structure, one that encompasses writers and readers (implied or actual). For example, in P. Oxy. 119 young Theon writes to old Theon, his father, expressing in ironic and sarcastic terms his disappointment that his father has not taken him along to Alexandria. Here are found distinct characters, a plot, and a setting.

Secondly, further reason why analysis of the New Testament has taken longer to develop is that not as many literary scholars (excluding biblical scholars for the moment) have turned their critical attention to interpreting the New Testament, and when they do, they have not been particularly well regarded. Scholars such as Kermode and Frye (see above) have been politely received but have failed except in the rare instance to affect the mainstream of interpretation. An exception to this is Wilder. A poet, Wilder was ahead of his time in his analyses, but was

29. See G.A. Deissmann, *Bible Studies* (trans. A. Grieve; Edinburgh: T. & T. Clark, 1923), pp. 1-59.

30. See, for example, J.L. White, *Light from Ancient Letters* (FFNT; Philadelphia: Fortress Press, 1986).

31. An important work is N. Petersen, *Rediscovering Paul: Philemon and the Sociology of Paul's Narrative World* (Philadelphia: Fortress Press, 1985), esp. pp. 43-88. Less convincing are J.P. Heil, *Paul's Letter to the Romans: A Reader-Response Commentary* (New York: Paulist Press, 1987) and M. Kitchen, *Ephesians* (New Testament Readings; London: Routledge, 1994).

able to excite interest in the symbolic function of language, as reflected in the later work of Perrin.[32]

A third possible reason why New Testament literary criticism has been long in developing is related to two tendencies also found in Old Testament criticism. One is to label readings as literary when they are nothing more than traditional readings with new labels. Much reader-oriented criticism and some deconstruction fits into this category. The jargon is literary but the results are still often either historical-critical or—perhaps worse—autobiographical. Another tendency is a dogged determination—sometimes in the face of fairly strong criticism—to persist with literary readings, even if they have little credibility (to say nothing of how they would fare outside the sphere of biblical studies).

One of the pervasive tendencies of much current literary interpretation of the New Testament—only recently rectified in small part, as indicated below—is its critical naivete. It is simply not enough to make claims for the 'final form of the text' or the 'reader's response', or the like, without knowing where these concepts come from, what they imply regarding text, author and reader, and how they are to be applied. Although much literary criticism as practised in literature departments in colleges and universities is moving away from an emphasis upon pure theory and back to historically-based criticism, this is only possible after having passed through a period of intense theoretical scrutiny and analysis. The kind of practical criticism that is being advocated in these departments is informed by and conversant with the major debates in critical theory of the last at least fifty or so years. The same cannot be said of much literary analysis in New Testament studies. An indication of this fact is the failure in many works to make clear what methods inform their readings. This is not to say that everyone must lay out an entire theoretical programme before offering a literary reading (these are noteworthily—and thankfully—lacking in secular literary criticism), but some awareness of the critical landscape should be evident, especially since 'literary criticism' is not a simplex phenomenon but a highly charged arena of debate. The offering of what are put forward as self-evident or implicitly clear readings especially of plot and character motivation, without any consideration of what counts for evidence in

32. See A. Wilder, *The Language of the Gospel: Early Christian Rhetoric* (New York: Harper & Row, 1964); *idem*, *The Bible and the Literary Critic* (Philadelphia: Fortress Press, 1991); N. Perrin, *Jesus and the Language of the Kingdom: Symbol and Metaphor in New Testament Interpretation* (Philadelphia: Fortress Press, 1976).

such models, often raises questions about how clear such readings really are. What these readings usually entail is a brutally and simplistically naive New Critical or formalist interpretation that assumes that the text is a self-contained artifact written in late twentieth-century English without reference to any historical or literary context and apart from any consideration of such a thing as authorial or textual intention or motivation.

b. *The Centre of Authority in Literary Interpretation*
The major question of all interpretation—whether it be literary or otherwise—is the centre of authority. By definition of the discipline involved, one must ask about the kind of evidence that is appealed to to arbitrate matters of interpretative dispute. To speak simplistically in the context of biblical studies, the centre of authority for historical criticism is the reconstructed historical context out of which the text emerged, with the text serving as a window to the past. The centre of authority for social-scientific criticism is the social structures that are reflected in or produced the text. For feminist criticism, the centre of authority is the complex of issues surrounding women writing, reading and being interpreted in a male-dominated culture. The centre of authority for liberation hermeneutics is the issue of the oppressed and their access to the avenues of power. For rhetorical criticism, the centre of authority is the means by which an audience is persuaded. The centre of authority for canonical criticism is the canonical shape of the text, either in its development or final form. And the centre of authority for linguistics is the set of syntagmatic, semantic, and pragmatic features that render a text into a cohesive discourse. All of these generalizations would need to be qualified if one were to analyse them in more detail. To compound the difficulty of analysis, each of these subsumes a variety of sub-methods. In that sense, each of these criticisms is not simplex but multiplex, though they share certain assumptions. But these generalizations are useful because they indicate some of the fundamental presuppositions of each method and how the various methods can be distinguished from each other. To understand a method or approach, one must analyse not only its praxis but its fundamental assumptions.

For literary criticism or criticisms, the centre of authority is the text as text.[33] From what has been said above, this can be understood to indi-

33. Exum and Clines call this 'foregrounding the textuality of the biblical literature' ('The New Literary Criticism', in Exum and Clines [eds.], *New Literary*

cate almost any written text (and has been so understood by a number of literary critics). This might seem like a presumptuous claim, since—apart possibly from linguistic criticism—it would seem to give this interpretative method a claim to priority. This kind of claim is one that many would argue is both prima facie evident and logically defensible. In dealing with the interpretation of any culture, including the ancient world, there is a variety of evidence available, none of it pre-interpreted. All of the remains—including archaeological finds—require interpretation. So far as self-conscious and explicit interpretation of the past is concerned, however, it is only the literary texts that offer direct help, and so they must be given priority.

One of the most helpful models for discussion of how the literary text functions as the centre of authority in literary criticism is an adaptation of the linguistic communication model of Jakobson.[34] He distinguishes the addresser, the message conveyed in its context in a particular linguistic code, and the addressee. When applied to literary texts, these three components become: the writer, the writing, and the reader. These three items can be re-expressed conceptually in terms of textual production, product and reception. Whereas this basic model can be applied to more than simply literary criticism (e.g. historical criticism focuses its attention upon the means of production of the text), here it will be used to speak only of literary criticism.[35]

Under the heading of writer or textual production, most contemporary literary criticism has not emphasized this as the centre of authority for interpreting texts. This kind of criticism is more usually associated with the romantic–humanist tradition, a kind of biographical criticism

Criticism, p. 11). Cf. M. Abrams, *The Mirror and the Lamp: Romantic Theory and the Critical Tradition* (New York: Oxford University Press, 1953), esp. pp. 8-29.

34. R. Jakobson, 'Closing Statement: Linguistics and Poetics', in T.A. Sebeok (ed.), *Style in Language* (New York: Wiley; Cambridge, MA: MIT Press, 1960), pp. 350-77, esp. p. 353; followed by Petersen, *Literary Criticism*, pp. 33-48; and R. Selden and P. Widdowson, *A Reader's Guide to Contemporary Literary Theory* (New York: Harvester Wheatsheaf, 3rd edn, 1993), p. 3. An approach more linguistic than literary is P.L. Danove, *The End of Mark's Story: A Methodological Study* (BIS, 3; Leiden: Brill, 1993).

35. For a recent survey of literary criticism, among many others see Selden and Widdowson, *Contemporary Literary Theory*; and from a biblical perspective, E.V. McKnight, *The Bible and the Reader: An Introduction to Literary Criticism* (Philadelphia: Fortress Press, 1985). I draw on them in the survey of criticisms below.

that emphasized the role of the author and how explicit authorial intentions govern interpretation. One of the few contemporary literary critics to argue for this position is Hirsch, although his theory is not nearly as simplistic as some of his interpreters in biblical studies make him out to be. First, Hirsch himself has undergone development in his thinking regarding the ability and desirability of determining authorial intention, making the concept a more difficult one to ascertain and use as a template for interpretation. Secondly, Hirsch does not claim that there is only one interpretation of a text, as he has been said to state. What he does claim is that texts often have multiple interpretations but that the authorial stance is the one that dictates which of these interpretations is correct.[36]

Under the heading of text or product, one can locate several kinds of criticism, including the kind of criticism once (and still usefully) called the New Criticism.[37] The New Criticism, developed in the 1920's in English-speaking critical circles, reacted against the romantic–humanist interpretative tradition. The focus shifted from the author to the work itself as a self-referring literary artifact. The emphasis in interpretation became an appreciation of the literary-artistic structure of the text in its own right, hence a rejection of the concept of paraphrase. The New Criticism was later influenced by Russian Formalism (e.g. Jakobson), which although earlier than the New Criticism had not been influential outside Russia until the late 1920's or 1930's, and especially in the 1940's after several leading figures fled the Soviet Union for the West. Russian Formalism brought a sociological dimension to interpretation that has not been

36. See E.D. Hirsch, Jr, *Validity in Interpretation* (New Haven: Yale University Press, 1967), clarified in *idem*, *The Aims of Interpretation* (Chicago: University of Chicago Press, 1976). Cf. also P.D. Juhl, *Interpretation: An Essay in the Philosophy of Literary Criticism* (Princeton: Princeton University Press, 1980).

37. The literature on the New Criticism is immense. Still useful are W.S. Scott, *Five Approaches of Literary Criticism* (New York: Collier, 1962), pp. 179-244; T.S. Eliot, *The Sacred Wood: Essays on Poetry and Criticism* (London: Methuen, 1960 [1920]); W. Empson, *Seven Types of Ambiguity* (London: Chatto & Windus, 1930); R. Wellek and A. Warren, *Theory of Literature* (New York: Harcourt, Brace & World, 3rd edn, 1956 [1942]); F.R. Leavis, *The Great Tradition* (New York: New York University Press, 1960); R.P. Blackmur, *Form and Value in Modern Poetry* (Garden City, NY: Doubleday, 1957). For critiques, see F. Lentricchia, *After the New Criticism* (Chicago: University of Chicago Press, 1980); and from a biblical standpoint, L.M. Poland, *Literary Criticism and Biblical Hermeneutics: A Critique of Formalist Approaches* (Chico, CA: Scholars Press, 1985).

picked up by many New Critics, especially in biblical studies, until lately, although it brought a greater attention to formal and quantifiable criteria by which the phenomena of texts may be evaluated (close reading). This factor was part of Russian Formalism's linguistic heritage, since several of its early proponents had been both linguists and literary critics (to make such a distinction may not have been possible at the time). In New Testament studies, the New Criticism was new when it first began to be used in the late 1970's.

Under the heading of textual reception, one can place reader-oriented criticism, and (lumped together here for the sake of convenience) deconstruction, poststructuralism and postmodernism, though there is distinction among them. Reader-oriented criticism[38] has proponents ranging widely over the span of what constitutes the reader. The common feature of reader-oriented criticism is the role of the reader in responding to the text or even playing a role in creating its meaning. Whereas in the criticisms mentioned above the reader is outside the process of creating meaning, but rather an observer and commentator, in reader-oriented criticism the reader is part of the process itself, so much so that some reader-oriented critics such as Fish go so far as to claim that without the reader there is no text. What is usually meant by such an extreme statement is that without readers texts have merely unrealized meaning potential, not actual meaning (although some would take this statement further). While some emphasize the psychological response of the reader, and others emphasize the so-called narratee (not the reader but a

---

38. The secondary literature is immense and growing here as well. See J.P. Tompkins (ed.), *Reader-Response Criticism: From Formalism to Post-Structuralism* (Baltimore: Johns Hopkins University Press, 1980); S.R. Suleiman and I. Crosman, *The Reader in the Text: Essays on Audience and Interpretation* (Princeton: Princeton University Press, 1980); W. Iser, *The Act of Reading: A Theory of Aesthetic Response* (Baltimore: Johns Hopkins University Press, 1978); *idem, The Implied Reader: Patterns of Communication in Prose Fiction from Bunyan to Beckett* (Baltimore: Johns Hopkins University Press, 1974); S. Fish, *Is There a Text in This Class? The Authority of Interpretive Communities* (Cambridge, MA: Harvard University Press, 1980); *idem, Doing What Comes Naturally* (Oxford: Clarendon Press, 1989); D. Bleich, *Subjective Criticism* (Baltimore: Johns Hopkins University Press, 1980). For a critique from a biblical perspective, see A.C. Thiselton, *New Horizons in Hermeneutics* (Grand Rapids: Zondervan, 1992), pp. 516-96, but with modifications: see S.E. Porter, 'Reader-Response Criticism and New Testament Study: A Response to A.C. Thiselton's *New Horizons in Hermeneutics*', *LT* 8 (1994), pp. 88-96.

hypothetical respondent), two forms of reader-oriented criticism have emerged from the rest. The first is dependent upon the work of Iser, who mediates a position between formalism and more radical reader-oriented approaches by claiming that while there is much that is stable in the meanings of texts, there is enough that is indeterminate to give the reader a role in the generation of meaning. The second form of reader-oriented criticism is perhaps best represented by Fish. He has developed his position, from an earlier position that emphasized how the way one understands a text can be affected by the placement of a single word ('affective stylistics'),[39] to a view that addressed plausibility of interpretation in terms of 'interpretive communities'.[40] Although the latter seems like a more radical development, as will be seen below, the former is in fact more potentially useful in generating readings of texts. Even though reader-oriented criticism per se has passed its peak in literary-critical circles, it is near its peak in New Testament interpretation. However, as will be seen below, what New Testament scholars mean by reader-oriented criticism is not always the same as what non-biblical scholars mean.

Deconstruction, poststructuralism and postmodernism,[41] although arguably distinct kinds of criticism, also share a number of common features regarding their view of language and the text, including often a jaundiced and world-weary pessimism regarding the fruitfulness of interpretation. Deconstruction as a literary method is dependent upon the work of Derrida, among others, especially as he had influence upon a number of American critics. Although each of these figures takes a

---

39. See Fish, 'Literature in the Reader: Affective Stylistics', in *Is There a Text?*, pp. 21-67.

40. See Fish, 'Interpreting the Variorum', in *Is There a Text?*, pp. 147-73.

41. Among many others, see J. Culler, *On Deconstruction: Theory and Criticism after Structuralism* (Ithaca, NY: Cornell University Press, 1982); C. Norris, *Deconstruction: Theory and Practice* (London: Methuen, 1982); J. Derrida, *Of Grammatology* (Baltimore: Johns Hopkins University Press, 1976); H. Bloom, *A Map of Misreading* (Oxford: Oxford University Press, 1975); G.H. Hartman, *Saving the Text: Literature/Derrida/Philosophy* (Baltimore: Johns Hopkins University Press, 1981); R. Barthes, *New Critical Essays* (trans. R. Howard; New York: Hill and Wang, 1980); M. Foucault, *The Order of Things: An Archaeology of the Human Sciences* (New York: Random House, 1970); *idem, The Archaeology of Knowledge and the Discourse on Language* (New York: Random House, 1972). For a biblical assessment, see T.J. Keegan, 'Biblical Criticism and the Challenge of Postmodernism', *BI* 3 (1995), pp. 1-14.

different orientation to what deconstruction means, each is in some way convinced that language is both more and less than the structuralist language-system of Saussure. It is more in that it can be seen to form a fragmented tapestry of endless regress, as texts suggest meanings other than and behind those that their authors thought that they were expressing. It is less in that the relation between signifier and signified is seen to be broken, with individual words made to carry their own weight in a given context, and often betraying their inadequacy to express meaning without becoming contradictory. Poststructuralism, at least as represented by Foucault, goes at least a step further (or back, depending upon one's perspective) and sees the power within discourses. Power structures govern what people are allowed and even able to say, so much so that these structures help to create the environment that welcomes or ignores ideas. These structures work at the individual and the social level, even though they may well not be perceived at the time.

All these literary criticisms are complexes of ideas held and exemplified by a number of different critics, so any attempt to form generalizations must take into account the rarity of finding any individual who matches a given profile. Various elements of these criticisms are to be found in other criticisms and in earlier forms of criticism as well. All of this makes it extremely difficult to describe their genetic and historical relationships. Nevertheless, describing their relationships, if only in brief outline, is probably worthwhile, because it helps to understand the influence upon a particular interpretative model. Throughout this discussion, it is important to note that there have been many other recognized schools of critical thought that are not represented here. The trials and errors of any academic discipline are clearly to be seen in literary criticism as well. What is described here are the triumphs of literary criticism, at least so far as they have been incorporated into current New Testament literary criticism. But mythic/archetypal criticism, moral criticism, the new historicism, psychoanalytic criticism, and the like, because of their relative neglect in New Testament studies, are not discussed, although if a fuller picture were drawn they too would need to be given their place.

Responding to the romantic–humanistic literary criticism, the New Criticism is a reaction against the notion of the overriding influence and importance of the author (hence reference to the 'intentional fallacy'). The emphasis upon text is consistent with the philosophical underpinnings of the New Criticism. Even though the New Criticism was not as overtly ideological as some more recent criticisms it is clearly indebted to logical positivism, with its emphasis upon self-evidential truths and empiricism. Reader-oriented criticism, despite protests from a number of its proponents, appears to be a direct development out of the New Criticism. Several proponents of reader-oriented criticism place a similar kind of emphasis upon the stability of the text and appreciate its structural qualities. Even those who minimize the distinction between literary and non-literary texts pay serious attention to close reading, and often assume that such a reading is self-evident (at least to them), a kind of positivism reminiscent of the New Criticism.

Whereas the romantic–humanistic, New Critical and reader-oriented methods of criticism have a distinctly Anglo-American feel about them—in their philosophical moorings, their frequent disregard for critical theoretical rigour, and their emphasis upon close readings (although this is not to say that all of their practitioners have been Anglo-American)—deconstruction and poststructuralist criticism have been more highly influenced by Continental thinking. In this sense, it is difficult to establish anything resembling a direct line from the New Criticism and reader-oriented criticisms to deconstruction and post-structuralism, except in those instances where the deconstructionists or poststructuralists are clearly rejecting their critical forebears. Instances of this are numerous. Instead, when one looks to the Continental influences, one sees them in several areas. One is in the area of philosophy where a much more existential approach is evident. Another is in the area of psychoanalysis which has had a profound influence upon post-structuralist thought. And a third is in the area of linguistics, which is probably the most important. These critical theories are methodologically aware of the structuralist linguistic assumptions that have influenced critical theory, but, more than that, they have consciously rejected many of the traditional linkages.

With this brief survey of twentieth-century criticism completed, it is possible to examine in more detail the kinds of criticism practised by New Testament scholars. The above context is important, however, for providing a necessary backdrop against which to examine the scholars cited below and to appreciate the kinds of criticism brought to their work.

3. *Models of Interpretation in New Testament Literary Criticism*

In this section, representative examples of each of the various forms of New Testament literary criticism will be briefly analysed. There will be no attempt at a complete representation of the work that has been done, or even of all of the work of a given author.[42] The goals of the exercise are to enable the reader to recognize these several kinds of criticism when they are encountered, and to assess the strengths and weaknesses of the given method, as well as the individual exposition.

Several features of New Testament literary criticism should be noted, however. The first is that many New Testament literary critics—even if they are somewhat critically naive—are quite self-conscious of being literary critics. Hence they keep reminding the reader that they are doing 'literary criticism'. Whether they are doing what secular literary critics would recognize as such is another thing. It is perhaps unfair to ask of New Testament literary critics to imitate the history of secular literary criticism, with its strengths and weaknesses. But if common terminology and approach are used, it is fitting to refine what one is doing in the light of how the most experienced practitioners handle such conceptual models. One thing is clear—secular literary critics are rarely as self-conscious. It appears—to speak very generally—that the more the critical landscape becomes full of a variety of methods, the more explicit New Testament literary critics will need to be in identifying their method or methods, not just that they are literary critics.

Secondly, New Testament literary critics, despite their claims to be doing 'literary readings', rarely push discussion forward from a methodological or theoretical standpoint. For many of them, the fact that they claim to be using a literary method seems to be sufficient to justify what they do. This may have been acceptable when modern literary criticism was new to the field of New Testament studies, and the early literary critics were pioneering the use of these methods. But these methods are sufficiently well integrated into the broad fabric of biblical studies that calling something literary, even with a more specific title, is

---

42. I purposely avoid the vast quantity of journal literature. For a more complete list, see M. Minor, *Literary-Critical Approaches to the Bible: An Annotated Bibliography* (West Cornwall, CT: Locust Hill, 1992). One must use caution, however, since Minor's definition of what constitutes literary criticism is extremely broad. Useful bibliographies are found within several of the volumes mentioned below.

probably not sufficient, especially when the interpretation itself still addresses traditional historical-critical questions, even in passing. The question must be raised, however, why it is that so few New Testament literary critics have raised what would seem to be a number of crucial questions regarding the use of literary models for interpretation, and for those who do, why they appear to be able to make the transition so easily. The major issues that would seem to need to be addressed are how it is that models of interpretation developed for modern literature can be used to interpret ancient literature, how it is that models of interpretation developed for self-consciously literary genres, such as poetry and drama, can be applied to forms such as letters, and how it is that methods designed for secular texts can be applied to religious or sacred documents, often the product not of a single individual as we conceive of a modern author but of an author as part of or equated with a religious community. Even where these questions have been faced, there is rarely theoretical advancement that shows how these models are germane to study of the New Testament.

Thirdly, New Testament literary critics often combine several different literary models, or successively try several different methods. For example, New Testament critics state that they are using a narrative and reader-oriented method, usually with these two criticisms then briefly defined. But where is the justification for the compatibility of these two methods? Is narrative criticism (see below), with its roots in the New Criticism and historical criticism, compatible with reader-oriented criticism, an explicit reaction against the New Criticism? They may work together, but this needs to be established, since these various methods represent explicit orientations and theoretical viewpoints that have been developed in the light of important interpretative exigencies. It is not self-evident that they are mutually informing.[43] Another approach is the sequential utilization of interpretative methods. This may avoid the problem of integrating potentially competing models, but it raises the question of interpretative allegiance. Although there is nothing to state that one must be allied to a particular viewpoint, the fact that the various views reflect different views of language and literature, the means of textual production, the relation of literature to the world, among others,

43. Cf. T. Eagleton, *Literary Theory: An Introduction* (Minneapolis: University of Minnesota Press, 1983), p. 198, who says that attempts to combine critical approaches are 'more likely to lead to a nervous breakdown than to a brilliant literary career'.

leads one to believe that there is more at stake for most literary critics than simply trying another method or approach. Criticism has something to do with the way critics see the world, literature, the human being, the interpretative task, and even God. This indicates, furthermore, that perhaps New Testament literary critics have often failed to grasp the seriousness of the interpretative enterprise. They have not realized the implications of their interpretations, the assumptions and presuppositions that dictate their interpretative vision, or the commitment needed to the interpretative task. It seems to reflect a view that criticism is simply a functional tool, to be used as long as it is useful or in contexts where it seems to promise results, rather than as a way of seeing and under-standing textual reality. It may also indicate that many of these critics have their own agendas, that is, they may be wanting to flirt with the novel and unique while retaining a different—and perhaps competing—set of agenda items as well.

Fourthly, a number of New Testament literary critics have tried to invent or at least to re-label some other forms of criticism. The most noteworthy example is narrative criticism (see below). Biblical scholars should be commended for thinking methodologically and attempting to develop a method that is explicitly biblical in orientation. However, one must wonder how distinct this method is and whether there are not other issues that have dictated its development, in particular a desire to ground the New Criticism in historical criticism. It is not that this is not a worthwhile or even necessary goal, but it does call into question the integrity of its practitioners so far as their literary interests are concerned. It seems too much like an attempt to package traditional historical criticism in the guise of the fashionable. One could argue that it would be better if important literary considerations were incorporated into historical criticism, thus keeping a larger number of scholars speaking a similar critical language.

Fifthly, New Testament literary critics do not seem to be as current with recent debate in literary criticism as one would hope. For example, genre studies still maintain an ambiguous status in New Testament studies, in particular in relation to the Gospels. The question of genre is a valid literary question to ask, but the criteria for assessment are historical-critical in New Testament studies, not literary.[44] Myth or

44. See, for example, C.L. Blomberg, 'The Diversity of Literary Genres in the New Testament', in Black and Dockery (eds.), *New Testament Criticism and Interpretation*, pp. 507-32.

archetypal criticism has essentially passed from the literary scene as a distinct kind of criticism, although it still makes regular appearances in biblical studies as if it were one of the competitive models in New Testament criticism.[45] For many biblical scholars deconstruction is the latest mode of criticism, something to be toyed with carefully despite the fact that its demise has already been announced in many literary circles.[46] Only a very few New Testament critics are seriously exploring the implications of a so-called poststructuralist perspective.[47] Attendance at a 'literary' session of a major New Testament conference and at a session of a major literary conference would result in a very different impression. Perhaps some of this can be accounted for by the relative newness of literary criticism to New Testament study. A more likely answer is that many of the questions and predispositions for conclusions of New Testament scholars (in particular their residual historical bent) do not encourage or even allow the kind of methodological approach reflected in secular literary criticism.

a. *New Criticism or Formalism*
The New Criticism or formalism has been by far the most important literary-critical method in New Testament study.[48] Its appeal is clear. It exalts the aesthetic qualities of the biblical text to the point of critical respectability, appears to provide an objective method of analysis and a grounds for assessment and evaluation of critical readings, does not get entangled with historical issues, and is compatible with a theology that is concerned with the biblical story. There are several manifestations of New Critical exegesis in New Testament study.

1. *Common-Sense Criticism.* Common-sense or phenomenological criticism has been and continues to be widely practised by New Testament literary critics. Although one could think by the orientation of such

45. See Stibbe, *John as Storyteller*, esp. pp. 121-23.

46. See J.T. Nealon, 'The Discipline of Deconstruction', *Publication of the Modern Language Association* 107 (1992), p. 1266; cf. S.D. Moore, *Mark and Luke in Poststructuralist Perspectives: Jesus Begins to Write* (New Haven: Yale University Press, 1992), pp. xviii-xix.

47. On liberation criticism and feminist criticism, see chs. 8 and 9 in this volume.

48. This is often what is equated with literary criticism. See C. Tuckett, *Reading the New Testament: Methods of Interpretation* (London: SPCK, 1987), pp. 174-75; S. McKnight, 'Appendix: Literary Criticism', in *Interpreting the Synoptic Gospels* (Grand Rapids: Baker, 1988), pp. 121-37.

works that they are theory-neutral (or at least wish to be seen to be so) or unconcerned with theory, or just simply reading the text (without getting hung up on abstractions), these readings are far from being without presuppositions. These kinds of readings seem to presuppose that the interpreter and the reader share the same assumptions regarding what a text is and what is important in a text, and that the same conclusions will become self-evident with the proper exegesis.

Representative of the common-sense approach is the work of Talbert. In some ways, he was a pioneer in literary studies of the New Testament, with his work on Luke–Acts and the genre of the Gospels.[49] His commentary on Luke[50] was one of the first to align itself with a literary perspective. However, whereas one might have hoped for one of the early efforts to be explicit about its method and the new course it was plotting, explicit comments regarding method are few. He states that the commentary will utilize 'a type of redaction criticism heavily influenced by nonbiblical literary criticism', although this literary criticism is not defined apart from the following: 'understanding large thought units... rather than focusing on the individual pieces of the narrative', 'close reading of the text',[51] and genre criticism, on which he spends almost sixty percent of the introduction in terms of ancient biography (see above). The same can essentially be said of his commentaries on the Corinthian letters[52] and John's Gospel. It is disappointing that, apart from virtually the same statement as cited above regarding not being a word by word commentary but 'concerned to understand large thought units',[53] there is no methodological discussion, in a commentary on arguably the most literarily-self-conscious of the Gospels.

49. C.H. Talbert, *Literary Pattern, Theological Themes and the Genre of Luke–Acts* (SBLMS, 20; Missoula, MT: SBL and Scholars Press, 1974); *What is a Gospel? The Genre of the Synoptic Gospels* (Philadelphia: Fortress Press, 1977).

50. C.H. Talbert, *Reading Luke: A Literary and Theological Commentary on the Third Gospel* (New York: Crossroad, 1982).

51. Talbert, *Luke*, p. 2, who acknowledges that he will make 'little reference to secondary literature', but indicates an indebtedness to the approach of C.H. Dodd (*Interpretation of the Fourth Gospel* [Cambridge: Cambridge University Press, 1958], part III on 'Argument and Structure').

52. C.H. Talbert, *Reading Corinthians: A Literary and Theological Commentary on 1 and 2 Corinthians* (New York: Crossroad, 1987), pp. xiii, xv, also eschewing secondary literature.

53. C.H. Talbert, *Reading John: A Literary and Theological Commentary on the Fourth Gospel and the Johannine Epistles* (New York: Crossroad, 1992), pp. xi, 3.

Similar is the work of Helms. On the back cover of his *Gospel Fictions* there is the hyperbolic claim that this is 'the first study of the Gospels based upon a demonstrable literary theory', although one does not readily find exposition of that theory. The author is concerned to show how the Gospels are 'fictional narrative', 'works of art deliberately composed as the culmination of a long literary and oral tradition', while tracing the use of extra-biblical sources.[54] Tannehill does not make the same kinds of grand claims. Tannehill seems to have been one of the earliest to offer a literary analysis of Luke–Acts, although explicitly eschewing concern for 'developing narrative theory',[55] something that he says is the 'result of extensive borrowing from non-biblical literary criticism'. He defines his understanding in terms of dealing primarily with character and plot within a narrative world, in which there are shared values and beliefs.[56]

This approach neither pushes forward methodological discussion nor increases literary understanding in terms of current categories; it recapitulates traditional critical insights in the guise of a modern literary approach.

2. *Defined Formalism.* The label defined formalism is given to a number of works that take an explicitly formalistic or New Critical perspective, reflected either through explicit statements to that effect backed by suitable secondary literature, or through their terminology and supportive secondary literature. There have been several recent studies that have illustrated an informed concern for theory and a close eye for detail in the text. The first reason for this is that the works seem to reflect a new generation of literary critics of the New Testament, a group that has been attuned to literary questions early in their professional training and careers. The second is that the evolution of the discipline, especially in

54. R. Helms, *Gospel Fictions* (Buffalo, NY: Prometheus, 1988).

55. R. Tannehill, *The Narrative Unity of Luke–Acts: A Literary Interpretation* (2 vols.; Philadelphia: Fortress Press, 1986, 1990), I, p. 1; cf. his earlier *The Sword of his Mouth* (Philadelphia: Fortress Press; Missoula, MT: Scholars Press, 1975), esp. ch. 1.

56. See also W.J. Kelber, *Mark's Story of Jesus* (Philadelphia: Fortress Press, 1979), p. 11; R.J. Karris, *Luke: Artist and Theologian: Luke's Passion Account as Literature* (New York: Paulist, 1985); L.W. Countryman, *The Mystical Way in the Fourth Gospel: Crossing over into God* (Philadelphia: Fortress Press, 1987); F.S. Spencer, *The Portrait of Philip in Acts: A Study of Roles and Relations* (JSNTSup, 67; Sheffield: JSOT Press, 1992), pp. 21-25; D.B. Taylor, *Mark's Gospel as Literature and History* (London: SCM Press, 1992).

terms of varying literary models, increasingly requires that one distinguish the position taken from other positions. The third is that the multifarious approaches available for study of the New Testament, along with a growing pressure for interdisciplinary research, demand that explicit criteria be stated to enable cross-disciplinary communication and understanding.

As mentioned above, although the New Criticism dominated literature departments for over forty years, and although much has mitigated its importance in critical debate, due to its influence on other criticisms as well as the entrenched practices of literature teachers, it appears that the New Criticism still has an important role to play in literary criticism. Thus, although the adaptation of New Critical method to New Testament interpretation has come fairly late, the method continues to have relevance.

One of the first and still one of the most important works in New Testament literary studies is Rhoads and Michie's *Mark as Story*.[57] First, it was co-written by a New Testament scholar and an English literature specialist. This overcomes one of the major shortcomings of early New Testament literary criticism—that the field is a foreign territory for so many, despite their interest in it. Secondly, the authors are explicit in their methodology, and label and describe what they are doing. Their notes and bibliography are extremely helpful in indicating the sources of their own thinking, many of the most important works in literary criticism, and much of the work to date in New Testament studies. The impression is that many subsequent literary interpreters have used Rhoads and Michie's references as the major sources of their own work. Thirdly, whereas much New Testament literary criticism reads like most work in New Testament studies, Rhoads and Michie's work reads more like a work in secular literary criticism. This has strengths and weaknesses to it. Whereas some might feel a bit lost without the kinds of markers that are traditional in the discipline, this style has the advantage of keeping the focus on literary questions.

In their introduction, the authors state that they wish to treat Mark as a 'unified narrative' drawing on 'the work of contemporary literary criticism' including analysis of the formal features of narrative. They claim that although these were developed for modern novels and the like, ancient narratives have the same features. The assumptions

57. D. Rhoads and D. Michie, *Mark as Story: An Introduction to the Narrative of a Gospel* (Philadelphia: Fortress Press, 1982).

regarding narrative are that it has unity, the narrator uses a consistent perspective, the plot and characters are coherent throughout, and various literary techniques for telling stories are used to create this narrative. In advocating discussion of the world of the story—and probably in the light of the general tenor of critical study of the Bible— the authors in their introduction include one italicized sentence: 'Unless otherwise identified as helpful historical information from the culture of the first century, all subsequent discussion about people, places, and events deals only with the story world of Mark's gospel'.[58]

One of those who seems to have been motivated by the work of Rhoads and Michie is the prolific Kingsbury. He has concentrated his efforts upon the Gospels, writing three books of interest in literary discussion, and a host of articles on Matthew. Although Kingsbury has concentrated upon Matthew, his two books on Mark and Luke take a similar approach.[59] One observes an evolution in Kingsbury's awareness of critical issues. For example, although his books on Mark and Luke are companion volumes, reference to secondary literature on literary topics is sparse in the volume on Mark but more plentiful in the one on Luke. Perhaps worth noting in response to Kingsbury's work is how a traditional higher critic looks at this kind of approach. In a lengthy article foreshadowing his book on Matthew, Kingsbury takes a literary-critical approach in which he uses literary analysis of Matthew to show how the narrator's, Jesus' and God's points of view coincide.[60] In the following article, the well-known Matthaean scholar Hill questions Kingsbury's neglect of the Synoptic issues when available for use, the lack of controls on evidence, and the subjectivity in the method.[61] Kingsbury's subsequent response re-states his previous conclusions and then simply determines that the two scholars disagree in their conclusions and their methods and he hopes that this will stimulate further discussion.[62] My

58. Rhoads and Michie, *Mark as Story*, pp. 2, 3, 4.

59. J.D. Kingsbury, *Matthew as Story* (Philadelphia: Fortress Press, 2nd edn, 1988 [1986]); *Conflict in Mark: Jesus, Authorities, Disciples* (Minneapolis: Fortress Press, 1989); *Conflict in Luke: Jesus, Authorities, Disciples* (Minneapolis: Fortress Press, 1991).

60. J.D. Kingsbury, 'The Figure of Jesus in Matthew's Story: A Literary-Critical Probe', *JSNT* 21 (1984), pp. 3-36.

61. D. Hill, 'The Figure of Jesus in Matthew's Story: A Response to Professor Kingsbury's Literary-Critical Probe', *JSNT* 21 (1984), pp. 37-52.

62. J.D. Kingsbury, 'The Figure of Jesus in Matthew's Story: A Rejoinder to David Hill', *JSNT* 25 (1985), pp. 61-81.

impression is that Hill gets the better of the debate, and for a very clear reason. Kingsbury does not go back and defend his theoretical position—he simply re-asserts it as if that were enough. Hill is very clear on what counts for evidence in his position, and uses this position to argue his line. Kingsbury falls back on agreeing to disagree. This may be an acceptable method when the position is acknowledged as valid and beyond dispute, but here leaves the impression that there is not much theoretical basis for the position, or that the position (as Hill raises the issue) has pre-decided its conclusions and is now simply looking for a way to assert them. When the critical method involves a repudiation or at least an ignoring of historical factors, in a field such as biblical studies, this is bound to raise questions.[63]

A study of irony from a New Critical perspective may give some idea of how these tensions can be resolved. The study of irony was greatly encouraged by the New Critics, because it proved (to their minds at least) to be one of the major unifying literary factors in creating the integrated shape of a work. Duke offers a study of irony in the Gospel of John.[64] In this book, Duke does several things that literary critics of the New Testament may want to learn from. The first is that he is explicit in defining his terms, with appropriate reference to suitable secondary literature. The second is that he is not concerned with creating an unmanageable task for himself, such as explicating the plot, character, setting, etc., of an entire Gospel. He is concerned to define a complex topic, irony. The third is that he illustrates how his theory enables him to read a variety of texts in John's Gospel, treating the readings under appropriate descriptive categories. This is not to say that all of his readings are equally plausible, but one gets the sense that there are explicit criteria here by which one could evaluate the success of his programme.[65]

---

63. Kingsbury's students have not improved on this. See D.R. Bauer, *The Structure of Matthew's Gospel: A Study in Literary Design* (JSNTSup, 31; Sheffield: Almond Press, 1988), pp. 12-13, his discussion of method; and D.J. Weaver, *Matthew's Missionary Discourse: A Literary Critical Analysis* (JSNTSup, 38; Sheffield: JSOT Press, 1990).

64. P.D. Duke, *Irony in the Fourth Gospel* (Atlanta: John Knox, 1985).

65. Less successful is J. Camery-Hoggatt's *Irony in Mark's Gospel: Text and Subtext* (SNTSMS, 72; Cambridge: Cambridge University Press, 1992). Although he attempts from a New Critical perspective to integrate an understanding of irony within a sociological framework, the study is flawed at several places (especially in terms of linguistic theory).

In New Testament literary criticism, one often sees reference to 'narrative criticism', as if this were a distinct form of criticism. This is what Powell argues. He admits that 'Secular literary scholarship knows no such movement as *narrative criticism*'. After describing what he considers the three forms of literary criticism in New Testament studies—structuralism, rhetorical criticism, reader-response criticism[66]— he defines narrative criticism. Although he claims that it corresponds to rhetorical criticism or reader-response in secular criticism (?), 'Biblical scholars, however, tend to think of narrative criticism as an independent, parallel movement in its own right'.[67] Powell's formulation needs serious scrutiny, however. First, putting aside the fact that literary critics have long been concerned with narrative even if they have not singled out a particular criticism to call it 'narrative criticism', the asserted uniqueness of narrative criticism raises a number of questions, especially regarding theoretical support. When investigated, it is evident that this so-called narrative criticism is only a sub-category of the New Criticism or formalism. This is shown by the fact that the major schema for defining narrative criticism, in terms of its attention to the implied reader and author as distinct from their real counterparts, is derived from Chatman and Booth.[68] Furthermore, the vast majority of other categories that Powell elucidates are the concerns of the New Criticism, including point of view, symbolism and irony, and various elements of plot. Lastly, Powell himself does not have a category for the New Criticism or formalism in his description of the field of New Testament literary criticism. When Powell defines literary criticism against historical criticism, it is in terms compatible with the New Criticism, including attention to the final form of the text, emphasis upon textual unity, and

66. I have serious questions whether structuralism and rhetorical criticism should be listed as literary criticisms, as noted above.

67. M.A. Powell, *What is Narrative Criticism?: A New Approach to the Bible* (London: SPCK, 1990), p. 19. See also Moore, *Literary Criticism and the Gospels*, pp. 51-55. On the shift in narrative analysis of the Bible, see H. Frei, *The Eclipse of Biblical Narrative: A Study in Eighteenth and Nineteenth Century Hermeneutics* (New Haven: Yale University Press, 1974); *idem*, 'The "Literal Reading" of Biblical Narrative in the Christian Tradition: Does it Stretch or Will it Break?', in F. McConnell (ed.), *The Bible and the Narrative Tradition* (New York: Oxford University Press, 1986), pp. 36-77, as well as other essays in the collection.

68. See S. Chatman, *Story and Discourse: Narrative Structure in Fiction and Film* (Ithaca, NY: Cornell University Press, 1978); W.C. Booth, *The Rhetoric of Fiction* (Chicago: University of Chicago Press, 2nd edn, 1983).

the text as an end in itself (or an aesthetic object). Powell places his narrative criticism in the category of 'objective' criticism (according to Abrams), where the New Criticism would be placed. Although one might wish to distinguish certain elements of biblical literary criticism, defining a separate kind of narrative criticism is not legitimate.

Some of the more interesting and enlightening studies of various literary dimensions of the New Testament have concentrated on narrative. For example, there have been several extensive studies of character development. Gowler studies the Pharisees as major characters in Luke–Acts, with the aid of a sociological/anthropological approach specifying shared cultural scripts.[69] Williams, using Mark's Gospel, analyses the use of the minor characters before Bartimaeus (Mark 10) and after Bartimaeus, with Bartimaeus forming the turning point in the narrative. Bartimaeus is the ideal minor character for Williams, seeing in him one who encapsulates what the author is trying to say about what it means to follow Jesus.[70] Carter's work on Matthew 19–20 employs three forms of criticism: historical-critical analysis, audience criticism and sociological criticism. His audience-oriented criticism is the most disappointing, because he utilizes a static concept of audience; his historical criticism is quite informative; but his sociological criticism is in many ways the most enlightening. However, this study could have been done simply in terms of historical-critical and sociological analysis, with the audience dimension incorporated into the horizons of beliefs of the sociological model.[71]

The most refined literary exegesis—and one that forms a transition from the New Criticism to reader-oriented criticism—is the treatment by

---

69. D.B. Gowler, *Host, Guest, Enemy, and Friend: Portraits of the Pharisees in Luke and Acts* (Emory Studies in Early Christianity; New York: Peter Lang, 1991).

70. J. Williams, *Other Followers of Jesus: Minor Characters as Major Figures in Mark's Gospel* (JSNTSup, 102; Sheffield: JSOT Press, 1994). Cf. his treatment of the women in 16.8, because of their response in fear. See also A.T. Lincoln, 'The Promise and the Failure: Mark 16.7, 8', *JBL* 108 (1989), pp. 283-300.

71. W. Carter, *Households and Discipleship: A Study of Matthew 19–20* (JSNTSup, 103; Sheffield: JSOT Press, 1994). See also D.B. Howell, *Matthew's Inclusive Story: A Study in the Narrative Rhetoric of the First Gospel* (JSNTSup, 42; Sheffield: JSOT Press, 1990); D.A. Lee, *The Symbolic Narratives of the Fourth Gospel: The Interplay of Form and Meaning* (JSNTSup, 95; Sheffield: Sheffield Academic Press, 1994); J.C. Anderson, *Matthew's Narrative Web: Over, and Over, and Over Again* (JSNTSup, 91; Sheffield: Sheffield Academic Press, 1994).

Darr of characterization in Luke–Acts.[72] Two of its virtues are worth noting. First, Darr is modest in the claims that he makes for his literary model. He realizes that much work that has approached the New Testament from a literary standpoint is not methodologically well defined. Rather than making the extravagant claims that often go along with many who invoke the reader-oriented paradigm, Darr, relying upon the classic work of Abrams, chooses instead to invoke a pragmatic approach (as opposed to objective, romantic, etc.). This means that he is not constrained by the kinds of expectations that typically go with reader-oriented criticism, which so often devolve into simply a characterization of the first-century audience, but he distinguishes his pragmatic or functionalist approach from those that are overly ideologically driven to make extreme claims regarding the dissolution of the subjective-objective divide. He appreciates the fact that, with Iser, the text sets the final parameters for interpretation of its meaning. He also recognizes the presupposition pool (what he calls 'extratext')[73] that readers bring to the task of interpretation as a factor that must be considered. Readers reading are not simply blank slates or completely impressionable. The second major contribution that Darr makes is that he approaches the problem of characterization not as an isolated problem or from consideration of a set of discrete texts from which to read-off a set of analyses, but as a textual factor inextricably interwoven with plot. Consequently, he selects three characters: John the Baptist, the Pharisees, and Herod. His exposition is varied (with the treatment of the Pharisees being the least satisfying because it is so episodic), but at its best it gives genuine insight into the characters involved and their contribution to the narrative of Luke–Acts.

Although the New Criticism may not be so new, so far as secular departments of literature are concerned (although as a revised formalism it has continued to be an important literary model), it is still alive and well so far as New Testament literary criticism is concerned. Having said this, however, it is not to say that every form of New Critical or formalist criticism approaches the text from the same theoretically

---

72. J.A. Darr, *On Character Building: The Reader and the Rhetoric of Characterization in Luke–Acts* (Literary Currents in Biblical Interpretation; Louisville: Westminster/John Knox, 1992). Cf. also M.A. Tolbert, *Sowing the Gospel: Mark's Literary World in Literary-Historical Perspective* (Minneapolis: Fortress Press, 1989).

73. Darr, *Character*, p. 22.

explicit standpoint, or is concerned with the same issues in interpretation. Although it is not necessary that one be theoretically explicit to be a successful interpreter, it does seem to be true that those who are theoretically well-informed provide more convincing readings of the text. The tendency is for New Critical readings to be combined with other models of interpretation, especially those that have developed from it (such as reader-oriented variations) and those sociologically based (realizing the goals of formalism?), which provides evidence for the abiding significance of the model, as well as undoubtedly prolonging its life through its continued critical evolution.

b. *Reader-Oriented Criticism*

Reader-oriented critics have consistently made the boldest claims for their literary approach to the New Testament.[74] The claims have been bold because they have introduced several new factors into interpretation. One is the formative or even determinative role that the reader is to play in interpretation. Another is that since readers are fundamentally involved in the production of meaning there is a resultant plurality of interpretation. But there is a large gap between bold claims and insightful exegesis using reader-oriented methods. Part of the problem is defining what constitutes reader-oriented criticism. The vast majority of biblical critics adopt a model of reader-oriented criticism that is arguably (as I have argued elsewhere)[75] no more than a modification of formalism. This takes two major forms. Some New Testament critics adopt the model of Iser. His concept of the implicit reader, similar to Booth's idea of the implied reader, is a hypothetical reader established by the boundaries of the text (the reader is text-immanent). Iser believes that there is a limit to plausible readings set by the parameters of the text, with the gaps in the text providing the places for subjectivity. This definition of reader-oriented criticism does not have the interpretative power to deliver the kind of significant change in approach or results that many of its advocates would claim, since interpretation is determined by the formalist agenda, with a few fine tunings. Fish, who has argued for ostensibly a much more radical proposal, in which he claims that the reader is wholly determinative in creating meaning, has criticized Iser's approach. The results in terms of productive interpretation

74. See two issues of *Semeia* 31 (1985) and 48 (1989).
75. S.E. Porter, 'Why Hasn't Reader-Response Criticism Caught on in New Testament Studies?', *LT* 4 (1990), pp. 278-92.

bear out his claim. An excellent example of Iser's kind of criticism is the important work of Culpepper.[76] His *Anatomy of the Fourth Gospel* is a highly insightful formalist reading of several important features of the Fourth Gospel (his work merits mention as one of the best New Critical analyses), but he devotes one chapter to a study of the implied author in terms of Iser's exposition and categories, along with insights from Chatman on narrative theory.

The second form of reader-oriented criticism in New Testament study confines itself to a particular kind of reader, usually the first-century reader. The claim is that the text was written at a particular time and that what the modern interpreter must do is to determine how that text influenced the original audience. Although close to a truncated form of reception theory, in many ways this model is indistinguishable from what historical critics would call audience criticism. In any case, it is far from the kind of radical paradigm shift that many reader-oriented critics would claim that it is. Implied by the concept of reader-oriented criticism is the role of the reader in interpretation, and to privilege the first reader is entirely arbitrary. This extended concept is not utilized in this particular model. Emphasis upon the original audience re-introduces historical reconstruction. If it is difficult to reconstruct the original time and place of writing (to say nothing of the author's intention), it is every bit as difficult to reconstruct the original audience, to say nothing of the original response of this audience to the work. Illustrating the difficulties of this approach is Beavis's treatment of Mark 4 in terms of the original audience of the Gospel.[77] Although she has some interesting insights, to arrive at these she must engage in extensive historical reconstruction regarding a hypothetical reader in the first century, and the educational system such a reader may have been exposed to. Beavis's reconstruction is not of any particular reader, or possibly even any reader of the Gospel, but of an educated Roman of the first century. The text becomes a pre-text for this exercise in historicism.

Fish's model of reader-oriented criticism remains the most distinct in the claims that he makes regarding what happens when readers read.

76. R.A. Culpepper, *Anatomy of the Fourth Gospel: A Study in Literary Design* (FFNT; Philadelphia: Fortress Press, 1988), esp. pp. 203-27. Cf. B.C. Lategan and W.S. Vorster, *Text and Reality: Aspects of Reference in Biblical Texts* (Atlanta: Scholars Press, 1985).

77. M.A. Beavis, *Mark's Audience: The Literary and Social Setting of Mark 4.11-12* (JSNTSup, 33; Sheffield: JSOT Press, 1989).

The major problem, as Brett has recently pointed out,[78] is that when it comes to interpreting, the tools that are used by Fishian readers, including the categories that are operative in their readings, are the same as other readers use, including many formalists, and even historical critics. It can be argued two different ways why this is so, either according to Fish's claim that this is simply the way reading occurs, or according to the claim of others that anti-essentialism is a bankrupt concept and that the distinction between subject and object is one that does not simply exist in the minds of readers but exists outside of readers as well. When it comes to interpretation, there are only a certain number of tools available by which to extract the meaning from the data. One may bring various secondary interpretative interests to this task, but the primary interpretative stance remains similar. To date, there are few if any who have taken up Fish's stance in a self-conscious and dedicated way. As Brett points out, however, Fish's early form of reader-oriented criticism, what he calls 'affective stylistics', a formalistic kind of reading that he claims to have moved beyond, has much greater potential as a profitable reading strategy. This chronological or sequential way of reading attempts to chronicle the change in understanding as a reader confronts the various phenomena of the text in the order in which they are confronted. Although the current Fish is making an epistemological claim regarding how one reads (e.g. essentialist vs. anti-essentialist), its results have been minimal for interpretation, whereas the older Fish, rejected by Fish himself, does not make an epistemological claim but has a better claim to being a form of reader-oriented criticism that has direct implications for insightful reading.[79]

Reader-oriented criticism has not caught on in a clear way in New Testament study. It has continued to produce criticism that either simply utilizes new language or amalgamates some of the features of reader-oriented criticism into an existing literary or historical framework. Fowler's work perhaps provides a representative case, since he has been one of the most enduring reader-oriented critics. His first work, *Loaves*

78. M.G. Brett, 'The Future of Reader Criticisms?', in F. Watson (ed.), *The Open Text: New Directions for Biblical Studies?* (London: SCM Press, 1993), esp. pp. 14-17.

79. See J. Staley, *The Print's First Kiss: A Rhetorical Investigation of the Implied Reader in the Fourth Gospel* (Atlanta: Scholars Press, 1988); cf. S.E. Porter, 'The Message of the Book of Job: Job 42:7b as Key to Interpretation?', *EvQ* 63 (1991), pp. 291-304.

and Fishes,[80] was an exploratory work, in which he combined elements of what he called reader-response criticism with historical criticism. Consequently, he was concerned for the way in which the author controls and directs the reader's experience of the Gospel.[81] Fowler puts a high emphasis upon authorial intention in creating meaning and subordinates the reader's involvement to the author's goals. His reader appears to be more text-immanent than is legitimate for reader-oriented criticism. Being an early work, it is perhaps understandable that Fowler did not take the concept of reader-oriented criticism further. In his recent work, *Let the Reader Understand*,[82] however, Fowler clarifies his approach by hinting at a more precise definition of reader-oriented criticism using Fish's 'affective stylistics', seeing how the movement of the narrative affects the reader. This is not altogether consistent, however. Fowler still invokes categories from the work of Booth and Chatman, both more formalist than reader oriented, and makes high claims for Mark's narrative being reader-oriented by nature.[83] He appears to endorse a hodgepodge of New Critical and later Fishian ideas that are not easily reconcilable:

> once the author finishes the text and gives it to the world, she [*sic*] no longer has control over it; thereafter the text has a life of its own. Once out of the author's hands, the text is totally dependent on its readers. Such life as it continues to enjoy flows from them. Unless the text is read and comes to life in the reading experience, it is simply a lifeless assemblage of paper, binding, and dried ink. The text has no life or meaning unless life and meaning are conferred upon it by a reader.[84]

It is unclear whether this is undue cynicism or hyperbole.

A similar kind of ambiguity pervades much of what is called reader-oriented criticism. Although there is a desire to find a model of interpretation that displaces the importance of the original author, and shifts the emphasis to the reader, this is virtually always a reader who is placed within a context different from the one of the current writer of the exposition, either in terms of the original reader or sometimes a

80. R.M. Fowler, *Loaves and Fishes: The Function of the Feeding Stories in the Gospel of Mark* (SBLDS, 54; Chico, CA: Scholars Press, 1981).

81. Fowler, *Loaves*, p. 149.

82. R.M. Fowler, *Let the Reader Understand: Reader-Response Criticism and the Gospel of Mark* (Minneapolis: Fortress Press, 1991).

83. Fowler, *Let the Reader*, p. 22.

84. Fowler, *Let the Reader*, p. 26.

hypothetical (and virtually always incredibly well-educated and nuance-sensitive) contemporary reader.

c. *Postmodernism, Poststructuralism and Deconstruction*
Discussion of postmodernism, poststructuralism and deconstruction[85] and their implications for interpretation of the New Testament has recently increased, although those responsible for the discussion are surprisingly few. Hence, in the light of its relatively recent use in the reading of texts, less space will be devoted to it, although the theoretical writing on the subject especially outside of biblical studies is immense.

One of the first to speak of the postmodernist agenda for biblical study was McKnight, who heralds the emergence of postmodern interpretation of the Bible by equating it with the emergence of reader-oriented criticism.[86] As evidenced by its place in literary criticism, it is questionable whether this is what truly distinguishes the postmodern agenda, especially since reader-oriented criticism, as seen above, is to a large extent a variation on the New Criticism.

Certainly the most important advocate of the postmodernist perspective, with its implications for deconstructive readings, is Moore. In his two recent volumes, *Mark and Luke in Poststructuralist Perspective* and *Poststructuralism and the New Testament*, he enters into the postmodern world by offering deconstructive readings. What emerges from these volumes is a number of clever insights, often arranged around recurring themes and motifs (and occasionally lurid wordplay). There are even occasional insights into texts, especially as he draws connections between them in ways that have not been emphasized before (e.g. his treatment of the woman at the well in John 4 and Jesus thirsting on the cross in John 19).[87] Perhaps more importantly, however, Moore draws attention to developments in literary-critical interpretation of the New Testament. Although his criticism goes beyond most others in his taking on the voice of deconstruction, his extreme approach well illustrates the

---

85. See S.D. Moore, *Poststructuralism and the New Testament: Derrida and Foucault at the Foot of the Cross* (Minneapolis: Fortress Press, 1994), pp. 131, 129, for several definitions, with bibliography.

86. E.V. McKnight, *Postmodern Use of the Bible: The Emergence of Reader-Oriented Criticism* (Nashville: Abingdon Press, 1988).

87. E.g. Moore, *Poststructuralism*, pp. 43-64. See also S.D. Moore, 'Are There Impurities in the Living Water that the Johannine Jesus Dispenses? Deconstruction, Feminism, and the Samaritan Woman', *BI* 1 (1993), pp. 207-27.

direction of much recent criticism in secular literary study that has not yet been explored by biblical critics. In some ways, we can be thankful that deconstruction has perhaps already passed its prime in secular literary study, although Moore has made a good effort to show what could have been.[88] What his discussion well illustrates is that the deconstructive agenda of postmodernism in many ways signals a return to criticism before the rise of literary-critical exegesis. One tenet of deconstruction is that the unity of the text is not assumed; in fact, the assumption is that the text is no more unified than anything else, and any assumed textual unity is disputed by the evidence.[89] Consequently, a number of different kinds of inconsistencies in the text emerge, including those of a linguistic, thematic and source-critical sort, with the various disjunctions easily providing the kind of evidence that early historical critics could have focused upon in support of various source- and form-critical theories. In this sense, there are commonalities between deconstruction and historical criticism. However, there is a major difference as well. Whereas the historical critic would use such textual discrepancies as a means of either reconstructing an earlier stage in the tradition or piecing together the orientation of a given author or community, deconstruction uses the evidence in a variety of other ways, most of them not wanting to go any further than the text itself. In this way, deconstruction is still a literary criticism. Discrepancies are used to reveal an inherent flawedness of the text that frustrates any attempt to get a firm hold on its interpretation. The text is said to subvert the best intentions of its interpreters.[90]

A clear example of this kind of interpretation is illustrated in Seeley's *Deconstructing the New Testament*.[91] At virtually every place in the New Testament he finds inherent unresolvable contradictions. For example, he finds the usual tension between Paul's statements in Romans 2 regarding the capability of one establishing righteousness through keeping of the law and later statements in Romans 3 and elsewhere that one is justified by faith apart from works. Similarly, in his discussion of John, Seeley finds that the author of the Fourth Gospel

88. An intention of Moore's *Mark and Luke*, pp. xiv-xvi, is to give deconstruction a chance in biblical studies.

89. See Moore, *Poststructuralism*, pp. 74-81. Contra E.P. Sanders and M. Davies, *Studying the Synoptic Gospels* (London: SCM Press, 1989), pp. 224-39, who put de-construction [sic] in part 4 under 'holistic readings'.

90. See Moore, *Poststructuralism*, p. 52.

91. D. Seeley, *Deconstructing the New Testament* (BIS, 5; Leiden: Brill, 1994).

appears to be making clear statements about the character of Jesus while these statements are found to be contradictory when examined more closely. Seeley's reading is as astute as anything a redaction critic would have come up with in finding the inherent contradictions in the text, while one is left with the impression that the biblical authors were all fairly dense, unable to construct a narrative that holds together. Interpreters who have attempted to solve these apparent difficulties have obviously been thwarted by the deconstructing text.

4. *Assessment of New Testament Literary Criticism*

To assess literary-critical interpretation of the New Testament is to ask the near-impossible. The reasons for this, as illustrated above, are that there is no such thing as a single literary-critical model of interpretation. There are many literary theories, each vying for its place in the critical marketplace. The most that can be offered here is a set of generalizations that attempt to capture some of the features that distinguish literary-critical readings from other kinds of readings, in particular historical-critical ones. After assessing its strengths and limitations, I offer a forecast for the future and a discussion of the ethics of interpretation.

a. *Strengths*
1. *Attention to certain kinds of details.* Literary-critical or close readings, especially New Critical ones concerned with narrative, have made readers aware of a new kind of detail. These details include such features as plot, character, and setting. As noted above, there have been several literary readings that have taken character, including minor characters, as the focus of attention. Other dimensions have proved equally insightful, such as discussion of plot and the motivation for action. There are already signs that some forms of redaction criticism are paying more attention to these textual features in their exposition of the theology of a writer.

2. *Recognition of the value of story.* Whereas much historical criticism, including redaction criticism, has worked in terms of propositional theology, including a given author's theological tendencies, literary criticism has brought to the fore that the story has value in and of itself. This has added several dimensions to exegesis, including a concern for the developing story as it unfolds, and recognition of a text's dynamics, rather than its being static. This insight has already been appropriated in

theology, where an individual's theological story is seen to be increasingly important.

3. *Emphasis upon textual integrity.* One of the hallmarks of much literary-critical exegesis, although one threatened in some ways by deconstruction, is the integrity of the text. The concept of textual integrity takes two forms in literary-critical circles. For many critics it means that the final form of the text is the object of critical scrutiny, without regard for any possible sources behind the text. Final-form criticism has come to distinguish the vast majority of literary critics, even if they are only concerned with a small portion of the final form of a given text. For others, textual integrity is a way of describing the critical position of many literary readers. That is, the majority of literary critics are textual maximalists, giving maximum credit to the phenomena of the text, over such things as sources, etc., as opposed to textual minimalists who skeptically question everything in the text. This concept is treated differently by deconstructionists, however, since one of the presuppositions of the method is that texts do not have inherent integrity but are built around contradiction.

4. *Interest in the writing, reading and reception process.* Having said above that literary critics are usually not concerned with sources, this is not to say that they are not concerned with the generation, interpretation and continuing significance of a text. The difference, however, seems to be that literary critics do not take texts and partition them into atomistic pre-existent elements, but explore the process by which they come about. This results in interest in writing, reading as one approaches and attempts to enter into the world of the text, and the reception process by which continuing generations of readers re-enter this textual world. This is an area that needs further development in New Testament literary exegesis.

5. *Expanded definition of literature.* Literary critics of the New Testament work with an expanded definition of literature. Whereas previous generations of biblical (and even some literary) critics tended to marginalize the New Testament because it was not thought to be suitably literary in character, the emergence of literary criticism of the New Testament has resulted in the re-definition of what constitutes literature to include at the least the Gospels and Acts. As mentioned above, the epistles are only now emerging as serious objects of literary consideration.

6. *A-historical orientation.* One of the arguable merits of literary

criticism is its a-historical orientation (not nonhistorical). This is not an assumption held by all literary critics, either overtly or inadvertently (e.g. those reader-oriented critics who interpret in the light of the original audience). It is fair to say, however, that the majority of literary critics are not concerned to place historical questions (such as did this really happen, where, at what time, involving whom, to what community of faith, etc.?) at the forefront of their interests. They are content to describe and elucidate the literary dimensions of the text, and to draw the boundaries of interpretation around this portrait, without feeling compelled to ask the further question of how this picture may gibe with historical reality.

7. *Text before theology.* Most literary-critical interpreters would question Wright's assertion that the justification of New Testament study is theology,[92] and argue instead that the text must take precedence. Not only do literary critics tend to resist examination of background and historical issues, but they also tend to shun foreground issues, that is, the use of the New Testament text simply as providing evidence or support for a New Testament theology. The text has an integrity of its own that warrants examination, not as a pre-text for creating a grand theological framework that runs the risk of overlooking significant textual phenomena.

8. *Interpreters freed from fear of failure.* On two accounts, literary-critical interpretation increases interest in interpretation by freeing the interpreter from the fear of failure. Literary-critical exposition is of such recent vintage that there is not as much likelihood that all of the reasonable interpretations of a text have already been done and re-done, a fear that many have regarding traditional historical-critical exposition. By its very nature literary-critical exposition frees the interpreter from the same kinds of constraints that usually attend to historical-critical exegesis, in so far as the interpretation need not fit a particular set of historical-critical assumptions.

9. *Methodological awareness.* Many outside of literary-critical circles would recognize that literary-critical exegesis has aided the entire field of New Testament studies because it has helped all interpreters to become more methodologically aware. This is not to say that before literary criticism there was not methodological awareness, but the burgeoning of literary-critical readings—which many see as a sign of the productivity

---

92. See S. Neill and N.T. Wright, *The Interpretation of the New Testament 1861–1986* (Oxford: Oxford University Press, 2nd edn, 1988), pp. 439-40.

of the model—has forced scholars to examine what is meant by interpretation. For example, the concept of an interpretative community has become important to all interpreters, in that literary criticism has not necessarily (although for some it has been treated in this way) set out to displace all other criticisms but has illustrated that, depending upon one's method, one will identify with similar-minded interpreters. A variety of other methodological issues have also been brought to all interpreters' attention by literary exegesis.

10. *Appreciation of how texts work*. With the kind of close attention being given to such things as character, plot, the role of the reader, even the assumption (or non-assumption) of textual unity, literary-critical exegesis has aided understanding of how texts work. The personification of the text in this way is not accepted by all literary critics, but there is a sense for many that the text does have a tangible role to play in setting the parameters for its own interpretation, and that a critic needs to work within these parameters. Consequently, the interpreter must learn how it is that any given text, and thus how texts in general, work, that is, how it is that they go about presenting their various features to the interpreter, and how it is that interpreters respond to them.

11. *Interesting readings*.[93] Perhaps the most important and enduring significance of literary-critical exegesis is a number of new and interesting readings of texts. Rather than simply working within the confines of traditional interpretation—whether established by the church or by a particular critical method—literary critics have expanded the boundaries of the viable interpretations of many passages. Sometimes this has taken the form of new readings of texts, while other times it has meant a new means of support for readings arrived at through other methods. In any case, these new readings, such as the emphasis upon the intricacies of the plot of a Gospel, the question of the character of an implied reader, etc., have been thought by many to offer new vistas for understanding the New Testament.

b. *Limitations*
There have been many limitations pointed out regarding literary-critical readings of the New Testament. One of the common flaws that can be

---

93. See D. Gunn, *The Story of King David: Genre and Interpretation* (JSOTSup, 6; Sheffield: JSOT Press, 1978), p. 88: 'In the end the test of the value of the interpretation is whether it enables the reader to see the text in ways that are new to him or her'.

noted in some of the work (historical critics are not immune from this) is that many interpreters do not appear to have sufficient linguistic ability to read the Greek text properly. Interpretations based on inaccurate understandings of the Greek text (or the English text, as it often turns out) cannot stand up to scrutiny however arrived at. Even the New Critics maintained that knowledge of the original language (whether sixteenth-century English, or ancient Greek) was pre-requisite for accurate interpretation. The limitations noted below are not this kind of error but are more systemically related to the approach itself.

1. *The history of criticism lost.* One of the limitations of literary-critical readings of the New Testament is that the history of criticism has been lost or outright rejected as irrelevant, in the same way that historical-critical questions are rejected. The reasons for this are several. For one, literary-critical interpretation, especially the vast majority that follows some form of the New Criticism, begins from a presupposition regarding the integrity and aloofness of the text, making its historical-contextual placement seem irrelevant. A second reason is that literary-critical exposition is to a large extent reacting against the historical-critical method that has dominated the last several hundred years of interpretation. When the historical-critical method is rejected, so is the history of interpretation that is built upon it.

2. *Ties with history lost.* In conjunction with the limitation noted above, it is also true that for much literary-critical interpretation ties with history are lost. The emphasis here is not upon the history of interpretation so much as the historicality of the text. Some of the more recent literary criticism has made an attempt to come to terms with this deficiency in much of the earlier literary criticism (see below), but there is a residual tendency to depreciate the relationship to history. What is neglected is that any text, no matter how artistic or literarily shaped, has an inherent historicality, in terms of at least the fact that an author (or even authors) wrote it in a particular place or time (even if this extended over a length of time), using a variety of language of some linguistic community, and it was read at least initially by readers in a given historical context who knew or understood the language, or at least sufficient to think that they were making sense of it. Furthermore, the matters referred to in any given text, in particular the various books of the New Testament, are historical people, places, events, etc., often mentioned without giving a full or even sufficient amount of supporting detail to understand them without further investigation. The result,

according to this limitation, is that there may at best be incomplete understanding and at worst complete misunderstanding of a passage or book if the historical dimension is not duly considered.

3. *Lack of explicit method and formal controls.* With any interpretative method, the question of methodological procedure and constraint must be raised. This is not to say that every interpreter must be a theoretician but that every interpreter must have a method—does have a method—whether or not realized. As pointed out above, however, many literary interpreters of the New Testament, especially up until fairly recently, have not been explicit in their method, treating the textual evidence as if it were self-evident, along with its interpretation. Within any method, there must be some consideration of what constitutes data, and how interpretations of these data are evaluated. These kinds of formal controls have been explicitly laid out by historical critics, and perhaps this has been part of the problem why some literary interpreters have chosen to go a separate way, since they have rejected some of the assumptions of historical criticism. This rejection, however, does not alleviate literary critics of elucidating their own standards of exposition, including criteria by which any given reading is to be evaluated. Most critics find the criterion of 'interest' alone to be insufficient.

4. *Preoccupation with labelling method but not identifying with it.* A shortcoming of some recent New Testament literary-critical exegesis has been the failure to grasp fully what a given method entails. This is seen in the areas of reader-oriented criticism and deconstruction. Interpreters have been anxious to adopt at least the labels of these methods and to call their interpretations examples of such a method, but they have failed to appreciate the complexities implied by the method in terms of its presuppositions and its resultant entailments. One is left with a method that is at best limited in its effectiveness since it does not conform to the expectations of the method, and at worst misleading and quite possibly inaccurate in terms of the reading it provides.

5. *Unenlightening and pedestrian readings.* Whereas many New Testament literary critics contend that their readings are quite insightful, offering all sorts of new considerations to the scholarly community, others have found them to be quite unenlightening, if not inaccurate, even if weighed by their own criteria (see the chapter on historical criticism). Many outside the guild of literary interpreters have not been brought to the same level of excitement by these readings as those within, finding some of the readings exercises in tedium or pointing out

the already evident. For those who evaluate the method on the basis of its ability to create new understandings, one might respond that this depends on the person for whom it is designed to be interesting.

6. *Neglect of important questions.* A common criticism of literary-critical exegesis is that it neglects important questions. Of course, this raises the issue of what constitutes an important question and for whom. This criticism is raised in the light of the history of interpretation, in which various recurring questions are seen to define the understanding of a given passage, and to neglect such questions renders a reading— almost by definition—inadequate. For example, regarding the Pauline opponents, the composition and character of the Pauline churches, or the nature of early Christianity as reflected by the Gospel accounts, failure to raise these questions and to provide an interpretation that addresses them could be seen as flawed. If emphasis is shifted to the kinds of questions that arise solely from the text, without reference to historical issues, such as the major themes or orientation of a given author, again historical exegesis works from the standpoint that there are certain issues that must be considered. Almost self-evident are the relations among the Synoptic Gospels. Most historical critics would consider it illegitimate to interpret, for example, the temptation narrative in Matthew or Luke without raising the questions of how this is handled in Luke differently from Mark and Matthew, especially since Mark would appear (according to standard Gospel criteria) to be the source of the account, and Matthew another interpretation. The ending of the Gospels and response to the empty tomb would be a similar example.

7. *Importation of method.* The question is often raised whether the utilization of interpretative methods developed for non-historical modern literature, such as novels, poems, etc., is appropriate for documents in the New Testament that, at least ostensibly, are historical and theological. The justification for development of the historical-critical method is that this method drew upon criteria developed in related historical disciplines, and then adapted them to interpretation of the texts of the New Testament. There is the further question of whether a method developed for non-historical literature is appropriate to sacred texts. For those who raise such objections, some would apparently be satisfied with more explicit methodological statements that show the compatibility of the method and the new context of usage; others would apparently reject the method altogether.

8. *What if story contradicts theology or history?* The question must

inevitably be raised regarding any method, but perhaps especially a method that takes such an avowedly a-historical position and emphasizes plurality of interpretation, what happens when the method arrives at conclusions that conflict with what are considered to be well-founded historical or theological conclusions? There are many different possible solutions, but the fundamental differences in the methods involved make it difficult to harmonize them. For example, whereas a number of literary critics might not find such a conclusion to be a problem, many historical critics would argue that their method, with its attempt to get back to the historical basis of the events involved, cannot advocate as a virtue the arrival at multiple conclusions. The situation with regard to theology is potentially even worse. So far, there has been no agreed upon method for even addressing—to say nothing of adjudicating—such disputes.

9. *Why do some scholars read the New Testament literarily?* There is persistent unease among historical critics regarding the motivations of at least some literary critics. The thought is that a good number of them have latched onto literary criticism as a way of avoiding the kinds of tough questions and methods that are associated with historical criticism. This limitation is in fact a criticism of two separate practices. On the one hand, it has long been suspected that a number of literary critics of the New Testament have adopted the method to avoid dealing with critical questions that might run contrary to their theologies. By adopting a literary model, for some it is possible to interpret the final form of the text and hence to avoid asking source- or form-critical questions, which might run up against various theological stances. On the other hand, some suspect that a number of literary critics of the New Testament have adopted such a stance because they have not been willing (or able?) to devote the kind of time and energy necessary to master the intricacies of the historical-critical method, with its attention to fine detail, multiple ancient cognate languages and literatures, rigorous historical method, etc.

10. *Eclecticism and its problems.* A final limitation to mention is the eclecticism often found in literary-critical exegesis. This criticism is not of eclecticism itself, since biblical studies is an eclectic discipline. The criticism here is that, while certain disciplines can be incorporated into the development of an appropriate method for interpretation of the New Testament, there are certain critical stances that may not be compatible and hence should not be included. Since New Testament studies is

historically based, it might be argued that besides the traditional historical-critical methods such other methods as sociological analysis, rhetorical analysis (drawing upon ancient models), liberation hermeneutics, to mention several of those treated in this volume, since they also have a distinct historical component, at least potentially can be integrated into New Testament study. But the avowedly a-historical presupposition of much literary-critical exegesis may well exclude it from integration, and hence it is inherently going to be a marginalized and quite possibly unimportant method for reading the New Testament.

c. *Forecast for the Future*

Having discussed the strengths and limitations of literary-critical exegesis of the New Testament it is perhaps appropriate to offer a brief glimpse at what I see as its future. I am not attempting to act as a prophet, but to look at the recent trends and offer some suggestive criticism regarding the developing discipline.

1. *Address the limitations above.* Literary exegetes of the New Testament must come to terms with the criticism raised above regarding their work. This is not to say that this will result in wholesale changes in the way the discipline of New Testament studies is conducted, and certainly not to say that literary criticism should be abandoned, only that for true progress to be made within the larger discipline, these issues must be addressed. When these issues are addressed, in the light of the already perceived strengths of literary-critical exegesis, there can be some productive rapprochement between the historical- and literary-critical areas of the discipline. More importantly, it is bound to result in the productive strengthening and developing of literary-critical methods. It seems to me that the following items should be given serious consideration. First, there needs to be continuing attention given to method. It would be ideal if more literary-critical interpreters of the New Testament moved to the forefront of theoretical discussion, not only in the biblical arena but ideally also in the general field of literary criticism. Failing this, more literary-critical exegetes need to come to terms with the development of secular literary criticism and become masters of its method. Secondly, reader-oriented criticism needs to come to terms with what it means to be reader-oriented, especially in the light of the manifest theoretical shortcomings of most such exegesis. The kind of half-way house that most reader-oriented critics live in is a shaky structure. It would be wise to move either back to the New Critical

house with its many different rooms or to some new development (although one cannot count on the deconstructive tract houses). Thirdly, and perhaps this reflects more my own preferences than any sort of objective analysis, I think that deconstruction and related so-called postmodern critical methods, now that they have had their say, and we know what they involve, will fade after an initial burst of energy. This is not to say that recent work has not been interesting and entertaining—it has. This is to say that it has not offered much insight into the text, because it has ended up exalting itself above the position of the text (mostly through redefining what a text is),[94] reverting to fallacious methods long rejected elsewhere (such as etymologizing), and becoming a form of autobiography more than anything else.

2. *Catch up with historical criticism.* Literary criticism of the New Testament is of sufficiently recent provenance that it continues to display the kind of excitement and enthusiasm often displayed in such disciplines. But historical criticism has had nearly two hundred years of sustained development and refinement. One of the tasks of literary criticism of the New Testament will be to increase its self-understanding both with regard to secular literary criticism and with regard to its place within the larger sphere of New Testament exegesis. In other words, literary criticism of the New Testament has a lot of growing up to do in relation to other interpretative methods. This is not to say that there are not many mature readings being offered of the New Testament; it is to say that currently the method has not yet been sufficiently tested by time in relation to its own endurance and the endurance of its readings.

3. *Integrate historical and literary readings.* The literary-critical analyses that I find most convincing are those that integrate a literary reading of the New Testament with a historical understanding. Although this kind of method has been shunned in some circles of literary criticism, it seems to me that if there is to be a useful dialogue between the sub-disciplines, such that literary criticism can profitably continue to influence historical criticism and historical criticism can provide the context for enlightened literary readings, literary criticism must appreciate the historicality of the New Testament in all of its facets. To illustrate this I offer brief summaries of four literary readings of four different texts.

a. *Opening of Mark's Gospel.* As noted above, the vast majority of

94. See D.A. Carson, 'On the Other Topics', in S.E. Porter and D.A. Carson (eds.), *Discourse Analysis and Other Topics in Biblical Greek* (JSNTSup, 113; Sheffield: Sheffield Academic Press, 1995), pp. 118-26.

literary interpretation has been concerned with the Gospels, either with broad sweeping expositions of the plot, setting and characters, such as those by Kingsbury, or with particularized studies that exegete individual characters or a class of characters, such as those produced by Darr and Williams. Few if any have noted, however, the literary *and* historical significance of the opening of Mark's Gospel. The Gospel begins with the words 'the beginning of the gospel about Jesus Christ, son of God'. There are many issues attendant upon this verse, including whether it serves as the heading for the entire Gospel or a portion of it. What has been overlooked is how the use of 'gospel' introduces a controlling Markan theme, carried forward by absolute use of the word on the lips of Jesus, with Jesus in 1.15, 8.35, 10.20, 13.10 and 14.9 proclaiming the good news. The 'good news' has significance, as few commentators have pointed out, because it helps to reinforce the Markan emphasis upon Jesus as the son of God, introduced in 1.1, developed in the Gospel, and explicitly reiterated by the Roman centurion at Jesus' death in 15.39. The conjunction of the two concepts of 'good news' and 'son of God' is also found in Hellenistic inscriptions with reference to Caesar as the son of god. The most noteworthy example is a 9 BCE inscription from Priene, erected during Caesar Augustus's life, which refers to the 'good news' regarding the birthday of 'the god' (OGIS 45B).[95] The conjunction of 'good news' and 'son of God' language in ancient Hellenistic inscriptions provides suitable historical evidence and context for the conjunction of these two concepts and ideas in Mark's Gospel. Their conjunction at the outset of the Gospel provides a controlling motif developed throughout it, even to the point of proclamation of Jesus as the son of God at his death, by none other than a Roman centurion. As a side-light this literary concatenation might well provide secondary evidence for the Roman origins of the Gospel. At the least it provides evidence for one who consciously crafts his Gospel in terms of religious and political terminology of the day, replacing Caesar with the genuine son of God, Jesus Christ.

b. *Luke 16.1-13 and the Unjust Steward.*[96] Whereas the previous

95. For citation of the abundance of data, see A. Deissmann, *Light from the Ancient East* (trans. L.R.M. Strachan; repr. Grand Rapids: Baker, 1978), pp. 338-78, esp. pp. 366-67.

96. This summarizes S.E. Porter, 'The Parable of the Unjust Steward (Luke 16.1-13): Irony *Is* the Key', in D.J.A. Clines, S.E. Fowl and S.E. Porter (eds.), *The Bible in Three Dimensions* (JSOTSup, 87; Sheffield: JSOT Press, 1990), pp. 127-53.

reading shows how historically-based literary features can provide a controlling formulation for treatment of an entire Gospel, historically-based literary criticism can also provide useful insight into a smaller pericope, such as a parable. The parable of the unjust steward has proved enigmatic, because a superficial reading of it in its Gospel context and in the context of the teaching of Jesus makes it sound like an endorsement of dishonest practices, since Jesus would be heard to praise a steward who has ostensibly survived through dishonest dealing with his master's accounts, once his previous dishonest practices are discovered. Although there have been various attempts to explain the steward's sharp practices, some of them appealing to supposed similar practices in the Jewish world, these all prove unsatisfactory. The resulting anomaly between the apparent meaning of a statement (such as Jesus' apparent endorsement of the steward's dishonest practices in v. 9) and what is clear from the context (Jesus does not elsewhere endorse dishonesty but condemns such behaviour especially regarding money) is a primary factor in determining the presence of irony. Irony, a category widely utilized in New Criticism, provides a clue to the parable. What Jesus is not saying to his listeners is to be shrewd like the steward (ignoring his cheating)[97] but he is saying to not think that one is being wise in trying to use earthly possessions to obtain a heavenly reward.[98] Thus the

97. As C.L. Blomberg contends in '"Your Faith Has Made You Whole": The Evangelical Liberation Theology of Jesus', in J.B. Green and M. Turner (eds.), *Jesus of Nazareth Lord and Christ: Essays on the Historical Jesus and New Testament Christology* (Grand Rapids: Eerdmans, 1994), pp. 90-91. Blomberg cites my study and claims: 'Porter complains that the steward's cleverness cannot be separated from his specific, ingratiating action, which forms an unworthy example (131), but he gives no reasons for this assertion, which is not self-evident' (p. 90 n. 81). It is unfortunate that Blomberg apparently only read a half page of the essay that is responding to the particular interpretation that he endorses (the traditional view, that the lord, probably Jesus, is commending the steward for his cleverness though not his dishonesty) rather than the entire essay, in which it is argued that the steward is an unworthy example. Two points remain to be made, however. First, one should note Blomberg's own defense (or lack of it) for the traditional interpretation: 'The most common interpretation throughout church history remains the best...' In other words, he offers little support, only assertion based on tradition. There is no argumentative force to his claim. Secondly, this particular interpretation is the reason that there is so much attention given to the parable, because most interpreters recognize that it is difficult if not impossible to separate the commendation of shrewdness from the way in which he was shrewd, that is, by further acting dishonestly once discovered to be dishonest.

98.   C. Brown, 'The Unjust Steward: A New Twist?', in M.J. Wilkins and

commendation Jesus offers is ironic, as is his further commentary in vv. 10-13. Thus this literary interpretation not only unifies the entire parable pericope (vv. 1-13) but brings consistency to Jesus' treatment of wealth here with the parables of the prodigal son and the rich man and Lazarus.

c. *Passover Motif in John's Gospel.*[99] Whereas the previous readings have looked internally for a literary framework to understand their respective texts, it is also possible to look outside the work to find the interpretative key. Such is the case with the use of the passover motif in John's Gospel. Although several recent commentators have found reference to the passover at various places throughout the Gospel, few have taken a sustained look at this concept as forming a consistent line of interpretation throughout the Gospel. In their recent works, Stibbe tries to create an integrated reading of John 18–19, combining literary (New Critical), generic, structuralist, and historical readings, but he clearly neglects the importance of the passover motif in ch. 19;[100] and Davies claims to provide a 'comprehensive reading' of the Fourth Gospel, making sense of its anthropology, history and theology, but she essentially only treats ch. 19 regarding the passover motif.[101] One need not argue that the passover motif is the most important or the only theme developed in the Gospel to realize its importance. Besides widespread reference in the Gospel to the passover feast, the following passages exemplify it: 1.29-36, especially vv. 29 and 36, at Jesus' baptism, 2.13-25 and the cleansing of the temple, ch. 6 and in particular the feeding of the five thousand and the bread of life discourse, 11.47–12.8 and

T. Paige (eds.), *Worship, Theology and Ministry in the Early Church* (JSNTSup, 87; Sheffield: JSOT Press, 1992), pp. 127-28, who apparently confuses irony with allegory in trying to insist that the 'heavenly tents' of v. 9 must refer to earthly abodes. Although he endorses the use of irony, his own solution is by far the least plausible, making the steward into a type of Jesus. The resultant inconsistencies with the Jesus of the rest of the New Testament render the solution a complete anomaly.

99.   This summarizes S.E. Porter, 'Can Traditional Exegesis Enlighten Literary Analysis of the Fourth Gospel? An Examination of the Old Testament Fulfilment Motif and the Passover Theme', in C.A. Evans and W.R. Stegner (eds.), *The Gospels and the Scriptures of Israel* (JSNTSup, 104; Sheffield: Sheffield Academic Press, 1994), pp. 396-428.

100.   See Stibbe, *Jesus as Story.*

101.   See M. Davies, *Rhetoric and Reference in the Fourth Gospel* (JSNTSup, 69; Sheffield: JSOT Press, 1992); cf. her *Matthew* (Readings; Sheffield: JSOT Press, 1993).

Caiaphas's prophecy and Jesus' anointing, 13.1–17.26 and Jesus' final meal with his disciples, and 19.32-42 and the death of Jesus, culminating with the quotation of the Old Testament in vv. 36-37 regarding no bone being broken. Although this could well be treated from a tradition-critical standpoint, showing how the passover tradition is formative for the structure of the Gospel, this can be combined with an intertextual literary analysis to see how the Gospel depicts Jesus as the perfect passover lamb. This can only be fully appreciated, however, if one knows of the passover from the Old Testament, and examines the motif throughout the entire Gospel, rather than confining oneself to one or two passages, especially those argued by earlier scholars.

d. *Romans 1–8 and Freytag's Pyramid.*[102] As mentioned above, there have been very few literary expositions of epistolary material in the New Testament. Apart from Petersen's treatment of Philemon, and a few treatments of individual passages in the epistles, there has been little systematic literary-critical exegesis. It is commonly agreed that Romans 1–8 forms an integrated literary unit, at least from 1.16 to the end of ch. 8. It is sometimes equated with the body of the letter, although chs. 9–11 should probably also be included in this section. Within chs. 1–8, justification by faith has since Luther traditionally been seen to be the most important concept. However, on the basis of a number of other factors, including the centrality of ch. 5 in the literary structure of chs. 1–8, the concentration of important vocabulary in ch. 5, and the use of 'reconciliation' language, it is arguable that ch. 5, with its exposition of reconciliation, defined in vv. 1 and 10-11 and exemplified in comparison of Adam and Christ, is the literary centre of interest. This is confirmed through use of a model from the nineteenth-century drama critic Gustav Freytag, who developed his so-called 'five part tragic pyramid'. He illustrates that a common plot structure involves five parts, with inciting action (Rom 1.16-17), increasing tension (1.18–4.25), climactic turning point (ch. 5), falling action (chs. 6-7) and resolution (ch. 8). According to this analysis, Paul's theme statement in 1.16-17 provides the inciting action. This is developed in terms of humanity's legal position as one of sinfulness, resolvable in legal terms only by justification (1.18–4.25). In language that combines legal and personal terminology, and which

102. This summarizes S.E. Porter, 'A Newer Perspective on Paul: Romans 1–8 through the Eyes of Literary Analysis', in M. Daniel Carroll R., D.J.A. Clines and P.R. Davies (eds.), *The Bible in Human Society: Essays in Honour of John Rogerson* (JSOTSup, 200; Sheffield: Sheffield Academic Press, 1995).

unites the pre-Christian with the Christian life, Paul introduces reconciliation, a complex theological concept focusing upon the relation of
humanity to God (ch. 5). This new relationship is explored in terms of
Christian behaviour in chs. 6–7, before being resolved by presenting the
life in the Spirit in ch. 8. Thus by the use of a model from secular literature, but in conjunction with the evidence of the biblical text, insight can
be gained into the developing literary argument of an epistle. This
outline of the argument not only satisfies literary criteria suggested by
the literary features of the letter but is in conformity with the epistolary
form, thus uniting a modern literary model with ancient epistolary study.

d. *The Ethics of Interpretation*

In the light of what has been said above, there is one last issue that
merits discussion—the ethics of interpretation.[103] The issue is essentially
what limits are there to the methods used to interpret the New
Testament and their resultant readings? In other words, are there certain
controls on interpretation, or is any method or reading legitimate, even if
it is offensive to others? This is an issue that has been addressed several
times recently. In her 1987 SBL presidential address, Schüssler Fiorenza
advocated what she calls a paradigm shift within the guild of biblical
scholars, so that they practice an ethics of historical reading (which
involves interpretation of the text within its historical context, as well as
providing a means of assessing and evaluating the values that emerge
from such interpretation), and an ethics of accountability (which is responsible for the choice of interpretative models used and the consequences of such an interpretation).[104] Jeanrond, although addressing a
more theological than biblical context in his theory of reading, recognizes the dynamic nature of the text, while limiting the possible
meanings of the text by the way that the text is structured. By the use of
a text-linguistic model, he states that all of the potential meaning is
organized and guided by an overriding sense of what the text has to say
and how it says it. For the reader, the interpretative task is limited by
genre, that is, by discovering and employing the conventions of a given

103. See, e.g., W.C. Booth, *The Company We Keep: An Ethics of Fiction*
(Berkeley: University of California Press, 1988). Cf. D.J.A. Clines, 'Possibilities and
Priorities of Biblical Interpretation in an International Perspective', *BI* 1 (1993), esp.
pp. 84-86.

104. E. Schüssler Fiorenza, 'The Ethics of Interpretation: De-Centering Biblical
Scholarship', *JBL* 107 (1988), pp. 3-17.

genre the reader is able to discern the meaning of the text as the author constructed it.[105] Fowl proposes that discussion dispense with talking about the meaning of texts, since there is no way to adjudicate between various proposed meanings, and talk instead about various interpretative interests. For example, one might talk about authorial intention, or issues of gender, or the like. Rejecting the notion that these various interests can be amalgamated into some kind of grand interpretation, he claims that many of the interpretative interests result in exclusive interpretations that are not apparently harmonizable. Communities of interpreters are the way of dealing with the resulting pluralism.[106] Finally, Young argues that what is necessary in interpretation is a recognition of the element of difference in a text, between what it might have meant to the original audience and what it might mean to interpreters today. Showing respect for each of these contexts is important in an ethical reading, and thus avoiding an arbitrary reading.[107]

Without resolving the question of the ethics of reading, several of the issues must be mentioned, especially in the light of the diversity of critical opinion on interpretation seen within this essay, to say nothing of the various approaches to interpretation offered in this volume. First, it is clear that all of those above, with the apparent exception of Fowl, are concerned not to leave interpretation open and arbitrary. Constraints cited include a concept of innate justice (Schüssler Fiorenza), a sense of inherent meaning (Jeanrond), and a historical-critical distance (Young). Fowl does not leave the situation entirely arbitrary, since he speaks of communities of interpreters, within which he outlines a procedure for adjudicating disputes within them (although it is not entirely clear why this should be done, or, if it can, why it cannot be applied to larger disputes, or whether he has clearly outlined a suitable procedure in the light of his own rejection of means of arbitrating between meanings). Secondly, in judging meanings, appeals are made to genre (Jeanrond), a sense of good will towards the text (Young), or interpretative

105. W.G. Jeanrond, *Text and Interpretation as Categories of Theological Thinking* (trans. T.J. Wilson; Dublin: Gill and Macmillan, 1988).

106. S.E. Fowl, 'The Ethics of Interpretation or What's Left over after the Elimination of Meaning', in Clines, Fowl and Porter (eds.), *Bible in Three Dimensions*, pp. 379-98; 'Texts Don't Have Ideologies', *BI* 3 (1995), pp. 15-34.

107. F. Young, 'The Pastoral Epistles and the Ethics of Reading', *JSNT* 45 (1992), pp. 105-20; cf. 'Allegory and the Ethics of Reading', in Watson (ed.), *Open Text*, pp. 103-20.

communities (Fowl). It is unclear where such concepts come from, whether they are an appeal to universal principles, in which case much more is needed to outline what these are, why others have not been able to find them and what implications they have for particular reading stances, or whether they are simply practical conventions, in which case they may simply reflect a utilitarian ethic with questionable normative force. Thirdly, if the attempt to establish an ethics of reading looks an awful lot like the critics above simply trying to justify their own personal preferences, such as re-asserting the validity of historical-critical reading, etc., then what of others who may have other personal preferences? Is there a sense in which anti-Semitic readings, or anti-women readings, or anti-Christian readings of the New Testament can be permitted or justified? It appears that the issue of a plurality of methods, with no clear means of arbitrating among them, leaves itself open to a host of abuses. It suffices to say that in the light of the multiplication of methods as well as the resultant readings, it is incumbent upon interpreters and their communities to discuss the issue of an ethics of reading. This may be the most important issue facing literary interpreters of the New Testament.

5. *Conclusion*

This essay has attempted to illustrate—through a brief history of literary interpretation of the Bible, a brief discussion of the methodological orientation and theoretical background of literary criticism in general, a representative survey of several works exemplifying literary-critical exegesis of the New Testament, a chronicling of the strengths and limitations of literary-critical exegesis, and a brief look to the future of the discipline—what is involved in the approach to New Testament exegesis called literary criticism. The future of the discipline is in many ways still undecided. There is the chance that there may be an implosion or backlash, in which the weight of so many different readings is seen to be counterproductive to interpretation. This may result in a swing back to emphasis upon the historical-critical method. The chances of this will probably be increased if much literary criticism resists connections with the more traditional interpretative disciplines. If literary criticism continues to develop a more explicit methodology or set of methodologies, with recognition of the historicality of the biblical text, there is probably a greater chance of more widespread acceptance and even endorsement of the kinds of readings that can emerge from these various literary-critical models.

RHETORICAL CRITICISM OF THE NEW TESTAMENT:
ANCIENT AND MODERN EVALUATIONS OF ARGUMENTATION

Dennis L. Stamps

1. *Introduction*

Traditionally, rhetoric has been understood as a particular kind of communication, the persuasive speech, with rhetorical criticism being the critical analysis of the formal qualities of the speech utilized to make the speech effectively persuasive.[1] In the history of biblical interpretation, the application of rhetorical criticism has gone through several stages. Most recently, the work of the so-called New Rhetoricians has formulated an understanding of rhetoric as the way all discourse induces or enhances an audience's adherence to certain values and hierarchies, that is, how all discourse functions as a form of persuasive argumentation.[2] As a consequence, rhetoric has become a ubiquitous term, applied to a wide range of discourse.[3] This shift has resulted in biblical studies applying different

---

1.   G.A. Kennedy, *Classical Rhetoric and its Christian and Secular Tradition from Ancient to Modern Times* (Chapel Hill, NC: University of North Carolina Press, 1980), pp. 3-24.

2.   E. Black, *Rhetorical Criticism: A Study in Method* (New York: Macmillan, 1965); C. Perelman and L. Olbrechts-Tyteca, *The New Rhetoric: A Treatise on Argumentation* (trans. J. Wilkinson and P. Weaver; Notre Dame: University of Notre Dame Press, 1969); W.J. Brandt, *The Rhetoric of Argumentation* (New York: Bobbs-Merrill, 1970); K. Burke, *The Rhetoric of Religion* (Berkeley: University of California Press, 1970); E.P.J. Corbett, *Classical Rhetoric for the Modern Student* (New York: Oxford University Press, 3rd edn, 1988); W. Nash, *Rhetoric: The Wit of Persuasion* (Oxford: Oxford University Press, 1989).

3.   Theoretical justification for using the term 'rhetoric' as a meta-label for discourse can be found in T. Eagleton, *Literary Theory: An Introduction* (Oxford: Basil Blackwell, 1983), esp. pp. 194-217; D. Leith and G. Myerson, *The Power of Address: Explorations in Rhetoric* (London: Routledge & Kegan Paul, 1989), pp. 114-48, 204-40. See also J.S. Nelson, A. Megill, and D.N. McCloskey (eds.), *The Rhetoric of the Human Sciences* (Madison, WI: University of Wisconsin Press,

rhetorical-critical models in order to analyse how the argument of a biblical text creates its persuasive effect.[4]

In order to understand how rhetorical criticism might be used as a way of approaching New Testament texts, it is necessary both to examine the current practice(s) of rhetorical criticism in New Testament studies and to attempt to posit a working definition of rhetoric. First, a review of recent developments in rhetorical criticism of the New Testament is offered. Secondly, the various strands of rhetorical criticism outlined in the first part are illustrated by examples of rhetorical critical practice. Thirdly, in response to the current practice(s) of rhetorical criticism in New Testament studies, a proposal is made for a rhetorical-critical theory and practice. Fourthly, the rhetorical-critical approach outlined in section three is applied to 1 Cor. 1.1-3. Finally, the current rhetorical criticism of the New Testament is critiqued in order to assess the strengths and weaknesses of such an interpretative approach.

2. Recent Developments in Rhetorical Criticism in New Testament Studies

The application of rhetorical criticism to the New Testament has a long history.[5] It extends back to the Early Church fathers who, trained in rhetoric, read many New Testament texts in order to analyse the persuasive style of the New Testament so that contemporary preachers could imitate this biblically-sanctioned rhetoric: a good example of this is St Augustine's *On Christian Doctrine* (Book 4). The renaissance of classical Greco-Roman rhetoric in the sixteenth century influenced the biblical exegesis of a number of the Reformers, including Luther and Calvin. And a strong legacy of rhetorical criticism of the New Testament

1986), and R.H. Roberts and J.M.M. Good, *The Recovery of Rhetoric: Persuasive Discourse and Disciplinarity in the Human Sciences* (Charlottesville, VA: University Press of Virginia, 1993).

4.　B.L. Mack, *Rhetoric and the New Testament* (Guides to Biblical Scholarship, NT Series; Minneapolis: Fortress Press, 1990), pp. 9-17; D.L. Stamps, 'Rhetorical Criticism and the Rhetoric of New Testament Criticism', *LT* 6 (1992), pp. 268-79.

5.　Recent summaries of the history of rhetorical criticism in New Testament studies include, D.F. Watson and A.J. Hauser, *Rhetorical Criticism of the Bible: A Comprehensive Bibliography with Notes on History and Method* (BIS, 4; Leiden: Brill, 1994), pp. 101-109; Mack, *Rhetoric*, pp. 9-24; F.W. Hughes, *Early Christian Rhetoric and 2 Thessalonians* (JSNTSup, 30; Sheffield: JSOT Press, 1989), pp. 19-30.

can be found in the German commentators writing in the late eighteenth century to the early twentieth century. It would be fair to say that much of this history of rhetorical criticism centred on an analysis of the literary and rhetorical devices that can be isolated in the New Testament as a form of style or ornamentation.[6]

The 'revival' of rhetorical criticism in biblical criticism in the late twentieth century has occurred through a number of influences. James Muilenburg, an Old Testament scholar, is credited with introducing the phrase, 'rhetorical criticism', into twentieth-century biblical studies with his writings in the mid 1950s.[7] His 1968 SBL presidential address, 'Form Criticism and Beyond', sounded a clarion call to go beyond form criticism by using rhetorical criticism.[8] He only vaguely defined what he meant, suggesting that the text should be approached as an 'indissoluble whole, an artistic and creative unity, a unique formulation'.[9]

Actually, slightly earlier, Amos N. Wilder introduced the concept of rhetoric for New Testament studies. Wilder's classic work published in 1964, *The Language of the Gospel: Early Christian Rhetoric*, introduced a form of rhetorical criticism which emphasized 'not so much... what the early Christians said, as how they said it'.[10] He, however, went further with respect to the text and its form in the preface to the 1971 reprint in which he suggested that Scripture's rhetoric was evidence of a particular and peculiar language event which put the reader in touch with the transcendent.[11]

Robert Funk took the insights of Wilder and gave them a specific application to the parable and the epistle in his book, *Language, Hermeneutic, and Word of God*.[12] In Funk's analysis, the parable is

6.   J. Botha, 'On the "Reinvention" of Rhetoric', *Scriptura* 31 (1989), pp. 15-18; A.H. Snyman, 'On Studying the Figures (*schēmata*) in the New Testament', *Bib* 69 (1988), pp. 93-107.

7.   J. Muilenburg, 'A Study in Hebrew Rhetoric: Repetition and Style', *VTSup* 1 (1953), pp. 97-111; and 'The Book of Isaiah: Chapters 40–66', in *The Interpreter's Bible* (New York: Abingdon Press, 1956), V, pp. 681-773.

8.   J. Muilenburg, 'Form Criticism and Beyond', *JBL* 88 (1969), pp. 1-18.

9.   Muilenburg, 'Form Criticism', p. 9.

10.   A.N. Wilder, *The Language of the Gospel: Early Christian Rhetoric* (New York: Harper & Row, 1964), p. 10.

11.   A.N. Wilder, *Early Christian Rhetoric: The Language of the Gospel* (Cambridge, MA: Harvard University Press, 1971).

12.   R.W. Funk, *Language, Hermeneutic, and Word of God* (New York: Harper & Row, 1966).

understood as a metaphor; the letter, as an oral conversation. In both instances, according to Funk, the form creates a language event in which a fresh experience or understanding of ultimate reality occurs. Funk's understanding of text and its meaning or sense is articulated in that phase of biblical theology known as the 'New Hermeneutic'.[13]

Possibly even more influential was E.A. Judge's article, 'Paul's Boasting in Relation to Contemporary Professional Practice'. In this seminal article he challenged New Testament scholarship to assess the rhetorical training of Paul and to assess the impact of Greco-Roman rhetoric upon the New Testament texts.[14]

Modern application of rhetorical criticism in New Testament studies, however, is better known for the critical perspective initiated by H.D. Betz. In 1974 he suggested that the whole of Galatians should be interpreted and analysed as a rhetorical discourse, an apologetic letter, which utilizes traditional ancient rhetorical categories of speech.[15] His application of ancient rhetorical criteria to a complete epistolary text has engendered a variety of responses[16] and has been severely criticized as methodologically questionable.[17]

In the mid 1980s, a classicist, George Kennedy, applied classical rhetorical criticism to the whole range of New Testament literature in his book, *New Testament Interpretation through Rhetorical Criticism*, suggesting a formulaic procedure for analysing textual units according to

13. J.M. Robinson and J.B. Cobb, Jr, *The New Hermeneutic* (New Frontiers in Theology, 2; New York: Harper & Row, 1964).

14. E.A. Judge, 'Paul's Boasting in Relation to Contemporary Professional Practice', *ABR* 16 (1968), pp. 37-50.

15. H.D. Betz, 'Literary Composition and Function of Paul's Letter to the Galatians', *NTS* 21 (1975), pp. 353-79; *Galatians: A Commentary on Paul's Letter to the Churches in Galatia* (Hermeneia; Philadelphia: Fortress Press, 1979).

16. Not least being imitation of his methodology: Hughes, *Early Christian Rhetoric*; C.A. Wanamaker, *The Epistles to the Thessalonians: A Commentary on the Greek Text* (NIGTC; Grand Rapids: Eerdmans, 1990); W. Wuellner, 'Paul's Rhetoric of Argumentation in Romans: An Alternative to the Donfried–Karris Debate over Romans', *CBQ* 38 (1976), pp. 330-51; T.H. Olbricht, 'An Aristotelian Rhetorical Analysis of 1 Thessalonians', in *Greeks, Romans and Christians: Essays in Honor of A.J. Malherbe* (ed. D. Balch, E. Ferguson and W. Meeks; Minneapolis: Fortress Press, 1990), pp. 216-37.

17. J. Smit, 'The Letter to Galatians: A Deliberative Speech', *NTS* 35 (1989), pp. 1-26; R.N. Longenecker, *Galatians* (WBC, 41; Dallas: Word Books, 1990), pp. cix-cxii; G.W. Hansen, *Abraham in Galatians: Epistolary and Rhetorical Contexts* (JSNTSup, 29; Sheffield: JSOT Press, 1989), pp. 58-71.

the theories of ancient rhetoric.[18] His easily applicable procedure for rhetorical criticism has spawned numerous rhetorical analyses of New Testament texts[19] and is a watershed manual in New Testament rhetorical criticism. Like Betz, Kennedy attempts to show how the New Testament texts are examples of the art of ancient Greco-Roman rhetoric and/or function in a manner similar to ancient rhetorical categories. Kennedy states the rhetorical critical task as follows:

> What we need to do is try to hear his [Paul's] words as a Greek-speaking audience would have heard them, and that involves some understanding of classical rhetoric... The ultimate goal of rhetorical analysis, briefly put, is the discovery of the author's intent and of how that is transmitted through a text to an audience.[20]

From this perspective, the New Testament supposedly was written and read in the context of Greco-Roman rhetoric and one can reconstruct that historical dimension in the text by identifying the classical-rhetorical units, classifying them, and thereby discerning their rhetorical function and intent in relation to the original situation, the original author, and the original audience. In distinction from Betz, however, Kennedy's understanding of the application of ancient oral rhetorical theory to written texts is also based on the premise that rhetoric is a universal means of discourse,[21] a factor which allows him to mix in some concepts of modern rhetoric.[22]

---

18. G.A. Kennedy, *New Testament Interpretation through Rhetorical Criticism* (Chapel Hill, NC: University of North Carolina Press, 1984).

19. D.F. Watson, *Invention, Arrangement, and Style: Rhetorical Criticism of Jude and 2 Peter* (SBLDS, 104; Atlanta: Scholars Press, 1988); W. Wuellner, 'Where is Rhetorical Criticism Taking Us?', *CBQ* 49 (1987), pp. 448-63; D.F. Watson (ed.), *Persuasive Artistry: Studies in New Testament Rhetoric in Honor of George A. Kennedy* (JSNTSup, 50; Sheffield: JSOT Press, 1991).

20. Kennedy, *New Testament Interpretation*, pp. 10, 12.

21. Kennedy, *New Testament Interpretation*, pp. 10-11. A detailed examination of this perspective on rhetoric and its use in New Testament studies is S.E. Porter, 'The Theoretical Justification for Application of Rhetorical Categories to Pauline Epistolary Literature', in S.E. Porter and T.H. Olbricht (eds.), *Rhetoric and the New Testament: Essays from the 1992 Heidelberg Conference* (JSNTSup, 90; Sheffield: JSOT Press, 1993), pp. 104-10.

22. It is important to note that M. Mitchell, *Paul and the Rhetoric of Reconciliation: An Exegetical Investigation of the Language and Composition of 1 Corinthians* (Hermeneutische Untersuchungen zur Theologie, 28; Tübingen: Mohr–Siebeck, 1991), pp. 7-19, as a student of Betz, begins to distance her purely historical rhetorical

W. Wuellner also has been influential in the application of rhetorical criticism to the New Testament.[23] In particular his appropriation of New Rhetoric and modern communication theory in his most recent writings has extended New Testament rhetorical criticism so that it includes any communication theory that helps illumine the way a text works to create its effect. Wuellner posits a form of rhetorical criticism that argues for a rhetoric revalued or rhetoric reinvented.[24] From this perspective, rhetoric is understood as a practical performance of power inseparable from the social relations in which both the rhetorical act is situated and the rhetorical critic is situated. Wuellner states his position as follows:

> ...as rhetorical critics (rhetorics as part of literary theory) we face the obligation of critically examining the fateful interrelationship between (1) a text's rhetorical strategies, (2) the premises upon which these strategies operate (gender in patriarchy or matriarchy; race in social, political power structures), and (3) the efficacy of both text and its interpretation; of both exegetical practice and its theory (= method).[25]

While Wuellner's definition of rhetoric is far from clear, his move away from rhetoric as the application of Greco-Roman categories to the New Testament or as a way to excavate the historical meaning is obvious.

To summarize, there are two distinct factors that have contributed to the resurgence of rhetorical criticism since the late 1960s. First, the search for ever more insightful ways to understand and reconstruct the historical context of the New Testament texts has played a key role in the development of rhetorical criticism.[26] The neglect of Hellenistic influences on the New Testament because of the over emphasis on Jewish backgrounds for interpreting the New Testament has contributed partially to the exploration of ancient Greco-Roman rhetoric. The

criticism from Kennedy, whom she feels has been influenced by the New Rhetoricians, Perelman and Olbrechts-Tyteca.

23. W. Wuellner, 'Hermeneutics and Rhetorics: From "Truth and Method" to "Truth and Power"', *Scriptura* S 3 (1989), pp. 1-54; *idem*, 'The Rhetorical Structure of Luke 12 in its Wider Context', *Neot* 22 (1989), pp. 283-310; *idem*, 'Rhetorical Criticism and its Theory in Culture-Critical Perspective: The Narrative Rhetoric of John 11', in *Text and Interpretation: New Approaches in the Criticism of the New Testament* (ed. P.J. Hartin and J.H. Petzer; NTTS, 15; Leiden: Brill, 1991), pp. 171-85; *idem*, 'Where is Rhetorical Criticism Taking Us?', pp. 448-63.

24. The fullest statement of Wuellner's understanding of rhetorical criticism is articulated in Wuellner, 'Hermeneutics and Rhetorics', pp. 1-54.

25. Wuellner, 'Hermeneutics and Rhetorics', p. 38.

26. Mack, *Rhetoric*, pp. 93-102.

prominence of rhetoric as a social practice in the Hellenistic world suggests to some New Testament critics that the New Testament authors and the original readers of the New Testament employed Greco-Roman rhetorical practice to construct and to interpret the New Testament texts. In this sense, ancient rhetorical theory and practice becomes another way to supposedly reconstruct in a more accurate manner the meaning and intent of the New Testament documents.

Secondly, sensitivity to hermeneutical issues in biblical interpretation has contributed to the use of rhetorical criticism as a way to approach the New Testament.[27] Such hermeneutical awareness has meant that interpreters increasingly recognize the full-orbed nature of a communicative event, whether oral or textual. Rhetoric in both its ancient and modern guises recognizes that a communication event like the New Testament texts entails a proper understanding of the author, the linguistic instantiation of the discourse, the audience, and the communicative situation or context.[28] In this sense, rhetorical criticism becomes one way to move beyond a purely content (what does the text mean?) approach to a New Testament text to an interpretative approach that respects the relationship between form, content and context.

3. *The Practice of Rhetorical Criticism in New Testament Studies*

As implied in the survey of the development of recent New Testament rhetorical criticism, there is no single overarching methodology to be found in the current practice of rhetorical criticism of the New Testament. Critical practice depends on whether one understands rhetoric as a purely historical phenomenon identified with ancient Greco-Roman rhetorical convention, as a universal communicative perspective identified with modern analyses of argumentation, or as some combination of the two.[29] Based on the previous survey, several of the different rhetorical-critical approaches to the New Testament will be examined.

The first rhetorical-critical approach is a historically-based rhetorical criticism. Since the historical paradigm still governs exegesis of the New Testament in the guild of New Testament studies,[30] it is not surprising

27. V.K. Robbins and J.H. Patton, 'Rhetoric and Biblical Criticism', *Quarterly Journal of Speech* 66 (1980), pp. 327-50.

28. Botha, 'Reinvention', pp. 23-26.

29. Watson and Hauser, *Rhetorical Criticism*, pp. 109-15.

30. See the discussion in R. Morgan with J. Barton, *Biblical Interpretation* (Oxford: Oxford University Press, 1988), pp. 44-200.

that the rhetorical criticism with a historical emphasis as advocated by Betz and Kennedy dominates most rhetorical-critical studies of the New Testament.[31] This stream of rhetorical criticism seeks to correlate the text with its supposed original historical context, specifically ancient Greco-Roman rhetoric.

This particular approach is interested in reconstructing the rhetorical form and function of the biblical text in its historically reconstructed situation. The text is analysed as a piece of ancient Hellenistic rhetoric according to the historical-rhetorical categories gleaned from ancient rhetorical handbooks[32] and ancient rhetorical compositions.[33] The rhetoric of the text, from this historical perspective, is a recovery of the original author's use of Greco-Roman rhetoric to persuade the original readers in the context of the original historical setting or rhetorical situation.

Actually there are two different historically-based rhetorical-critical perspectives. The 'Betz' school sees Greco-Roman rhetorical analysis as one part of a complete package of historical criticism. As a student of Betz, Margaret Mitchell, states, 'Rhetorical Criticism...is one of the panoply of tools which bear the name "historical-critical method"'.[34] Betz himself has trailblazed this approach in his two Hermeneia commentaries, on Galatians and on 2 Corinthians 8 and 9, and in an important article assessing the place of rhetoric in Paul's theology.[35] In

31. See Stamps, 'Rhetorical Criticism', pp. 272-74, for a fuller discussion of how rhetorical criticism has been assimilated into the historical-critical method.

32. Greco-Roman rhetorical theory based on the handbooks, in general, dealt with five aspects of the practice of rhetoric: invention, arrangement, style, memory, and delivery. Convenient explanations and definitions of these five aspects can be found in Mack, *Rhetoric*, pp. 25-48; Kennedy, *New Testament Interpretation*, pp. 12-33; Watson, *Invention*, pp. 8-28; Hughes, *Early Christian Rhetoric*, pp. 30-50. See also the very helpful volume, J.J. Murphy, *A Synoptic History of Classical Rhetoric* (Davis, CA: Hermagoras Press, 1983).

33. Mitchell, *Paul*, pp. 8, 9: 'In reconstructing the Greco-Roman rhetorical tradition for comparison with New Testament texts it is imperative that the ancient rhetorical handbooks not be the sole source... The directions which the rhetorical handbooks provide must always be tempered and compared with actual speeches and other rhetorical compositions from the Greco-Roman world, so that the fluidity and variety of possibilities of rhetorical composition in Greco-Roman antiquity can be brought to bear on the analysis.'

34. Mitchell, *Paul*, p. 7.

35. Betz, *Galatians*; *idem*, *2 Corinthians 8 and 9: A Commentary on Two Administrative Letters of the Apostle Paul* (Hermeneia; Philadelphia: Fortress Press,

each case, Betz seeks to demonstrate that such rhetorical analysis is the best way to reconstruct the argumentative intent of Paul and to reconstruct the historical situation behind the New Testament texts.

Besides the work of Betz, the most comprehensive application of this rhetorical critical approach is the work of Mitchell, *Paul and the Rhetoric of Reconciliation*.[36] Mitchell seeks to avoid one of the major criticisms of Betz—that his rhetorical analysis is not based on an actual extant rhetorical text-type—by correlating her analysis of 1 Corinthians with a deliberative letter in the vein of political rhetoric as found in the speeches and writings of Isocrates, Demosthenes, and others.[37] Mitchell goes on to use ancient rhetorical categories to demonstrate the thematic unity of 1 Corinthians by showing the consistent use of the language about factionalism, language that appears to be directly borrowed from ancient political rhetoric, and to prove the argumentative unity or literary integrity of 1 Corinthians by an analysis of the invention and arrangement of the letter body.

The second historically-based perspective, the 'Kennedy' school, while remaining resolutely historical in perspective, seeks to restate the interpretative goal in exclusively rhetorical terms, and according to classical or Greco-Roman rhetorical terms at that. In particular, Kennedy focuses on the verbal reality of the text and its original persuasive power in its original historical context:

> Rhetoric cannot describe the historical Jesus or identify Matthew or John; they are probably irretrievably lost to scholarship. But it does study a verbal reality, our text of the Bible, rather than the oral sources standing behind that text, the hypothetical stages of its composition, or the impersonal workings of social forces, and at its best it can reveal the power of those texts as unitary messages.[38]

1985); *idem*, 'The Problem of Rhetoric and Theology according to the Apostle Paul', in *L'apôtre Paul: Personalité, style et conception du ministère* (ed. A. Vanhoye; BETL, 17; Leuven: Leuven University Press, 1986), pp. 16-48.

36. See n. 22.

37. Mitchell, *Paul*, pp. 21-23. However, the letters she cites to prove her rhetorical text-type are actually literary letters and less like the Greek friendly letter or personal letter which the Pauline epistles seem to correspond to in epistolary convention; on this distinction, see D.E. Aune, *The New Testament in its Literary Environment* (Library of Early Christianity, 8; Philadelphia: Westminster Press, 1987), chs. 5 and 6.

38. Kennedy, *New Testament Interpretation*, pp. 158-59.

Watson, in his book *Invention, Arrangement and Style*, provided the first comprehensive application of Kennedy's methodology to the epistles of Jude and 2 Peter.[39] He first sets forth an amplification and simplification of Kennedy's rhetorical theory, which also draws heavily on ancient rhetorical handbooks to provide clarification and definition of the rhetorical terms and categories he uses.[40] He adopts a five step approach to analyse any rhetorical argument: (1) determine the rhetorical unit, either a self-contained textual unit or an entire book; (2) define the rhetorical situation, that is the person, events and exigence that precipitated the rhetorical response; (3) determine the species of rhetoric (judicial, deliberative or epideictic) and the rhetorical problem or stasis; (4) analyse the invention (argument by ethos, pathos and logos), arrangement (the ordering of the argument according to the components such as the *exordium* or introduction, the *narratio* or statement of facts, the *probatio* or main body of the argument, and the *peroratio* or the conclusion), and style (the use of figures of speech and other such devices to shape the speech according to the needs of the invention); and (5) evaluate the rhetorical effectiveness of the rhetorical response in addressing the rhetorical situation.

Watson analyses Jude in the following way. The rhetorical unit is the letter as a whole. The situation is 'the infiltration of the church or churches by a doctrinally and ethically divergent group'.[41] The species of rhetoric for Jude is deliberative. The invention or argument of the letter is classified as follows: the *exordium* (v. 3); the *narratio* (v. 4); the *probatio* with three proofs (vv. 5-16); the *peroratio* (vv. 17-23). Interestingly and questionably, he labels the epistolary prescript as 'quasi-*exordium*' (vv. 1-2) and the letter closing, a doxology, as 'quasi-*peroratio*' (vv. 24-25); these two literary units of letter do not easily conform to the classical oral rhetorical model Watson uses as the basis of his analysis. Through the application of his rhetorical-critical theory, Watson not only wants to illumine the rhetorical nature of the argument, but to solve the problems of literary integrity and dependency between Jude and 2 Peter.[42]

Both historically-oriented rhetorical approaches embody a full-orbed understanding of the New Testament text as a persuasive communicative

39. See n. 19.
40. Watson, *Invention*, pp. 1-28.
41. Watson, *Invention*, p. 29.
42. Watson, *Invention*, pp. 147-88.

event, albeit as it happened in relation to the original author, the original audience and the original situation and as understood exclusively from a theory of ancient Greco-Roman rhetoric. In both approaches, interesting and helpful readings are given of the way the argument of the texts coheres and addresses the historical exigence that motivated the epistolary response. More problematic is whether such rhetorical analyses actually solve matters like the literary integrity of a text. Demonstration of the inter-relatedness of a text according to an ancient rhetorical model of speeches cannot prove that the original author conceived the textual argument in the same way or that such inter-relatedness is not a product of a later editor or later editors.

Another rhetorical-critical perspective practised in New Testament studies is found in the work of W. Wuellner. Wuellner advocates the priority of rhetoric over hermeneutics.[43] This reprioritization not only constitutes the re-invention of rhetoric, but also the complete abandonment of the interpretative task as presently practised in New Testament studies:

> It made a revolutionary difference to take the familiar notion, that human beings in general, and religious persons in particular, are hermeneutically constituted, and replace it with the ancient notion familiar to Jews and Greeks alike, that we are rhetorically constituted. We have not only the capacity to understand the content or propositions of human signs and symbols (= hermeneutics); we also have the capacity to respond and interact with them (= rhetorics).[44]

For Wuellner and others like him, the rhetoric of a text is the power of a text to effect, in Kenneth Burke's terms, social identification and transformation in every act of reading.[45] The operative rhetoric is dependent upon the immediate social context of any reading (whether ancient or modern) and of the readers, emphasizing the ideology of the text as a practical exercise of power.[46]

---

43. Wuellner, 'Hermeneutics and Rhetorics', pp. 29-38.

44. Wuellner, 'Hermeneutics and Rhetorics', p. 38.

45. K. Burke, *A Rhetoric of Motives* (Englewood Cliffs, NJ: Prentice-Hall, 1950), pp. 49-59.

46. Wuellner's definition of rhetoric is far from clear. W. Wuellner, personal letter: 'What I find myself doing is avoiding the conventional approach of moving from theory to practice; from definition to application. Instead, I want to move toward a theory and with it a definition of rhetoric (and hermeneutic) which arises from practice.'

There have been a number of significant studies based on this under-standing of rhetoric. F. Siegert in *Argumentation bei Paulus* analyses Romans 9–11 according to the rhetorical categories of C. Perelman and the New Rhetoric.[47] Similarly, A.C. Wire in *The Corinthian Women Prophets* examines the role of Christian women prophets in 1 Corinthians using the rhetorical theory of C. Perelman and the New Rhetoric.[48] In *The Agency of the Apostle*, J.A. Crafton uses Kenneth Burke's dramatic theory of rhetoric to analyse Paul's response to conflict in 2 Corinthians.[49] E.A. Castilli employs the literary and social theory of Foucault to analyse the imitation language of Paul in her work, *Imitating Paul: A Discourse of Power*.[50] All of these works examine the argument of the text in modern rhetorical categories in order to elucidate the persuasive effect of the text without necessary recourse to ancient rhetorical convention and without being a-historical in their elucidation of the argument.

A third rhetorical-critical approach is a hybrid. It generally utilizes many of the categories of rhetoric as posited by ancient Greco-Roman rhetorical theory and combines it with some other communication theory in order to unpack the nature of the argument and rhetorical situation. For instance, K. Berger's *Formgeschichte des Neuen Testaments* classifies the literary forms in the New Testament using the insights of modern linguistics, particularly a theory of genre, and using the ancient rhetorical classification of the three species of ancient rhetoric.[51] B. Johanson, in *To All the Brethren*, examines the rhetoric of 1 Thessalonians based on a concept of ancient rhetoric and modern text-linguistic theory.[52] Similarly, R. Jewett assesses the communication intent and effect of 1 and 2 Thessalonians using epistolary theory, ancient rhetoric, New Rhetoric concepts and text-linguistics in *The Thessalonian*

47. F. Siegert, *Argumentation bei Paulus: Gezeigt an Röm 9–11* (WUNT, 34; Tübingen: Mohr–Siebeck, 1985).

48. A.C. Wire, *The Corinthian Women Prophets: A Reconstruction through Paul's Rhetoric* (Philadelphia: Fortress Press, 1990).

49. J.A. Crafton, *The Agency of the Apostle: A Dramatistic Analysis of Paul's Responses to Conflict in 2 Corinthians* (JSNTSup, 51; Sheffield: JSOT Press, 1991).

50. E.A. Castilli, *Imitating Paul: A Discourse of Power* (Literary Currents in Biblical Interpretation; Louisville: Westminster/John Knox, 1991).

51. K. Berger, *Formgeschichte des Neuen Testaments* (Heidelberg: Quelle & Meyer, 1984).

52. B.C. Johanson, *To All the Brethren: A Text-Linguistic and Rhetorical Approach to 1 Thessalonians* (ConBNT, 16; Uppsala: Almqvist & Wiksell, 1987).

Correspondence.[53] In a very different vein, S. Pogoloff, in *Logos and Sophia: The Rhetorical Situation of 1 Corinthians*, breaks new ground, drawing on the literary theory of Stanley Fish, philosophical hermeneutics, and classical rhetoric to develop a theory of situational rhetoric which explores the interplay between textual form, content and historical exigencies in 1 Corinthians 1–4.[54] All of these studies are concerned to elucidate the argument of the text by using different communication theories to illumine the complex communication components that contribute to the text's persuasive effect.

4. *Special Issues in the Practice of Rhetorical Criticism of the New Testament*

The practice of rhetorical criticism in New Testament studies raises two special issues which need further explanation. One is the relationship of ancient Greco-Roman rhetorical theory to the epistolary practice of New Testament letters. The second is the application of rhetorical criticism to the Gospels.

New Testament Epistolary Literature and Ancient Rhetorical Theory
The relationship between ancient rhetorical theory and practice and the Greek epistolary literature is highlighted by the problem noted in Watson's rhetorical analysis of Jude—what does one do with the distinctly epistolary parts? This is a problem all practitioners of rhetorical criticism face when analysing New Testament epistles, especially those rhetorical critics who only use a rhetorical theory based on Greco-Roman rhetoric. In order to consider this issue, two aspects demand consideration: (1) what was the perceived relationship between Greco-Roman rhetorical theory and practice and letter writing in the first century CE?,[55] and (2) what is the actual approach modern rhetorical critics are adopting in practice?

53. R. Jewett, *The Thessalonian Correspondence: Pauline Rhetoric and Millenarian Piety* (FFNT; Philadelphia: Fortress Press, 1986).
54. S.M. Pogoloff, *Logos and Sophia: The Rhetorical Situation of 1 Corinthians* (SBLDS, 134; Atlanta: Scholars Press, 1992).
55. This issue is thoroughly addressed in the following important essays: C.J. Classen, 'St Paul's Epistles and Ancient Greek and Roman Rhetoric', in Porter and Olbricht (eds.), *Rhetoric and the New Testament*, pp. 265-91; Porter, 'Theoretical Justification', pp. 100-22; J.T. Reed, 'Using Ancient Rhetorical Categories to Interpret Paul's Letters: A Question of Genre', in Porter and Olbricht (eds.), *Rhetoric and the New Testament*, pp. 292-324.

The primary sources for determining the relationship between Greco-Roman rhetoric and Greek epistolary practice are (1) a work on epistolary theory, *On Style* (*De Elocutione*), attributed to Demetrius of Phalerum, probably dating from the first century BCE;[56] (2) the epistolary handbook, *Epistolary Types* (Τύποι Ἐπιστολικοί), also falsely ascribed to Demetrius of Phalerum, often designated as Pseudo-Demetrius, dated somewhere in the period 200 BCE to 300 CE;[57] (3) the epistolary handbook, *Epistolary Styles* (Ἐπιστολιμαῖοι Χαρακτῆρες), falsely attributed to Libanius, dated from the period 400–600 CE;[58] (4) in addition there are the remarks about letter writing and rhetoric in the letters of Cicero, Seneca, and other similar practitioners of rhetoric.[59] In the third century BCE to the third century CE, the period in which the Greek letter tradition thrived, there is almost no mention of letter writing in any extant handbook of rhetoric; and in the epistolary handbooks and theorists, rhetoric and letter writing are always differentiated in theory and practice. Though letter writing eventually became a topic in rhetorical handbooks, it is not until the middle ages that this occurs.[60]

56. For Greek text and English translation, see A. Malherbe, *Ancient Epistolary Theorists* (SBLSBS, 19; Atlanta: Scholars Press, 1988), pp. 16-19; discussion on the text, p. 2. Dating of the document ranges from third century BCE to first century CE; Malherbe's argument for first century BCE seems convincing, *Ancient Epistolary Theorists*, p. 5.

57. For Greek text and English translation, see Malherbe, *Ancient Epistolary Theorists*, pp. 30-41; discussions on the text, pp. 3-4; the problem of dating, p. 4.

58. For Greek text and English translation, see Malherbe, *Ancient Epistolary Theorists*, pp. 66-81. Another manuscript tradition attributes the text to Proclus, with both possibly stemming from a common source. For discussion of the text, see Malherbe, *Ancient Epistolary Theorists*, pp. 5-6.

59. On Cicero, see Malherbe, *Ancient Epistolary Theorists*, pp. 2-3, and pp. 20-27 for selected Latin texts and English translation. On Seneca, see Malherbe, *Ancient Epistolary Theorists*, p. 3, and pp. 28-29 for selected Latin texts and English translation. On other epistolary theorists, see Malherbe, *Ancient Epistolary Theorists*, pp. 2-6.

60. Kennedy, *Classical Rhetoric*, pp. 161-94; and the survey in Hughes, *Early Christian Rhetoric*, pp. 27-29, whose remark, 'The fact that letter writing is so firmly established in the mediaeval appropriation of Graeco-Roman rhetoric suggests that the composition of letters may have been more than a peripheral concern in the actual practice of rhetors, particularly in the Hellenistic period', neglects the development of written rhetoric in the post-Hellenistic period which distinguished the theory and practice of rhetoric in the middle ages.

Demetrius's *On Style* (first century BCE) is the first significant discussion of letter writing by any Greco-Roman rhetorician. The comments are made as an excursus (223-235) in the general discussion on 'plain style' (ἰσχνός) and appear to be a response to a theory of letter writing stemming from Artemon,[61] the editor of Aristotle's letters, that letters should be written in the manner of a dialogue (223). Demetrius corrects Artemon, 'The letter should be a little more studied than the dialogue, since the latter reproduces an extemporary utterance, while the former is committed to writing and is (in a way) sent as a gift' (224). Demetrius's point is that letter writing is distinctly different from spoken discourse. Further, Demetrius clearly distinguishes letters from oration. As opposed to oration, letters should not: (a) imitate conversational style (226); (b) be too long or stilted in expression (228); (c) employ certain types of ornamental devices or arguments (229, 231, 232); (d) address certain topics (230). Hence, with regard to style, Demetrius clearly distinguishes letter writing from anything oratorical.

The premier Roman letter writer, Cicero (first century BCE), made several comments regarding letter writing.[62] But he nowhere writes as if he had a systematic theory of epistolography, most of the comments on letters being dispersed incidently in his corpus of writings.[63] Significantly, there are no comments about letter writing in any of his writings on rhetoric (*De Inventione, De Oratore, Partitiones Oratoriae, Brutus*, and *Orator*). While many of Cicero's letters show affinity with

---

61. H. Koskenniemi, *Studien zur Idee und Phraseologie des griechischen Briefes bis 400 n. Chr.* (Suomalaisen Scientiarum Fennicae, 102.2; Helsinki: Suomalainen Tiedeakatemia, 1956), pp. 24-27, suggests that the reference to Artemon, and other references in the excursus on Aristotle's letters, is evidence that Artemon wrote a theoretical essay on epistolary theory in a rhetorical discussion. But Demetrius's reference to Artemon is not necessarily an actual reference to an actual source; in addition, Koskenniemi over-reads the other references to Aristotle to suggest that all such references stem from the Artemon source, so K. Thrade, *Grundzüge griechisch-römischer Brieftopic* (Zetemata, 48; Munich: Beck, 1970), pp. 20-22, and Malherbe, *Ancient Epistolary Theorists*, p. 2.

62. For example, as noted in Malherbe, *Ancient Epistolary Theorists*, p. 2, Cicero makes a distinction between public and private letters (*Pro Flacco* 16.37), mentions the genre of epistles (*Ad Familiares* 4.13.1), suggests jesting be avoided in certain types of letters (*Ad Atticum* 6.5.4), and states that letters convey the presence of an absent friend (*Ad Familiares* 3.11.2).

63. Malherbe, *Ancient Epistolary Theorists*, p. 2, thinks Cicero knew such theory and handbooks; however see Porter, 'Theoretical Justification', pp. 112-13, for a contrary and more probable position.

rhetorical features and composition, this is due to the fact that friendly letter writing was for him an artistic and aesthetic exercise:[64]

> That there are many kinds of letters you are well aware; there is one kind, however, about which there can be no mistake, for indeed letter writing was invented just in order that we might inform those at a distance if there were anything which it was important for them or for ourselves that they should know. A letter of this kind you will of course not expect from me... There remain two kinds of letters which have a great charm for me, the one intimate and humorous, the other austere and serious (*Ad Familiares* 2.4.1).

Two other important practitioners of rhetoric make comments about letter writing, again generally making a distinction between letters and oratory. Seneca (first century CE) associates letters with conversation, and conversation is distinct from oration (*Epistulae Morales* 75.1-2). Quintilian (first century CE) remarks that letters and conversation should be of a 'looser texture' than the closely 'welded and woven' style of oration (*Institutio Oratoria* 9.4.19-22).

In fact the first rhetorician to include letter writing as a part of a theory of rhetoric is Julius Victor, in his work, *Ars Rhetorica* 27 (fourth century CE). Yet, even in this case, it is an appendix (*De Epistolis*), and only discusses the matter of style. As Malherbe notes, 'While epistolary style is here, then, part of a rhetorical system, it can nevertheless be argued that the fact that it is relegated to an appendix shows that it does not properly belong in a discussion of rhetoric'.[65]

The two epistolary handbooks, *Epistolary Types* and *Epistolary Styles*, though providing extensive discussions on the matter of epistolary practice, are distinctly not developing a system of rhetorical theory with respect to letter writing. Both handbooks posit the appropriate letter style for particular epistolary situations, and provide sample letters to illustrate such style. *Epistolary Styles* dates between the fourth and sixth century CE (well past the particular period in which the New Testament was written), and it is interesting that in comparison with the earlier handbook, *Epistolary Types*, both in theory and in the number of types of letters proposed, the latter handbook is greatly developed suggesting that epistolary theory had become more complex. So while both handbooks are concerned with developing a theory of letter writing and as a consequence with the rhetorical matter of selecting the proper

---

64. S.K. Stowers, *Letter Writing in Greco-Roman Antiquity* (Library of Early Christianity, 5; Philadelphia: Westminster Press, 1986), pp. 32-35.

65. Malherbe, *Ancient Epistolary Theorists*, p. 3.

response to a situation, in particular selecting the type of letter appropriate to the sender's relationship with the addressee and the particular occasion, neither specifically relates letter writing to the five traditional aspects of rhetorical practice: invention, arrangement, style, memory and delivery; or to the three traditional species of rhetoric: judicial, deliberative and epideictic.[66]

In sum, based on the evidence of the epistolary theorists, the ancient rhetoricians who comment on letter writing, and the epistolary handbooks, the only matter which overlapped between epistolary theory and the practice of rhetoric was the matter of style. Even when style was discussed, it never was discussed in the technical terms found in rhetorical handbooks. Further, when matters of style were addressed, it was always to distinguish epistolary style from the style of rhetorical oration.

The current study and analysis of New Testament letters according to the categories of Greco-Roman rhetoric has resulted in a certain amount of confusion about the relationship between the epistolary nature and the rhetorical nature of the text.[67] L. Thurén has noted at least three major

66. Reed, 'Using Ancient Rhetorical Categories', pp. 294-314, surveys what each epistolary theorist and rhetorician states about letter writing and relates it to each of the five aspects of rhetoric and the matter of species. He concludes that what overlap exists between epistolary traditions and rhetorical practices is primarily functional and not formal. However, Hughes, *Early Christian Rhetoric*, p. 27, suggests that some of the letter types in the handbooks represent a direct borrowing of technical rhetorical terminology from rhetorical handbooks; for instance the 'advising' (συμβουλευτικός) letter type is related to the species of deliberative (συμβουλευτικόν) rhetoric. But as Reed ('Using Ancient Rhetorical Categories', pp. 299-301) notes, 'the similarities are probably due to common communicative practices in culture'; and common terminology possibly represents common cultural concerns and situations which could be addressed by a variety of communication modes. Further, the 'names' for the letter types have more divergent terms than synonymous terms with respect to ancient rhetorical terminology. The fact of semantic overlap does not prove a singular theoretical perspective operating in both practices.

67. The essential problem resides in classifying the letters as a mixed genre. H. Hübner, 'Der Galaterbrief und das Verhältnis von antiker Rhetorik und Epistolographie', *TLZ* 109 (1984), pp. 241-50, sees Paul's letters as real letters, but also having aspects of speeches; but K. Berger, 'Apostelbrief und apostolische Rede: Zum Formular frühchristlichen Briefe', *ZNW* 65 (1974), pp. 190-231; *idem*, 'Hellenistische Gattungen im Neuen Testament', in *ANRW* II.25.2 (ed. H. Temporini and W. Haase; Berlin: de Gruyter, 1984), pp. 1031-432; and Kennedy, *New Testament Interpretation*,

scholarly approaches to the problem of how the epistles are seen in relation to Greco-Roman rhetoric.[68] The first approach sees rhetorical conventions as having only secondary applicability to New Testament epistles, which are primarily authentic examples of Greek epistolary practice.[69] The second approach sees the epistles as primarily forms of rhetorical speeches, which incidently have an epistolary frame.[70] The third approach views epistolary and rhetorical categories as referring to separate dimensions of the letter as a form of communication with the entire letter capable of being analysed by either set of categories or by some combination.[71]

While each New Testament letter deserves a separate evaluation, with regard to the Pauline letters which constitute the majority of New Testament epistles, the issue appears fairly straightforward. Analysis of the Pauline opening and closing suggests that they are genuine Greek letters which function within a real or authentic epistolary situation.[72] The opening and closing are not artificial devices which frame a general treatise or 'speech'. Furthermore, the specific epistolary situation inscribed in the opening and closing of the Pauline letters is a consistent aspect of the entire epistolary discourse. But to recognize the epistolary nature of the Pauline letter does not exclude using rhetorical criticism,

pp. 86-87, regard the letters as primarily speeches with epistolographic openings and closings.

68. L. Thurén, *The Rhetorical Strategy of 1 Peter: With Special Regard to Ambiguous Expressions* (Åbo: Åbo Akademi, 1990), pp. 57-64.

69. Advocated by J.L. White, 'Saint Paul and the Apostolic Letter Tradition', *CBQ* 45 (1983), pp. 433-44; W. Doty, *Letters in Primitive Christianity* (Guides to Biblical Scholarship; Philadelphia: Fortress Press, 1975); and Hübner, 'Der Galaterbrief'.

70. As advocated by Berger, 'Hellenistische Gattungen', pp. 1327-40; and Kennedy, *New Testament Interpretation*, pp. 86-87; cf. Betz, *Galatians*.

71. Thurén, *Rhetorical Strategy*, pp. 63-78. Other studies recognize the integrity of epistolary features throughout the letter, but use rhetorical categories to analyse these features, so Johanson, *To All the Brethren*, pp. 61-63; M. Bünker, *Briefformular und rhetorische Disposition im 1.Korintherbrief* (Göttinger Theologische Arbeiten, 28; Göttingen: Vandenhoeck & Ruprecht, 1983), pp. 11-18; F. Schnider and W. Stenger, *Studien zum neutestamentlichen Briefformular* (NTTS, 11; Leiden: Brill, 1987).

72. See D.L. Stamps, *The Rhetorical Use of the Epistolary Form in 1 Corinthians: The Rhetoric of Power* (JSNTSup; Sheffield: Sheffield Academic Press, [forthcoming]), ch. 3.

even categories of Greco-Roman rhetoric, as a way to analyse the persuasive effect of the entire letter.[73]

The main thrust of many applications of Greco-Roman rhetorical categories to Pauline letters lies in the conviction that it was the intention of the sender(s) to utilize ancient rhetorical theory in the construction of the letter-text. The result of this interpretative perspective is to regard the Pauline letters as written forms of oral rhetoric. The problem scholars cannot solve is where the rhetorical intent begins—in the letter opening or in the letter body.[74] But as argued above, the theoretical justification for regarding ancient letters as intended instances of Greco-Roman rhetorical practice is at least problematic, if not completely unfounded.

The matter is not as straightforward for all New Testament epistles. The letter to the Hebrews presents a particular problem with its lack of an epistolary prescript yet having a concluding epistolary postscript.[75] Equally problematic in terms of the relationship between epistolary form and rhetoric is 1 John with no epistolary conventions.[76] Revelation also presents a complicated interpretative knot in its mix of genres: letters, visions, and prophecies, etc.[77]

What all this suggests regarding New Testament epistles is that both in theory and in practice the relationship between Greco-Roman rhetoric and Hellenistic epistolary convention is not a simple formulaic matter of analysis. The recognition that rhetorical criticism according to the categories of Greco-Roman rhetorical theory is only one means of analysing the argumentative function of the various epistolary units is a helpful corrective to those who insist that New Testament letters are intended instances of ancient rhetorical practice. The application of a theory of

73. Hansen, *Abraham*, pp. 21-71, esp. p. 56: 'I intend to use the parallels which are applicable from the rhetorical handbooks simply as descriptive tools'.

74. Mitchell, *Paul*, p. 22 n. 5: 'Thus by my definition a "deliberative letter" is a letter which employs deliberative rhetoric in the letter body... This does not mean, however, that the epistolary formulae (salutation, thanksgiving) do not play a rhetorical function homogenous with the argument in the body of the letter.'

75. Aune, *New Testament*, pp. 212-14, suggests Hebrews is a hortatory sermon later circulated with an epistolary postscript.

76. For a rhetorical analysis of 1 John, see D.F. Watson, 'Amplification Techniques in 1 John: The Interaction of Rhetorical Style and Invention', *JSNT* 51 (1993), pp. 99-123; and H.-J. Klauck, 'Zur rhetorischen Analyse der Johannesbriefe', *ZNW* 81 (1990), pp. 205-24.

77. E. Schüssler Fiorenza, *The Book of Revelation: Justice and Judgment* (Philadelphia: Fortress Press, 1985), ch. 7.

ancient Greco-Roman rhetoric to a New Testament letter does not imply that the letter is a form of oral discourse, rather it recognizes the general applicability of rhetorical criticism to written discourse. This perspective leaves open the possibility of using other theories of rhetoric to achieve the same end—to assess the argumentative or persuasive function of various epistolary units.[78]

The Rhetorical Criticism of the Gospels

Using a rhetorical-critical approach for the Gospels presents a different set of problems. Since the Gospels are commonly labelled as a form of narrative discourse, a different kind of discourse than the epistles, the application of the categories of Greco-Roman rhetoric used for speech type discourse seems inappropriate. Yet it is appropriate to consider what Robert Tannehill calls the 'narrative rhetoric' of the Gospels, because as narrative they tell a story and 'the story is constructed in order to influence its readers and particular literary techniques are used for this purpose'.[79] The decision is whether to assess this narrative rhetoric based on ancient rhetorical categories or by a different rhetorical approach.

As narrative literature the Gospels are often interpreted through the use of various forms of literary criticism.[80] In conjunction with this 'literary criticism', the perspective of rhetoric is often slipped in. This literary understanding of rhetoric is generally linked to the seminal work of W.C. Booth, *The Rhetoric of Fiction*, who analyses the author's narrative technique—narration, point of view, plot—in order to assess the 'author's means of controlling his reader'.[81] All four Gospels have

78. Classen, 'St Paul's Epistles', p. 268: 'When one turns to the categories of rhetoric as tools for a more adequate and thorough appreciation of texts, their general structure and their details, one should not hesitate to use the most developed and sophisticated form, as it will offer more help than any other. For there is no good reason to assume that a text could and should be examined only according to categories known (or possibly known) to the author concerned.' An interesting example of a modern theory of rhetoric being applied to the New Testament is J.J. Murphy, 'Early Christianity as a "Persuasive Campaign": Evidence from the Acts of the Apostles and the Letters of Paul', in Porter and Olbricht (eds.), *Rhetoric and the New Testament*, pp. 90-99.

79. R.C. Tannehill, *The Narrative Unity of Luke–Acts: A Literary Interpretation*. I. *The Gospel according to Luke* (Philadelphia: Fortress Press, 1986), p. 8.

80. See the chapter on literary criticism in this volume.

81. W.C. Booth, *The Rhetoric of Fiction* (Chicago: University of Chicago Press, 2nd edn, 1983), p. xiii.

been analysed using such a rhetorical understanding of narrative in order to investigate how the story is told to create certain effects on the reader.[82] In the end, these studies use a limited understanding of rhetoric: narrative rhetoric that is based primarily on an aesthetics of the imagination rather than on a concept of argumentation or persuasion.

In *New Testament Interpretation through Rhetorical Criticism*, Kennedy applies his method of rhetorical criticism using Greco-Roman rhetorical categories to parts of the Gospels. The Sermon on the Mount (Mt. 5–7) and the Sermon on the Plain (Lk. 6) are interpreted as a form of deliberative rhetoric, and the Farewell Discourse (Jn 13–17) as a form of epideictic rhetoric.[83] He also analyses the distinctive rhetorical characteristics of each of the four Gospels.[84] For instance, Kennedy labels Mt. 1.1-17 as a *proem*; the stories or incidents (Mt. 1.18–4.25) which follow are the *narratio* and function as forms of external proof. Interwoven in these incidents are internal proofs of logical argumentation, enthymemes (1.20; 2.2; 2.5; 2.13; 2.20; 3.2; 4.6; 4.17). Next, the Sermon on the Mount functions as the proposition (*partitio*) for the whole of the Gospel, which makes much of the rest of the Gospel the proof or *confirmatio*.[85] Such a rhetorical analysis of a Gospel can only be analogical to the Greco-Roman speech pattern, and is heuristic at best.

A more fruitful rhetorical-critical approach to the Gospel material has been to assess smaller blocks of didactic or speech discourse found in the Gospel stories. A form of argumentation found in the ancient world, the *chreia*, has proved particularly applicable to Jesus' teaching.[86] A *chreia* is a memorable saying (or action) attributed to a famous character or

82. D.B. Howell, *Matthew's Inclusive Story: A Study in the Narrative Rhetoric of the First Gospel* (JSNTSup, 42; Sheffield: JSOT Press, 1990); D. Rhoads and D. Michie, *Mark as Story: An Introduction to the Narrative of a Gospel* (Philadelphia: Fortress Press, 1982); Tannehill, *Narrative Unity of Luke–Acts*; and J.L. Staley, *The Print's First Kiss: A Rhetorical Investigation of the Implied Reader in the Fourth Gospel* (SBLDS, 82; Atlanta: Scholars Press, 1988).

83. Kennedy, *New Testament Interpretation*, chs. 2 and 3.

84. Kennedy, *New Testament Interpretation*, ch. 5.

85. Kennedy, *New Testament Interpretation*, pp. 101-104, gives an analysis of Matthew.

86. J.R. Butts, 'The Chreia in the Synoptic Gospels', *BTB* 16 (1986), pp. 132-38; B.L. Mack and V.K. Robbins, *Patterns of Persuasion and the New Testament* (Foundations and Facets: Literary Facets; Sonoma, CA: Polebridge, 1989); V.K. Robbins, 'The Chreia', in *Greco-Roman Literature and the New Testament* (ed. D.E. Aune; SBLSBS, 21; Atlanta: Scholars Press, 1988), pp. 1-23.

authority and is usually regarded as a form of cultural wisdom.[87] Understanding how ancient rhetors analysed *chreia* is based in part on the rhetorical exercises described in Hermogenes' *progymnasmata* (preliminary exercises) and on the elaboration of a *chreia* by Aelius Theon of Alexandria. Their theories about the nature and use of a *chreia* form the basis for much of the rhetorical criticism of the *chreia* found in the Gospels.

Mack gives an example of a *chreia* from the sabbath controversies, Mk 2.23-28.[88] Mack calls this an instance of judicial rhetoric in which the argument is a rebuttal of the accusation of illegality, that is, that it is illegal to eat on the sabbath. The argument is as follows: narrative, v. 23; argument, vv. 25-26 with the maxim (*chreia*), v. 27; conclusion, v. 28. Unlike most instances in classical literature in which the pithy saying is given at the beginning, the Gospels' *chreia* generally have the maxim near the end. Instances of the *chreia* in the Gospels closely resemble the form-critical category, the pronouncement story. Given these observations, it is questionable whether the Greco-Roman practice of *chreia* was the progenitor for the sayings of Jesus found in the Gospels, but rather provides a way to appraise the argumentative technique of pronouncement stories.[89]

A more iconoclastic form of rhetorical criticism of the Gospels is advocated by V.K. Robbins.[90] His socio-rhetorical analyses of Mark and other Gospel pericopes are complex sociological and ideological examinations of the ancient literary forms and patterns and of the ancient

---

87. M.L. Stirewalt, *Studies in Ancient Greek Epistolography* (SBLRBS, 27; Atlanta: Scholars Press, 1993), p. 44, also pp. 43-64. See the helpful surveys of the *chreia* in Mack, *Rhetoric*, pp. 43-47; Watson and Hauser, *Rhetorical Criticism*, pp. 116-19; R.F. Hock and E.N. O'Neil, *The Chreia in Ancient Rhetoric. I. The Progymnasmata* (SBL Texts and Translations, 27; Atlanta: Scholars Press, 1986).

88. Mack, *Rhetoric*, pp. 52-53.

89. The relationship between pronouncement stories and *chreia* is analysed in V.K. Robbins, 'Pronouncement Stories From a Rhetorical Perspective', *Forum* 4 (1988), pp. 3-32.

90. V.K. Robbins, *Jesus the Teacher: A Socio-Rhetorical Interpretation of Mark* (Philadelphia: Fortress Press, 1984); *idem*, 'The Woman Who Touched Jesus' Garment: Socio-Rhetorical Analysis of the Synoptic Accounts', *NTS* 33 (1987), pp. 502-15; *idem*, 'The Reversed Contextualization of Psalm 22 in the Markan Crucifixion: A Socio-Rhetorical Analysis', in *The Four Gospels 1992: Festschrift Frans Neirynck* (ed. F. Van Segbroeck, C.M. Tuckett, G. Van Belle, J. Berheyden; BETL, 50; Leuven: Leuven University Press, 1992), pp. 1161-83.

cultural traditions and influences imbedded in the Gospels in order to determine how the Gospel stories changed social attitudes and promoted certain actions. Mark's Gospel represents effective rhetoric because it posits an image of Jesus as an extraordinary human teacher, an understanding of discipleship, and a teaching/learning cycle, all of which are compatible with the cultural ideological and communication norms of the Hellenistic world.

In many ways the application of rhetorical criticism to the Gospels is still in the early stages. At this point, it seems the approach that views the Gospels as a form of narrative rhetoric holds more promise than the approach that attempts to apply the rhetorical features found in speeches.

5. *A Proposal for a Rhetorical-Critical Approach to the New Testament*

After this survey and analysis of the current practices and problems of rhetorical-critical approaches to the New Testament it remains to discuss what might be meant by 'rhetoric' in a rhetorical-critical approach to the New Testament, in particular to offer a definition that is broader than the application of ancient Greco-Roman rhetorical theory to the New Testament that currently dominates biblical rhetorical criticism. The proposal which follows is not meant as an effort to provide a comprehensive method of rhetorical criticism that meets all the peculiar interpretative demands of the New Testament. It is meant to provide a foundational understanding of how rhetoric might be conceived as an interpretative approach to the New Testament. First, certain ideas about the nature and scope of rhetoric in texts are explored. Then, based on these ideas about rhetoric, several possible rhetorical-critical strategies are suggested.

The Nature and Scope of Rhetoric in Texts
Historically, rhetoric has been understood as an act of persuasion.[91] In that sense rhetoric is an action and a theory about how to achieve that action. It is in these terms that Chaim Perelman's theory of the 'New Rhetoric' focuses on rhetoric as argumentation, with the argumentative goal being to 'induce or to increase the mind's adherence to the theses

91. Two histories of rhetoric from different perspectives are Wuellner, 'Hermeneutics and Rhetorics', pp. 2-29; B. Vickers, *In Defense of Rhetoric* (Oxford: Clarendon Press, 1988), pp. 1-479.

presented for its assent'.[92] Similarly, Eagleton's literary theory suggests that rhetoric is concerned with the kinds of effects which discourses produce and how they produce them.[93] In both instances, texts are conceived as forms of power and performance 'at the point of consumption'. Rhetorical criticism, then, seeks to lay bare both the means of power and the ways of the performance, in order to expose the kinds of effects a discourse produces and how they are produced.

The words 'power', 'performance', and 'effect' suggest a possible way to understand the distinct nature of rhetoric and to clarify the relationship between hermeneutics and rhetoric, a much needed area of re-exploration.[94] Rhetoric is distinct from the inter-subjectivity of understanding as foundational to hermeneutics and more directly related to what D. Klemm calls the 'hermeneutics of existence'.[95] M.J. Hyde and C.R. Smith make a provocative suggestion along these lines:

> The primordial function of rhetoric is to 'make-known' meaning both to oneself and to others. Meaning is derived by a human being in and through the interpretative understanding of reality. Rhetoric is the process of making-known that meaning... Ontologically speaking, rhetoric shows itself in and through the various ways understanding is interpreted and made known... If the hermeneutical situation is the 'reservoir' of meaning, then rhetoric is the selecting tool for making known this meaning.[96]

This explanation of the relationship between hermeneutics and rhetoric, particularly the idea of rhetoric as making meaning known to oneself and to others, pinpoints the social dimension of rhetoric. In Mikhail Bakhtin's terms, this means rhetorical criticism as a way of reading is not a 'dialogic relationship with an object'.[97] Rhetorical reading constitutes the confrontation between 'two consciousnesses and two subjects', which creates 'contextual meaning' that requires a responsive

---

92. Perelman and Olbrechts-Tyteca, *New Rhetoric*, p. 4.

93. Eagleton, *Literary Theory*, p. 205.

94. See Wuellner, 'Hermeneutics and Rhetorics', pp. 1-54; and H. Geissner, 'Rhetorik und Hermeneutik', *Rhetorik* 4 (1985), pp. 85-100.

95. D.E. Klemm, *Hermeneutical Inquiry*. II. *The Interpretation of Existence* (American Academy of Religion Studies in Religion, 44; Atlanta: Scholars Press, 1986), pp. 1-6.

96. M.J. Hyde and C.R. Smith, 'Hermeneutics and Rhetoric: A Seen but Unobserved Relationship', *Quarterly Journal of Speech* 65 (1979), pp. 348, 354.

97. M. Bakhtin, *Speech Genres and Other Late Essays* (trans. V.W. McGee; University of Texas Press Slavic Series, 8; Austin: University of Texas Press, 1986), p. 144.

understanding and includes evaluation.[98] An illustration of this is suggested by W. Brueggemann in his comments on the texts regarding Babylon in the Old Testament: 'In each case the text is a deliberate act of combat against other views of public reality which live through other forms of rhetoric'.[99] J. Habermas suggests that such rhetorical power works because there exists a community convention to utilize and manipulate in the spheres of both meaning and expression.[100] Part of the rhetorical power of a text is its ability to utilize convention, either by following or flaunting such convention, in order to construct or identify a social reality in each linguistic moment.[101] Rhetorical criticism, then, requires an explication of a text's performance as part of the construction of a social reality and as a means to challenge social conventions.

The social dimension of the rhetoric of texts raises the question of the evaluative function of rhetorical criticism. Rhetoric recognizes that no discourse is objectively neutral. The humanistic reconception and revival of rhetoric along the lines found in Brian Vickers' *In Defense of Rhetoric*, and even Perelman's *The New Rhetoric*, is romantically naive about the ideological, even the theological, nature of all discourse.[102] Instead, rhetorical criticism must employ a Platonic suspicion of rhetoric in texts; yet, at the same time, it must accept the fact that all texts (including critics' sub-texts) as rhetoric are authoritative power performances with distinct ideological effects. This evaluative side of rhetoric

98.   Bakhtin, *Speech*, pp. 111, 125; also Wuellner, 'Hermeneutics and Rhetorics', p. 23.

99.   W. Brueggemann, 'At the Mercy of Babylon: A Subversive Rereading of the Empire', *JBL* 110 (1991), p. 18.

100.   J. Habermas, 'On Hermeneutics' Claim to Universality', in *The Hermeneutics Reader* (ed. K. Mueller-Vollmer; Oxford: Basil Blackwell, 1986), pp. 294-319.

101.   The relationship of discourse (verbal and textual) to social reality is a complex question. An interesting contribution to the debate is M. McGuire, 'The Structural Study of Speech', in *Explorations in Rhetoric* (ed. R.E. McKerrow; Glenview, IL: Scott Foresman, 1982), pp. 1-22. See also W. Jeanrond, *Theological Hermeneutics: Development and Significance* (New York: Crossroad, 1991), pp. 67-68, 105-10.

102.   Vickers, *In Defense of Rhetoric*. The ideology of all texts is explored in G. Kress and R. Hodge, *Language as Ideology* (London: Routledge & Kegan Paul, 1979); and F. Jameson, *The Political Unconscious: Narrative as a Socially Symbolic Act* (Ithaca, NY: Cornell University Press, 1981). For application to biblical studies, see D. Jobling and T. Pippin (eds.), *Ideological Criticism of Biblical Texts* (Semeia, 59; Atlanta: Scholars Press, 1992).

demands that the ethics of interpretation become a forthright aspect of critical dialogue. Rhetorical criticism, then, requires that a text and its interpretation be accountable for their ethical consequences and political functions.[103]

In summation, rhetoric is an aspect of all discourse. Rhetoric is both the ways and means a text produces its effects and the kinds of effects a text produces. Rhetoric is not merely about formal and ornamental argumentation, but about argumentation as one aspect of the persuasive power of a text. Furthermore, all texts are rhetorical in that all texts are ideological: they are the presentation of a social construct of reality to the reader. Rhetorical criticism, then, is not the cold, objective analysis of forms of arguments and the truth or non-truth of their conclusions, but the exposure and the critical evaluation of a text's means to power and of a text's ideological presumption.[104]

Rhetorical-Critical Interpretative Strategies

Rhetoric and rhetorical criticism as conceived above negate any effort to establish a singular, definitive rhetorical-critical method. There are many different rhetorical-critical perspectives and methods one could adopt to assess the way a text creates its effect and the effect a text creates. With this broad rhetorical-critical goal in view, Wuellner is correct to state, 'Rhetorical criticism is not a set of analytical techniques, not a set of approaches or methods of interpretation, which when applied, will produce interpretations or solve interpretative problems'.[105] Rhetorical criticism as a critical discourse based on a theory of rhetoric, however, provides a way to establish various interpretative strategies or various readings of a text.

One particular interpretative strategy is based on what H. Lausberg calls the *aptum*.[106] The *aptum* is a term which designates rhetoric's concern for the relationships which exist between the speaker, the speech, and the audience, for which one can substitute the communication

103. An advocacy and example of this stance is put forth by E. Schüssler Fiorenza, 'The Ethics of Interpretation: De-Centering Biblical Scholarship', *JBL* 107 (1988), pp. 3-17; see also Jeanrond, *Theological Hermeneutics*, pp. 110-11, 116-18.

104. The most helpful discussion and application of this understanding of rhetoric is found in D. Jasper, *Rhetoric, Power and Community: An Exercise in Reserve* (Louisville: Westminster/John Knox Press, 1993).

105. Wuellner, 'Hermeneutics and Rhetorics', p. 33.

106. H. Lausberg, *Handbuch der Literarischen Rhetorik* (2 vols.; Munich: Hueber, 1960), I, pp. 54ff. and 258.

coordinates author, text, and reader. These relationships can be stated as follows: the relationship between speaker/author and speech content/text, the relationship between speaker/author and audience/reader, and the relationship between speech content/text and audience/reader.[107] What a theory of rhetoric would suggest is that these relationships are inscribed or entextualized in every text. Part of the rhetoric of a text, then, is the way the text creates, establishes and utilizes these relationships to persuade the audience/reader. A critic who adopts the rhetorical-critical stance reads a text by constructing or reconstructing the *aptum* and from that analyses and evaluates the effects which discourses produce and how they produce them. A rhetorical critic should be sensitive both to the rhetorical dynamics of the *aptum* inscribed in the text and to the critic's own critical stance with respect to the communication situation.

Besides the *aptum*, Greco-Roman rhetorical theory posits the role of *ethos*, *logos*, and *pathos* as aspects of the persuasive nature of communication. *Ethos* refers to the speaker's appeal to his own moral character and other aspects of his life which enhance the speaker's credibility.[108] *Logos* refers to the modes of reasoning used within a speech such as induction or deduction.[109] *Pathos* refers to the emotional reaction of the audience as a means of persuasion or proof.[110] Theoretically, each of these corresponds with the respective communication coordinates, *ethos* with the speaker, *logos* with the speech or discourse, and *pathos* with the audience. Consequently, rhetorical criticism maintains that all communication has these argumentative appeals. There is no communication without all three elements of *ethos*, *logos*, and *pathos*.[111] This understanding of rhetorical appeals being a part of all texts challenges the idea that argumentation can be separated from presentation, or that content (*verba*) can be separated from form (*res*). If one cannot separate content from its presentation, there is no longer any necessary prioritizing of philosophy or *logos* over rhetoric.[112] Rhetorical

107.   Jeanrond, *Theological Hermeneutics*, p. 111. The *aptum* is similar to what Jeanrond labels 'the conditions of communication in which text and reader meet'.

108.   Aristotle, *Rhetoric* 1.2.1356a.3-4, 1.8.1366a.6; Cicero, *De Oratore* 2.43.182-84; Quintilian, *Institutio Oratoria* 6.2.8-19.

109.   Aristotle, *Rhetoric* 1.2.1356b.8; Cicero, *De Inventione* 1.31-41.

110.   Aristotle, *Rhetoric* 1.2.1356a.3, 5; Cicero, *De Oratore* 2.42.178, 2.44.185-87; Quintilian, *Institutio Oratoria* 6.2.20-24.

111.   See Brandt, *Rhetoric of Argumentation*, pp. 16, 218-26.

112.   Vickers, *In Defense of Rhetoric*, pp. 148-213; also Wuellner, 'Hermeneutics and Rhetorics', pp. 24-33.

criticism, then, encourages the exposure of the various kinds of argumentation or persuasive techniques associated with (but not necessarily defined by) the terms *ethos, logos,* and *pathos.*

The use of the *aptum* and the three modes of persuasion are only two ways in which rhetorical theory suggests interpretative strategies or ways to evaluate the text critically. Another strategy is examining the structure or arrangement of a text. The structure or arrangement of texts can be contrasted with the disposition of rhetorical arguments as suggested by Greco-Roman rhetorical theory: a speech has the basic pattern of *exordium, narratio, confirmatio,* and *conclusio.*[113] The effect of a text based on its structure or arrangement also can be evaluated against the genres or species of classical rhetoric: judicial, deliberative, and epideictic.[114] Another way to evaluate the effect of texts is using the rhetorical theory of style, which pertains to the selection of words and how word groups are put together.[115] The point is that these theories of ancient rhetoric provide a way to classify the organization and the potential effect(s) of a text. As categories they provide heuristic devices or classificatory rubrics rather than theoretical absolutes concretized in their historical formulations by ancient Greco-Roman rhetoricians. The work of the New Rhetoricians has shown how these classical theories can be expanded, if redefined, by modern philosophical and linguistic discussion.[116]

In summary of the above, what is meant by rhetorical criticism? It is the attempt to analyse, interpret, or read a literary text by examining the text in terms of the inscribed three relationships of the *aptum* within the context of a defined rhetorical situation in order to uncover the

---

113. Aristotle, *Rhetoric* 3.13.4; Cicero, *De Oratore* 2.80.326; Quintilian, *Institutio Oratoria,* 3.9.1-5. For secondary discussions, see Mack, *Rhetoric,* pp. 41-43; Kennedy, *New Testament Interpretation,* pp. 23-25; Watson, *Invention,* pp. 20-21; and Hughes, *Early Christian Rhetoric,* pp. 32-43.

114. Aristotle, *Rhetoric* 1.3.1358b.3, 1359a.9; Cicero, *De Inventione* 1.5.7, 2.4.12-59.178; *De Oratore* 2.81.333-85.349; Quintilian, *Institutio Oratoria* 2.21.23, 3.3.14-15, 3.4. See secondary discussions in Kennedy, *New Testament Interpretation,* pp. 19-20; Watson, *Invention,* pp. 9-10.

115. Aristotle, *Rhetoric* 3.1-12; Cicero, *De Oratore* 3.5.19-20.73, 3.25-27, 3.37-55; Quintilian, *Institutio Oratoria* 8-9. See secondary discussions in Kennedy, *New Testament Interpretation,* pp. 25-30; Watson, *Invention,* pp. 22-26. An example of rhetorical-criticism based on style is Porter, 'Theoretical Justification', pp. 116-22.

116. Perelman and Olbrechts-Tyteca, *New Rhetoric, passim*; Brandt, *Rhetoric of Argumentation,* pp. 24-69; Black, *Rhetorical Criticism,* pp. 10-90.

persuasive effect(s) a text creates. It is also the evaluation of the ways a text presents its argumentation or persuasive appeals whether explicitly or implicitly, formally or indirectly. Simply put, it examines the way discourses are constructed and operate to create certain effects.

6. *An Application of Rhetorical Criticism to the Opening of 1 Corinthians*

Using the concept of rhetoric given above, this section seeks to demonstrate a rhetorical-critical analysis of the opening of 1 Corinthians.[117] As a textual unit, it is self-contained—1 Cor. 1.1-3. In terms of literary form, it is epistolary: the opening of 1 Corinthians is a typical, Greek letter opening with three parts, the sender, the addressee, and the salutation, in the form, 'A to B, greetings'. Without direct recourse to any ancient rhetorical categories the opening is interpreted against the backdrop of ancient Greek letter-writing practice in order to assess and evaluate the rhetorical effect created by the language of the text and by the use of epistolary convention. Each part of the letter opening of 1 Corinthians will be interpreted separately.

The Sender
Typical of most Greco-Roman letters, except letters of petition, the sender is named first in 1 Corinthians: Παῦλος κλητὸς ἀπόστολος Χριστοῦ Ἰησοῦ διὰ θελήματος θεοῦ καὶ Σωσθένης ὁ ἀδελφός ('Paul, a called apostle of Christ Jesus through the will of God, and Sosthenes, the brother'; 1 Cor. 1.1). For a Greek friendly letter, the qualification of the sender by a title would have been unusual, especially from someone whom the recipients knew. The name immediately followed by two nominatives, κλητός and ἀπόστολος ('called' and 'apostle'), would have signaled a more formal epistolary context and invoked an official tone since most letters where the sender is titled belong to official correspondence.[118]

Understanding the title depends primarily upon the lexical interplay between the words 'Paul' and 'apostle'. 'Paul' represented the historical

---

117. Stamps, *Rhetorical Use*, ch. 4, provides a detailed rhetorical analysis of 1 Cor. 1.1-9.

118. J.L. White, 'Epistolary Formulas and Cliches in Greek Papyrus Letters', in *SBLSP* (2 vols.; ed. K. Richards; Missoula, MT: Scholars Press, 1978), II, pp. 292-93.

person who had come and ministered among them, someone of whom they had a present perception based on a past experience. Among the readers, each person's perception varied depending on the individual's experience. Into that perspective is introduced the term 'apostle'. 'Apostle', whether a previous self-designation or a new one, singles out a specific aspect of the relationship: the person Paul is a special envoy or messenger to the Corinthians.[119]

The commission is specifically identified with Christ Jesus—'apostle of Christ Jesus'. The sender comes as a designate of Christ Jesus, not the church in Jerusalem or any other human power.[120] The sender identifies himself and his role with Christ Jesus, who has become the object of faith and devotion for the recipients, thus invoking a shared religious context. In addition, the whole apostolic role is endowed with divine significance by the additional qualification, 'through the will of God'.[121]

This special authoritative role of the sender is highlighted in the comparative designations which follow in the letter opening. Paul is a called apostle; Sosthenes is a brother; the Corinthians are called to be saints. The apostolic designation is unique to Paul and implies a special relationship to God and to the Corinthians. As apostle to the Corinthians, he wields authority. Being divinely called endows this apostolic status with divine significance and enhances the sender's authority because of its transcendent source.

A final element of the sender designation is the reference to Sosthenes. How the readers would have perceived the co-sender here is difficult to determine as it was not a common epistolary convention.[122] If it is meant as a reference to a co-author, there are no clues to joint authorship in the letter, especially noticeable by the use of the first-

119. The debate over what the word, 'apostle', signified at the time of the writing of 1 Corinthians is whether the word meant an established office or institution or whether it was a functional title. A summary of the etymology of the word and the New Testament use of the word concluding that the word was a functional title is D. Muller, 'Apostle', *NIDNTT*.

120. H. Conzelmann, *1 Corinthians* (trans. J.W. Leitch; Hermeneia; Philadelphia: Fortress Press, 1975), p. 20.

121. G.D. Fee, *The First Epistle to the Corinthians* (NICNT; Grand Rapids: Eerdmans, 1987), p. 29.

122. In extant epistolary literature there are few examples of the use of a co-author/sender; cf. Cicero, *Ad Atticum* 11.5.1. G.J. Bahr, 'Paul and Letter Writing in the First Century', *CBQ* 28 (1966), pp. 476-77, examines the phenomenon in first-century CE epistolary literature.

person singular (compare 1 Thessalonians which uses the first-person plural). If Sosthenes was well known to the Corinthians, there is no evidence in the letter. The inclusion of him as a co-sender and the designation as '*the* brother' possibly imply Sosthenes is a co-worker with Paul.[123]

The familial language in the New Testament suggests that the title, ἀδελφός ('brother'), was a common term for a fellow Christian.[124] If so, the letter is endorsed by another Christian. It emanates from Paul as apostle, but also from his co-worker. This inclusion of a co-sender depreciates any claim to exclusive authority; and, it safeguards the authority through the endorsement of a co-worker.[125] In this sense, the letter carries official weight because both what is said and what is expected are protected by and made accountable to a larger community.

Address

In typical Greek letter form, the addressee is named after the sender in 1 Cor. 1.2: τῇ ἐκκλησίᾳ τοῦ θεοῦ τῇ οὔσῃ ἐν Κορίνθῳ ἡγια-σμένοις ἐν Χριστῷ Ἰησοῦ, κλητοῖς ἁγίοις, σὺν πᾶσιν τοῖς ἐπικα-λουμένοις τὸ ὄνομα τοῦ κυρίου ἡμῶν Ἰησοῦ Χριστοῦ ἐν παντὶ τόπῳ, αὐτῶν καὶ ἡμῶν ('to the church of God which is at Corinth, to the ones having been sanctified in Christ Jesus, called saints, with all the ones who call on the name of our Lord Jesus Christ in every place, theirs and ours'). 1 Corinthians contains the longest address of the Pauline letters. Epistolary convention allows an expanded address, but the expansion found in this address is longer than usual. In addition the

123. Fee, *First Corinthians*, pp. 30-31. The article could imply Sosthenes was known by the Corinthians with a possessive translation, 'your/our brother', but this does not necessarily mean he is the Sosthenes of Acts 18.17, as the name was common. E.E. Ellis, 'Paul and his Co-Workers', *NTS* 32 (1970–71), pp. 437-52, suggests that the use of the article indicates a co-worker with Paul.

124. The term, 'brother', is used approximately 130 times in Paul for fellow Christians. The word is not exclusively Christian in its theological significance as it was used in other religious contexts conveying brotherhood or familial overtones. H.V. von Soden, ἀδελφός, *TDNT*, I, pp. 144ff., provides a thorough discussion of the word but over-reads the theological significance.

125. Little work has been done on the significance of Paul's regular mention of co-workers, however, see Doty, *Letters*, p. 30; Schnider and Stenger, *Studien*, pp. 4-7. For a historical and sociological discussion of their role, see B. Holmberg, *Paul and Power: The Structure of Authority in the Primitive Church as Reflected in the Pauline Epistles* (Philadelphia: Fortress Press, 1978), pp. 57-67.

elaborations pertain to the community, and the terms are not stereotypically familial, but religious.

The phrase, τῇ ἐκκλησίᾳ τοῦ θεοῦ τῇ οὔσῃ ἐν Κορίνθῳ ('the church of God which is at Corinth'), serves as the basic dative of address. The genitive, 'of God', attributes or relates the ἐκκλησία to God, denoting source and ownership. This basic address is qualified in three ways. All three qualifications clarify and expand upon the religious concept of the phrase, 'the church of God'.

The first qualification, ἡγιασμένοις ἐν Χριστῷ Ἰησοῦ ('those who are sanctified in Christ Jesus'), is an expression found only in the address of 1 Corinthians. The effect of the phrase is to place the individual in apposition to the collective appellation, 'church of God': note the change in number from singular to plural which particularizes the dative of address. The perfect participle, ἡγιασμένοις, recalls all the contingencies or processes which have made sanctification a reality for the individual.[126] The word implies how the reader has come to be a member of this Christian assembly.[127] The dative prepositional phrase, 'in Christ Jesus', provides the particular Christian context for sanctification.[128] The participle as a modifier also endows a particular religious status on the addressee by asserting that the 'those' alluded to in the participle are identified with all that the word, ἡγιασμένοις, conjures up: 'set apart', 'consecrated', 'made holy'. The use of a participle identifies the reader(s)-cum-church as 'the sanctified ones'.

In the second descriptive phrase, κλητοῖς ἁγίοις ('called saints'), the author draws on a frequent concept in the Pauline addresses. With respect to 1 Corinthians, the phrase is nearly synonymous with the previous phrase. In both phrases, the same root idea of holiness is present. This second phrase, though, is more focused on the status than the

126. Commentators over-read the use of the perfect tense attempting to specify the past event which caused the sanctification: F.F. Bruce, *1 and 2 Corinthians* (NCB; Grand Rapids: Eerdmans, 1971), p. 30, confession of faith; A. Robertson and A. Plummer, *First Epistle of St Paul to the Corinthians* (ICC; Edinburgh: T. & T. Clark, 2nd edn, 1914), p. 2, baptism. For a recent and more helpful grammatical analysis of the Koine perfect tense, see S.E. Porter, *Idioms of the Greek New Testament* (Biblical Languages: Greek, 2; Sheffield: JSOT Press, 1992), pp. 39-42.

127. So C.K. Barrett, *A Commentary on the First Epistle to the Corinthians* (HNTC; New York: Harper & Row, 1969), p. 32.

128. The dative is ambiguous being both locative and instrumental; see C.F.D. Moule, *Idiom Book of New Testament Greek* (Cambridge: Cambridge University Press, 1959), pp. 75-81.

process. The two words, κλητοῖς and ἁγίοις, almost stand together to create two equal substantives ('called persons', 'holy people'), though grammatically κλητοῖς is probably best understood as a 'verbal' adjective. The Corinthians are designated as holy people by virtue of their divine calling.[129] Still, the phrase endows the addressees with the status of being both called and saints.

The final characterization of the addressee by the sender is an ambiguous enlargement of the letter's address, σὺν πᾶσιν τοῖς ἐπικαλουμένοις τὸ ὄνομα τοῦ κυρίου ἡμῶν Ἰησοῦ Χριστοῦ ἐν παντὶ τόπῳ, αὐτῶν καὶ ἡμῶν ('[together] with all those who call on the name of our Lord Jesus Christ in every place, theirs and ours'). The phrase associates the Church of God at Corinth with the larger Christian community.[130] The effect of bringing in the larger community creates a relational tension. While the association of the Corinthian church with the Church at large creates a sense of solidarity and unity, it also invokes a need for conformity through such unity. This religious solidarity and conformity serves the rhetoric of 1 Corinthians well; it acts as a major premise for instructing the Corinthians on traditional Christian beliefs (4.17; 7.17; 9.16; 14.33-36) and for enjoining them to an obligatory church-wide charitable service to the churches of Jerusalem (16.1-4).[131]

Another aspect to this prepositional phrase is the implicit solidarity established between the sender and the addressee. The phrase, '...our Lord Jesus Christ...theirs and ours', sets up a foundational relational basis for the rhetoric of the letter. The author/sender sets up the following relational triangle in the letter opening: Christ Jesus has called and sent Paul as an apostle to the Corinthians; Jesus Christ is the mutual Lord of both parties in the letter opening, and he is the mutual Lord of the worshipping church at Corinth and elsewhere. But, the relational perspective that is central to the letter opening—signified in five places

129. Barrett, *First Corinthians*, p. 32: 'The fact of the calling is as significant as that of the holiness'. Fee, *First Corinthians*, translates the phrase, 'God's holy people'. See also Moule, *Idiom Book*, pp. 95-96.

130. The main interpretative problem with this phrase is deciding whether it modifies the dative of address or the immediately preceding κλητοῖς phrase. Most probably the use of ἁγίοις prompted the mention of the larger 'holy' community. See Robertson and Plummer, *First Corinthians*, pp. 2-3; L. Morris, *1 Corinthians* (TNTC; Grand Rapids: Eerdmans, 1985), p. 36.

131. This suggestion comes from Barrett, *First Corinthians*, p. 33, but from his exegesis of the previous phrase.

(1.2, 3, 7, 8, 9)—is that which is implied in 'our Lord'.[132]

A rhetoric of power operates through this relational triangle established in the address.[133] The shared lordship implies a mutual submission. But a functional distinction operates—while under Christ's lordship both sender and addressee are called, one is designated apostle, the other, saints. This effectively works out into an authoritative hierarchy: Jesus Christ is Lord of the Church, Paul is an apostle of Jesus Christ to the Church, and the Corinthians are a part of the Church. The author is at pains in several places in the letter to spell out, defend, and even impose this hierarchy (1.17; 2.1-5; 3.5-11; 4.1-7, 14-17; 9.1-2). This spiritual hierarchy is part of the authorial perspective which is created and imposed in the letter opening.

Greeting

The Pauline letter greeting or salutation is formulaic in a majority of the Pauline epistles: χάρις ὑμῖν καὶ εἰρήνη ἀπὸ θεοῦ πατρὸς ἡμῶν καὶ κυρίου Ἰησοῦ Χριστοῦ ('grace and peace to you from God our Father and [the] Lord Jesus Christ'), with only a minor variant found in Galatians and an abbreviated form in 1 Thessalonians. For a Greek-speaking audience, this epistolary greeting would have been very unconventional to the standard, one word greeting, χαίρειν. From an authorial perspective, the greeting was stereotypical, and probably a deliberate play upon Greek convention. This distinctly Pauline greeting created three possible effects: novelty, a religious context, and a personal and communal context.

The audience would immediately have noticed the deviation from the standard epistolary greeting. The novelty itself would secure the reader's attention. The double nominative greeting ('grace and peace'), the pronouns, the length of the greeting, all these would draw the reader in, subverting any sense of the familiar.

The perspective which the sender created for the audience centred around the religious nature of the greeting. This religious nature was primarily evoked through the words 'grace' and 'peace'. However, the religious connotations are not necessarily straightforward until the ἀπό

---

132. Fee, *First Corinthians*, p. 35; L. Belleville, 'Continuity and Discontinuity: A Fresh Look at 1 Cor. in the Light of First-Century Epistolary Forms and Conventions', *EvQ* 59 (1987), p. 18.

133. G. Shaw, *The Cost of Authority: Manipulation and Freedom in the New Testament* (London: SCM Press, 1983), p. 62.

phrase; χάρις and εἰρήνη were both good Greek words for denoting well-being.[134] It is from the syntactical relationship between the words 'grace' and 'peace' and the prepositional phrase that the Christian content of the greeting emerges: the substantives, grace and peace, represent those things that come from God the Father and Jesus the Lord. The personal pronoun, ἡμῶν (our), modifying 'God the Father', secures a reference to the shared locus of faith which existed between the sender and recipients.

The third aspect, the personal and communal nature of the greeting, emerges from the use of the second-person and first-person personal pronouns, ὑμῖν and ἡμῶν. Greetings by convention were third person.[135] The explicit personalization of the greeting, 'to you', continues the familiar/friendly letter pretext found in the letter opening in general. Both pronouns affirm that a relationship exists between the two parties, and that the sender wishes it to go forward.

The reader confronted with this distinctive Pauline greeting reads it against convention and in context. Doing so, the greeting is probably understood as both a greeting and a health wish of sorts in which the sender invokes a Christian sense of well-being.[136] This greeting wishes the letter recipients the favour and rest which comes from God the Father and from the Lord Jesus Christ. The greeting being so distinctively Christian in content continues to establish an official religious tone for the letter. The greeting is either presumptuous or prescriptive, either by assuming that the sender and addressee share in the Christian experience of grace and peace or by declaring that the letter is open to those who receive this Christian salutation as a shared perspective. Either way, by transforming the conventional greeting, the religious ideas and values embedded in the greeting are given a special textual presence.

Summary: The Rhetorical Effect of the Letter Opening and the Relationship between Paul and the Corinthians
The opening, as a literary presentation, creates a textual characterization of the sender and the addressee. The sender thereby both entextualizes

134. H.H. Esser, 'Grace', *NIDNTT*; see also Conzelmann, *1 Corinthians*, p. 24 n. 44.

135. J.M. Lieu, '"Grace to you and Peace": The Apostolic Greeting', *BJRL* 68 (1985–86), pp. 163, 165; White, 'Epistolary Formulas', pp. 295-99.

136. J.L. White, 'The Structural Analysis of Philemon: A Point of Departure in the Formal Analysis of the Pauline Letter', in *SBLSP* (2 vols.; ed. K. Richards; Missoula, MT: Scholars Press, 1971), I, pp. 29-30.

his envisaged relationship with the recipients and prescribes the rhetorical identity for the reader, and thus sets forth the rhetorical stance or dynamic for the rest of the letter.

The sender part of the opening is official and authoritative. The title sets the official tone. The selective presentation of the sender as an apostle emits authority. That authority is deflected from being self imposed authority to divine authority by the stress on the divine origin of the apostolic commission.

The rhetorical effect of the address in creating the identity of the reader is significant especially in terms of the rhetorical tension it creates among the author, text and reader. There are two dimensions to this rhetorical tension. First, a reader must decipher and respond to the relational perspectives entextualized or presented in the text itself. Secondly, the readers must decide their response to the text itself as they adopt or reject the assigned role of the addressee. This response is explicitly called for in letters as the reader decides whether to identify with the named addressee.

Much of this rhetorical tension comes from the implicit power play operative in the address. This power play is achieved through two different alterations or manipulations of the conventional Greco-Roman address. First, the use of religious categories instead of the traditional familial descriptions of the addressee heightens the rhetorical tension. As with so much religious language, the stated religious designations for the addressee come across as authoritative assertions or declarations conveying an implicit understanding not requiring definition or explanation.[137] This type of language contributes to the official tone of the address, whereas the standard familial categories would create a more friendly ambiance.

A second deviation from the traditional epistolary address is the use of a community address as opposed to the conventional individual address. This creates a tension between the individual reader and the addressee as a corporate body. The primary aspect of this tension when combined with the nature of the religious language is that the individual member of the community as a reader is forced through the assertive religious descriptions of the community to evaluate a host of relationships

---

137. Kennedy, *New Testament Interpretation*, pp. 6, 104-107; Leith and Myerson, *Power*, pp. 17-22; C. Perelman, *The Realm of Rhetoric* (trans. W. Kluback; Notre Dame: University of Notre Dame Press, 1982), pp. 81-105.

entextualized in the letter. The rhetorical tension creates an existential tension in relational terms.

First, there is the relationship with God. Before individual readers can properly consider themselves members of the community, they must examine their relationship to God in Christ. Then, secondly, as one so 'sanctified', individual readers must determine how they relate to that community which is designated as 'Church of God', etc. Furthermore, as a member of the community, the relationship with the wider Christian community outside Corinth must be considered. Through the dynamics of the letter itself, that is the sender/recipient relationship inherent in all letters, and through the relational overtones in the word, 'our', the reader is confronted with their relationship to the sender. In summary, the literary presentation of the addressee forces individual readers to evaluate their own individual identity in relation to the qualities, characteristics, and relationships which are selectively set out in the text for the addressee.

The greeting reinforces the religious context which has been established in the naming of the sender and addressee. Again, the change from the stereotypical conventional greeting highlights the religious nature of the language. 'Grace and peace', while words of well-being, are concepts said to come from God and his agent, Jesus Christ. The personal pronouns personalize the greeting so as to affirm and to emphasize the existing and ongoing relationship between the letter parties. The personal pronouns also reinforce the religious context implying that it is mutual or shared and that it is assumed as the basis for the textual communication.

Through the authority of the assertive language of naming and through the relational tension embedded in the opening, the sender creates a rhetoric of power which forces the audience into the identity prescribed in the text. Identification with both the community and the quality of existence described becomes the criterion for becoming a reader of this text. To dissent is to step out of the world of the text; to assent is to accept the relationship between the sender and addressee as entextualized and prescribed by the sender.

7. A Critical Assessment of the Theory and Practice of Rhetorical Criticism in New Testament Studies

The discussion and example of rhetorical criticism above have included a number of critical evaluations of the present practice of rhetorical criticism in New Testament studies. Rather than repeat these criticisms, in this final section some of the broader positive and negative aspects of the theory and practice of rhetorical criticism are explored in order to offer a critical assessment of the rhetorical-critical approach to the New Testament.[138]

The key issue in relation to rhetorical criticism is whether to perceive its critical practice as a method or as an interpretative perspective. At present there is more than one rhetorical-critical practice being used in the interpretation of the New Testament. The question is whether such diversity represents methodological conflict or whether such diversity indicates a potential reconception of rhetoric.

Certainly at present there is a distinct effort to define rhetorical criticism as a specific interpretative methodology.[139] The foundation of this methodology is the application of the categories of Greco-Roman rhetorical theory to biblical texts. Yet, there is disagreement as to the extent to which these categories should control the methodology, as illustrated by the different approaches critics adopt with respect to the degree of rhetoric in the epistles. In the main, whatever methodology is identified it is generally seen as a supplement to the panoply of historical-critical approaches to the New Testament.[140]

Part of the problem with the effort to define a singular methodology for rhetorical criticism is the limitation of the categories of Greco-Roman

138.   For other evalutions, see Robbins and Patton, 'Rhetoric', pp. 327-50; Wuellner, 'Where is Rhetorical Criticism Taking Us?', pp. 448-63; C.C. Black II, 'Keeping up with Recent Studies. XVI. Rhetorical Criticism and Biblical Interpretation', *ExpTim* 100 (1989), pp. 252-58; *idem*, 'Rhetorical Questions: The New Testament, Classical Rhetoric, and Current Interpretation', *Dialog* 29 (1990), pp. 62-70; J. Lambrecht, 'Rhetorical Criticism and the New Testament', *Bijdragen* 50 (1989), pp. 239-53; Mack, *Rhetoric*, pp. 93-102; and most importantly, W. Wuellner, 'Biblical Exegesis in the Light of the History and Historicity of Rhetoric and the Nature of the Rhetoric of Religion', in Porter and Olbricht (eds.), *Rhetoric and the New Testament*, pp. 492-513.

139.   Black, 'Rhetorical Criticism', pp. 256-57, in his critical evaluation of rhetorical criticism concludes by endorsing Kennedy's method, in part because '…Kennedy's proposal incorporates an articulated procedure. His is truly a method, not merely an interpretative perspective.'

140.   Lambrecht, 'Rhetorical Criticism', p. 248: 'Perhaps one better sees the new rhetoric as an enriching segment of the larger and more encompassing historical-critical method'. Others like Black, 'Rhetorical Criticism', p. 257; and Mack, *Rhetoric*, p. 93, see rhetorical criticism as providing a critical method which bridges literary, sociological, and historical concerns.

rhetorical theory. As discussed above, the Gospels present an example of this limitation. Is it theoretically possible to apply a theory of oral speech construction and evaluation to the range of biblical genres: narrative, epistles, prophecy, history, etc.? Furthermore, additional thought needs to be given to the potential differences in concept and strategy that might exist between a Greco-Roman theory of rhetoric, Jewish rhetoric and Christian rhetoric. So while one may theoretically assent to the idea that rhetoric is a dimension to all discourse, it seems methodologically questionable to assess the rhetoric of all texts according to the categories of one very particular theory of rhetoric, Greco-Roman rhetorical theory.

The methodological issue is confused, however, by the attempt to integrate the perspective on rhetoric supplied by the New Rhetoricians, which essentially sees all discourse as employing persuasive techniques.[141] From this emerges a variety of definitions of rhetoric, some of which go beyond a Greco-Roman theory of rhetoric. So at present, it is necessary when engaging in rhetorical criticism to define what one means by rhetoric. For many, the lack of clarity regarding a definition of rhetoric is a distinct hindrance to the critical approach. On the other hand, many see the lack of a final definition for rhetoric and the fluidity of methodology as enabling the critical approach, because it allows rhetorical criticism to be defined by an interpretative perspective that can adapt to the variety of text-types and to a broad range of communicative situations or contexts.[142]

If one sees rhetorical criticism as an interpretative perspective rather than a method based on the categories of Greco-Roman rhetorical theory, then it is possible to use a wide range of rhetorical theories to appraise a New Testament text. Rhetorical criticism would thus generally be defined by its attempt to identify the textually-embedded strategies that seek to persuade the reader, to assess the effectiveness of these strategies, and then to evaluate the ideological positions to which the reader(s) is being moved.

There are several advantages to adopting this more general interpretative perspective with respect to the rhetorical criticism of the New Testament. Primarily, it respects the textuality of biblical discourse in

141. Many practitioners of rhetorical criticism and many evaluators of rhetorical criticism see the importance of the insights of the New Rhetoric, but struggle with the implications of these insights, which entail an understanding of rhetoric that is broader than Greco-Roman rhetoric.

142. Wuellner, 'Biblical Exegesis', pp. 511-13.

which form and content are inseparable. Rhetorical criticism does not discard the structure, style and argumentative features of a text in order to recover the historical data and theological content of a text.[143]

Equally, rhetorical criticism entails a respect for the full-orbed nature of a communicative situation. It is possible to assess the textual strategies of the New Testament in terms of the original situation, the present context, or any other identifiable communication situation: 'rhetorical criticism takes the historical moment of a human exchange seriously in order to assess the quality of an encounter and the merits of an argumentation'.[144] The advantage of a rhetorical-critical perspective is that it recognizes that the important rhetorical features and their effectiveness must be reconsidered when a text is placed in a different context.

Another advantage of a rhetorical interpretative perspective is that it provides a way to consider and assess the explicit ideology of the New Testament texts. The persuasive nature of the New Testament is not limited to its logic or reason or the convincing nature of its theological propositions. The power of the New Testament equally resides in its appeal to authority and experience and to an all-embracing spiritual world-view or understanding of reality. Rhetorical criticism exposes these appeals and allows them to be critically evaluated as to their past and present effectiveness.[145]

In conclusion, rhetorical criticism is still an emerging discipline. There are many issues of method which await further clarification. Equally, some of the claims of rhetorical critics in terms of the exegetical problems they claim to solve await further evaluation. However, rhetorical criticism in all its guises is opening up a fresh understanding of the persuasive nature of the New Testament by exposing the textual strate-

143. Black, 'Rhetorical Criticism', p. 257; Lambrecht, 'Rhetorical Criticism', pp. 247-48.

144. Mack, *Rhetoric*, p. 101. I have used this quotation to endorse a continuum of historical moments in which New Testament texts are read, though Mack limits the historical moment to the original reading of a New Testament document.

145. Two different perspectives on this point are Black, 'Rhetorical Criticism', p. 257: 'The intelligent application of rhetorical principles does promise augmented insight into that quality of scripture so obvious to its readers yet so elusive to its critics: the power to instill and to enhance the life of faith'; and Mack, *Rhetoric*, p. 102: 'Rhetorical criticism may therefore be the strongest challenge yet to the notion that critical scholarship and biblical hermeneutics should and will always come out together in support of some traditional definition of the Christian faith'.

gies employed within these texts and providing a critical faculty for assessing the impact of the argument of these texts in a variety of interpretative contexts. The following quotation sums it up for the present: 'A new rhetoric and a new rhetorical criticism are in the process of emerging, and need to be cultivated, not once, nor once and for all, but ever anew, to enable readers of sacred scriptures to let the reading and critical study of those texts do its work: "transforming society"'.[146]

146. Wuellner, 'Biblical Exegesis', p. 513.

CANONICAL CRITICISM: AN INTEGRATED READING OF BIBLICAL TEXTS FOR THE COMMUNITY OF FAITH

Kent D. Clarke

1. Introduction

Although canonical criticism began its development approximately twenty-five years ago, this relatively young approach to biblical interpretation has been for the most part out of reach for both the student and scholar of New Testament studies.[1] This elusive element can be attributed to a number of different reasons. First, virtually all of the initial dialogue concerning canonical criticism has been initiated by Old Testament scholars who have applied the methodology to the Old Testament canon, distancing the field from those involved in New Testament research.

Secondly, canonical criticism is not often presented or discussed in introductory biblical textbooks, and, except for those who are more immediately involved in its dialogue, has, therefore, left the discipline relatively obscure until more recent times (in fact, Brevard Childs, the prominent Old Testament scholar, has written the *only* New Testament introduction completely dedicated to canonical criticism). When this approach is presented in the standard introductory texts, the discussion is usually more technical in nature, inadequately dealt with, unsympathetic to the approach, or not fully understood by the author, and thus rendered arduous to the newcomer in the field.[2]

---

1. James A. Sanders states that although canonical criticism had precursors in the 1960s, the publication of his book *Torah and Canon* (Philadelphia: Fortress Press, 1972) seems to have marked its inception. James Barr likewise states that the publication of Sanders's *Torah and Canon* may be regarded as the first full work in the genre. For these statements, see Sanders, *Canon and Community: A Guide to Canonical Criticism* (Philadelphia: Fortress Press, 1984), p. 61; and J. Barr, *Holy Scripture: Canon, Authority, Criticism* (Oxford: Clarendon Press, 1983), p. 156.

2. An exception is the fine work of Mikeal C. Parsons, whose explanation of

A third reason for canonical criticism's slow emergence into New Testament studies lies in a lack of consensus as to what the discipline actually is, and what tasks it should accomplish, or, for that matter, whether canonical criticism is even a worthy approach to biblical studies.[3] This ambiguity is expressed both in matters of terminology (how it is defined), and methodology (how it is performed). The goal of this chapter is to remove some of the present ambiguity and to present canonical criticism as one valid and effective approach to New Testament study. This will be accomplished by discussing its pre-history and rise as an interpretative discipline, by clarifying and comparing the various methods of particular practitioners, and by applying the principles of canonical criticism to a selected portion of the New Testament. Perhaps the most appropriate place to begin is with a simplistic working definition of canonical criticism: Canonical criticism is a method of study that seeks, as its primary goal, to interpret the biblical text in its canonical context and in relationship to the believing community of faith.

2. *The History and Development of Canonical Criticism*

Several factors have brought about the emergence and development of canonical criticism. A growing dissatisfaction with the historical-critical method and the rapid decline of the Biblical Theology Movement were the primary contributors to canonical criticism's 'coming of age'. It is essential that the reader has at least a general understanding of these two areas of biblical interpretation prior to any discussion of canonical criticism.

Critical Methodology and Historical Criticism
Perhaps the most significant factor that brought about a transition from the premodern to the modern period of biblical interpretation has been the acceptance of a critical methodology for study of the Bible. Prior to the development of this critical methodology the primary task of the

canonical criticism formed my initial understanding of the discipline and has hence allowed me to further develop my views and methodology. See M.C. Parsons, 'Canonical Criticism', in D.A. Black and D.S. Dockery (eds.), *New Testament Criticism and Interpretation* (Grand Rapids: Zondervan, 1991), pp. 255-94.

    3.   Christopher Tuckett, in his evaluation of canonical criticism, states that 'Firstly, it must be said that, however much is claimed for the value of the new approach, the results are often rather meager...' See C. Tuckett, *Reading the New Testament: Methods of Interpretation* (London: SPCK, 1987), p. 170.

exegete focused upon explaining the 'plain sense' of Scripture. Authorship and dating of the various biblical books generally corresponded to the Early Church traditions, and most Christians believed that the Bible described events as they had actually occurred. Literal chronologies of the Bible were developed that placed creation close to 4000 BCE, and harmonies of the Gospels were produced that would thereby provide a type of biography of the life and times of Jesus.[4]

Gradually, however, this 'literalist' approach to the study of the Bible began to change. With the dawning and influence of the Enlightenment, which rejected the traditional, authoritative, and dogmatic approaches of the church's biblical interpretations, a new freedom developed that allowed the Bible to be studied with a critical mind. Paul Hazard, the late French historian (1878–1944), described how questions about truth became extremely important in seventeenth-century Europe, after centuries in which Christian beliefs had been taken almost for granted:

> What men craved to know was what they were to believe, and what they were not to believe. Was tradition still to command their allegiance, or was it to go by the board? Were they to continue plodding along the same old road, trusting to the same old guides, or were they to obey new leaders who bade them turn their backs on all those outworn things and follow them to other lands of promise? The champions of Reason and the champions of Religion were…fighting desperately for the possession of men's souls, confronting each other in a contest at which the whole of thoughtful Europe was looking on.[5]

Edgar Krentz states that:

> The rationalist Enlightenment radicalized the claim of reason and history; as a result it placed the claims of religion outside the realm of reason. In this division Orthodox theology lost its foundations in history. The cleft between reason and history triumphed among the learned—including the theologians—and removed the basis of orthodoxy's epistemology.[6]

This growth of critical methodology, which was marked by an open ended quest for truth rather than by a quest for truth tied within the

---

4. As recently as the 1600s, such leaders of the church as Archbishop James Ussher, who understood the days of Genesis 1 to be literal twenty-four hour periods, confidently asserted that the week of creation had taken place on October 18-24, 4004 BCE. Adam, he said, was created on October 23 at 9.00 a.m., Greenwich Mean Time.

5. P. Hazard, *The European Mind 1680–1715* (Harmondsworth: Penguin Books, 1973), pp. 8-9.

6. E. Krentz, *The Historical-Critical Method* (Philadelphia: Fortress Press, 1975), p. 21.

bounds of one's orthodoxy, placed the Bible under the scrutiny of scientific thought, empiricism, and rational investigation. New interpretative methods were developed in order to deal with the more difficult texts and to answer the numerous discrepancies which an honest reading of the Hebrew and Greek Scriptures produced. One of these new interpretative methods, historiography, gave rise to what was called historical criticism, which attempted, among other things, to verify the authenticity or spuriousness of various documents. This method was used as early as the time of Laurentius Valla, who in 1440 affirmed Nicholas of Cusa's claim that the 'Donation of Constantine' was not authentic. This document, which purportedly had been written by Constantine the Great and later sent to Pope Sylvester I, had been used by the Roman Catholic Church to support its claims to temporal lordship over central Italy. However, beginning with the critical study of Valla, and many others thereafter, the erroneous nature of the document was established.

If historical criticism could be used to verify the authenticity or spuriousness of the 'Donation of Constantine', could it not also be used to solve the perplexing questions inherent in the biblical books as well? Did Moses actually write the first five books of the Old Testament? Did the events recorded in the Bible actually take place as written? By the middle of the eighteenth century, a historical-critical method was developed by Johann Salamo Semler (1725–1791) that emphasized the importance of a historical interpretation of the biblical text over a theological interpretation.[7] With the work of Semler, often regarded as the father of modern critical study, the era of modern historical-critical investigation of the Bible had begun.

The broad discipline of historical criticism covers a number of subcategories within biblical studies. Textual criticism (also known as lower criticism) can be defined as the science and art that compares all the known manuscripts of the Bible in order to trace the history of variations within the biblical text and to discover its original form and wording. Source criticism seeks to reconstruct the non-extant literary sources that were used by the early authors and editors of the Bible as they formed their works. Form criticism strives to go behind the literary sources of the Bible to the earlier period of oral tradition, for the purpose of

---

7. Semler's *magnum opus* was a four-volume work on the free investigation of canon (1771–1775). It called for a purely historical-philological interpretation of the Bible in light of the circumstances that surrounded the origin of the various books, with little concern for edification. See Krentz, *Historical*, pp. 18-19.

isolating the various oral forms that gave rise to the written sources. Tradition criticism, somewhat related to form criticism, investigates and compares the several interpretations or understandings of the more important oral traditions recorded in the Bible. And finally, redaction criticism generally focuses upon larger textual units, and concerns itself with how a biblical author or editor used his sources in shaping and altering his final work.[8]

Today, historical criticism is taken for granted. It would be not only impossible, but undesirable to turn back to the interpretative methods of the precritical age. Stephen Neill comments that '...the liberty of the scientific and critical approach has established itself almost beyond the possibility of cavil'.[9] R.P.C. Hanson goes further in stating that '...the battle for the acceptance of historical criticism as applied to the Bible has been won'.[10]

Some scholars claim that the methods used in biblical research are undeniably similar to those used by contemporary historians. In view of this, historical criticism has often been called into question, and in some regards, rightfully so. It has been, in part, this very questioning and the ensuing disappointment with historical criticism that has led to the development of canonical criticism as an interpretative method of the Bible. Mikeal C. Parsons, writing in relation to historical criticism, states:

> Canonical criticism emerged, in part, in response to a growing sense of the inadequacy of the historical-critical method in dealing with the message of the biblical texts. This dissatisfaction has ranged from those who wish to abandon the historical-critical method altogether to those who wish to subordinate historical criticism to some other interpretative matrix (such as the canon).[11]

---

8. For an excellent survey and introduction to the various types of biblical criticism, the reader is referred to the Guides to Biblical Scholarship series published by Fortress Press. Both Sanders's *Canon and Community* and Krentz's *The Historical-Critical Method* are works in this series. See also J. Rogerson, *Old Testament Criticism in the Nineteenth Century* (Philadelphia: Fortress Press, 1985). For a good beginning introduction to historical criticism and other critical methods, see also D.J.A. Clines, 'Methods in Old Testament Study', in J. Rogerson (ed.), *Beginning Old Testament Study* (London: SPCK, 1983), pp. 26-43.

9. S. Neill, *The Interpretation of the New Testament 1816–1961* (London: Oxford University Press, 1966), p. 338.

10. R.P.C. Hanson, *Biblical Criticism* (Baltimore: Penguin Books, 1970), p. 13.

11. Parsons, 'Canonical', p. 255.

Historical criticism is primarily concerned with reconstructing the events and history lying behind the biblical texts. By focusing upon these events and histories, the actual texts themselves have often been neglected. It becomes increasingly difficult to interpret the text when one is primarily concerned with the historical events that took place *behind* the text. In order to understand this history, the scholar/historian must look *through* the biblical text, and, in so doing, the text can become of little relevance. It is proper and natural to desire a knowledge of the history giving rise to the biblical texts, but in this quest for history, it is claimed that the Bible becomes a book of sources for historical reconstruction.[12] In other words, the Bible is used as a tool for reconstructing the past with little regard given to the actual meaning of the texts. By approaching the Bible as a source for the history of religion, a genuinely theological treatment cannot be successfully accomplished. In this light, historical criticism is often guilty of removing the Bible from the context of the community of faith and placing it into the scholar's and historian's study. The Bible's relevance and meaning is no longer developed through its use and interpretation in the church or synagogue, but instead, its relevance and meaning for the believing community is often lost as it becomes a source for reconstructing Jewish and Christian history. Although historical criticism can rightly be called biblical study, in that it makes use of the biblical texts, some scholars claim it cannot properly be called a method of biblical interpretation if one defines this as an approach that primarily concerns itself with exegeting the meaning of the text.

Historical criticism has often assumed that the correct meaning of a text is the original author's intended meaning. Often historical criticism has sought to recreate this original meaning. In fact, generations of scholars have concerned themselves with reconstructing the oldest written texts, the oral traditions that preceded them, and the historical conditions and events that gave rise to them. This was done mostly for the purpose of discovering the original author's intended meaning and aim. Yet some claim that the more detailed these reconstructions become, the more speculative and subjective in nature they are.[13] In fact,

12. See Clines, 'Methods', p. 39.

13. See, among others, M.C. Callaway, 'Canonical Criticism', in S.L. MacKenzie and S.R. Haynes (eds.), *To Each its Own Meaning: An Introduction to Biblical Criticisms and their Application* (Louisville: Westminster/John Knox Press, 1993), p. 123.

it is often stated that historical criticism tends to present and discuss the often widely differing views of scholars rather than the texts themselves.[14] Because of this subjectivity, it is concluded that the believing community should not necessarily be tied down to any 'original' meaning as established by historical criticism.

Historical criticism has been overwhelmingly concerned with *diachronic* interpretation of the biblical text (interpretation based upon the historical setting of the text, its origin, and its process of transmission), rather than with *synchronic* interpretation (interpretation based upon the text itself and its final form). In reality, it may not be an over-exaggeration to make the point that most biblical scholars who advocate historical criticism operate on the principle that the text (the only objective datum available) must be interpreted and understood only after an investigation into the process by which it came into being. The understanding of this process will always remain at least somewhat, if not completely, hypothetical and speculative.

Diachronic study and the inquiry into the biblical text's process of transmission, as endorsed by historical criticism, has led to a focus concerned with microscopic analysis rather than telescopic analysis. In other words, the individual sources, traditions, literary forms, redactional units, and even lone words have been considered more important, and, in fact, have been singled out for biblical interpretation over and above the completed and final canonical form of the text. This has, again, caused distortions of meaning and subjectivity in interpretation. Numerous scholars feel that the Bible must be interpreted with methods that focus on the whole of Scripture, and that its final form and canonical composition must be the primary governing task of the exegete. While every scrap of external information is potentially valuable for the interpretation of the Bible, the surprising thing is how little is, in reality, significant. To understand Amos or Micah well, a paragraph or two of historical and social background probably suffices (and much more is largely guesswork); to interpret Matthew or Luke it can hardly be necessary to learn about the historical origin of these books (valid though such an inquiry may be in itself), since we have no kind of certainty about such matters. To seek the 'author's intention', indeed, can lead us no deeper into the meaning of these works than to ask directly about meaning, disregarding almost entirely questions of date and authorship except on

---

14. See R. Smend, 'Questions about the Importance of the Canon in an Old Testament Introduction', *JSOT* 16 (1980), p. 49.

the broadest scale. The vast bulk of the data we need for interpretation is contained in the works themselves.[15]

The Biblical Theology Movement

Critical methodology and historical criticism brought about a new manner of viewing Scripture, particularly the Old Testament. Scholars influenced by these critical approaches began to question whether the Bible told one what God was like and what he had done. Instead, it was said that the Bible was to be read as history, recording what the Israelites *thought* God was like and what they *thought* he had done. In many ways this is where the issue still stands today, and as John Barton explains, it has created some difficulties for Christian believers and communities of faith, both past and present:

> In gaining an objective knowledge of the historical development of religious beliefs in Israel, we seem to have lost the Bible as a book of faith; and the Old Testament has ceased to be a problem by becoming, from the believer's point of view, more or less an irrelevance. The history of the religious beliefs of the ancient Israelites is, no doubt, a very interesting subject for scholars to study, but so are a great many other things, and it is not at all clear why students of *theology*—still less ordinary Christians—should continue to concern themselves with the Old Testament, if this is all it can inform them about.[16]

It has been the goal of Old Testament theology and the Biblical Theology Movement, both past and present, to bring some type of reconciliation between the Old Testament as a text used by Jews and Christians to establish theology (to provide information about God), and the history of the Israelite religious belief as developed by critical study (to provide a historical reconstruction). Over the years numerous models have been presented in an attempt to accomplish this amalgamation. The Biblical Theology Movement was one of these.[17]

The Biblical Theology Movement arose with much enthusiasm in the 1940s, flourished in the 1950s, and greatly declined in the 1960s. The

15. Clines 'Methods', pp. 36-37.

16. J. Barton, 'Old Testament Theology', in Rogerson (ed.), *Beginning Old Testament Study*, p. 91.

17. For a survey and critique of the Biblical Theology Movement see the works of G.E. Wright, *God Who Acts* (London: SCM Press, 1958); J. Barr, *The Semantics of Biblical Language* (New York: Oxford University Press, 1961); and B.S. Childs, *Biblical Theology in Crisis* (Philadelphia: Westminster Press, 1970). See also the titles in footnote 19.

movement was primarily interested in the special character and nature of the Bible, its difference from any other type of literature or system of thought, its relation to the Church and its proclamation, the unity of the Bible and the relation of the Old Testament to the New, and its place in the witness of the Church.[18] At the same time, the movement emphasized that the God of the Bible was a God who acted in history, and, therefore, historical criticism, which focused upon this history, was the most appropriate method of biblical interpretation.

It was from the epochal and magisterial works of Walter Eichrodt and Gerhard von Rad that the Biblical Theology Movement developed.[19] Both of these men sought to write a theology of the Old Testament by formulating one overarching theme (or 'family likeness') that unified each Old Testament book. Two criteria were enlisted to bring about this purpose: (1) the idea or theme must be found in the Scriptures alone, and (2) the idea or theme must be found to a greater or lesser degree in each Old Testament book.[20] Clearly the task was to be accomplished by focusing explicitly upon what each biblical writer had *said* regarding God, Israel, and his surrounding world. Eichrodt developed the unifying biblical theme of 'covenant', while von Rad presented his theme of 'salvation history'. Extending from the work of these two scholars, the Biblical Theology Movement sought to establish its unifying biblical theme not on what the writers had explicitly said, but rather upon the shared assumptions *underlying* what they had said. In other words, the Old Testament, in fact, the entire Bible as a whole, was perceived as being less a matter of all its writers agreeing in what they asserted, and more a feature of their agreement in underlying *thought* patterns.[21]

Along with disillusionment with historical criticism, the collapse of the Biblical Theology Movement, with its close dependence upon historical criticism, also contributed to canonical criticism's emergence. Mary C. Callaway, writing about the decline of the Biblical Theology Movement that thus gave way to the rise of canonical criticism, colorfully concludes with these words:

18. Barr, *Holy Scripture*, p. 131.

19. See W. Eichrodt, *Theology of the Old Testament* (London: SCM Press; Philadelphia: Westminster Press, 1967), and G. von Rad, *Old Testament Theology* (Edinburgh: Oliver & Boyd; New York: Harper & Row, 1962–65). For a good introduction relating to the pursuit of an Old Testament theology and its relationship to the Biblical Theology Movement, see Barton, 'Old Testament', pp. 90-112.

20. Callaway, 'Canonical', p. 122.

21. Barton, 'Old Testament', pp. 100-101.

Like a variety of garments dyed various shades of the same hue, the books of the Bible could be unified by their tincture with a unifying theological concept. For Walter Eichrodt this concept was covenant, for Oscar Cullmann the biblical idea of time, for Gerhard von Rad salvation history. But the multiplicity of theories, and the failure of any of them to construct a roof wide enough to cover all the idiosyncratic residents of the Bible, began to suggest that the search for the unifying idea of scripture was ill-conceived. The recalcitrant books of the Bible were made of different fabrics and would not all take a single dye.[22]

By the mid 1960s, the Biblical Theology Movement had been undermined. James Barr, in his work entitled *The Semantics of Biblical Language*, had clearly demonstrated that the use of etymologies and the derivation of thought patterns from particular Hebrew words were far from objective, and, indeed, were based on highly problematic issues. Brevard Childs followed suit in *Biblical Theology in Crisis* by claiming that the movement's failure could be directly traced to its preoccupation with history. Subsequent work in the field revealed its many similarities with neoorthodoxy and disclosed that the apparently distinctive ideas of the Old Testament were not as distinctive as the Biblical Theology Movement had claimed.[23] Despite its name, the movement was not always biblical, and in reality, it was at times quite unbiblical.

It has been in the attempt to alleviate the numerous problems present in historical criticism and the Biblical Theology Movement that canonical criticism has sprung forth. In bold contrast to historical criticism and the Biblical Theology Movement, canonical criticism has at its heart the task of interpreting the Bible based primarily upon: (1) the biblical texts alone, (2) the completed and final canonical form of the Bible in its entirety, and (3) the normative context of the believing community of faith.

3. *Major Practitioners of Canonical Criticism*

A discussion of canonical criticism must undoubtedly take into account its primary advocates and practitioners. And although there are numerous scholars who sympathize with and to some degree utilize the approach, two in particular stand out above the others as the principal

22. Callaway, 'Canonical', p. 122.

23. M.G. Brett, *Biblical Criticism in Crisis?* (Cambridge: Cambridge University Press, 1991), pp. 1-2.

developers and defenders of canonical criticism. However, as will be seen, the canonical approach of Brevard S. Childs and the canonical process of James A. Sanders, in spite of having foundational similarities, display distinctive differences and stand at separate ends of the canonical spectrum.

The Canonical Approach of Brevard Childs
Brevard Childs is Sterling Professor of Divinity in Old Testament at Yale University, having studied under such influential Old Testament scholars as W. Eichrodt, W. Baumgartner, G. von Rad, and W. Zimmerli. Although primarily a professor of Old Testament, he has read more widely in New Testament studies than many New Testament scholars! It is important to note that although Childs has been well recognized as one of the most proficient practitioners of historical criticism, he is now one of those who has become dissatisfied with the method.[24]

Although the approach being addressed in this chapter has been referred to as 'canonical criticism', Childs has expressed a dislike for this term because it associates the method with those of historical criticism (source criticism, form criticism, redaction criticism, etc.). Childs would rather use the term 'canonical approach':

> The approach which I am undertaking has been described by others as 'canonical criticism'. I am unhappy with this term because it implies that the canonical approach is considered another historical critical technique which can take its place alongside of source criticism, form criticism...and similar methods. I do not envision the approach to canon in this light. Rather, the issue at stake in relation to the canon turns on establishing a stance from which the Bible can be read as sacred scripture.[25]

Childs's canonical approach can be most adequately outlined by presenting his developing thought through chronological summaries of a number of his more important publications. The discussion begins with his works on historical criticism.

Childs's Early Works (1958–1969): Although Childs's early works deal primarily with historical criticism, one can see traces of his later

24. For similar background and bibliography on Childs, see Parsons, 'Canonical', pp. 256-57; Brett, *Biblical Criticism*, pp. 229-30, and G. Tucker, D. Petersen, and R. Wilson (eds.), *Canon, Theology, and Old Testament Interpretation: Essays in Honor of Brevard S. Childs* (Philadelphia: Fortress Press, 1988).
25. B.S. Childs, *Introduction to the Old Testament as Scripture* (London: SCM Press, 1979), p. 82.

views in this material. In fact, as Mark Brett rightly suggests, there are at least four principles of biblical interpretation present in Childs's early monographs that would, more or less, be later introduced into his future publications as well.[26] These four principles are: (1) one should view the Scriptures as a progressive theological 'refinement' from the Old Testament to the New Testament,[27] (2) theological reference should be accorded higher privilege than historical realities,[28] (3) descriptive exegesis (based on historical criticism) should relate to historical realities while constructive exegesis (based upon normative theological meaning) should relate to theological realities,[29] and (4) historical reconstruction, authorial intention, and reference to the past event are of little relevance to exegesis.[30] One should keep in mind that these four early interpretative 'seeds' were to later produce the more mature principles and statements of Childs's canonical approach.

Biblical Theology in Crisis (1970): In his book *Biblical Theology in Crisis*, Childs, after providing a history and description of the move-

26. See Brett, *Biblical Criticism*, pp. 31-38, where the following four points and their relating footnotes have been developed. See esp. B.S. Childs, 'Interpretation in Faith: The Theological Responsibility of an Old Testament Commentary', *Int* 18 (1964), pp. 432-49; *Myth and Reality in the Old Testament* (London: SCM Press, 1960); *Memory and Tradition in Israel* (London: SCM Press, 1962); and *Isaiah and the Assyrian Crisis* (London: SCM Press, 1967). Already at this early stage, Childs's article 'Interpretation in Faith' clearly revealed and articulated his dissatisfaction with historical criticism. One can begin to see Childs's emphasis on interpretation that focuses upon the whole canonical text and final form, as well as, if not more important than, authorial intention and historical reconstructions.

27. This is to be differentiated from progressive revelation where the Old Testament is subordinated in light of the 'purer revelation' present in the New Testament. Childs here insisted that one must read both the Old Testament and New Testament in light of each other. However, there is a progressive theological refinement of biblical tradition. This was to later give way to Childs's emphasis on the final form and text of Scripture rather than textual prehistory.

28. Childs maintained that 'biblical' or 'theological' reality could not be scientifically proven; therefore, historicity could not be used as a criterion for theological reality. In view of this, Childs said that the received biblical tradition of the final form, refined through theological discussion, should have priority in exegesis.

29. These two categories ensued by questioning what role historical criticism had in providing meaning for theological reality. These two aspects of reality are not to be identified with each other, nor entirely separated. In many ways, they remain in tension.

30. This point tends to align Childs with literary criticism and New Criticism's 'formalism'.

ment, attacks it, along with its historical agenda that had caused the Bible to be separated from the community of faith.[31] Childs, who draws together a barrage of both old and new criticisms, concludes that the Biblical Theology Movement, with its outright historical focus, failed. He attributes this failure primarily to the fact that the movement refused to take into serious consideration the relationship between both Old and New Testaments acting in and forming one complete canonical context. Childs concludes this book by presenting a new type of biblical theology, one which gives up its preoccupation with historicity and historical reconstructions, and instead emphasizes all the scriptural traditions of the entire Christian canon, both Old and New Testaments.

Exodus (1974): Childs, in his commentary on Exodus, goes on to explain that he does not share the hermeneutical view of those who suggest that biblical exegesis is an objective, descriptive enterprise, controlled solely by scientific criticism, to which the Christian theologian can at best add a few homiletical reflections for piety's sake. Childs continues by explaining that the separation of descriptive (what the text meant) and constructive (what the text means) elements of exegesis undermines the theological task of understanding the Bible.[32] However, far from abandoning the historical considerations of these scholars, as some mistakenly assume Childs has done, he does acknowledge the continued importance of dealing seriously with the biblical text in its original setting within the history of Israel. He claims that use of this historical research is important to exegesis, but should be subjugated to a model of interpretation that sees the Bible as canonical Scripture within the theological discipline of the Christian Church. Briefly stated, exegesis that is both descriptive and constructive in nature is essential for biblical interpretation.

---

31. After dealing a harsh blow to biblical theology in *Biblical Theology in Crisis*, Childs argues in a number of later publications not dealt with here that a canonical approach to the Bible can not only revive biblical theology, but is the normative means for exploration of the theological dimensions of the biblical text. See the noteworthy, yet often criticized, works by Childs, *Old Testament Theology in a Canonical Context* (London: SCM Press, 1985); and *Biblical Theology of the Old and New Testaments* (London: SCM Press, 1992). For a number of reviews of the latter title, see T.E. Fretheim in *CBQ* 56 (1994), pp. 324-26; and R. Bauckham in *BI* 2 (1994), pp. 246-50.

32. B.S. Childs, *Exodus* (London: SCM Press, 1974), p. ix. In a review of various commentaries on Exodus, one scholar claims, 'It is without doubt the best modern commentary at present'. See C.S. Rodd, 'Which is the Best Commentary? VIII. Exodus', *ExpTim* 98 (1987), pp. 359-62.

The heart of the commentary, Childs claims, is the section entitled 'Old Testament Context'. This section deals with the text in its final form, which is its 'canonical shape', while at the same time recognizing and profiting from the variety of historical forces which were at work in producing this final shape of the canon. Childs states:

> From a literary point of view there is a great need to understand the present composition as a piece of literature with its own integrity. The concentration of critical scholars on form-critical and source analysis has tended to fragment the text and leave the reader with only bits and pieces. But an even more important reason for interpreting the final text is a theological one. It is the final text, the composite narrative, in its present shape which the church, following the lead of the synagogue, accepted as canonical and thus the vehicle of revelation and instruction... In my judgment, the study of the prehistory has its proper function within exegesis only in illuminating the final text.[33]

Although Childs's canonical approach is not yet expressed in its full maturity, his foundational presuppositions are clearly evident. Again, Childs's predominant focus is sharpening.

Introduction to the Old Testament as Scripture (1979): With the publication of this book, which was accepted with varying degrees of enthusiasm, Childs's canonical approach was for the first time presented in its full maturity.[34] However, one can clearly hear the distinct echoes of his earlier works, although presented in a somewhat clearer and more vivid manner. Childs's emphasis on interpretation, which is based upon the final form of the text and placed into the context of the community of faith, is again stressed. He comments on both the final form and the community of faith:

> The reason for insisting on the final form for scripture lies in the peculiar relationship between text and people of God which is constitutive of the canon. The shape of the biblical text reflects a history of encounter between God and Israel. The canon serves to describe this peculiar relationship and to define the scope of this history by establishing a beginning and an end to the process... The significance of the final form of the biblical text is that it alone bears witness to the full history of revelation... It is only in the final form of the biblical text in which the normative history has reached an end that the full effect of this revelatory

---

33. Childs, *Exodus*, pp. xiv-xv.
34. See Childs, *Introduction*.

history can be perceived... But it is the full, combined text which has rendered a judgment on the shape of the tradition and which continues to exercise an authority on the community of faith.[35]

Clearly, one reason for the mixed reception of this book lies in Childs's much firmer and more vocal subordination of historical criticism to the canonical approach. Parsons, commenting on this very point, affirms that Childs 'has so modified the purposes of the historical critical method that many of his critics think he has in fact abandoned the historical critical method altogether'.[36] Although it is undeniably clear that Childs greatly limits the task of historical criticism, especially in light of his canonical approach, it is erroneous to assume that historical considerations have no part in his methodology. He states:

> Throughout this Introduction I shall be criticizing the failure of the historical critical method, as usually practiced, to deal adequately with the canonical literature of the Old Testament. Nevertheless, it is a basic misunderstanding of the canonical approach to describe it as a non-historical reading of the Bible. Nothing could be further from the truth![37]

This work introduces the newest concept to be crystallized in Childs's canonical approach. It is referred to as 'canonical shaping'. Childs defines canonical shaping as an interpretative structure which the biblical text has received from those who formed and used it as sacred Scripture. Parsons clarifies this definition by referring to canonical shaping as the selection, collection, and ordering of biblical material.[38] However, those who did the selecting, collecting, and ordering of this material have purposely obscured their own identity, and in so doing have also blurred their editorial motivations and those processes by which the text was reworked. Yet their primary goal for shaping the text has not been obscured. It was the main intention of these editors to shape the biblical traditions of the past into a form that would enable these traditions to be transmitted in such a way that their authoritative claims could be laid upon all successive generations.[39]

---

35. Childs, *Introduction*, pp. 75-76.
36. Parsons, 'Canonical', p. 259.
37. Childs, *Introduction*, p. 71.
38. Parsons, 'Canonical', p. 260.
39. In some ways this is similar to redaction criticism in that early textual editors sought to reshape or 'layer' the biblical texts in order to update or contemporize an older tradition. For a fuller discussion of Childs's canonical shaping, see Childs, *Introduction*, pp. 77-79. Perhaps a number of examples of canonical shaping can be

The New Testament as Canon: An Introduction (1984): Having written an introduction to the Old Testament completely committed to a canonical approach, Childs's next task was to verify whether or not his approach could be upheld and adequately applied to the New Testament as well. With the publication of *The New Testament as Canon*, Childs successfully accomplished what most Old Testament scholars would never undertake.[40] In keeping with his previous Old Testament publications, Childs shows remarkable insight and understanding into both New Testament background and exegesis. In this work, Childs provides his readers with the clearest expression to date of the canonical approach. Following a discussion of the role of canon in the New Testament, Childs gives further clarity to aspects such as historical criticism and canonical shaping. However, without doubt, the most important addition to this introduction is a small (and some would say inadequate) section dealing entirely with the methodology of his canonical approach. It is here that Childs begins to provide much needed answers to questions such as: How does the canonical approach affect exegesis? What factors, perspectives, or rules govern the study of individual books? How does one proceed? This methodology will be presented later in this chapter.

Criticism of Childs's Approach
At least two elements in Childs's canonical approach have attracted considerable criticism, and at times this criticism has been fervent and spirited. First, as was previously mentioned, Childs is accused of limiting historical criticism to such an extent that many claim he has abandoned the discipline. Some scholars insist that Childs's approach has completely turned its back upon the last two centuries of historical criticism, and, in fact, modern critical study of the Bible as a whole. To these individuals, it appears that Childs is re-advocating a precritical view of exegesis with its emphasis on the 'plain sense' of Scripture. Others feel that Childs has developed a domineering view of exegesis within his canonical approach. These scholars claim that Childs has sometimes appeared methodologically totalitarian in that he seems to overwhelm the entire interpretative discipline by pressing everyone into his service.

Secondly, Childs is also criticized by some who accuse him of not

observed in, but by no means restricted to, the following passages: Exod. 12.26ff.; Deut. 31.9; Jn 20.30-31; and Rev. 1.1-3.

40. B.S. Childs, *The New Testament as Canon: An Introduction* (Valley Forge, PA: Trinity Press International, rev. edn, 1994 [1984]).

really developing a new exegetical method after all, but instead, they claim that the canonical approach relies upon other such disciplines as: (1) biblical theology—with its focus upon the unique normativity of the Bible, (2) form criticism—with its stress upon literary genre and biblical forms and units, (3) redaction criticism—with its emphasis upon shaping and final form and (4) a number of the newer literary-critical methods— which push aside diachronic study and authorial intention in order to focus strictly upon the integrity of the text alone. In fact, a number of scholars conclude that when separated from the results of these disciplines, the canonical approach really does not add a great deal of new insight into exegetical methodology or biblical interpretation. While it may be true that change often encounters adversity, there is some truth to these criticisms leveled at Childs and his canonical approach. The legitimacy of these claims may be further highlighted as the discussion turns to the canonical process of James Sanders.

The Canonical Process of James Sanders
James A. Sanders is Elizabeth Hay Bechtel Professor of Intertestamental and Biblical Studies at the School of Theology, Claremont, California, Professor of Religion at the Claremont Graduate School, and President of the Ancient Biblical Manuscript Center in Claremont. In addition to his work on canonical criticism, he has labored extensively with the Qumran scrolls in assessing their importance and impact upon biblical studies.[41] Sanders's academic training has been rather diversified in its scope. Although he originally intended to pursue a doctoral degree in New Testament, he ended up earning, under the direction of the well-known Jewish scholar Samuel Sandmel, a PhD in Hebrew Bible and early Judaism.[42]

Whereas Childs explains his methodology as 'the canonical approach', in the attempt to distinguish it from historical and biblical criticism, Sanders eagerly embraces the term 'canonical criticism' in order to

41. For works of this nature by Sanders, see such articles as 'Palestinian Manuscripts 1947–1967', *JBL* 86 (1967), pp. 431-44; 'Palestinian Manuscripts 1947–72', *JJS* 24 (1973), pp. 74-83; *The Dead Sea Psalms Scroll* (Ithaca, NY: Cornell University Press, 1967); and *The Psalms Scroll of Qumran Cave 11 (11QPs^a)* (DJD, 4; Oxford: Clarendon Press, 1965).

42. For a fuller autobiographical statement by Sanders, and a current bibliography of his work in canonical criticism, see his book, *From Sacred Story to Sacred Text* (Philadelphia: Fortress Press, 1987), pp. 1-3, and 198-99 respectively.

show its necessary relationship to these various types of criticism. He states that:

> Canonical criticism is therefore not just another critical exercise. It is not only a logical evolution of earlier stages in the growth of criticism but it also reflects back on all the disciplines of biblical criticism and informs them all to some extent. Canonical criticism is dependent on all that has gone before in this line, but what has gone before may now be dependent to some extent on canonical criticism. If biblical criticism is to be redeemed from its own failings and from the serious charges being leveled against it, it should embrace this additional disciplinary and self-critical stance.[43]

Like Childs's canonical approach, Sanders's canonical process will also be discussed through a chronological presentation of his more important publications.

Torah and Canon (1972): Sanders explains that this book began as an attempt to look at the Bible holistically. He describes this as focusing upon the Bible's shape and function, rather than seeking its unity (as in biblical theology). In *Torah and Canon*, Sanders first called biblical scholars to the task of canonical criticism, which he defined as giving careful attention to the origins and function of canon as held in conjunction with biblical criticism.[44] At this point, Sanders's goal for canonical criticism was to pick up the results of source, form, and tradition criticism (which focus upon smaller biblical units), redaction criticism (which focuses upon larger biblical units), and comparative midrash by asking what the function or authority was of the ancient tradition in each context where it was cited.[45] How was the ancient tradition used in its new context? To what ends did the biblical writer put the story when he cited it? How did he apply it to the situation he describes? What were his

43. Sanders, *Canon*, p. 19.
44. Sanders, *Torah*, p. XV.
45. Comparative midrash is defined by Sanders as 'the function of an ancient or canonical tradition in the ongoing life of the community which preserves those traditions and in some sense finds its identity in them. When one studies how an ancient tradition functions in relation to the needs of the community, he is studying midrash. Any definition of midrash which limits its scope to the citation and use of an actual biblical passage is deficient... The New Testament is, in one perspective and to a limited degree, a compilation of midrashim on the Old Testament, the only ancient authority that the New Testament writers recognize or cite.' For further information, see Sanders, *Torah*, pp. xiv-xv, and the article by R. Le Deaut, 'A Definition of Midrash', *Int* 25 (1971), pp. 259-82.

hermeneutical rules? How did other biblical writers make use of the same tradition? Sanders uses canonical criticism to answer how and why the biblical books received the shape and form in which we inherit them. Sanders builds upon the premise that the ancient biblical writers and later editors specially shaped and formed the biblical material in order to furnish an interpretative 'timelessness' that would allow both them and successive generations to find their identity in the biblical texts. Through dynamic analogy and contemporization, the community sees its current tensions, between what it is and what it ought to be, in the tensions which Israel and the Early Church also experienced. By correctly reading the Bible the believing community sees itself on the same pilgrimage that Israel was making from its enslavements to its freedom.[46]

In *Torah and Canon*, Sanders took these concepts and applied them to a study of the Pentateuch. He questioned why the Torah ended with Deuteronomy (thus forming the Pentateuch) and not Joshua (thus forming the Hexateuch). Most of the ancient biblical traditions and early Jewish credal statements which tell of God's blessing and promise to the Patriarchal fathers commence with the exodus from Egypt and consummate in the conquest of Canaan (Exod. 15.1ff.; Deut. 6.20ff.; 26.5ff.; 33.1ff.; Josh. 24.2ff.). Why then was the book of Joshua—which records the ultimate fulfillment of God's promise and blessing through the giving of the promised land to his people—excluded from the other books of the Torah? With Joshua's absence from the Torah, not only does this form an unnatural end to the story, but the Torah completely reinterprets Israel's foundational traditions. There is no fulfillment to God's promises in the Torah. Instead, God's people, who are now without their leader Moses, are left encamped in the enemy territory of Moab without the blessing of the promised land. How could this be? Sanders, relying upon the past work of historical critics, extends canonical criticism from their insights and offers an answer to the dilemma. Utilizing the results of source, form, and especially redaction criticism, Sanders presents the possible theory that the final editing of the Torah was accomplished by a group of Priestly editors exiled in Babylon during the sixth century BCE. By focusing upon the canonical shape of the Torah, Sanders explains that these editors purposely excluded the book of Joshua, thereby truncating the original Torah account, in order to contemporize it for themselves and future genera-tions. For the exiles in Babylon, who no longer possessed their promised

46. Sanders, *Torah*, pp. xv-xvi.

land and who had, therefore, lost their basis of identity, the old readings of the Torah which included the book of Joshua would, no doubt, be of little, if any comfort. With Joshua placed outside the Torah, thus forming the Pentateuch, the Priestly editors afforded a new interpretation of the past traditions by placing the fulfillment of the promise of a homeland in the future. The canonical Torah redirected Israel's emphasis and basis for identity from the land which they had lost, and placed it upon the law, which they could never lose.

Canon and Community: A Guide to Canonical Criticism (1984): In *Canon and Community*, Sanders takes his earlier work and fashions it into two major foci.[47] The first focus, which can be clearly seen in and extending from *Torah and Canon*, he calls the 'canonical process'. Whereas Childs emphasizes the primary importance of the biblical texts in their final form, Sanders draws attention to the various earlier steps of textual and canonical development that gave rise to this final form. In Sanders's view of canonical criticism the final form is an important stage; however, despite it being the last stage of canonization, it is only one of many previous stages.

The second focus that Sanders emphasizes, and that which is most helpful for an understanding of his methodology, is not unrelated to the canonical process. 'Canonical hermeneutics' is that task undertaken by the current believing community whereby they seek to get in touch with their ancestors in the faith who formed and shaped the canon. This is accomplished by tracing the history of function of a community tradition, or in other words, studying the pattern of interpretation that the ancient communities used in adapting their Scriptures for us.[48] In order to perform this task, which Sanders notes is both diachronic and synchronic in perspective, he develops what he calls the 'triangle'.[49] The triangle, which is simply a hermeneutical model, is reproduced below, along with a brief summary of Sanders's explanation:

47. See Sanders, *Canon*.

48. For this point, see also Parsons, 'Canonical', p. 265.

49. This triangle, along with its canonical hermeneutic, was previously developed by Sanders in his work entitled 'Hermeneutics in True and False Prophecy', in G.W. Coats and B.O. Long (eds.), *Canon and Authority: Essays in Old Testament Religion and Authority* (Philadelphia: Fortress Press, 1977). The triangle has also been reproduced in the fifth chapter of Sanders's book *Sacred Story*.

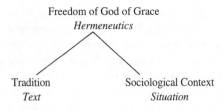

Freedom of God of Grace
Hermeneutics

Tradition   Sociological Context
Text   *Situation*

Sanders explains that the bottom left angle represents the tradition or text being called upon, recited, or alluded to, both in antiquity and in our modern reading of Scripture. Emphasis here is placed upon the careful discernment of meanings in a text's literary context. All the applicable tools of biblical criticism are needed here.[50]

The bottom right angle of the triangle represents the historical and sociological context being addressed, again, both in antiquity and in modern times, according to what the focus of interest or study may be. Emphasis here is placed upon careful discernment of sociological context and the needs of the people being addressed. Once more, all the pertinent tools of historical criticism are needed. It is here that we attempt the careful recovery of the situations of our ancestors in the faith, those believing communities which found value in the traditions and shaped them into canon. Sanders notes that it is as important to discern and exegete the sociological context as it is to exegete the text.[51]

And finally, the top angle represents the hermeneutics by which the tradition functions in the contexts of both past and present communities. Emphasis here is placed upon the careful discernment of the canonical hermeneutics used in the ancient canonical process that provide the necessary guidelines and boundaries of modern interpretation. Sanders concludes by stating that canonical criticism focuses especially upon the unrecorded hermeneutics which lie in and between all the lines of biblical texts. It is the hermeneutics used which determine, in large measure, the meaning of the text.[52]

From Sacred Story to Sacred Text (1987): This book consists of nine previously published essays written by Sanders from 1975–1980.[53] A tenth essay, which forms the climax of the book, is presented here for the first time. Perhaps the most recent addition to Sanders's canonical

50. Sanders, *Canon*, pp. 77-78.
51. Sanders, *Canon*, p. 78.
52. Sanders, *Canon*, p. 78.
53. See Sanders, *Sacred Story*.

process is his definition of canonical criticism as a 'theocentric monotheizing hermeneutic'. This concept, which had its birth in *Torah and Canon* and was further elaborated upon in *Canon and Community*, constitutes the heart of Sanders's tenth and final essay in *From Sacred Story to Sacred Text*. By utilizing this theocentric monotheizing hermeneutic, Sanders emphasizes that the Bible, rather than being poly-theistic literature, is instead monotheistic literature. However, the nation of Israel, in keeping with her ancient neighbors who thought in poly-theistic terms, often tended to be a polytheizing people who struggled in attempting to monotheize against this cultural norm. Sanders explains that the Bible may be viewed as the result of many efforts over 1500–1800 years to monotheize in the face of this massive cultural backdrop of polytheism. In fact, he claims that this is the Bible's principle and basic hermeneutic shape. Not only was it difficult for ancient Israel to monotheize, but as Sanders states, the human psyche has not changed in this regard but still finds it hard to monotheize even today. Therefore, to monotheize is to engage in a resistance movement against a dominant mode of thinking, whether in biblical antiquity or in the present. It is this theocentric monotheizing that allows the modern believing community to contemporize the Bible for new situations in ways that run parallel to the ancient believers that preceded us. In obeying the canonical mandate to monotheize, the believing community unites both descriptive (what the text meant) and constructive theology (what the text means), and therefore, like Childs, Sanders believes that he is able to overcome the problems created by biblical theology and historical criticism.

Criticism of Sanders's Process

Sanders's canonical process is criticized to a much lower degree than the canonical approach of Childs. This is undoubtedly due to Sanders's more acceptable amalgamation of historical and canonical criticism, whereas Childs chooses to distance the two disciplines, often at the expense of historical criticism. However, Sanders's canonical methodo-logy is not without its own problems. The primary contention brought against his methodology is its subjective and highly speculative nature. Sanders's various reconstructions of the canonical process, although thought-provoking and interesting, are often criticized for their lack of objective proof and support, which is admittedly difficult to find in the study of canon. In light of this, many feel that Sanders's reconstructions of the canonical process, which form the heart of his methodology, lack the substance upon which to build a new method of biblical criticism and exegesis. Furthermore, Sanders's explanation that it was Israel's need for identity that brought upon the canonical shaping of the biblical texts, and his presentation of concepts such as stability and adaptability, are again criticized for their subjectivity and for ignoring other possible interpretations. Perhaps one final attack directed at Sanders is his lack of explanation as to how the various tenets of canon criticism fit and function together. His emphasis upon canonical process, canonical hermeneutics, and theocentric monotheizing often seem to constitute three different methodologies rather than one integrated interpretative approach.

A Comparison of Childs and Sanders
Often confusion arises among those trying to understand canonical criticism because they too closely try to associate the differing views of Childs and Sanders. Robert Wall clarifies why these two methodologies cannot be completely integrated:

> The differences between Childs and Sanders should not be minimized or their approaches collapsed together under the rubric 'canonical criticism'. Childs views the canon *qua* static text, sacred in its final form. His approach necessarily is more literary, ahistorical and 'Protestant'. Sanders on the other hand approaches the canon *qua* dynamic tradition. The Bible is understood as the deposit of a community's struggle with its identity; its religious function is as a paradigm of how the current church should respond to God in its ongoing and analogous struggles. Sanders's approach, then, is necessarily more historical, pastoral and 'catholic'.[54]

This quotation reveals several of the numerous differences that exist between Childs and Sanders. As has been emphasized, Childs separates his canonical approach from historical criticism, while Sanders openly embraces the numerous disciplines of historical criticism. This is one foundational difference between the two scholars. A second distinction that separates these two individuals is Childs's emphasis upon *product* versus Sanders's emphasis upon *process*. This is also explained in terms of Childs's synchronic focus (interpretation based upon the text itself and its final form) versus Sanders's diachronic focus (interpretation based upon the historical setting of the text, its origin, and its process of transmission). Whereas Childs places exegetical stress upon the final

54. R.W. Wall and E.E. Lemcio, *The New Testament as Canon: A Reader in Canonical Criticism* (JSNTSup, 76; Sheffield: JSOT Press, 1992), p. 142 n. 2.

form of the text, which is the end result of the canonical process, Sanders tends to highlight the actual canonical process that gave us the final texts. Thus Childs is said to base his canonical approach upon synchronic interpretation, while Sanders bases his canonical process more fully upon diachronic interpretation.

One last area of difference that exists between Childs and Sanders, in direct relation to the above considerations, deals with the area of hermeneutics. Childs's canonical approach, with its stress upon the final canonical text, places hermeneutical emphasis upon this final biblical form. For Childs, it is the Bible in its final textual form that must act as the focal point for the modern church's interpretation. Sanders's canonical process places hermeneutical emphasis upon the various ways in which biblical writers called upon, recited, or alluded to the Torah/Gospel story along its path towards final canonization. For Sanders, modern interpretation must focus upon this historical process because it is here, especially, that one discovers the decisive clues in how to use the Bible in the church's life. In order to give further clarity to the differences between Childs and Sanders, the following chart seeks to place their methodologies on a canonical continuum set within the wide realm of biblical study and criticism.[55]

Despite these differences that clearly separate Childs and Sanders, they do hold in common a number of foundational concepts regarding canonical criticism. Perhaps it is from this mutual platform that all future inquiries into canonical considerations will be launched. First, both Childs and Sanders agree that historical criticism, as practiced in the past, has fallen into bankruptcy and is in need of some type of corrective. This corrective is to come in the form of a new exegetical method—some form of canonical criticism. Secondly, both agree that the biblical canon, whether in its canonizing process or in its final form, must act as the primary basis of hermeneutics and exegetical interpretation. Thirdly, both scholars wish to see the Bible returned to its normative position and function within the believing community of faith. It is in this

---

55. It should be noted that this continuum represents the differing methodologies of Childs and Sanders only in a general manner. It is designed to give the reader a broad allocation of the two scholars' approaches within biblical criticism, and should not be interpreted as a hard and firm placement. In some respects, Childs and Sanders may even disagree with the corresponding placement of their respective views; however it does relate, in a general manner, their methodologies and those of similar substance and praxis.

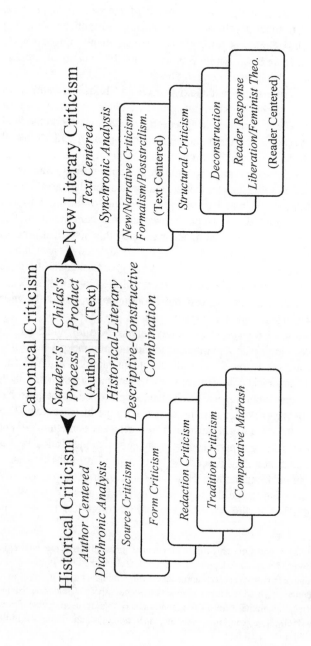

Canonical Criticism

Historical Criticism ◄───── Sanders's | Childs's ─────► New Literary Criticism
Author Centered   Process | Product   Text Centered
Diachronic Analysis   (Author) | (Text)   Synchronic Analysis

                    Historical-Literary
                    Descriptive-Constructive
                    Combination

Historical Criticism side:
- Source Criticism
- Form Criticism
- Redaction Criticism
- Tradition Criticism
- Comparative Midrash

New Literary Criticism side:
- New/Narrative Criticism Formalism/Poststrcltism. (Text Centered)
- Structural Criticism
- Deconstruction
- Reader Response Liberation/Feminist Theo. (Reader Centered)

environment that the biblical texts were first given shape, form, and meaning, and, therefore, reciprocally provided shape, form, and meaning in those communities that found in them their identity and the very meaning of life. Fourthly, Childs and Sanders both see canonical criticism as having a theological focus. The Bible witnesses primarily to a theological reality rather than a historical reality. To see the Bible as a source for the history of religion rather than a theological document is to erroneously understand its central function.

Other Practitioners of Canonical Criticism

The canonical interests of both Brevard Childs and James Sanders have been examined in some detail within this essay. However, although these two scholars have been recognized as the chief figures in the development of canonical criticism, other individuals have made considerable contributions to the field as well, and deserve recognition. Mark Brett has endeavored to balance and extend Childs's canonical approach, and in so doing, has brought further credibility to it.[56] James Dunn has taken the discussion between Childs, Sanders, and other Old Testament scholars, and has placed it into the realm of New Testament studies.[57] Both F.A. Spina and Gerald Sheppard have written helpful works that seek to compare and somewhat amalgamate the views of Childs and Sanders.[58] Mikeal Parsons's essay has opened canonical criticism up to a broader audience due to its thorough, articulate summary and application of the discipline.[59] The ongoing and outstanding work of Robert Wall and Eugene Lemcio has perhaps been the most faithful and concentrated effort to apply canonical criticism to the New Testament.[60] Wall and Lemcio have sought to synthesize and extend the work of

---

56. See above Brett's *Biblical Criticism*.

57. J.D.G. Dunn, 'Levels of Canonical Authority', *HBT* 4 (1982), pp. 13-60.

58. F.A Spina, 'Canonical Criticism: Childs Versus Sanders', in W. McCown and J.E. Masset (eds.), *Interpreting God's Word for Today: An Inquiry into Hermeneutics from a Biblical-Theological Perspective* (Anderson, IN: Warner, 1982), pp. 165-94; and G. Sheppard, 'Canonical Criticism', in the *Anchor Bible Dictionary* (New York: Doubleday, 1992), I, pp. 861-86.

59. See above Parsons's essay 'Canonical'.

60. See above Wall and Lemcio's *New Testament* and R. Wall's forthcoming chapter entitled 'Reading the New Testament in Canonical Context', in J.B. Green (ed.), *Hearing the New Testament: Strategies for Interpretation* (Grand Rapids: Eerdmans, 1995).

Childs and Sanders, and in so doing have articulated a number of thoughtful and exciting considerations.

4. *Canonical Methodology*

Those seeking to understand canonical criticism have often encountered a considerable amount of confusion. This puzzlement has resulted not only because the discipline offers differing methodologies, but also because these methodologies are far from rigorously explained. How does canonical criticism affect actual exegesis? What are the principles, guidelines, and rules for canonical interpretation? How does one proceed to incorporate canonical criticism in order to understand the biblical texts? Unfortunately, these questions have not been adequately dealt with by canonical critics, and more than one scholar echoes something of the following words:

> …Childs himself has failed to provide a coherent exegetical theory. That is to say, he has not yet provided a sufficiently clear and explicit discussion of the interpretative interests and concepts that shape the canonical approach. This lack of coherent theory has turned out to be one of the major obstacles to a balanced appreciation of his work.[61]

This criticism is equally worthy of Sanders as it is of Childs.[62] Suffice it to say, at this point in the study of canonical criticism, explanations of the discipline's methodology seem to emphasize more a particular perspective from which one reads the biblical texts, rather than a helpful explanation of clear and concise systematic procedures. And although this is beginning to change, canonical criticism, at present, functions more as a foundational assumption from which one begins exegesis, rather than as a development of actual principles and methodologies that aid one in performing exegesis from a canonical standpoint.[63] Regardless

---

61. Brett, *Biblical Criticism*, p. 27. See also Barr's criticism in *Holy Scripture*, pp. 133-34.

62. The following figures may serve to emphasize the point. In Childs's *New Testament*, only six of over five-hundred and fifty pages are devoted specifically to a concentrated explanation of methodology (pp. 48-53). In Sanders's *Canon*, only two of seventy-eight pages are given directly to a concentrated methodological presentation (pp. 77-78).

63. It is essential to note that canonical criticism does not necessarily propagate a new method of doing exegesis. Instead, canonical criticism attempts to accomplish biblical exegesis by focusing on the final textual form (thus Childs), and the process

of the present methodological dilemma, this chapter will now attempt to explicate the principles and tenets of canonical criticism as defined by Childs with his emphasis upon the final form of the text, and, as defined by Sanders, with his attention to the canonical process.

Childs's Product: The Final Canonical Form[64]

For Childs, interpretation begins with the final canonical form of the Bible. The pre-history and post-history of the text are subordinated to this final form. Childs's focus upon the final canonical form as his basis for exegesis can be broken down into two primary areas, the first being canonical shape and the second being canonical placement or position.

1. Canonical Shape (Immediate Context)

Canonical shaping attempts to discover traces within the text itself as to how the biblical author intended the material to be understood. Canonical shaping takes seriously the author's expressed intentions. At this point, exegetical considerations focus upon one particular biblical book, or the smaller units that make up that book (i.e. immediate context). One scholar has applied the term 'micro-canonical analysis' to this task.[65] Childs provides a description of several key principles or methods that might serve as indicators of canonical shaping, and thereby reveal matters such as authorial intention.

a. *Structure of the book.* The structure of the book, Childs remarks, is one of the first places the reader ought to look for indications of canonical shaping. He adds that 'the formal means by which the material is ordered affects the content of the book in an integral way'.[66] Therefore, an understanding of the book's structure is vital to the comprehension of its content. Childs states further that any analysis of the structure which, in fact, eliminates portions of the book should be viewed with suspicion.[67] In this regard, the book of Philippians provides

of canonization (thus Sanders). It is often the procedures which govern this 'canonical exegesis' which lack coherent explanation.

64. This section makes extensive reference to Childs's chapter entitled 'Methodology of Canonical Exegesis', in *New Testament*, pp. 48-53.

65. Donn F. Morgan first uses this term in his article entitled 'Canon and Criticism: Method or Madness?', *ATR* 68 (1986), pp. 83-94, esp. p. 87.

66. Childs, *New Testament*, p. 49.

67. Childs, *New Testament*, p. 49.

a good example. Debate concerning the apparent disunity of Philippians has led some scholars to conclude that the book actually consists of a combination of at least three separate letters. Whereas historical criticism, especially redaction criticism, focuses upon why the book's editors gave Philippians its particular final shape, Childs's canonical approach would stress interpretation based upon this final shape and form of the biblical text, just as previous communities of faith have done. It is the final form that has acted as the normative basis for providing meaning within believing generations. Other such New Testament books as 2 Corinthians would be treated in like manner.[68]

b. *Prescripts, conclusions, and titles.* 'The purpose of the author', says Childs', 'is often most clearly stated in the prescript, or in the conclusion'.[69] Perhaps the two clearest New Testament prescripts are those found in Lk. 1.1-4 and Acts 1.1-5. The Lukan prescript informs the reader that the author wrote for the following reason: 'Therefore, since I myself have carefully investigated everything from the beginning, it seemed good also to me to write an orderly account for you, most excellent Theophilus, so that you may know the certainty of the things you have been taught'. The prescript in Acts stems directly from its Lukan counterpart and even provides an important and concise summary of the author's message in Luke. Childs also explains that the lack of a prescript in a book can often give important clues as to how it now functions. The most obvious example here is the book of Hebrews. Its lack of a definite prescript has occasioned ambiguity over the authorship and background of the book, and in turn, this ambiguity has posed numerous difficulties for interpretation. Although authorship was most often ascribed to the apostle Paul for some 1200 years, since the Reformation this has been widely contested. One of the arguments against Pauline authorship is the very fact that Hebrews omits a prescript, whereas one common feature among Paul's writings is the inclusion of a prescript in which he identifies himself.[70]

The concluding words of a book often provide a summary of the

68. See Childs's discussion of Philippians for these very points in *New Testament*, pp. 331-37. See also Childs's discussion of 2 Corinthians and its canonical shape in *New Testament*, pp. 291-96; and Parsons's explanation of 2 Corinthians in 'Canonical', pp. 275-76.

69. Childs, *New Testament*, p. 49.

70. See also Parsons's discussion of the Ephesians prescript, 'Canonical', p. 276.

author's key thoughts and purpose, as well as clues to the overall canonical setting. In the conclusion of the book of John (20.31), the author records his purpose with these words: 'But these are written that you may believe that Jesus is the Christ, the Son of God, and that by believing you may have life in his name'.[71] Such conclusions as the closing words of Col. 4.7-18 provide the reader with clues to the canonical setting. Here one finds not only information relating to the specific situation and setting of the author and his companions (imprisonment), but also instructions for the reading of Paul's letter, and similarities with personalities mentioned in Philemon—perhaps matters of consequence in considering authenticity and epistolary canonization.

Along with structure, prescripts, and conclusions, consideration of a book's title can also supply additional clues as to its canonical shape. Although not part of the original autographs, titles, having likely been included or added in the last stages of the canonizing process, often provide insight into the overall function of the book and its use in defining faith and life in the early believing communities. Although the book of Hebrews is without a prescript, its early title, which reads 'The Epistle of Paul the Apostle to the Hebrews', was likely added in the early second century in order to aid it through the canonizing process and to ensure its final place within the Pauline corpus. Numerous scholars have been critical of the title because the book of Hebrews itself does not follow the traditional literary form of an epistle, its claim of Pauline authorship is highly contested, and the Hebrew addressee cannot be confirmed by the content of the book. Therefore, these scholars all but negate the role of the title for interpretation. The canonical approach, however, seeks to make sense out of the title because it reveals something of the canonical placement of Hebrews at the end of the Pauline corpus but just prior to the General Epistles.[72] The title also provides additional clues relating to the book's function and role in the early Christian church.[73]

71. Based upon the results of literary criticism, numerous scholars conclude that ch. 21 of John is a later addition. Both Jn 20.30-31 and 21.24-25, they would claim, indicate that ch. 21 was added to the already finished Gospel. Again, canonical criticism would stress looking at the book of John in its final canonical form, thus including ch. 21. See Childs, *New Testament*, pp. 141-42.

72. It should be noted that P[46], the second Chester Beatty biblical papyrus, places Hebrews before 1 and 2 Corinthians. This discrepancy regarding the canonical placement of particular books will be dealt with later in the chapter.

73. See also Parsons's explanation of the book of Hebrews, 'Canonical', pp. 276-77.

c. *Role of addressee.* 'A frequent indication of how the New Testament seeks to transcend its original historical context', says Childs, 'lies in carefully observing the function of the addressee of a composition'.[74] At times the original disciples are portrayed in their historical context. In these instances, it is only through what Childs calls 'subtle analogies' that the later readers and church universal are addressed. On other occasions, the disciples become an 'obvious transparency' through which the biblical message is to be applied to succeeding communities of faith. Childs also notes that often the change from a singular form to a plural form, such as 'I' to 'we', denotes a shift in the scope of the audience.[75]

d. *Matter of authorship.* Although not directly related to canonical shaping, one should mention authorship as an important consideration within the canonical approach. Yet Childs makes sure to clarify that canonical questions dealing with authorship do not follow along the same lines as the traditional arguments between 'conservatives and liberals'. In dealing particularly with Ephesians and the Pastoral Epistles, Childs is at ease with the concept of pseudonymity. He allows for this by distinguishing between the 'historical' Paul, the actual personage of history whom Ephesians and the Pastorals reveal little of, and the 'canonical' Paul, who is clearly seen in these books. For Childs, it is not the Paul of history, but the Paul of the canon who brings the community to faith. Canonical criticism, Childs states, 'seeks to explore the role of a canonical portrait of Paul...which is only partially congruent with a critical reconstruction of the historical apostles.'[76]

2. *Canonical Placement or Position (Broader Context)*
Whereas canonical shaping places exegetical emphasis upon one particular biblical book or the smaller units that make up that book, canonical

---

74. Childs, *New Testament*, p. 52.

75. One of Childs's clearest applications of this point concerns the 'we' passages of Acts where he states that the use of the first person plural 'serves to bridge the gap between the original author and the subsequent reader'. See Childs, *New Testament*, p. 234. See also Childs's example for 1 John, on pp. 485-86. Likewise, Wall uses this type of principle in his evaluation of Jas 4.13–5.6. See Wall, 'Reading the New Testament in Canonical Context'.

76. Childs, *New Testament*, p. 52. Childs's distinction between the 'canonical' author and the 'historical' author is somewhat problematic. This issue of authorship will be discussed more extensively later in the chapter.

placement or position draws interpretational insights from where a given book is placed or positioned in relationship to the other books within the canon. Childs claims that 'At times the larger corpus exerts a major influence by establishing a different context from that of a single composition'.[77] The term 'macro-canonical analysis' has been used to define this broader canonical context.[78] By reading a book holistically, that is, within its broader canonical context, valuable insights can be gained that assist the interpreter in his task. Robert Wall has articulately and extensively commented on this facet of canonical criticism:

> The shaping of the New Testament reflects the actual practice of the church, which came to recognize after a period of some time (two or three centuries) that particular collection of inspired writings, arranged in such a way as to maximize its usefulness, as the rule of Christian faith for the formation of the faithful. While the interpreter should not place too much importance on the order of writings within the New Testament, such a perspective does allow one to construct...an overarching 'canon-logic' that provides an added dimension of meaning to the whole New Testament and to individual compositions within it.[79]

The longer ending of Mark's Gospel, when seen in relationship to the other three Gospels, serves to illustrate this point. Textual criticism has utilized the criteria of both external and internal evidence in order to verify that Mark's longer ending is most likely a later addition to the text. Whereas modern scholarship has tended to discard the longer ending of Mark because of its apparent late addition to the earliest biblical witnesses, canonical criticism, especially when considering matters of canonical placement, has attributed significance to these passages and the early tradition they represent. Childs notes: 'If from a historical perspective Mark's Gospel provided the primary source for Matthew and Luke, there is at least one highly important example within the canonical process of the reverse influence at work'.[80] Instead of discrediting the longer ending as historical criticism has tended to do, Childs claims, no doubt controversially, that canonical criticism with its emphasis upon placement and position attempts to make sense out of these passages in the larger context of all four Gospels. One seeks to understand what role

77. Childs, *New Testament*, p. 52.
78. Morgan, 'Madness', p. 88.
79. Wall and Lemcio, *New Testament*, p. 279.
80. Childs, *New Testament*, p. 94.

Mark plays in its final canonical form and the context of the community of faith.

Further considerations of canonical positioning have also sought to address issues such as how the Gospel of Matthew serves to unite the Old and New Testaments, whether Acts was separated from Luke in order to form a natural bridge between the Gospels and the Pauline letters, and what canonical role the Pastoral Epistles played within the larger context of the Pauline corpus.

Numerous scholars have criticized this emphasis upon canonical position, and there is validity to their concern.[81] Canonical criticism must not only face the results of textual criticism, but must also consider the question of which canon is to be adopted as the basis for providing the broader canonical context. For the Old Testament, should it be the Masoretic text, the Greek Septuagint, or the Christian Old Testament? For the New Testament, does one adopt the Protestant canon, the Catholic canon, or the Coptic canon? And these represent only a few of the options available. The problem is even further compounded when one considers the unlimited number of translations. Despite the fact that these issues continue to be somewhat problematic in the development of a mature canonical methodology, there is hope and good reason to believe that they will be resolved. Scholarly criticism continues to aid the canonical critic in developing a sound methodology.

Sanders's Process: Historical Canonization

One should not think of Sanders's canonical process in the same terms as Childs's canonical approach. Sanders's methodology cannot be as clearly outlined as has been Childs's methodology. It has not been Sanders's task to provide a historical reconstruction of the complete canonical process. It has not been his goal to formalize a method that, through consistent application, supplies the exegete with interpretational insights recovered from an investigation into the canonizing process of Scripture. Instead, he has utilized the tools of historical criticism in order, through informed speculation, scholarly inference, and creative reconstruction, to explain how an understanding of the canonical process provides hermeneutical clues for the modern interpreter and the community of faith as they seek to contemporize the message of the Bible. What Sanders has done with the canonical process is unique and based

81. For example, see Tuckett, *Reading*, p. 182 n. 11; and J. Barr, 'Childs' Introduction to the Old Testament as Scripture', *JSOT* 16 (1980), p. 22.

somewhat on individualistic subjectivity, rather than upon a firmly established methodology. In other words, Sanders does not provide his readers with a consistent methodological basis that allows one to determine the hermeneutical insights gleaned throughout the historical process of canonization. Sanders's 'Triangle' does not form a concerted effort to provide this methodological outline. Instead, in Sanders's own words, the triangle 'helps the searcher keep in mind the necessary and essential interrelatedness of the three major factors [tradition and text, sociological context and situation, and hermeneutics] *always* involved in the canonical process...'[82] These factors are largely revealed through the application of historical criticism. Even then, Sanders states, 'Unfortunately, there are not enough clear data at some points along that path to fill in what is needed at the three points of the triangle'.[83] The presentation of Sanders's canonical process is further compounded in the New Testament, as Sanders has not clearly applied his canonical process to these texts.[84] Sanders concludes that:

> The principal tools of canonical criticism are tradition history and comparative midrash, with constant attention to the hermeneutics which caused the authoritative tradition being traced to function in the sociological context where repeated or recited. It is tracing the history of function of a community tradition or a wisdom tradition that puts the current believing communities in touch with their ancestors in the faith who formed and shaped the canon. The perspective is both diachronic and synchronic. The focus is the canonical process.[85]

Again, Sanders stresses that the history of a book's canonizing process often reveals insights into the history of its interpretation. These insights can then be employed in order to provide exegetical guidelines for the contemporization, interpretation, and application of the biblical texts in today's believing communities. The canonical process and formation of the Bible have long been an area of interest to biblical scholars. A number of valuable works have been written on the subject,

82. Sanders, *Canon*, p. 77.
83. Sanders, *Canon*, p. 77.
84. In this respect, the work of Wall and Lemcio has served as an extension of Sanders's canonical process. Both scholars have provided pertinent exegetical insights taken from their consideration of the New Testament canonical process. These insights are then applied by Wall and Lemcio to the interpretation of the biblical texts in a contemporary context. See examples in Wall and Lemcio, *New Testament*.
85. Sanders, *Canon*, p. 77.

and should be consulted when relating the canonical process to canonical criticism.[86]

Although the relationship between Sanders's canonical process and Childs's canonical approach is presently in dispute, not only by canonical critics but by historical critics as well, it is clear in the minds of some scholars that considerations of the canonical process must be included in what might be called the broader discipline of canonical criticism. Whether this is right or wrong must yet be hammered out; nevertheless, Sanders's process in some ways acts as a precursor to Childs's approach. And although they cannot be easily or simplistically amalgamated, their relationship must be wrestled with and further established. Perhaps the scholarly consensus will eventually conclude that both methodologies should continue as separate entities. However, it seems more likely that to deny the canonical process a place within canonical criticism would be to discard a potentially valuable interpretational tool.

5. *A Canonical Reading of John's Apocalypse*

This section applies canonical criticism to a reading of the book of Revelation. It should be stated at the onset, however, that the scope of this chapter does not permit an exhaustive assessment of a canonical reading of Revelation. Instead, this section will serve to paint a number of broad, yet colorful, brush strokes upon the canvas of canonical criticism in the hopes of revealing several of the disciplines' more foundational considerations and techniques when used as a method of biblical exegesis. Elements from both Childs's canonical approach and Sanders's canonical process will be directly incorporated into the discussion. However, the work of Wall and Lemcio will be used to define and extend Sanders's insights since they, probably more than any other canonical critics, stress the importance of incorporating Sanders's process into Childs's product, and have provided balanced and insightful examples of this amalgamation. For Wall and Lemcio, both canonical process and canonical product are constitutive of the entire field of canonical criticism.

Wall brilliantly summarizes the dilemma encountered by the believing

---

86. See the formidable collection of books discussing canon such as those by K. Aland, W. Barclay, F.F. Bruce, H. von Campenhausen, H.Y. Gamble, E.J. Goodspeed, A. von Harnack, E. Käsemann, J. Knox, B.M. Metzger, C.F.D. Moule, R.E. Reuss, A. Souter, and B.F. Westcott.

community of faith that seeks to use the book of Revelation in order to inform its faith (orthodoxy) and life (orthopraxy):

> More often than not, the church has treated Revelation as an esoteric writing, whose meaning is found by cipher and, if found at all, is located outside of history or at its very end. Modern scholarship has hardly done better, preferring to locate Revelation's meaning in the first century... Few have tried to relate Revelation in any practical way to the current life and faith of God's people... Few have tried to read Revelation as a canonical book, whose message while shaped by first century contingencies continues to effect an important model for understanding faith today. As a result, few try to make meaning of Revelation in ways which cohere with the church's intent for its canon.[87]

Although canonical criticism cannot, nor should it make claim to solve all the problems of biblical interpretation, especially those inherent to John's Apocalypse, the issues presented by Wall can be addressed by looking at the book of Revelation through the eyes of a canonical critic. This requires attention to the three previously mentioned considerations: (1) Canonization of Revelation (canonical process), (2) Canonical position of Revelation (broader context), and (3) Canonical shape of Revelation (immediate context).

Canonization of Revelation (Canonical Process)
The Christian community has struggled throughout the centuries to make sense of the book of Revelation's prophetic message and to make application of its 'hidden truths'. The history of its canonization is equally problematic, and this is without doubt the result of the Early Church's battle in deciding upon its usefulness. The respected Roman Presbyter Gaius, whom Eusebius (265–339 CE) claimed was a 'very learned man' (*Hist. eccl.* 6.20.3), rejected Revelation as canonical when in the early third century he firmly denounced the apocalyptic views of the Montanists and their ecstatic use of the book.[88] Sometime between 315–40 CE, Eusebius himself placed Revelation in both his 'ὁμολογούμενοι' (list of universally-accepted canonical books) and his 'νόθοι' (list of spurious noncanonical books), thus showing something of Revelation's divided acceptance. Metzger rightly explains Eusebius's motives for including the Apocalypse under two differing classes:

87. Wall and Lemcio, *New Testament*, p. 274.
88. B.M. Metzger, *The Canon of the New Testament* (Oxford: Clarendon Press, 1987), pp. 104-105.

As a historian Eusebius recognizes that it is widely received, but as a churchman he has become annoyed by the extravagant use made of this book by Montanists and other millenarians, and so is glad to report elsewhere in his history that others consider it to be not genuine.[89]

On the other hand, Hippolytus (c. 200–35 CE) entered into the controversy by disagreeing with the Roman Christian Gaius, and accepted Revelation as canonical. The patristic writer Irenaeus of Lyons (c. 180 CE) quotes extensively from the book in his *Adversus Haereses (Against Heresies)*. Similar to Irenaeus is Theophilus, the Bishop of Antioch (c. 200–35 CE), who used the book in order to refute the heretical claims of Hermogenes. Cyprian, Bishop of Carthage, who was martyred in 258 CE, freely refers to John's Apocalypse. Origen (185–254 CE) not only accepts the work as canonical but firmly attests to its authentic authorship by John the Apostle. And the Latin Father Tertullian, who would later join the Montanist sect, uses Revelation in the mid-second century CE to combat Marcion's heresies.

Clearly the strongest opposition to Revelation's inclusion in the canon comes from the Eastern church. Cyril of Jerusalem (c. 315–86 CE), Gregory of Nazianzus (329–89 CE), and Amphilochius of Iconium (after 394 CE) all rejected the use of the Apocalypse. In like fashion, John Chrysostom (c. 347–407 CE), the remarkable exegete from the school of Antioch, resolutely rejected the book of Revelation, and, therefore, held a canon identical to the Peshitta—the Syriac version used in Antioch at this time. Theodoret (c. 393–466 CE), a later successor of Chrysostom at the Antioch school, likewise held to a Bible resembling the Syriac Peshitta. In fact, the earliest Bible in the Eastern Syrian church, Tatian's Diatessaron, excluded the book of Revelation from its pages. In Armenia, the first kingdom to accept Christianity as its official religion, the Armenian church no later than the fifth century CE placed Revelation in the apocryphal Acts of John, thereby denying its canonicity until the twelfth century.[90] The Georgian church followed suit, doing without the Apocalypse until St Euthymius translated it from either Greek or Armenian in the tenth century. Even today, some Nestorian churches and the Greek Orthodox Church of the East follow the Peshitta, and, therefore, exclude Revelation from their canon of Scripture. However, the issue has not always been so 'cut and dried' for the Eastern church. To complicate matters in the East, there were a

89. Metzger, *Canon*, p. 205.
90. Metzger, *Canon*, p. 223.

number of important churchmen who did accept the canonicity of Revelation. The expositions of Didymus the Blind (c. 398 CE) include quotations from John's Apocalypse, and thus at least reveal its usefulness to him if not its canonical status. More significantly, Athanasius of Alexandria (c. 296–373 CE), the most prominent fourth-century theologian, includes Revelation in a canon that is, for the first time, identical to the same twenty-seven canonical books of today. As well, both the early Coptic (Bohairic) church and the Ethiopic church accepted Revelation as canonical Scripture.

The Western church does not fare any better in its decision-making regarding the canonicity of the Apocalypse. Lucifer of Calaris (d. 370 CE), Ambrose of Milan (339–97 CE), and Tyrannius Rufinus of Aquileia (c. 345–410 CE) all consider the book to be canonical, while others like Philaster, Bishop of Brescia (d. c. 397 CE), lists the Scriptures of the New Testament without including Revelation.[91] Jerome (c. 346–420 CE), the great scholar and writer of the Vulgate, includes Revelation in his New Testament, yet in a letter dated 414 CE he claims that the Apocalypse, along with Hebrews, is still disputed by some. It should be noted that Jerome, like Athanasius, includes in his New Testament the same twenty-seven canonical books of today. Augustine (354–430 CE), the most influential Western church father, writing in his *De doctrina christiana*, includes Revelation in the canon; however, it is followed by the book of James. Augustine's involvement in the Synod of Hippo (393 CE), the Synod of Carthage (397 CE), and a second Synod of Carthage (419 CE) further allowed him to influence canonical decisions. Recorded in the statutes of these synods are the words: 'And further it was resolved that nothing should be read in church under the name of the divine Scriptures except the canonical writings'.[92] The statutes were then followed by a list of canonical books, again, identical to the twenty-seven canonical books of today. John's Revelation was included among them.

As history progressed, the final shape of the canon was steadily reaffirmed, and had, by the middle ages, become solidified. However, a

---

91. Philaster does not include Revelation or Hebrews in his list, although evidence from the other references in his work ascribe apostolic authority to both books. Perhaps Philaster's list of canonical books also reflects the division of his day. See both Metzger, *Canon*, p. 233; and F.F. Bruce, *The Canon of Scripture* (Glasgow: Chapter House, 1988), p. 223.

92. Bruce, *Scripture*, p. 233.

division of consensus still existed over a number of particular books; Revelation was one of these. Further on into the Reformation, the Apocalypse could still not escape its disputable background, as Luther well reveals. In his 1522 New Testament, Luther recognizes the canonicity of the Apocalypse, yet he gives it a secondary status, claiming that it 'lacks everything that I hold as apostolic or prophetic'.[93] It is clear that Luther mistrusted Revelation because of its obscurity. 'A revelation', said he, 'should be revealing'.[94] Thus other reformers were influenced by such views. Both Johannes Oecolampadius (1482–1531 CE) and Jacob Thomas de Vio (1469–1534 CE) made it clear that Revelation was not to be placed upon the same level as the other canonical books.[95] De Vio himself refused to deal with Revelation because, as he confessed, he was unable to penetrate its mysteries.[96] Even John Calvin (1509–64 CE), who wrote commentaries on nearly every book of the New Testament, neglected, along with 2 and 3 John, to write on Revelation. With Huldreich Zwingli (1484–1531 CE), the discussion comes around full circle from where it began. Like Gaius and Eusebius, Zwingli denigrates the Apocalypse claiming that he 'takes no account of it, for it is not a book of the Bible'.[97] Gaius, Eusebius, and Zwingli asserted that Revelation presented too many problems for interpreters, and had, therefore, caused the eruption of pagan superstitions.

As one looks back upon the canonizing process of Revelation, a number of key themes emerge over and over again. First, although the book has been included in the canon, its most eager acceptance has often come from the sectarian and outer fringe Christian communities who have often used it to excessively espouse their millenarian, apocalyptic views. Secondly, Revelation's usefulness for informing the church's faith and life has, especially in light of the first consideration, long been disputed. An understanding of these insights into Revelation's canonical process can assist and inform the canonical critic. When the canonical process is amalgamated to canonical criticism, the task of interpretation takes on a slightly broader scope. Wall concludes:

93. Bruce, *Scripture*, p. 244.

94. Bruce, *Scripture*, p. 244.

95. A. Souter, *The Text and Canon of the New Testament* (London: Gerald Duckworth, 1965), p. 185; and Metzger, *Canon*, p. 240.

96. Metzger, *Canon*, p. 240.

97. B.F. Westcott, *A General Survey of the Canon of the New Testament* (Cambridge: Macmillan, 1889), p. 487.

Throughout history, certain groups of believers have elevated the importance of Revelation as their 'canon within a canon' either to promote a sectarian sociology or to justify an extreme interest in eschatology. For other believers, the presence of Revelation in the New Testament is a mere technicality; in practice, Revelation is never used to nurture believers or to measure their fidelity to the rule of faith. Whenever any part of the whole canon is excluded from the actual practice of Christian nurture, distortions in the church's witness to the gospel will result. A canonical perspective toward Revelation accepts its message as constitutive for and necessary to a vital faith.[98]

Canonical Position of Revelation (Broader Context)

The book of Revelation is not an entity unto itself. Only when Revelation is interpreted within the broader framework of the entire Christian Scriptures, constituting both Old and New Testaments alike, can one come to appreciate its unique role and contribution in shaping the faith and life of the church. The final form of the New Testament canon is the product of an intentional process. 'In this sense', says Wall, 'neither the inclusion of Revelation within the New Testament canon nor its specific location within the New Testament canon are the results of arbitrary and abstract decisions made by a few'.[99] This being so, the fact that the book falls at the very end of the biblical canon is a profound statement on its consummating role within the canon. In other words, canonical criticism places emphasis upon Revelation as the concluding chapter and final summation of the entire Bible. Wall exclaims, '...Revelation is the Bible's "conclusion" and should be interpreted as such. The most important theological convictions found in Revelation are highlighted when it is read as the concluding chapter in God's cosmic struggle with evil powers.'[100] Extending this further, in many ways the Bible can be seen as one long story, with the book of Revelation acting as the summation of that story which began in the

98. Wall and Lemcio, *New Testament*, p. 278. The phrase 'a canon within a canon' has often been used at this point to explain the differing levels of authority and inspiration ascribed to various books within the biblical canon. In this manner, both the Pentateuch and the Gospels have often been accorded a higher status, while other books such as Revelation and James have been accorded a lower status. Although some books, due to their biblical content, may inform and instruct to a greater degree the community of faith, to subordinate others to a biblical hierarchy is antagonistic to the goal of canonical criticism.

99. Wall and Lemcio, *New Testament*, p. 279.

100. Wall and Lemcio, *New Testament*, p. 280.

book of Genesis. Whereas humanity is first separated from God in Genesis, Revelation tells of the final restoration of humanity to God. All that falls in between these two points in the biblical canon serves to unfold the continuing process of God's cosmic plan of redemption which begins in covenant and culminates in Christ. Again, in no way does this place less importance upon those books that are situated between the Bible's beginning (Genesis) and end (Revelation). The concept or emphasis of a canon within a canon is to be refused. A canonical critic tends to see Genesis and Revelation functioning as an *inclusio*, or two 'bookends' inside of which fall the other sixty-four books of Scripture. Indeed, this inclusio can be observed in some detail. Note the following comparisons and contrasts:

In the beginning God created the heavens and the earth. (Gen. 1.1)	A new heaven and earth. (Rev. 21.1)
God called the darkness night. (Gen. 1.5).	There will be no night. (Rev. 21.25)
God gathered the waters and called this sea. (Gen. 1.10)	No longer any sea. (Rev. 21.1)
God created the sun and moon. (Gen. 1.16)	There will be no sun or moon. (Rev. 21.23)
The first Adam. (Gen. 2.7)	Reign of the new Adam. (Rev. 19.11)
Humanity's primeval home by a river. (Gen. 2.10)	Humanity's eternal home by a river. (Rev. 22.1)
The Deceiver appears. (Gen. 3.1, 4)	The Deceiver's defeat. (Rev. 20.10)
The increase of pain. (Gen. 3.16)	There will be no pain. (Rev. 21.4)
The ground is cursed. (Gen. 3.17)	There will be no curse. (Rev. 22.3)
The introduction of death. (Gen. 3.19)	There will be no death. (Rev. 21.4)
Banished from the tree of life. (Gen. 3.22-24)	The tree of life reappears. (Rev. 22.2)
Driven from God's presence. (Gen. 3.24)	They will see his face. (Rev. 22.4)

The interpretation of Revelation is not only assisted by reading it in its fixed canonical position and relationship to Genesis, but also in its general canonical relationship to a number of other biblical writings or collections of writings. Continuing with the Old Testament, Childs points out that 'Although the book of Revelation is completely saturated with the Old Testament...the writer did not employ a method of citations, but creatively adapted the ancient traditions to his own purpose'.[101] This is clearly evident when one examines the 'seven bowl plagues of God's

---

101. Childs, *New Testament*, p. 509.

wrath' (Rev. 15–16), which echo something of the Exodus plagues bestowed upon Egypt (Exod. 7–11). When comparing the two pericopes, it is difficult to dispute that the Exodus account was reincorporated, or in the least alluded to, in the vision of the bowl judgments of Revelation. This reveals significant considerations for a canonical reading of Revelation. Historical criticism and biblical scholarship have tended to conclude that the book was written when Christians were entering a time of persecution.[102] The Roman authorities had begun to enforce the cult of emperor worship, and increased hostility fell upon those Christians who, refusing to bow to Caesar, worshipped Christ alone. Therefore, in a situation of crisis similar to that of ancient Israel and the prophets, it is appropriate that the author of Revelation provides encouragement and hope for his audience by use of an Exodus typology, just as the earlier Israelite generations had likewise done. As in the Exodus account, so, too, in Revelation. God's sovereignty would eventually triumph, humanity's evil would be judged, and God's faithful people would be liberated. At the same time, there was further incentive for the Christian to remain faithful during persecution. For those believers who wished to return to 'Egypt' or 'Babylon', and who were inclined to disregard God's 'eternal gospel', the vision of the seven bowl plagues was also a warning to repent in order to escape their own judgment.[103]

Going further, the Apocalypse has a number of close affinities with the Old Testament prophets, and upon close inspection, one finds that much of its vocabulary, symbolism, and prophetic nature issues forth directly from these. The most apparent example of this lies in Revelation's use of the prophetic book of Daniel. It is from here that John identifies the risen Christ with Daniel's 'son of man' image. Childs emphasizes that:

> ...the writer of Revelation has radically reinterpreted the book of Daniel in light of his christology. God's decisive event in defeating the cosmological power of evil lies in the past. In the event of the cross, God's reign was forever established and Satan defeated. Indeed the church continues to suffer in tension under persecution, but it lives in the confidence that

102. The two most likely periods for Revelation's composition include the latter part of Nero's reign (54–68 CE) or the latter part of Domitian's reign (81–96 CE). A small number have held to a period during Vespasian's reign (69–79 CE). Most scholars would date the book c. 95 CE.

103. Wall and Lemcio, *New Testament*, p. 295.

victory has already been won. The apocalyptic imagery of Daniel now
serves the function of identifying the defeated enemies of God and of the
church who act from an earthbound perspective as if they were still in
control.[104]

By making such a statement, Childs is able to throw off the concrete
historical situations referred to in both Daniel and Revelation. Although
both books were written to address a time of great crisis, and although
the writers of both books revealed a message of judgment followed by
salvation, each contained within a particular historical situation, the soon
expected and final cataclysmic end described in both books did not
occur. For Daniel, the reign of Antiochus IV Epiphanes did not result in
the coming of the Antichrist. So, too, in Revelation, the reign of either
Nero or Domitian, although persecuting the church as never before, did
not give way to the imminent consummation described in the
Apocalypse. In light of this, the contemporaries of both Daniel and
Revelation projected both books into the future and regarded their
prophetic utterances as yet unfulfilled. Childs explains, rightly or
wrongly, that 'such a move has failed to reckon with the hermeneutical
guides within the book of Revelation which the canonical process has
provided in order to aid its future appropriation by the community of
faith'.[105] He goes on to explain that the original author of Revelation
had already purposely enabled successive generations of believers to
appropriate its prophecies, and, therefore, to project its fulfillment into
the future is not only unnecessary, but wrong. Although Revelation
referred to a specific historical situation, the author's use of the traditional apocalyptic scenario freed the text from its historical ties, and thus
allowed, as in Daniel, each successive generation to be challenged to
endure in the midst of opposition. Like Daniel, the author of Revelation
chose to incorporate the medium of apocalyptic symbolism, and by
doing so, greatly aided, although likely unknowingly, in providing a
vehicle for the book's continued canonical function. This apocalyptic
symbolism was such as to continue to function kerygmatically while
allowing its inner historical events and background to become purposely
obscured, and, therefore, inoperative for later readers.[106] Wall is likewise
able to throw off the historical elements of Revelation and thus allow for
its contemporization, although in a manner differing from Childs. He

104. Childs, *New Testament*, pp. 514-15.
105. Childs, *New Testament*, p. 514.
106. Childs, *New Testament*, p. 515.

explains that while John had seven specific Christian congregations in mind (Rev. 2–3), there is reason to believe that the number seven, a number symbolizing wholeness or completeness which occurs all throughout the vision, alludes to a universal significance and timeless audience. He also draws attention to the fact that the majority of communities in the canonizing church, in recognition of the book's inspiration, and, therefore, usefulness in developing the faith and life of successive generations, included it in their biblical canon. Wall then concludes:

> The point is this: the interpreter should not assume that Revelation is esoteric writing, relevant only for an ancient Christian people doing battle with the evil forces of the Roman empire. The proper hermeneutical judgment, consistent with its author, is that Revelation is useful in forming Christian faith for today.[107]

One cannot dismiss the strong lines of continuity that also exist between Revelation and the book of Ezekiel. Not only are both writers prophets, but both are exiles, Ezekiel to Babylon and John to Patmos. Both are commanded to eat divinely-given scrolls that tasted as sweet as honey. And finally, both are then ordered to prophecy (Ezek. 3.1-4; Rev. 10.9-11). Wall legitimately points out that these similarities suggest that John understands his own commission and current situation in the context of Ezekiel: 'sharply put, John views himself as a latter day Ezekiel'.[108] The prophecies of both individuals contain relatively similar messages: the wicked will be cursed while the righteous will be blessed. Again, as in the Exodus typology used by John, the unrevealed words of the seven thunders contained in the little scroll (Rev. 10.4), acting somewhat like the bowl plagues, serve to warn the wicked that punishment is imminent, while at the same time encouraging the church to remain pure even under trial, thereby resulting in their blessing.

Many modern scholars would hold that the author of Revelation purposely cited or borrowed from the Old Testament prophets for at least two reasons: first, in order to provide an enhanced, yet familiar eschatological and apocalyptic medium with which his readers would be familiar, and secondly, to give further credibility and authority to his message. However, not only did the prophets guide and shape the words of the author of Revelation, but perhaps a reciprocal element occurred in

107. Wall and Lemcio, *New Testament*, p. 288.
108. Wall and Lemcio, *New Testament*, p. 292.

which Revelation itself provided a somewhat new foundation from which one viewed the prophets. Although it is important to recognize this textual continuity, canonical criticism makes more of this 'intertextual dialogue' by asserting, on the one hand, that the author of Revelation understood his composition to be in fundamental agreement with his biblical canon, the Old Testament Scriptures. His interpretation and description of his visions located him within Israel's biblical traditions. On the other hand, the allusions made by John to Israel's biblical traditions link up with visionary images, but further extend these by recognizing that something new and strange has occurred in the death and exaltation of God's messiah. In other words, there is an *apocalypsis* of meaning that 'distorts' the biblical tradition as it had been received from 'official' Judaism and spins it off in a new and more 'Christian' direction.[109] Although there are affinities and intertextual continuities between Revelation and the Old Testament prophets, John's Apocalypse seeks to push forward a new frontier with fresh meaning and implication for Christians. '[T]he central point to make, and indeed the heart of the canonical issue for the book of Revelation', says Childs, 'is that the New Testament writer offered a profound reinterpretation of the whole Old Testament in the light of his understanding of Jesus Christ'.[110] It is perhaps here that Sanders's emphasis upon comparative midrash finds a basis of application. John's obvious use and reinterpretation of a number of significant Old Testament traditions encourages his readers to understand Revelation's prophecies with renewed hope and perseverance, while at the same time clearly placing them among the formative and inspiring traditions of Israel's past. In this way there is a reciprocal relationship between both Testaments. While the old informs the new, the new continues to develop the old.[111]

The final concern that must be dealt with in this section is the consideration of Revelation's canonical setting within the New Testament. Clearly its apocalyptic themes have a kinship with other endtime sections of the New Testament such as Matthew 24 and parallels, 2 Thessalonians 2, and 2 Peter 3. Again, the basic outline follows that of Daniel with the

109. Wall and Lemcio, *New Testament*, p. 290.

110. Childs, *New Testament*, p. 509.

111. It should be noted that Childs disagrees with this midrashic concept, at least in this particular setting. He explains that the author of Revelation uses the Old Testament in a prophetic sense rather than in a midrashic sense. See Childs, *New Testament*, p. 509.

persecution, perseverance, and salvation of the faithful occurring along-side the rise of the Antichrist, his eventual defeat, and the judgment of the wicked. Once again, this shows that while the traditions of the ancient prophets are upheld, although reshaped by a new christological perspective, there is a deep apocalyptic hope within the church and Revelation, likely written later than all the above and forming the con-clusion to the Bible, acts as the final word on apocalyptic expectations for all future communities of faith.

One must also turn to the relationship between Revelation and the other Johannine books. A quick perusal of the commentaries reveals no lack of discord in matters concerning authorship. Suffice it to say, however, that recent scholarship has been more willing to focus atten-tion upon thematic similarities as well as stylistic and linguistic com-monalities. This is especially true when relating Revelation to the Gospel of John and 1 John. Some now claim that the simple differences between Gospel, epistle, and apocalypse may be enough justification in itself to nullify the previous discrepancies held by numerous scholars.[112] This ongoing matter of authorship will be addressed from a canonical perspective in the next section.

Canonical Shape of Revelation (Immediate Context)
Canonical shaping attempts to discover traces within the text itself as to how the biblical author intended the material to be understood. If authorial intentions are expressed, these are taken seriously. Whereas canonical position focuses upon Revelation's broader canonical relation-ship to other books in the canon, canonical shape concerns itself with Revelation itself, and the smaller units that make up the book.

The structure of a book is one of the first places the reader ought to look for indications of canonical shaping. The formal means by which the material is ordered affects the content of the book in an integral way. Therefore, an understanding of Revelation's structure can prove helpful to the comprehension of its content. In view of the book's perceived duplications and discrepancies, many scholars of the past questioned Revelation's unity.[113] Literary considerations were, therefore, mobilized

112. For further discussion of these issues, see Wall and Lemcio, *New Testament*, pp. 282-86.

113. See such works as C. von Weizsacker's *The Apostolic Age of the Church* (1895), pp. 173-205; and J. Wellhausen's *Analyse der Offenbarung Johannis* (1907). See also Childs, *New Testament*, p. 505.

in an attempt to answer the problematic issues related to the book's lack of unity. Numerous solutions were proposed, each based upon various source, form, and redactional insights. Some even concluded that Revelation had been compiled over a long period of time from a number of fragmentary sources, its literary history resembling something of Wellhausen's documentary hypothesis for the Pentateuch. Suffice it to say that although these various inferences sought honestly and critically to explain the formation of Revelation, the book's original unity was not strongly upheld. The actual structure of the book has also long been in dispute. The symbolic significance of the number seven, representing completeness in biblical thought, has figured prominently in the book. The centrality of this numerical figure is obvious, and based upon this symbolic centrality, many have claimed that the overall structure of Revelation polarizes around seven grand visions. Childs finds that 'The major problem with this analysis is to explain the interpolations and expansions which seem to disregard this scheme'.[114] Although the issues of Revelation's unity and structure will continue to be a matter of debate, for the canonical critic several key considerations must be maintained. First, and of importance to the issue of Revelation's unity, exegesis must focus primarily upon the final form of the book rather than upon its underlying sources. Secondly, the broad structure of the book, as already mentioned, must be seen in close relationship to the traditional pattern for apocalyptic literature, with Daniel especially acting as Revelation's guide.

Also important for the canonical shape and immediate context of Revelation is its heading or title 'The Revelation of St John', and subsequently the book's authorship. Although not part of the original autograph, this title, which was added in the later stages of the canonizing process, provides insight into the overall function of Revelation and its continued use by successive communities of faith. Based upon historical grounds, one must conclude that Revelation's title is a later addition made by canonical editors; however, it has definite theological and canonical implications. The title attests to the fact that the Early Church viewed Revelation as authoritative in shaping her faith and life, authentic at least in prophetic task and message if not authorship, and one part of

114. Childs, *New Testament*, p. 509. Wall also notes that 'Some commentators on Revelation have been themselves persuaded by, but are not very persuasive about, the symbolic and structural significance of the number seven...' See Wall and Lemcio, *New Testament*, p. 282 n. 10.

a larger theological context from which the book was to be read. Childs adds to this last point:

> The title provides an additional context from which the book is to be read. At first it is surprising that such a title should be used because it appears to disagree with the actual introduction which ascribes the Apocalypse to Jesus Christ. However, the editor's purpose is clear, and is not intended to contest the ultimate source of the visions. The book of Revelation is to be read in conjunction with the larger Johannine corpus. The point is not to harmonize the book of Revelation with the Gospel of John, but rather to affirm that there is a larger canonical unity to the church's scriptures which is an important guideline to its correct theological understanding. For the last book of the Bible such a canonical control is especially needful.[115]

When understood in this manner, those modern biblical translators who change the title to 'The Revelation of Jesus Christ' in order to correspond to the book's introduction change the canonical intentions and the overall function of Revelation as it has been used by successive generations of believers. Likewise, those who retain the title but claim that the author John is other than Jesus' apostle, although rightly subscribing to historical considerations, confuse the more theological concerns which canonical criticism emphasizes. The title of Revelation reflects the ancient tradition of the canonizing agents and the Early Church who ascribed authorship to the Apostle John.[116]

For some this issue of authorship no doubt seems problematic. Therefore, it is appropriate to discuss the matter from a canonical perspective. Until the period of modern critical scholarship, it was essentially unanimous that the Apostle John had written the book of Revelation.[117] Today, however, it seems that there are a number of approaches to this issue of authorship, some of which center around differing concepts of apostolic authenticity and authority. Generally,

115. Childs, *New Testament*, p. 517.

116. See also Wall and Lemcio, *New Testament*, p. 283.

117. One should note the exceptions to this. Both Dionysius (d. 265 CE) and Eusebius (d. 340 CE) investigated matters of style and grammar between Revelation and the Gospel of John, and each concluded that the Apostle John had not written Revelation. Eusebius claimed that a second John, John the Presbyter, had written the book. It should also be pointed out that their rejection of the traditional norm was based more on practical reasons such as Revelation's theological excesses and problematic issues of interpretation rather than pure historical considerations. For this point, see Metzger, *Canon*, p. 205 n. 38; and Wall and Lemcio, *New Testament*, p. 284 n. 13.

those who defend apostolic Johannine authorship of Revelation do so on the grounds of a stricter sense of authenticity. In other words, for any given writing to be included initially in the canon, and then to subsequently provide continued authority for the church, it had to bear the seal of authentic apostolic authorship. Individuals in this camp would conclude that the Apostle John must have written Revelation since its inspiration, canonicity, and authority are tied to its authenticity.

On the other hand, a majority of canonical critics would, like Childs, make some type of distinction between the 'canonical' author (with emphasis upon a theological perspective), and the 'historical' author (with emphasis upon a historical perspective) of Revelation. This camp would conclude that one should not blindly accept the stated authorship of any given biblical book on the basis of a strict definition of canonical authenticity. Instead, one might also claim authenticity, not only on the grounds of antiquity, but also on the grounds of consistent orthodoxy. Here the claim is made that the early Christian criterion of apostolic authenticity referred to the congruence of a book's message with its memory of the apostle's witness to Christ. If one subscribes to this concept of consistent orthodoxy, and it is fair to note that there are some problems with it, then authentic authorship ceases to be as vital an issue for canonicity. As long as any given book upheld apostolic theology and tradition, it could be rightfully included in the canon regardless of its author. Although these arguments can be applied to numerous other biblical books, there are a number of further considerations that apply particularly to the authorship of Revelation and to this dilemma of definition. Revelation itself makes no specific claim to apostolic Johannine authorship, but rather to authorship by one simply named John. Therefore, although contrary to the predominant Early Church tradition, some have found a way around the issue by concluding that the author of Revelation was, in fact, John the Presbyter, rather than John the Apostle. One could further conclude that whether the John at Patmos was the son of Zebedee or the Presbyter really does not matter. Instead, the author's appeal throughout Revelation is not to apostolic authority but to prophetic inspiration, from whence his authority derives.

A number of considerations are introduced when one reads Revelation from a canonical-critical perspective. These deal with matters concerning the role of the addressees, the book's introduction or prescript (Rev. 1.1-3), and its conclusion or epilogue (Rev. 22.6-21). Concerning the first issue, it has already been pointed out that one must understand the addressees of Revelation, the seven churches, as a universal representative or typology of future communities of faith. Whether one makes use of apocalyptic symbolism (Childs) or numerical symbolism and canonizing factors (Wall), for canonical criticism it is important that the book of Revelation transcends its historical addressee and influences the faith (orthodoxy) and life (orthopraxy) of its contemporary audience.

Moving on to the last two issues, it is often in the prescript and/or the epilogue where the purpose of the author is most clearly stated. Wall contends that Revelation's prescript, and perhaps also the epilogue, function in two primary ways. First, the prescript authorizes the prophet's composition for Christian edification, since it is rooted in divine revelation. Secondly, the prescript introduces three hermeneutical clues by which the composition is most profitably read. Revelation must be read as an apocalypse (Rev. 1.1), as the word of God and testimony of Christ (Rev. 1.2), and as words of prophecy (Rev. 1.3). If these hermeneutical guides are not followed, says Wall, the meaning of Revelation is distorted, and so the formation of the faith community. When this happens, the intended role of the canonical Revelation is denied.[118]

Childs thinks that the prescript in Revelation is written in a different voice from that of the author (v. 4). For Childs it seems clear that the introduction was a later addition by someone belonging to the community of faith who had received the book. The addition of this introduction by a later disguised editor provided a canonical guideline that enabled Revelation to be removed from its historical moorings and situation, and thus function as authoritative Scripture for all generations long after the author. Childs also notes that the prescript serves to indicate the purpose of the book—that being to give testimony to Jesus Christ concerning what must soon take place.[119]

The conclusion of a book often summarizes or reemphasizes main ideas, goals and issues. And, in fact, the epilogue in Revelation repeats many of the themes presented in the introduction. In this way, as in the discussion regarding the broader context of Genesis through to Revelation, the book's prescript and epilogue function again as an immediate canonical inclusio. The epilogue echoes the prescript by affirming the truth of God's words through his prophet, promising

118. Wall and Lemcio, *New Testament*, p. 283 n. 11.
119. Childs, *New Testament*, pp. 516-17.

blessing to those who adhere to these words, and encouraging the book's readers that Christ's coming is soon. Childs adds one additional thought to the warning of vv. 18-19. He states that 'From the beginning the formula served to reinforce the authority which the book claimed. The book of Revelation was never simply a tract for the times or an occasional letter which later was assigned a religiously authoritative status, rather its author laid claim to its being divine revelation at the outset.'[120]

6. *Conclusion*

This essay has attempted to present canonical criticism as a valid approach to biblical exegesis. And although the method in discussion is not without its flaws and weaknesses, it seems that canonical criticism in one form or another can be used as a valuable tool by biblical scholars in their search for textual meaning. Future work in the study of this discipline will, of necessity, have to focus upon several fronts. First, the methodological impasse that exists between canonical critics such as Childs and Sanders will have to be confronted. Whether this impasse will be assailed through a synthesis of both scholars' views, as some have deemed adequate, or through a new presentation of canonical principles, which will undoubtedly be based upon the past work of both Childs and Sanders, is yet to be seen. Perhaps some will even conclude that both methodologies have validity in their own right, and, therefore, the methodological diversity should remain. Secondly, the strained relationship between historical criticism and canonical criticism must be reconciled. Only negligent thinking would render the past two-hundred years of critical research obsolete. And although historical criticism has proven inadequate on numerous occasions, it is doubtful that canonical criticism will be able to step in as the sole champion of biblical interpretation. Instead, the canonical approach may provide a necessary and foundational corrective to historical criticism. That the discipline be subordinated to historical criticism is perhaps, again, fallacious thinking. However, it will once more be the work of future scholars to determine whether canonical criticism should act on par with historical criticism, or whether historical criticism should be subordinated to canonical criticism. Regardless, the issue of canon must be taken seriously. That the canon functions as the normative means by which theological exegesis occurs

120.   Childs, *New Testament*, p. 516.

appears to be a valid insight of canonical criticism. Canonical criticism can establish important checks and balances that greatly reduce interpretative excesses. At the same time, the discipline may well aid in restoring the crumbling foundation for believing communities who have seen their source of faith and life, the Bible, lowered to the position of merely another historical source that aids in scholarly reconstructions. The words of James Sanders are an apt testimony to what canonical criticism may offer to the community of faith and scholar alike:

> Canonical criticism may perhaps be the corrective to what happened because of the Enlightenment, when the Bible was taken from the church lectern into the scholar's study. The movement of canonical criticism is that of the scholar's being openly willing to be a servant of the believing communities. Not those believing communities who are so frightened of Enlightenment study... They have not taken the necessary prior steps; they have not demonstrated the depth of faith necessary to be 'honest to God'. They live by the fear that the faith will disappear if they allow honesty... On the other hand, it is for those faithful who have discerned the hand of God in the Enlightenment just as the ancient biblical authors discerned the hand of God in the international Wisdom they learned from others. It may help those faithful to discern the immense power for truth the Bible conveys...[121]

121. Sanders, *Canon and Community*, p. xvi.

MODERN LINGUISTICS AND THE NEW TESTAMENT:
A BASIC GUIDE TO THEORY, TERMINOLOGY, AND LITERATURE

Jeffrey T. Reed

1. *Introduction*

In terms of an organised, programmatic agenda for the linguistic analysis
of biblical texts, New Testament scholars are well behind their Old
Testament counterparts. This state of affairs exists despite the fact that
there are a wide array of linguistic analyses of the New Testament which
have been and continue to be published (although mostly in the area of
semantics);[1] yet it can almost go without saying that such studies have
had little impact on the wider scholarly guild. In the 1989 publication of
The New Testament and its Modern Interpreters linguistic approaches to
the New Testament are limited to nine pages under the somewhat anti-
quated heading 'Philology' (pp. 127-36), approximately two pages
primarily on Erhardt Güttgemanns's use of transformational-generative
grammar as a challenge to fundamental issues of form and redaction
criticism (pp. 164-65), and brief mention of structuralism, post-structuralism, semantic field theory, and discourse analysis (pp. 166-67, 180-82,
186-89).[2] Even these narrow discussions reveal that there is no clear
consensus on what New Testament linguistics entails. Part of the problem stems from the diversity of modern linguistics[3] itself and, hence, the

---

1. Many of these studies are carried out in organised settings, e.g. the SBL
section on Biblical Greek Language and Linguistics, international forums and publications overseen by the Summer Institute of Linguistics and the United Bible
Societies, academic work and publications in Uppsala and in South Africa (on the
latter see esp. articles in *Neotestamentica*).

2. E.J. Epp and G.W. MacRae SJ (eds.), *The New Testament and its Modern
Interpreters* (Atlanta: Scholars Press, 1989).

3. Modern linguistics typically is claimed to have begun with the posthumous
publication of F. de Saussure's notes and lectures on linguistics at the turn of the
century: F. de Saussure, *Course in General Linguistics* (trans. W. Baskin; New
York: McGraw-Hill, 1966 [translation of 1916]).

dilemma of choosing a coherent model that will appeal to scholars with little or no formal linguistic training. Despite this diversity, most New Testament linguistic studies are patterned after the theories of Ferdinand de Saussure (structuralism), Noam Chomsky (transformational-generative grammar), or Kenneth Pike (tagmemics). These linguists represent only the tip of the iceberg when one considers the likes of Edward Sapir, Leonard Bloomfield, Louis Hjelmslev, J.R. Firth, M.A.K. Halliday, Teun van Dijk, Walter Kintsch, and Peter Hartman—and this list is far from comprehensive.[4] Another reason for the lack of linguistic influence on New Testament studies stems from the myth that questions of Greek grammar have all been resolved. So J.J. van Rensburg disdains, 'In many circles it is deemed unnecessary to investigate Greek grammar because—so it is argued—all of the major problems were solved in the 19th century.'[5] Ironically, the fallacy of this myth is exposed by the many questions still perplexing modern linguists today. If questions of *modern* languages are still partly unresolved, then issues surrounding the language of the New Testament,[6] which has not had nearly the same

4. R. de Beaugrande, *Linguistic Theory: The Discourse of Fundamental Works* (London: Longman, 1991), pp. 4-5, who surveys the above linguists, laments that he could not discuss over 68 other scholars who have significantly advanced the study of modern linguistics.

5. J.J. (Fika) Janse van Rensburg, 'A New Reference Grammar for the Greek New Testament: Exploratory Remarks on a Methodology', *Neot* 27 (1993), pp. 133-52; on the need for continual research regarding New Testament grammar and semantics, see esp. E.A. Nida, 'Implications of Contemporary Linguistics for Biblical Scholarship', *JBL* 91 (1972), pp. 73-89; R.J. Erickson, 'Linguistics and Biblical Language: A Wide-Open Field', *JETS* 26 (1983), pp. 257-63; J.P. Louw, 'New Testament Greek: The Present State of the Art', *Neot* 24 (1990), pp. 159-72; S. Wong, 'The Nature of the Greek of the New Testament: Its Past and Present', *Scriptura* 32 (1990), pp. 1-27; S.E. Porter, 'Keeping Up with Recent Studies. 17. Greek Language and Linguistics', *ExpTim* 130 (1991), pp. 202-208; and S.E. Porter and J.T. Reed, 'Greek Grammar since BDF: A Retrospective and Prospective Analysis', *FN* 4 (1991), pp. 143-64.

6. Without arguing the point here, I understand the Greek of the New Testament to be essentially the same as that of the Greek used throughout the Greco-Roman world of its day, i.e. Hellenistic or koiné Greek. This equation is made at the level of 'code' (competence), but factors such as dialect, register, and idiolect often produced different manifestations (performance) of this code, including those with Semitic interference. For key scholarly opinions on the debate, see S.E. Porter (ed.), *The Language of the New Testament: Classic Essays* (JSNTSup, 60; Sheffield: JSOT Press, 1991).

modern linguistic resources devoted to its understanding, are surely far from entirely resolved. Of course, the application of modern linguistic approaches to New Testament texts will not amount to a rewriting of biblical scholarship, but it will surely challenge several presuppositions used in exegesis and at least call for more methodological clarity when it comes to writing, for example, such a monumental work as a commentary.[7]

This essay is intended as a basic guide to the terminology, theory, and literature of several key linguistic disciplines that are relevant for New Testament studies. This is done by defining key concepts, naming key theorists and their works, suggesting linguistic principles useful for exegesis, and relating the concepts to actual New Testament examples. The first area surveyed—semantics—is at least somewhat familiar to most biblical scholars. However, the next two—pragmatics and socio-linguistics—have had less impact on New Testament scholarship. Discourse analysis, the final topic covered, brings together several features of the other disciplines into a more coherent hermeneutic. Finally, one aspect of discourse analysis, viz. information flow theory, is applied to Paul's letter to the Philippians. Due to space, I have unfortunately had to omit other potentially relevant areas of linguistics: e.g. psycho-linguistics; corpus linguistics; formal grammar; functional grammar; historical linguistics; literature and linguistics; philosophy of language; ethnography; translation theory; artificial intelligence; applied linguistics. For surveys and bibliographies of these and many other areas of linguistics see especially the *International Encyclopedia of Linguistics*.[8]

2. Semantics

Semantics has arguably had more influence on New Testament studies than any other field of modern linguistics. Several monographs and essays have been devoted to the subject and now a lexicon based on

---

7. Whether one accepts his linguistic model or not, W. Schenk, 'Hebräerbrief 4.14-16: Textlinguistik als Kommentierungsprinzip', *NTS* 26 (1980), pp. 242-52 and *Die Philipperbriefe des Paulus* (Stuttgart: Kohlhammer, 1984) are attempts at such methodological clarity; but few commentators have followed his lead.

8. W. Bright (ed.), *International Encyclopedia of Linguistics* (4 vols.; Oxford: Oxford University Press, 1992). For definitions of key linguistic terms, see D. Crystal, *A Dictionary of Linguistics and Phonetics* (Oxford: Basil Blackwell, 3rd edn, 1991).

modern semantic theory is available.[9] *Semantics*, a term coined in the late nineteenth century, is defined by J. Lyons as 'the study of meaning',[10] involving the study of both how language is used to express meaning and how it is interpreted as meaning.[11] Such a definition results in an expansive scope of inquiry for semanticists; indeed, it is difficult to divorce semantics from any other linguistic enterprise (as was eventually acknowledged by generative grammarians). J.P. Louw notes that semantics 'is concerned with far more than merely the meanings of

9.   See esp. J. Barr, *The Semantics of Biblical Language* (Oxford: Oxford University Press, 1961); D.D. Steinberg and L.A. Jakobovicz, *Semantics: An Interdisciplinary Reader in Philosophy, Linguistics and Psychology* (Cambridge: Cambridge University Press, 1971); E.A. Nida and C.R. Taber, *The Theory and Practice of Translation* (Leiden: Brill, 1974); A.C. Thiselton, 'Semantics and New Testament Interpretation', in *New Testament Interpretation: Essays on Principles and Methods* (ed. I.H. Marshall; Exeter: Paternoster Press, 2nd edn, 1979), pp. 75-104; G.B. Caird, *The Language and Imagery of the Bible* (London: Gerald Duckworth, 1980); A. Gibson, *Biblical Semantic Logic: A Preliminary Analysis* (New York: St Martin, 1981); J.P. Louw, *Semantics of New Testament Greek* (Atlanta: Scholars Press, 1982); M. Silva, *Biblical Words and their Meaning: An Introduction to Lexical Semantics* (Grand Rapids: Zondervan, 1983); J.P. Louw and E.A. Nida, *Greek–English Lexicon of the New Testament Based on Semantic Domains* (2 vols.; New York: United Bible Societies, 1988); P. Cotterell and M. Turner, *Linguistics and Biblical Interpretation* (Downers Grove, IL: InterVarsity Press, 1989), chs. 2–5; and for a list of word-study fallacies common in biblical studies, see D.A. Carson, *Exegetical Fallacies* (Grand Rapids: Baker, 1984), ch. 1.

10.   J. Lyons, *Introduction to Theoretical Linguistics* (Cambridge: Cambridge University Press, 1968), p. 400.

11.   Standard works include S. Ullmann, *The Principles of Semantics* (Glasgow: Jackson, 1951); *idem*, *Semantics: An Introduction to the Science of Meaning* (Oxford: Basil Blackwell, 1962); J.J. Katz, *Semantic Theory* (New York: Harper & Row, 1972); E.A. Nida, *Componential Analysis of Meaning* (The Hague: Mouton, 1975); *idem*, *Exploring Semantic Structures* (Munich: Fink, 1975); R. Kempson, *Semantic Theory* (Cambridge: Cambridge University Press, 1977); J. Lyons, *Semantics* (2 vols.; Cambridge: Cambridge University Press, 1977); G. Leech, *Semantics: The Study of Meaning* (Harmondsworth: Penguin Books, 1981); F.R. Palmer, *Semantics: A New Outline* (Cambridge: Cambridge University Press, 1981); K. Allan, *Linguistic Meaning* (2 vols.; London: Routledge & Kegan Paul, 1986); and D.A. Cruse, *Lexical Semantics* (Cambridge: Cambridge University Press, 1986). I do not discuss here logical approaches to semantics such as truth-conditional and model-theoretic semantics; on which see M.J. Cresswell, *Structured Meanings: The Semantics of Propositional Attitudes* (Cambridge, MA: MIT Press, 1985).

words' and that 'semantics extends over sentence boundaries';[12] hence, it is possible to ask what a word, sentence, or discourse 'means'. Thus, semantic theory is not simply relevant to dictionary-making; it affects much of what constitutes New Testament hermeneutics.

What is meant when it is said that a word 'means' something? This is perhaps the essential problem of semantics and it has several potential answers.

1. First, to say that a word 'means' something implies that a choice has been made by a speaker/author.[13] This has become a commonly cited maxim of modern linguistics.

Principle: *Meaning implies choice.*[14]

What is said in a particular context communicates 'meaning' because it has been chosen from a meaningful system of other possible expressions. However, this principle can be misconstrued if it is not also remembered that much of discourse is redundant, that is

Principle: *Texts typically transmit less information than the sum of their linguistic parts.*

Such redundancy 'serves to reduce the likelihood of an error in the reception of the message resulting from the loss of information during the transmission'.[15] The redundancy principle warns against the assumption that closely related words used in the same linguistic context must always have their own distinctive meanings.

2. Most linguists differentiate between two aspects of lexical meaning: reference and sense.[16] *Reference* is that type of meaning in which a speaker 'refers to' an object in the real world, that is, the relationship which holds between words and material objects. Of course, this definition of meaning is only partly adequate, since not every word refers to some object in the 'real' world. For example, the words 'love'

---

12. Louw, *Semantics*, p. 3.

13. In the remainder of the essay, 'speaker' also implies 'author' and 'listener' implies 'reader' unless specifically stated.

14. Lyons, *Theoretical Linguistics*, pp. 413-14.

15. J. Caron, *An Introduction to Psycholinguistics* (trans. T. Pownall; New York: Harvester Wheatsheaf, 1992), p. 5.

16. See Lyons, *Theoretical Linguistics*, pp. 424-28.

and ἐλπίς do not necessarily refer to material entities. Furthermore, the same word may be used to refer to different objects in different contexts (i.e. 'I like your *shoes* better than my *shoes*'). The concept of reference is closely related to that of *denotation*, viz. what a word stands for in the abstract (i.e. the class of properties shared by a word). For example, 'tree' denotes in part a class of objects sharing the properties of being plants and having trunks. Again, there are obvious limitations to this approach to meaning. For example, what is the denotation of 'chair'? Are chairs stationary objects that have legs and are used to sit on? Does this mean that a rocking chair is not part of the class of 'chairs'? Whereas reference and denotation concern the relationships words have with the external world, *sense* refers to the meaningful relationships a word has 'intralinguistically' (i.e. with other parts of the language system). Again the principle of 'meaning implies choice' is important here. So J. Lyons defines sense: 'By the *sense* of a word we mean its place in a system of relationships which it contracts with other words in the vocabulary'.[17] On the one hand, New Testament exegetes may use archaeological studies in order to determine the *referential* and *denotative* meaning of words such as the weapons ῥομφαία, μάχαιρα, λόγχη, and ὑσσός. Most semantic analyses, however, have to do with the 'sense' of a word and thus raise questions of linguistic and situational context, concepts which are now treated in more detail.

3. The linguistic concepts of *paradigmatic* and *syntagmatic* analysis and *slots* and *fillers* are one way of determining sense relations of words. According to such approaches, a sentence may be treated functionally as a series of grammatical slots which may be filled with a variety of actual instances of language. For example, there may be subject slots, verb slots, adverb slots, and complement slots. In Greek, a subject slot may be filled with an infinitive clause, a nominal phrase, or even a single article. To fill a slot, a speaker will choose an actual grammatical form from the paradigm of choices. R. de Beaugrande calls this paradigm of choices the *virtual* system of the speaker, that is, the speaker's linguistic code or language (*langue*, competence, language system)—the shared meaning-system. What the speaker actually chooses and fills the slot with is the *actual* system (*parole*, performance, language use). The virtual system is composed of 'elements whose potential is not yet put to use, e.g. the repertories of sounds, grammatical forms, sentence patterns, concept names, etc., which a particular language

17. Lyons, *Theoretical Linguistics*, p. 427.

offers its users'; in contrast, a text is an actual system, 'a functional unity created through processes of decision and selection among options of virtual systems'.[18] What is important to remember is that what the speaker chooses from the virtual system is constrained by the co-text (i.e. surrounding linguistic items) and context (i.e. situation and culture). There is, in other words, an interplay between the *system* of language and the *use* of language in the production and interpretation of discourse:

> On the one hand, the 'system' of the language as known to the communicative participants determines what items, relations, and significances they assign to any instance of language in use. On the other hand, the steadily accruing body of experience with language use is both the source of that knowledge and a continual influence upon it. In this sense, the use of language provides experience and the system provides categories.[19]

I would add to de Beaugrande's observation the point that both co-text and 'experience' (mental scripts of culture) influence choices from the system. The following sentence may help to illustrate this: 'I gulped down the _____'. The missing element in the preceding sentence may be filled with various linguistic elements from the English virtual system (e.g. water, lemonade, drink). These elements represent paradigmatic choices. However, not any element from the virtual system may fill this slot, and some options are even less likely than others. The item 'millet mixed with mud' is not a likely candidate for the missing element. But it would be a more likely candidate if 'the pig' were the subject. Nor would 'I' likely gulp down a 'brick' or 'a dog running through the park'. These may seem amusing, but they serve to demonstrate that the linguistic co-text, or syntagmatic choices, influences paradigmatic choices. In other words, that which *fills* the various *slots* of a sentence is in part determined by what elements fill the surrounding discourse. Lyons provides some informative English examples: 'At one extreme, we have adjectives like "good" or "bad" in English which can be used in collocation with almost any noun; at the other extreme, we find an adjective like "rancid", which may be predicated of butter and little else'.[20] This is all to say that

---

18. R. de Beaugrande, *Text, Discourse and Process: Toward a Multidisciplinary Science of Texts* (ed. R.O. Freedle; Advances in Discourse Processes, 4; Norwood, NJ: Ablex Publishing Company, 1980), p. 16.

19. De Beaugrande, 'Text Linguistics through the Years', *Text* 10 (1990), p. 13.

20. Lyons, *Semantics,* I, pp. 262-63.

Principle: *The production and interpretation of sentences/utterances (indeed, of all levels of discourse) are dependent upon the principles of selection and combination.*

The following diagram illustrates this principle in an elementary way.

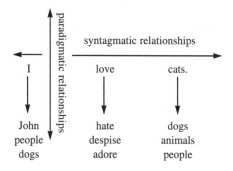

Three basic types of paradigmatic relationships exist between words: synonymy; antonymy; and hyponymy.[21] *Synonymy* refers to a paradigmatic relationship in which lexical items share similar meanings (but not necessarily totally synonymous ones), that is, words from the same semantic domain. *Antonymy* refers to a paradigmatic relationship in which lexical items are dissimilar in meaning. It is not that antonyms are totally unrelated in meaning but that they differ in one or only a few semantic features while sharing others, that is, there is negativity and similarity. Some antonyms are *privative* in that one of the lexemes denotes the positive property and the other denotes the absence of that property (e.g. 'known' vs. 'unknown', πιστός vs. ἄπιστος). Other antonyms are *equipollent*, that is, contrasting lexemes which share a positive property (e.g. both ἄρσην 'male' and θῆλυς 'female' have gender but different genders). These two types of antonyms may be further subdivided into three categories. *Gradable* antonyms include those words which are used to compare two or more objects with respect to their possession of a certain property (e.g. ψυχρός 'cold' and ζεστός 'hot' compare the temperature of objects). *Complementary* antonyms, in contrast, are not gradable (e.g. 'female' and 'male' or νεκρός 'dead' and ζωή 'alive'). *Converse* antonyms, as the label suggests, involve words such as ἀγοράζω 'buy' and πωλέω 'sell' (i.e. *I*

21. For a detailed discussion, see Lyons, *Theoretical Linguistics*, pp. 446-70.

buy shoes is the converse of *I am sold shoes*) or ἀνήρ 'husband' and γυνή 'wife'. The third type of sense-relation, *hyponymy*, refers to paradigmatic relationships in which one lexical item is included in the total semantic range of another item (but not vice-versa), allowing for a hierarchy in lexical systems. For example, 'Labrador' is a hyponym of 'dog', 'dog' is a hyponym of 'animal', 'animal' is a hyponym of 'living beings', and so on. Similarly, οὖς 'ear' is a hyponym of σῶμα 'body'. The one is included in the semantic range of the other which in turn is included in the semantic range of another, and so on. Hyponymy may be further distinguished according to *contracting* types (e.g. '*People* got on and off the bus. At the news-stand *school children*, returning home, bought candy.') and *expanding* types ('*Diamonds* may be a girl's best friend, but then *jewellery* can be expensive'.).

One method of specifying these three types of paradigmatic sense-relations is by *componential analysis*, which originated in anthropology, in semantic field theory, and especially in the Prague school's *distinctive feature analysis* of morphology. In componential analysis, the various components or features of meaning which make up a word are separated into constituent semantic parts. Two or more closely related words are then described as either having or not having the various components. Often, only a few semantic components demarcate two paradigmatically related words. However, such slight distinctions may prove important for understanding why one word is used in a particular context rather than another. Two simplistic componential analyses illustrate the approach.

	Animate	Male	Single	Possibility of Marriage
Bachelor	+	+	+	+
Monk	+	+	+	-

	Animate	Human	Adult	Male
ἀνήρ	+	+	+	+
γυνή	+	+	+	-

Componential analysis is not without valid criticism, however, as the above examples reveal. First, another analyst may want to create more sense-relations to describe these words than I have. Some componential analyses may become so expansive that they no longer provide a meaningful description of a word (e.g. a bachelor could be labelled a 'thing'). Different interpreters might come up with componential analyses which share only some of the same components—as was vividly revealed to me after giving such assignments to students. Secondly, the components of a componential analysis are often arbitrary. For example, 'possibility of marriage' may be a general description of a bachelor, but when 'bachelor' is used in the phrase 'bachelor party' the sense of *imminent* marriage is also present. This example reveals that componential analysis tends to create the impression that words mean something apart from actual contexts. Despite these problems, this method does force exegetes to be precise about their understanding of a given word's 'meaning'.

4. Semantics is not, as stated above, relegated only to the study of lexical meaning. A semantic analysis also encompasses grammatical meaning, which is quite important in the case of an inflected (or 'fusional') language such as Greek. Thus, λόγος and λόγον have different 'meanings'. The inflections add a certain 'sense' to the meaning of the lexical root. Inflections are not the only grammatical influence upon lexical semantics. For example, the word ἀκούω can take its object in the accusative or genitive case. J.H. Moulton has deemed this significant for interpreting the Acts accounts of Paul's 'conversion'. He maintains that there is no contradiction in the two accounts (Acts 9.7 and 22.9) if the 'well-known distinction between the accusative and genitive with ἀκούω' is recognized.[22] In Acts 9.7 ἀκούοντες...τῆς φωνῆς, accordingly, the genitive indicates that those with Paul heard the sound but did not distinguish the words; thus, they did not understand the voice when they heard it (22.9 τὴν...φωνὴν οὐκ ἤκουσαν τοῦ λαλοῦντος). In sum,

Principle: *Grammar and lexis both contribute to the senses of words; consequently, syntax and semantics (form and function) are inseparable components of a semantic analysis of discourse.*

An important consequence of this principle relates to the common distinction between deep structure and surface structure, a tenet sometimes employed by transformational-generative linguists and biblical scholars.[23] While it is possible to conceive of the difference between an

---

22. J.H. Moulton, *A Grammar of New Testament Greek*. I. *Prolegomena* (Edinburgh: T. & T. Clark, 3rd edn, 1908), p. 66; for discussion and alternative explanation, see F.F. Bruce, *The Acts of the Apostles* (Grand Rapids: Eerdmans, 1951), p. 199.

23. See Louw, *Semantics*, pp. 67-89.

author's intended theme (deep structure) and the way in which this theme is actualized in discourse (surface structure), the only recourse to the deep structure of an ancient text is through the surface structure. A semantic analysis of New Testament discourse is first of all based on a linguistic theory (presupposed or explicit) of surface structures.

5. It is now a generally agreed upon principle of biblical exegesis that *context* plays a key role in the semantics of individual words. That is, words acquire meaning when they are used in a context. Context can be more usefully divided into the concepts of co-text (the surrounding linguistic context, e.g. word, phrase, clause, pericope, discourse), context of situation (the immediate situation in which the discourse occurs), register (the genre of the discourse), context of culture (shared world view), and idiolect (a person's individualized world view). All of these factors influence the speaker's choice and the listener's interpretation of linguistic meaning. This all goes to say that an empirical study of language should be based upon the use of 'language-utterances in the multifarious situations of everyday life'.[24] Or to quote Wittgenstein's famous slogan: 'Do not look for the meaning of a word, look for its use'. Hence,

Principle: *Words as physical objects do not 'possess' meaning, they are 'attributed' meaning by speakers and listeners in a context.*

Consequently, it is becoming more commonplace in New Testament studies to emphasize the polyvalence of discourse; that is, texts allow for a multitude of interpretations. Rather than debate the validity of this claim (human experience verifies the point), it would seem more beneficial for New Testament semantics to focus on *why* it is that words can mean something in particular at all (another principle which human experience verifies). That is, what linguistic and sociological influences account for the fact that speakers are often able to communicate at least in part what they intend to communicate? That which restricts possible semantic interpretations is precisely the above notion of context.[25] (a) The co-text (viz. morphemes, words, clauses, sentences, paragraphs, and discourses) limits the possible senses of linguistic expressions (paradigmatic options) by means of the syntagmatic structure. (b) The

24. Lyons, *Theoretical Linguistics*, p. 411.
25. Cf. the study of 'dimensions of the meaning of a discourse' in Cotterell and Turner, *Linguistics*, pp. 77-105.

immediate (and to a certain degree unique) context of situation limits possible meanings primarily by means of the pragmatic principle of relevance (see below on pragmatics). (c) Registers (genres) also confine meaning by bringing to mind stereotypical situations in which certain linguistic choices reflect the situation (see below on sociolinguistics). (d) The context of culture (world view) restricts potential meanings by means of cognitive mental scripts through which experience is filtered (and which experience, including linguistic experience, may modify); that is, a speaker's mental script of a social convention might determine what kinds of paradigmatically-related words may be employed in that context. Any speaker or reader might break these linguistic and cultural conventions (which allows for an infinite number of possible intentions and interpretations), but this can be done only with the result of creating new collocations, new world views, and new registers, which is simply another means of organizing and hence restricting meaning.

6. Lastly, due to the importance of the Greek lexical system for a semantic interpretation of New Testament discourse, dictionaries have played a central, determinative role in New Testament studies.[26] Until recently, standard New Testament dictionaries have hardly been based on principles of modern semantics. For this reason, a tool like Louw and Nida's *Greek–English Lexicon* is invaluable, although it has not had much influence as of yet on exegetical studies. Despite the title, this work offers much more than the standard lexicon. It seeks to partition New Testament Greek words into their semantic domains and sub-domains, that is, various sense-relations distinguishing words from one another.[27] This lexicon is characterized by functional categories, many of which represent cultural phenomena. For example, rather than listing words in their alphabetical order, Louw and Nida order them according to meaningful categories such as Geographical Objects and Features, Maritime Activities, and Household Activities. Under each category (domain), further subdomains may also be delineated. Under the category of Geographical Objects and Features, for example, are the sub-categories (subdomains) of Universe/Creation, Regions Below the Surface of the Earth, Heavenly Bodies, Atmospheric Objects, The

---

26. For a history of New Testament lexicography, see J.P. Louw, 'The Present State of New Testament Lexicography', in *Lexicography and Translation* (ed. J.P. Louw; Roggebaai: Bible Society of South Africa, 1985), pp. 97-117.

27. For a detailed statement on the purpose and theoretical moorings of the lexicon, see their 'Introduction', *Greek–English Lexicon*, I, pp. vi-xx.

Earth's Surface, Elevated Land Formations, Depressions and Holes, and so on. By grouping words according to functional categories, Louw and Nida reveal an essential function of words, viz. a means of storing and communicating human knowledge of culture and experience. More importantly, under each category (domain or subdomain) words are listed according to a hierarchy, that is, words with the most general meaning are listed first and those with the most narrow meanings last (from generic to specific)—a hyponymous approach to language. For example, under the category of Household Activities, οἰκονομέω ('to manage and provide for a household') is listed first and σαρόω ('to sweep by using a broom') last. In other words, sweeping with a broom conveys a more specific household activity. Hopefully, this will not be the last edition of this lexicon. Most notably, it needs to (i) broaden the semantic domains to include other words from Hellenistic Greek; (ii) re-evaluate interpretations of individual words based on new literary evidence and wider scholarly exegesis; and (iii) provide examples from extra-biblical literature.[28] Despite these current limitations, future lexicons will hopefully employ similar theoretical frameworks.

3. *Pragmatics*

Pragmatics is defined by Robert C. Stalnaker as 'the study of linguistic acts and the contexts in which they are performed'.[29] Its modern usage originated in the philosopher Charles Morris who demarcated three branches of semiotics (the science of signs): syntax, semantics, and pragmatics.[30] According to Morris, syntax concerns 'the formal relation

---

28. For other criticisms, see J.A.L. Lee, 'The United Bible Societies' Lexicon and its Analysis of Meanings', *FN* 5 (1992), pp. 167-89; for a response, see J.P. Louw, 'The Analysis of Meaning in Lexicography', *FN* 6 (1993), pp. 139-48.

29. R.C. Stalnaker, 'Pragmatics', in *Semantics of Natural Language* (ed. D. Davidson and G. Harman; Dordrecht: Reidel, 2nd edn, 1972), pp. 380-97. Besides the other works cited below, see also E. Bates, *Language and Context: The Acquisition of Pragmatics* (New York: Academic Press, 1976); D. Sperber and D. Wilson, 'Pragmatics', *Cognition* 10 (1981), pp. 281-86; G.M. Green, *Pragmatics and Natural Language Understanding* (Hillsdale, NJ: Erlbaum, 1989); and J.L. Mey, *Pragmatics: An Introduction* (Oxford: Basil Blackwell, 1993). In addition, *Journal of Pragmatics* (since 1977) contains a wealth of up-to-date research on pragmatics.

30. C.W. Morris, *Foundations of the Theory of Signs*, in *International Encyclopedia of Unified Science* (ed. O. Neurath, R. Carnap, and C. Morris; Chicago: University of Chicago Press, 1938), pp. 77-138; reprinted in C.W. Morris, *Writings*

of signs to one another', semantics 'the relations of signs to the objects to which the signs are applicable', and pragmatics 'the relation of signs to interpreters'.[31] The pragmatic study of language seeks to understand how the context in which an utterance is made affects the interpretation of that utterance. In pragmatics, then, particular attention is given to language structure (lexico-grammar) *and* context of situation. So Stephen C. Levinson, in his influential work, provides a working definition of pragmatics: 'Pragmatics is the study of those relations between language and context that are grammaticalized, or encoded in the structure of a language'.[32] In this definition of pragmatics, Levinson has made an appeal that pragmatics should take seriously the role of the lexico-grammar in the contextual interpretation of discourse. He admits that his restriction of pragmatics to linguistic matters does not reflect all of current practice,[33] but his approach is very suggestive for New Testament linguistics which only has recourse to the texts in which the original contexts were encoded. Based on Levinson's definition,

Principle: *A reconstruction of a discourse's context should at least partly be explained in terms of the lexico-grammar of the discourse.*

The converse of this principle is equally applicable to grammarians of New Testament Greek.

Principle: *An explanation of the grammar of a particular part of discourse should take into account the context.*

These general principles become more specific when one turns to two major areas of pragmatic research: *deixis* and the closely related concepts of *presupposition* and *speech acts*.

on the General Theory of Signs (The Hague: Mouton, 1971). This tripartite approach to linguistics has influenced several biblical scholars (e.g. Schenk, *Philipperbriefe* and D. Hellholm, *Das Visionenbuch des Hermas als Apokalypse: Formgeschichtliche und texttheoretische Studien zu einer literarischen Gattung. I. Methodologische Vorüberlegungen und makrostrukturelle Textanalyse* [ConBNTS, 13; Lund: Gleerup, 1980]), but has been abandoned by many discourse analysts for being too compartmentalized to explain real discourse.

   31. Morris, *Foundations*, p. 6.

   32. S.C. Levinson, *Pragmatics* (Cambridge: Cambridge University Press, 1983), p. 9.

   33. Levinson, *Pragmatics*, p. 11.

Deixis

Deixis refers to the ability of language users to employ linguistic forms to 'point to' or 'indicate' elements of the *co-text* (i.e. surrounding linguistic elements) and/or *context* (i.e. situational elements). Levinson describes it as 'the ways in which languages encode or grammaticalize features of the *context of utterance* or *speech event'*.[34] Deictic indicators may be usefully divided into three categories: person, time, and place.

Person deixis refers to the grammaticalizing in discourse of the participants (persons or objects) involved in the context.[35] Languages often allow for naming conventions in order to identify participants. Generally, some nominal form performs this role. Pronouns then take over to make the discourse less redundant. Other means of signalling participants in Greek include the article and verbal suffixes (e.g. first, second, third person, singular and plural). Person deixis not only concerns the referents of a discourse, but also the roles played by those referents. Typical roles include *spokesperson(s)* and *recipient(s)*. The spokesperson produces the discourse, but can also be distinguished from its *source*. Indirect discourse is one way in which a spokesperson shifts to another person as the source of a message. For example, in 1 Cor. 12.16 the anatomical 'ear' is the source of a direct discourse ('Because I am not an eye, I do not belong to the body' ὅτι οὐκ εἰμὶ ὀφθαλμός, οὐκ εἰμὶ ἐκ τοῦ σώματος) which is recounted by the spokesperson, Paul (indeed the actual source of the direct discourse). Paul at times appeals to this distinction between spokesperson and source. In 1 Cor. 7.10 he gives a command to married persons, adding that it is not his command but the Lord's. Later in the letter he gives his own opinion regarding the pursuit of marriage by virgins (1 Cor. 7.25). In one case the source is the 'Lord'; in another he is the implied source. Just as the spokesperson may not be the source of a message, the recipient may not be the *target* of address. For example, although 1 Timothy is addressed to Timothy some have argued that the intended target comprised a wider circle of Christians.[36]

34. Levinson, *Pragmatics*, p. 54.
35. See M.A.K. Halliday, *Language as Social Semiotic: The Social Interpretation of Language and Meaning* (London: Edward Arnold, 1978), p. 132; *Introduction to Functional Grammar* (London: Edward Arnold, 1985), pp. 168-69.
36. For discussion, see J.T. Reed, 'To Timothy or Not: A Discourse Analysis of 1 Timothy', in *Biblical Greek Language and Linguistics: Open Questions in Current Research* (ed. S.E. Porter and D.A. Carson; JSNTSup, 80; Sheffield: JSOT Press, 1993), pp. 90-118.

Recipients may be either *ratified* or *unratified*. To draw upon
1 Timothy, if the author's real target was the larger church body (1 Tim.
4.13), he may have only wanted part of that group to hear his letter (e.g.
elders and presbyters)—the ratified recipients of the letter. These leaders
(including Timothy) were then expected to see that the message
eventually reached the entire community.

Temporal deixis is another important way in which discourse is tied to
a context of situation.[37] According to one grammatical model of the
Greek language, verb tenses serve as temporal indicators in discourse.
Recent research in verbal aspect of the Greek verb either abandons or
significantly downplays the idea of time in the verbal tense-forms.[38] This
debate is far from over, and presently there are exegetes from all three
schools of thought (temporal, *Aktionsart*, aspect), and some with mixed
categories. The point, however, is that the interpretation of tense-forms as
temporal deixis is disputed. Some less-disputed deictic indicators of time
include adverbs (e.g. τότε, νῦν, μέχρι), anaphora (e.g. demonstratives),
and references to places (spatial and temporal deixis are closely related).
All three classes are helpful for establishing temporal relationships
between the discourse and the implied context of situation. The first
class represents a type of direct temporal indication; the others are
indirect. Analysis of temporal deixis is complicated by the point of view
of the speaker. For example, if a letter is read containing the sentence
'Now I will tell you what I think about your new book', does the word
'now' refer to the point in time at which the letter was written or the
point in time at which it was read? Similarly, does the aorist ἔγραψα in
1 Cor. 5.11 (νῦν δὲ ἔγραψα ὑμῖν...) refer to the time when the letter
was written or the time it was read. In deictic terms, the distinction is
between the 'moment of utterance (or inscription) or coding time (or
CT)' and the 'moment of reception or receiving time (or RT)'.[39]
Temporal deixis is even relative for the speaker, since at the precise

---

37. Halliday, *Functional Grammar*, p. 176.
38. See esp. the persuasive, although somewhat distinct, arguments in the publica-
tions of B.M. Fanning, *Verbal Aspect in New Testament Greek* (Oxford: Clarendon
Press, 1990); K.L. McKay, *A New Syntax of the Verb in New Testament Greek:
An Aspectual Approach* (Studies in Biblical Greek, 5; New York: Peter Lang, 1994);
S.E. Porter, *Verbal Aspect in the Greek of the New Testament, with Reference to
Tense and Mood* (Studies in Biblical Greek, 1; New York: Peter Lang, 1989); and
J.W. Voelz, 'Present and Aorist Verbal Aspect: A New Proposal', *Neot* 27 (1993),
pp. 153-64.
39. Levinson, *Pragmatics*, p. 73.

point in time when the word 'now' or ἔγραψα is actually written, the author has not yet finished writing the clause. The point being emphasized here is that grammatical forms do not provide *absolute* indicators of time. They are *relative* to anchorage points determined by the speaker. The anchorage points may be interpreted differently by the listener.

Levinson defines *place* deixis as 'the specification of locations relative to anchorage points in the speech event'.[40] The characteristic feature of place deixis is that it concerns the spatial locations of persons/objects relative to other persons/objects. An example of this may involve a speaker (anchorage point) pointing to an object across the room (relative location). This may be done explicitly by naming or describing locations, as in the sentence 'The school is twenty miles away from the library' and in Mt. 14.24 τὸ δὲ πλοῖον ἤδη σταδίους πολλοὺς ἀπὸ τῆς γῆς ἀπεῖχεν 'the boat by this time was many furlongs away from the land'. Locations may also be specified relative to the location of a speaker, as in the sentence 'The dog is fifty feet away from here' and in Jn 4.16 ὕπαγε φώνησον τὸν ἄνδρα σου καὶ ἐλθὲ ἐνθάδε 'go, call your husband, and come here'. In both examples, 'here' and ἐνθάδε refer to something outside of the discourse. 'Here' and ἐνθάδε are the anchorage points around which other objects are relatively located. As in temporal deixis, place deixis is relative to the speaker, that is, the speaker determines the anchorage point around which other entities are located. Again, the listener may interpret the anchorage points differently.

Presupposition and Implicature

The concept of *speech acts*, originating in the works of the philosophers Ludwig Wittgenstein, J.L. Austin, H.P. Grice, and John Searle,[41] and the

40. Levinson, *Pragmatics*, p. 79; cf. Halliday, *Functional Grammar*, p. 160.

41. L. Wittgenstein, *Tractatus Logico-Philosophicus* (trans. D.F. Pears and B.F. McGuiness; London: Routledge & Kegan Paul, 1961); J.L. Austin, *How to Do Things with Words* (London: Oxford University Press, 1962); H.P. Grice, 'Logic and Conversation', in *Syntax and Semantics 3: Speech Acts* (ed. P. Cole and J. Morgan; New York: Academic Press, 1975), pp. 41-58 (part of H.P. Grice, *Logic and Conversation* [unpublished manuscript of the William James Lectures, Harvard University, 1967]); J.R. Searle, *Speech Acts: An Essay in the Philosophy of Language* (Cambridge: Cambridge University Press, 1969); for applications of speech act theory to the New Testament, see esp. A.C. Thiselton, 'The Parables as Language Event: Some Comments on Fuchs's Hermeneutics in the Light of Linguistic Philosophy', *SJT* 23 (1970), pp. 437-60; T. Aurelio, *Disclosures in den Gleichnisse*

closely related concepts of *presupposition* and *implicature* have already resulted in more methodologically precise discussions of New Testament texts and their situational contexts.

Austin, for example, highlighted the ways in which speakers *do* something through *performative* utterances (e.g. 'I hereby declare you husband and wife'), or direct speech acts. In indirect speech acts, the illocutionary force of the utterance (e.g. yes-no question in 'Can you help me out here?') distorts its intended function (e.g. a request). Pragmatics is concerned with the principles used by listeners to draw inferences from utterances and their contexts in order to interpret them. One such principle is the so-called rule of 'common conversation':

Principle: *Make the strongest relevant claim justifiable by your evidence.*[42]

Using this principle, it would be possible to infer B from the assertion of A in the following sentence (1 Cor. 4.18 RSV):

A: 'Some are arrogant (as though I were not coming to you).'
B: 'Some are not arrogant.'

B is not derived from A by logical entailment since A could be true even when B is false as in 'Some are arrogant; indeed, all are arrogant'. B is derived pragmatically from A based on the rules of 'common conversation'. Accordingly, Paul's choice of the weaker statement (ἐφυσιώθησάν τινες) *implicates* that he was not in a position to assert a stronger one (e.g. ἐφυσιώθησαν πάντες). In other words, he makes

---

Jesu: Eine Anwendung der Disclosure-Theorie von I.T. Ramsey, der modernen Methaphorik und der Sprechakte auf die Gleichnisse Jesu (Regensburger Studien zur Theologie, 8; Frankfurt: Lang, 1977); E. Arens, *Kommunikative Handlungen: Die paradigmatische Bedeutung der Gleichnisse Jesu für eine Handlungstheorie* (Düsseldorf: Patmos, 1982); J.N. Vorster, 'Toward an Interactional Model for the Analysis of Letters', *Neot* 24 (1990), pp. 107-30; and the articles in *Semeia* 41 (1988); J.G. Du Plessis, 'Why Did Peter Ask his Question and How Did Jesus Answer Him? Or: Implicature in Luke 12.35-48', *Neot* 22 (1988), pp. 311-23; *idem*, 'Speech Act Theory and New Testament Interpretation with Special Reference to G.N. Leech's Pragmatic Principles', in *Text and Interpretation: New Approaches in the Criticism of the New Testament* (ed. P.J. Hartin and J.H. Petzer; NTTS, 15; Leiden: Brill, 1991), pp. 129-42.

42. R.M. Harnish, 'Logical Form and Implicature', in *An Integrated Theory of Linguistic Ability* (ed. T.G. Bever *et al.*; New York: Crowell, 1976), p. 362.

the strongest relevant claim justifiable by his evidence.

Grice's theory sets forth a more comprehensive approach to pragmatic implicature. His general principle is called the *co-operative principle*.

Principle: *Make your conversational contribution such as is required, at the stage at which it occurs, by the accepted purpose or direction of the talk exchange in which you are engaged.*[43]

This principle assumes that the goal of speakers is to communicate successfully their message. The speaker must, therefore, cooperate with the audience. Four maxims further clarify what it means for the speaker to cooperate.

Quantity:	Make your contribution as informative as is required (for the current purposes of the exchange). Do not make your contribution more informative than is required.
Quality:	Do not say that which you believe to be false. Do not say that for which you lack adequate evidence.
Relation:	Be relevant.
Manner:	Be perspicuous. Avoid obscurity of expression. Avoid ambiguity. Be brief (avoid unnecessary prolixity). Be orderly.

This is not an exhaustive list (so claims Grice), but it represents the most significant principles or maxims which speakers supposedly adhere to when communicating. (Of course these maxims can be broken, perhaps for the purpose of concealing meaning, but not without frustrating the communicative process.) Consider the following exchange between a student and a teacher:

A: I've got the worst headache.
B: There's a bottle of aspirin in my drawer.

Several conversational assumptions occur in this brief interchange; a few may be noted. B would not be acting relevantly if there was an empty bottle of aspirin in the drawer. The speaker assumes that the bottle is not empty. The quality of A's statement would be invalid if the student had a stomach-ache instead of a headache. B assumes that A sincerely means

43. Grice, 'Logic and Conversation', p. 45 (emphasis mine).

what A is saying. Of course the student could be lying, but this would be a purposeful avoidance of the cooperative principle for some ulterior motive. This is what makes the cooperative principle difficult to use at times, since the analyst does not always know whether the speaker is being honest or dishonest. Another difficulty in applying this principle is irony, in which meaning and expression are not directly related. According to Grice's principles it might be argued that effective irony is simply a case of recognizable relevancy.

Some conversational implicatures become conventionalized (*conventional implicata*), that is, they are associated with certain lexical and grammatical constructions.[44] Because they are socially conventionalized, these implicatures are *pragmatic presuppositions*: 'propositions whose truth [the speaker] takes for granted, or seems to take for granted, in making his statement'.[45] These presuppositions are based on a *common ground* shared between speaker and listener in a given context. In any given utterance there may be conventional implicata which are presupposed by speaker and listener and also assertions or propositions which add information to the common ground. For example, the author's following utterance in A (Lk. 18.15 RSV) may be reduced to the assertion of B.

> A: '...they were bringing even (καί) infants to him that he might touch them.'
> B: 'They were bringing infants to him that he might touch them.'

Whereas the proposition B has been *added* to the common ground of author and reader, 'even' *implies* that they brought others to Jesus and that children were least likely to be brought. In other words, 'even' contributes a presupposition to the communicative context which the speaker considers non-controversial (i.e. it is presupposed as part of the context).

In sum, the above cursory treatment of pragmatic theory suggests several hermeneutical principles for New Testament interpretation: (i) communication should be informative enough (not too little but not too much); (ii) it should be relevant with respect to the context and the

44. See L. Karttunen and S. Peters, 'Conversational Implicature', in *Presupposition* (ed. C.-K. Oh and D.A. Dinneen; New York: Academic Press, 1979), pp. 1-56.

45. R.C. Stalnaker, 'Pragmatic Presuppositions', in *Semantics and Philosophy* (ed. M.K. Munitz and P.K. Unger; New York: New York University Press, 1974), pp. 197-214.

theme(s) of the discourse; (iii) it should be brief and sufficiently clear. It is not unreasonable to suppose that New Testament authors would have been accountable to abide by such principles, at least with respect to their audience. The cooperative principle, along with the goal of informativeness, truthfulness, relevancy, and clarity, provides a standard upon which exegetes may argue for a particular interpretation of a text and its context. In addition, they are useful for reader-response analyses of New Testament texts, since readers' interpretations are also influenced by the cooperative principle. Indeed all of the above communicative principles may be summed up under Sperber and Wilson's single axiom of relevance:[46]

Principle: *The speaker tries to make the utterance as relevant as possible to the hearer.*

4. *Sociolinguistics*

Whereas the term 'sociology of language' emphasizes the 'sociological' aspect of language, 'sociolinguistics' typically highlights the 'linguistic' side of social behaviour. *Sociolinguistic* studies generally seek to understand the social significance of language *usage*,[47] including such topics of

---

46. D. Sperber and D. Wilson, *Relevance: Communication and Cognition* (Oxford: Basil Blackwell, 1986).

47. Some informative works include D.H. Hymes (ed.), *Language in Culture and Society* (New York: Harper & Row, 1964); J.J. Gumperz and D.H. Hymes (eds.), *Directions in Sociolinguistics* (New York: Holt, Rinehart and Winston, 1972); W. Labov, *Sociolinguistic Patterns* (Philadelphia: University of Pennsylvania Press, 1972); D.H. Hymes, *Foundations in Sociolinguistics: An Ethnographic Approach* (Philadelphia: University of Pennsylvania Press, 1974); M. Sanches and B. Blount (eds.), *Sociocultural Dimensions of Language Use* (New York: Academic Press, 1975); M. Gregory and S. Carroll, *Language and Situation: Language Varieties and their Social Contexts* (London: Routledge & Kegan Paul, 1978); P. Brown and S. Levinson, 'Social Structure, Groups and Interaction', in *Social Markers in Speech* (ed. K. Scherer and H. Giles; Cambridge: Cambridge University Press, 1979), pp. 291-347; R.A. Hudson, *Sociolinguistics* (Cambridge: Cambridge University Press, 1980); P. Trudgill, *Sociolinguistics: An Introduction to Language and Society* (Harmondsworth: Penguin Books, rev. edn, 1983); J.P. Louw (ed.), *Sociolinguistics and Communication* (UBS Monograph Series, 1; New York: United Bible Societies, 1986); N. Fairclough, *Language and Power* (London: Longman, 1989); *idem*, *Discourse and Social Change* (Cambridge: Polity Press, 1992). For application to the New Testament, see F.P. Cotterell, 'Sociolinguistics', *Vox Evangelica* 16 (1986), pp. 61-76.

research as interactional sociolinguistics, power and language, social dialect, and social structure and language. Such interests have resulted in cross-fertilization with pragmatics.

Sociolinguistic studies have shown that the idea of an isolated, fixed language does not do justice to the facts. Rather, *varieties of language* exist within and across cultural groups. Only in the case of *standard languages*, perhaps such as Hellenistic Greek, should one think of a *language* in contrast to what is typically termed *dialect*. A standard language, or *code*, is shared by a group of people. Such linguistic codes provide a way to communicate despite regional and social *dialects*. In other words, whereas the code is shared by the larger society, dialects are unique to various groups of users of the code.[48] Dialect is commonly thought of in terms of pronunciation; however, other factors determine dialectical varieties such as spelling, vocabulary, and gestures. Variant spelling practices probably due to pronunciation differences, as found in ancient papyri, reveal such dialectical varieties in Egypt. Such dialects (or varieties of language) should be pictured on a continuum with opposite poles representing the greatest disparity between the varieties. If two varieties of language are closely positioned together on the continuum, they are readily understood by the different speakers. Two varieties of language on opposite ends of the continuum are less intelligible to the different users of the code. Although the similarities among the dialects on the continuum are recognizable, R.A. Hudson argues that the individual instances on the continuum should not be called a particular language. 'The concept "language X" has no part to play in sociolinguistics—nor, for exactly the same reasons, can it have any place in linguistics.'[49] Accordingly, it might be argued that there is no such thing as *the* language of the New Testament, but only varieties of language in the New Testament. At most, there is a shared linguistic code underlying these varieties.

Two key factors—regional and social—affect changes in varieties of languages. Regional factors refer to the geographical locations of the language users. Geographical isolation often results in unique developments of a language variety (e.g. phonological peculiarities). Social factors, such as gender, age, education, and status, all affect the development of varieties of language. In addition, the particular needs of

48. Hudson, *Sociolinguistics*, p. 48.
49. Hudson, *Sociolinguistics*, p. 37.

social groups may result in the modification of the standard language. For example, all legal terms used in the Roman judicial system may not have been part of the public's vocabulary, but they were a vital part of the variety of language used by lawyers and orators. Similarly, early Christian groups likely developed their own varieties of language; in addition, the evidence suggests that the native languages of Palestinian and diaspora Jews did interfere with their use of Greek.[50]

Hudson argues that standard languages are the only examples of language in which one should speak of 'a language X'.[51] A standard language is a variety of language that has become the assumed, widespread language of choice. It may simply be a variety of language that has been accepted (for various reasons) by a larger group of speakers. With the rise of Alexander's empire, koiné Greek (originally the Attic dialect) first developed as the standard variety of language of the empire, with the result that communication took place across dialectal and cultural varieties. This linguistic *code* was eventually shared throughout regions of the Roman empire, allowing for cross-cultural communication.

Individual speakers not only learn the standard language and varieties of language necessary to communicate, but they also acquire language based on their own personal experience, resulting in a somewhat idiosyncratic *idiolect* or personal variety of language. All the experiences and events of an individual's life give rise to an evolution of linguistic structures in the brain. This might involve, for example, particularities in pronunciation, intonation, rate of delivery, vocabulary, or sentence structure. More importantly, certain language users might recognize the idiolects of others and attach social significance to them. Paul's idiolect, both written and spoken, clearly evoked certain types of cognitive and emotive responses (cf. 2 Cor. 10.10).

50. On the latter point, see the informative article by M. Silva, 'Bilingualism and the Character of Palestinian Greek', *Bib* 61 (1980), pp. 198-219; he demonstrates cogently that on the level of *langue* (language system) New Testament Greek is part of the koiné Greek used throughout the Roman empire of the day, but that on the level of *parole* (language use) it shows signs of Semitic influence. On the former point, however, I am unaware of any comprehensive attempt to compare the linguistic varieties of early Christian documents to reveal potential sociological (or regional) differences—a macro and micro-stylistic evaluation of the New Testament and other Christian documents.

51. Hudson, *Sociolinguistics*, p. 37.

Studies of language varieties and code can assist in the debate over the language of the New Testament. But another area of sociolinguistics, register/genre, is more useful in the analysis of actual texts. Whereas standard languages and varieties of languages are determined by broad sociological factors, *register* or *genre*[52] have to do with more narrow, limited sociological factors. More specifically, whereas a variety of language refers to *language according to user*,[53] register refers to *language according to use*. Registers correspond to linguistic expressions occasioned by common, social activities (e.g. telephone conversations; teacher–pupil interchange; doctor–patient appointments; or ancient letters). They are a means of 'doing things' with language. Consequently, registers are one of the most important ways of relating language to the context of situation. Register has been defined as *a configuration of meanings which is associated with a particular situation*.[54] Communicants are able to identify the situation by means of these configurations of meanings (e.g. 'once upon a time', epistolary formulas), often by the time the first few words of a discourse are spoken. It usually takes only a few seconds, for example, when turning on the radio, to identify whether we are listening to a sermon, sports broadcast, news broadcast, disc jockey, commentary, talk show, quiz programme, or interview. Halliday's definition hits at the essence of the concept of register:

> A register can be defined as a particular configuration of meanings that is associated with a particular situation type. In any social context, certain semantic resources are characteristically employed; certain sets of options are as it were 'at risk' in the given semiotic environment. These define the register. Considered in terms of the notion of meaning potential, the register is the range of meaning potential that is activated by the semiotic properties of the situation.[55]

52. The terms are used interchangeably here, the only difference being that register concerns primarily the social context of a 'way of speaking' and genre concerns primarily the spoken or written manifestation of that context in a 'way of speaking'.

53. Hudson, *Sociolinguistics*, pp. 48-49.

54. M.A.K. Halliday and R. Hasan, *Language, Context, and Text: Aspects of Language in a Social-Semiotic Perspective* (Oxford: Oxford University Press, 1989), pp. 38-39.

55. M.A.K. Halliday, *Learning How to Mean—Explorations in the Development of Language* (London: Edward Arnold, 1975), p. 126.

Halliday is suggesting that changes in the context of situation contribute to changes in the use of language. Speakers conform their discourse to the context of situation, and consequently draw upon accepted forms of language which others recognize as appropriate for that situation. Ethnographers have argued that 'much of language use, like a grammar, is rule governed'.[56] Registers, accordingly, may be treated as rule-governed structures of language use. Consequently, these linguistic structures invoke corresponding interpretations by listeners, that is, they provide for predictability. 'Appropriateness for the situation', for example, was an important aspect of rhetorical and epistolary theory in Greco-Roman traditions. The same communicative principle (which is likely a universal principle along the lines of Grice's 'cooperative' principle) *prima facie* governed the production of New Testament discourses.

This principle of predictability required by a register involves primarily five aspects of discourse: (i) subject-matter (the semantic content of the discourse); (ii) situation-type (or context of situation); (iii) participant roles (who is communicating with whom; what are the differences or similarities in age, gender, and other social variables); (iv) mode (e.g. persuasive, explanatory, and imperative discourses); and (v) medium (spoken or written).[57] Languages develop standard formulas in order to express these features of the discourse. The following diagram illustrates the fundamental choices of generic formulas made by an author. Once a particular situation invokes a choice of register, the author may choose to support or reject standard conventions (formulas). If they are supported, the author must then choose both between obligatory or optional formulas *and* between canonical or modified ones. These types of choices involve eight basic questions: (i) what elements must occur (obligatory)?; (ii) what elements may occur (optional)?; (iii) where must they occur?; (iv) where may they occur?; (v) how often must they occur?; (vi) how often may they occur?; (vii) what function must they have?; and (viii) what function may they have?

56. J.J. Gumperz, *Discourse Strategies* (Studies in Interactional Sociolinguistics, 1; Cambridge: Cambridge University Press, 1982), p. 155.

57. R. Hasan, 'Code, Register and Social Dialect', in *Class, Codes and Control II: Applied Studies towards a Sociology of Language* (ed. B. Bernstein; London: Routledge & Kegan Paul, 1973), p. 272.

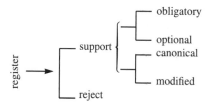

5. *Discourse Analysis*

Discourse analysis, a rapidly-growing, influential discipline of modern linguistics, may provide the type of comprehensive methodological framework necessary for modern linguistics to become a usable hermeneutic for 'non-linguistic' New Testament scholars.[58] Indeed, discourse analysis involves all of the above disciplines of linguistics and several others. This is not to say that discourse analysis is an entirely unified theory of language without theoretical discrepancies among its proponents. It does, however, possess certain tenets which provide a coherent framework for those working in the field as well as a growing body of theoretical and practical literature which has hardly been tapped by New Testament scholars. There is a recognition by discourse analysts that its success depends upon its acceptance of and willingness to inter-act with different scientific disciplines in order to understand language. In a 1990 special tenth anniversary issue of the journal *Text*, Deborah Tannen admits that discourse analysis 'may seem almost dismayingly diverse', but then goes on to suggest that 'an attitude of catholicism

58. See the following works: T. van Dijk, *Some Aspects of Text Grammars* (The Hague: Mouton, 1972); W. Dressler, *Einführung in die Textlinguistik* (Tübingen: Niemeyer, 1972); J.E. Grimes, *The Thread of Discourse* (The Hague: Mouton, 1975); J.M. Sinclair and R.M. Coulthard, *Towards an Analysis of Discourse* (Oxford: Oxford University Press, 1975); T. van Dijk, *Text and Context* (London: Longman, 1977); H.F. Plett, *Textwissenschaft und Textanalyse: Semiotik, Linguistik, Rhetorik* (Heidelberg: Quelle & Meyer, 2nd edn, 1979); R. de Beaugrande and W. Dressler, *Introduction to Text Linguistics* (London: Longman, 1981); J.J. Gumperz, *Discourse Strategies*; Brown and Yule, *Discourse Analysis*; R.E. Longacre, *The Grammar of Discourse* (New York: Plenum, 1983); M. Stubbs, *Discourse Analysis: The Sociolinguistic Analysis of Natural Language* (Oxford: Basil Blackwell, 1983); M. Coulthard, *An Introduction to Discourse Analysis* (London: Longman, 2nd edn, 1985); T.A. van Dijk (ed.), *Handbook of Discourse Analysis* (4 vols.; London: Academic Press, 1985); L. Polyani (ed.), *The Structure of Discourse* (Norwood, NJ: Ablex, 1987); D. Schiffrin, *Approaches to Discourse* (Oxford: Basil Blackwell, 1994).

toward the necessary diversity of the field' is one of its greatest strengths.[59] This 'interdisciplinary attitude' could prove advantageous for biblical scholars, since most will find that they are already familiar with one or more of the major academic disciplines influencing discourse analysis. Nevertheless, its expansiveness or perhaps the mere fact that it is primarily a *linguistic* discipline explains why it has had only marginal influence on mainstream biblical scholarship.[60]

It is impossible in the short span of this essay to survey theories of discourse analysis. It is, however, possible to mention certain key tenets of discourse analysis and to apply one aspect of the theory—viz. information flow—to a New Testament text.

The term *discourse analysis* at its broadest level refers to *the study and interpretation of both the spoken and written communication of humans.*[61] It is analysis that takes seriously the role of the speaker, the text, and the listener in the communicative event. The 'discourse' part of the term might comprise a twenty-volume history of the world or a one-word exchange between a parent and child. The boundary of a *discourse*, then, is probably best treated as whatever language users decide, or 'texts are what hearers and readers treat as texts'.[62] Speakers

59. D. Tannen, 'Discourse Analysis: The Excitement of Diversity', *Text* 10 (1990), pp. 109, 111; cf. T.A. van Dijk, 'The Future of the Field: Discourse Analysis in the 1990s', *Text* 10 (1990), pp. 135-38.

60. Informative theoretical approaches to biblical discourse analysis include: K. Callow, *Discourse Considerations in Translating the Word of God* (Grand Rapids: Zondervan, 1974); Cotterell and Turner, *Linguistics and Biblical Interpretation*; D.A. Dawson, *Text-Linguistics and Biblical Hebrew* (JSOTSup, 177; Sheffield: Sheffield Academic Press, 1994); Hellholm, *Das Visionenbuch des Hermas als Apokalypse*; B. Johanson, *To All the Brethren: A Text-Linguistic and Rhetorical Approach to 1 Thessalonians* (ConBNTS, 16; Stockholm: Almqvist & Wiksell, 1987); S.H. Levinsohn, *Discourse Features of New Testament Greek: A Coursebook* (Dallas: Summer Institute of Linguistics, 1992); J.P. Louw, 'Discourse Analysis and the Greek New Testament', *BT* 24 (1973), pp. 101-19; *idem*, 'Reading a Text as Discourse', in *Linguistics and New Testament Interpretation: Essays on Discourse Analysis* (ed. D.A. Black; Nashville: Broadman Press, 1992), pp. 17-30; W. Pickering, *A Framework for Discourse Analysis* (Arlington, TX: Summer Institute of Linguistics and University of Texas at Arlington, 1980).

61. Cf. Stubbs, *Discourse Analysis*, pp. 1, 9-10.

62. G. Brown and G. Yule, *Discourse Analysis* (Cambridge: Cambridge University Press, 1983), p. 199; cf. Tannen ('Discourse Analysis', p. 109): 'Discourse—language beyond the sentence—is simply *language*—as it occurs, in any context…in any form'.

and listeners determine when a communicative event begins and when it ends. Occasionally, the terms *text linguistics* (*Textwissenschaft*) and *text grammar* refer to the same type of analysis, but specifically that of written texts. Hence some reserve the term *discourse* solely for speech (including paralinguistic features) and the term *text* for the written use of language. In current practice the two are rarely distinguished, as Robert de Beaugrande notes: 'Although "text linguistics" and "discourse analysis" originally emerged from different orientations, they have steadily converged in recent years until they are usually treated as the same enterprise...'[63] For some, the term 'text linguistics' is too narrow and more comprehensive terms have been suggested, such as 'text studies', 'text science', and 'textology'. Nevertheless, 'discourse analysis' is generally the preferred term, although at times giving way to the broader term 'discourse studies'. The following four tenets, although cursory in scope, help put flesh on this skeletal definition of discourse analysis.

1. Discourse analysts take seriously the roles of the speaker, the audience, and the text in the communicative process. On the one hand, discourse analysts seek to *interpret the speaker's role in the production of discourses*. Much of discourse analysis has been concerned with naturally occurring texts and, consequently, how *original* speakers create those texts and how *original* listeners process texts. In addition to the speaker's role, discourse analysts also seek to *interpret the listener's comprehension(s) of and response(s) to the discourse*. Stubbs comments on the impulse to interpret: 'Hearers and readers have a powerful urge to make sense out of whatever nonsense is presented to them'.[64] They may not 'get it right', but they attempt to understand and, more than that, to understand 'correctly'. Brown and Yule summarize this two-part tenet appropriately:

> We shall consider words, phrases and sentences which appear in the textual record of a discourse to be evidence of an attempt by a producer (speaker/writer) to communicate his message to a recipient (hearer/reader). We shall be particularly interested in discussing how a recipient might come to comprehend the producer's intended message on a particular occasion, and how the requirements of the particular recipient(s), in definable circumstances, influence the organization of the producer's

63. R. de Beaugrande, 'Text Linguistics and New Applications', *Annual Review of Applied Linguistics* 11 (1990), p. 26 n. 1.
64. Stubbs, *Discourse Analysis*, p. 5.

discourse. This is clearly an approach which takes the communicative function of language as its primary area of investigation and consequently seeks to describe linguistic form, not as a static object, but as a dynamic means of expressing intended meaning.[65]

2. The discourse analyst is also guided by the tenet to *examine language at a linguistic level larger than the sentence.*[66] This is perhaps the most distinguishing, if not best known, characteristic of the theory. Discourse analysts have forsaken the long-lived taboo in linguistics that the study of grammar is to be confined to the boundary of the sentence. T. Givón criticizes those who have not moved beyond this restrictive approach to language:

> It has become obvious to a growing number of linguists that the study of the syntax of isolated sentences, extracted, without natural context from the purposeful constructions of speakers is a methodology that has outlived its usefulness.[67]

This principle of discourse analysis stands in contrast to the fact that linguistics 'has traditionally been restricted to the investigation of the extent of language which can comfortably be accommodated on the average blackboard'.[68] Similar criticism may be redirected at much of biblical scholarship's continuing preoccupation with interpreting 'words' and their 'meanings' and the fact that traditional grammars of the last two centuries say little about discourse functions of Greek.

3. A third tenet of discourse analysis is that *discourse should be analysed for its social functions and, thus, in its social context.*[69] This has resulted in a strong marriage between discourse analysis and the fields of pragmatics and sociolinguistics. As Brown and Yule state,

> Any analytic approach in linguistics which involves contextual considerations necessarily belongs to that area of language study called *pragmatics*. 'Doing discourse analysis' certainly involves 'doing syntax and semantics', but it primarily consists of 'doing pragmatics'.[70]

65. Brown and Yule, *Discourse Analysis*, p. 24.
66. Cf. Stubbs, *Discourse Analysis*, pp. 6-7; D. Schiffrin, 'The Language of Discourse: Connections Inside and Out', *Text* 10 (1990), p. 97.
67. T. Givón, 'Preface', in *Syntax and Semantics Volume 12: Discourse and Syntax* (New York: Academic Press, 1979), p. xiii.
68. M. Phillips, *The Lexical Structure of Text* (Discourse Analysis Monograph, 12; Birmingham: University of Birmingham: English Language Research, 1989), p. 8.
69. See especially the work of Gumperz, *Discourse Strategies*.
70. Brown and Yule, *Discourse Analysis*, p. 26.

M.A.K. Halliday has made this tenet central to his theory of language and discourse: 'Language is as it is because of its function in social structure'.[71]

4. That there is a relationship grammatically, semantically, and pragmatically between the various parts of a given text, and that there is some thematic element which flows through it, allows a listener to recognize discourse as a *cohesive* piece of communication rather than a jumble of unrelated words and sentences. How is it, then, that speakers go about forming texts into a cohesive unit? How do they combine relatively unrelated words and sentences into a meaningful whole? Discourse analysts repeatedly seek answers to such questions, attempting to *identify how a language is used to create cohesive communication.* Labov describes the task similarly: 'The fundamental problem of discourse analysis is to show how one utterance follows another in a rational, rule-governed manner—in other words, how we understand coherent discourse'.[72]

A few caveats are in order regarding the above portrait of discourse analysis. First, the above tenets will certainly evolve over time and perhaps lose some of their importance in the future. Nevertheless, they have made discourse analysis what it is and they represent many of the questions being asked about discourse. These tenets, of course, do not characterize all that discourse analysis entails; in addition, their application to actual texts by discourse analysts is certainly much more involved than the above portrait suggests. Furthermore, I have failed to mention other well-studied features of discourse analysis: for example, the study of the sequencing of sentences in texts; the study of the structural organization of texts and their parts; the study of discourse as an entity which develops in time; the study of the statistical properties of various types of texts; the study of the ways in which the grammatical, organizational and rhetorical choices made by the creators of texts have determined their rhetorical or aesthetic effect.

As already stated, discourse analysis brings together several principles of semantics, pragmatics, sociolinguistics, and psycholinguistics. These are treated in the following summary as various levels of language and culture which influence the production and consumption of discourse. The 'words' of a discourse are part of a *linguistic code* shared by a

71. M.A.K. Halliday, *Explorations in the Functions of Language* (London: Edward Arnold, 1973), p. 65.
72. Labov, *Sociolinguistic Patterns*, p. 252.

group of people, but they are also part of a *variety of language* shared by various subgroups of society. Furthermore, these words reflect the *idiolect* of a particular author. These three levels reflect a whole semiotic system (*context of culture*) which is stored in the cognitive structures (mental scripts) of the mind. In addition, every discourse is part of a unique historical context[73]—a *context of situation*—which is revealed generically by the register and particularly by its own lexico-grammatical structure. The *co-textual* level of discourse begins to affect discourse production and processing as soon as the first word is spoken or written. The initial word then influences the possible combinations of other words and in turn the resulting clause influences the construction of ensuing clauses (syntagmatic and paradigmatic choices). These clauses may or may not be grouped into a cohesive unit (what is commonly called a paragraph), which in turn influences the construction of other units. Both co-textual (text-internal) and contextual (text-external) factors, therefore, play a role in the analysis of a particular linguistic item in a discourse. These various levels help clarify what it means to claim that discourse analysis is an attempt at understanding language beyond the level of the clause, yet without neglecting the semantic importance of the clause itself. As a hermeneutical maxim, these levels determine the linguistic choices made in the production and comprehension of discourse. They are represented in the following diagram.

Standard Language/Code Variety of Language/Dialect Idiolect	*Context of Culture*
Genre/Register	*Context of Situation*
Discourse (Paragraph) Sentence (Clause) Phrase/Group Word	*Co-text*

Influences on Linguistic Choice

It now remains to apply one particular area of discourse analysis to a New Testament text, viz. the study of information flow. The concept of *information flow*, fundamentally intrinsic to discourse structure, is an intentional metaphor used to refer to *the ongoing change in status of*

---

73. Halliday and Hasan, *Language, Context, and Text*, p. 42.

discourse entities through time.[74] The study of information flow is not per se concerned with the *ideas* (themes) of discourse but with how speakers' and listeners' perceptions change throughout the discourse regarding the *status* of those ideas. Information flow may affect several choices of Greek discourse, including word order, pronominalization, and tense/aspect.[75] It is an important example of how discourse may influence morphological and syntactical choices and one that has received little study with respect to New Testament discourse.

The order of entities in discourse has received considerable attention by linguists studying given versus new information and the role of themes and topics in discourse. Such approaches were a focus of early representatives of the Prague School, especially V. Mathesius,[76] developed further under the *functional sentence perspective* by, for example, J. Firbas.[77] Along similar lines, T. Givón and E.F. Prince provide heuristic models for analysing information patterns in New Testament discourse.

The use of language in a referential manner in discourse follows a basic principle whereby (i) a linguistic item maintaining a topic/theme may employ a 'leaner' semantic content (e.g. pronouns), but (ii) a linguistic item re-establishing a prior topic/theme requires a 'richer' semantic content (e.g. full noun phrase).[78] T. Givón's *iconicity principle*

74. Some important studies on the subject include W.L. Chafe, 'Givenness, Contrastiveness, Definiteness, Subjects, Topics, and Point of View', in C.N. Li (ed.), *Subject and Topic* (New York: Academic Press, 1976), pp. 25-55; H.H. Clark and S.E. Haviland, 'Comprehension and the Given–New Contrast', in *Discourse Production and Comprehension* (ed. R.O. Freedle; Norwood, NJ: Ablex, 1977), pp. 1-40; P.J. Hopper, 'Aspect and Foregrounding in Discourse', in *Discourse and Syntax* (ed. T. Givón; New York: Academic Press, 1979), pp. 213-42; E.F. Prince, 'Toward a Taxonomy of Given–New Information', in *Radical Pragmatics* (ed. P. Cole; New York: Academic Press, 1981), pp. 223-55; T. Givón (ed.), *Topic Continuity in Discourse* (Amsterdam: Benjamins, 1983); J. Firbas, 'On the Dynamics of Written Communication in the Light of the Theory of Functional Sentence Perspective', in *Studying Writing: Linguistic Approaches* (ed. C.R. Cooper and S. Greenbaum; Beverly Hills, CA: Sage, 1986), pp. 40-70; R. Tomlin (ed.), *Coherence and Grounding in Discourse* (Amsterdam: Benjamins, 1987).

75. In spoken language, information flow has been related to intonation and stress patterns as well.

76. V. Mathesius, 'Zur Satzperspektive im modernen Englisch', *Archiv für das Studium der Neueren Sprachen und Literaturen* 155 (1929), pp. 202-10.

77. See esp. Firbas, 'Dynamics', pp. 40-70.

78. Cf. D. Kies, 'Marked Themes with and without Pronominal Reinforcement:

states the inverse principle: 'The more disruptive, surprising, discontinuous or hard to process a topic is, the more coding material must be assigned to it'.[79] That is, as topic continuity decreases, there tends to be a progression from referents which are not coded (zero-anaphora), to those coded by pronouns, to those coded with full noun phrases. Notably, this principle is based on cross-language studies and thus has potential relevance for New Testament discourse analysis.[80] Givón also suggests a useful quantitative approach to the analysis of topic information in discourse, based on three criteria: (a) *referential distance*, the number of clauses between the previous occurrence of the topical entity and its current occurrence; (b) *potential distance*, the existence of competing topical entities within the last few clauses; and (c) *persistence*, the number of clauses after the current one in which the topical entity continues to be included. The assumption of the iconicity principle is that speakers/authors generally attempt to remove potential confusion from the discourse.

An approach similar to Givón's and one that is a useful taxonomy for New Testament discourse analysis is that of E.F. Prince.[81] She distinguishes between three types of participants with respect to *information status*: new, evoked, and inferable. When a speaker introduces *new* 'entities' into the discourse (i.e. the first use of a discourse entity), they will be either brand-new or unused. A *brand-new* entity is not previously known by the audience and is typically introduced by means of an indefinite expression or a full noun phrase. Brand-new entities may be *anchored* (i.e. linked to another discourse entity) or *unanchored*. An *unused* entity is known to the audience (based on their knowledge of the context of situation or culture) but is not at the forefront of their consciousness at the time of utterance. The second class of participants is *evoked* (i.e. already in the discourse). They are either (a) situational or

Their Meaning and Distribution in Discourse', in *Pragmatics, Discourse and Text: Some Systemically-Inspired Approaches* (ed. E.H. Steiner and R. Veltman; London: Pinter, 1988), p. 71.

79. T. Givón, 'Topic, Pronoun, and Grammatical Agreement', in Li (ed.), *Subject and Topic*, p. 18.

80. See his *Topic Continuity in Discourse*.

81. Prince, 'Toward a Taxonomy', pp. 883-907. W. Chafe ('Cognitive Constraints on Information Flow', in *Coherence and Grounding in Discourse* [ed. R. Tomlin; Amsterdam: Benjamins, 1987], pp. 21-51) provides a similar model—a cognitive-pyschological approach—of active, semi-active, or inactive information in the speaker's and listener's consciousness.

(b) textual. Situationally-evoked entities are interpreted via access to the context of situation. Words like ἐγώ or σύ, for example, may be associated with a situationally-based entity (external reference). Textually-evoked entities are interpreted based on the co-text. Typically this involves an entity that has already been introduced in the discourse and is now being interpreted with recourse to that former entity through a referential marker (e.g. a pronoun or verbal suffix) or zero-anaphora (i.e. ellipsis or an infinitive with no marked subject). The third class of participants is *inferables*. These are participants which the speaker believes the listener can *infer* from a discourse entity already introduced or from other inferables. These are usually expressed by means of a full noun phrase with a meaning similar or hyponymous to another discourse entity (e.g. τέκνον in Phil. 2.22 is an inferable of Τιμόθεον in v. 19).

Due to the confines of the present essay, the following application of the above models to Philippians is presented in a summary manner. In particular, attention is focused on two of the main participants in the discourse (viz. Paul and the Philippians).

When investigating information flow in the Pauline letters (and I suspect the same is true of narrative discourse), it is beneficial to distinguish between main and peripheral participants.[82] Main participants play a central role in the discourse, usually appearing throughout the text (although not in every section). Peripheral participants play a secondary role (in the case of a letter, typically anyone who is not the author or audience), usually appearing only occasionally in the text and only in a supportive role to the main plot or argument. Without much explanation here, I consider the main participants of the letter to the Philippians to be Paul and the Philippians (sender and recipient), as identified by the epistolary prescript (1.1; Timothy is subsequently excluded from the implied author's role) and manifested in the prevalent use of first-person singular and second-person plural pronouns and verbal suffixes. Paul's letter to the Philippians consists of approximately

---

82. *Participants* are understood here as the persons, objects, abstracts expressed in discourse in contrast to finite verbal *events* (participles in Greek may play the role of participant and event); see Halliday, *Functional Grammar*, pp. 168-69. As a functional basis for the distinction between main and peripheral participants in language, I appeal primarily to the theory of cohesive chains (peripheral, relevant, and central tokens) in M.A.K. Halliday and R. Hasan, 'Text and Context: Aspects of Language in a Social-Semiotic Perspective', *Sophia Linguistica* 6 (1980), esp. pp. 50-59.

307 clauses,[83] of which approximately 90 may be treated as embedded (or rank-shifted) clauses (mostly participle or infinitive clauses). In 113 of all clauses (37%) Paul is the implied subject—indicated by name, pronoun, verbal suffix, or zero-anaphora. In 66 clauses (22%) the Philippians (as a collective group) play the role of subject. In eight clauses (2.6%), both Paul and the Philippians are treated as a collective subject (i.e. first-person plural). The remaining 120 clauses (39%) have peripheral subjects, the most frequent being 'God' (16×) and 'Jesus Christ' (13×). It is clear from this quantitative analysis that Paul and the Philippians, as participants, play a vital role in the topical information flow of the letter.

With respect to the iconicity principle it is first of all necessary to keep in mind the feature of referential distance, that is, the number of clauses between the previous occurrence of the topical entity and its current occurrence. The greater the referential distance the more likely the need for more coding when reintroducing an already introduced participant— see, for example, 'God' in 2.9 (full noun phrase then verbal suffix) and 2.13 (full noun phrase). A number of observations regarding the iconicity principle in Philippians follow, mostly with respect to the use of *grammatical subjects*.[84] (1) In the case of *main participants* (Paul and the Philippians), the iconicity principle is fairly straightforward: (a) new (either brand-new or used) participants are introduced with a full noun phrase (1.1 Παῦλος...τοῖς ἁγίοις...ἐν Φιλίπποις); and (b) evoked and inferable main participants receive less coding, either with a verbal suffix,[85] zero-anaphora,[86] or pronoun. The use of pronouns for main

---

83. Clauses are defined formally here as linguistic units which typically contain a verb. This includes embedded clauses such as those created by infinitives and participles. For example, the clause ὁ ἐναρξάμενος ἐν ὑμῖν ἔργον ἀγαθόν is both its own clause unit as well as an embedded subject of the main verb ἐπιτελέσει (1.6). Those clauses which do not contain a verb, however, still stand out in relation to surrounding clauses with verbs, i.e. the subjects and complements of a verbless clause may be distinguished by surrounding verb clauses. When I speak of clauses here, then, I am speaking of a formal unit, without trying to define it functionally.

84. Participants which are not grammatical subjects are almost always encoded with pronouns if they are main participants or with full noun phrases if they are peripheral participants. An exception to peripheral encoding occurs when a secondary participant has considerable referential persistence (such as 'Jesus' in Phil. 2.5-11), in which cases subsequent references are made with third-person pronouns.

85. 1.3; 1.4; 1.6; 1.7; 1.8; 1.9; 1.10; 1.11; 1.12; 1.16; 1.18 [2×]; 1.19; 1.20; 1.22

participant subjects occurs (a) in clauses with verbs (participles and especially infinitives) which do not have suffixes for indicating person and/or number (1.7 [2×]; 1.10; 1.12), (b) for the purpose of comparison and contrast with other participants (2.4 [2×];[87] 2.18; 2.19; 2.24; 2.28; 3.3; 3.4 [2×]; 4.15),[88] and (c) for the purpose of focus/emphasis (3.13 [2×]; 4.11; 4.15).[89] An inferable full noun phrase (usually a vocative) may be used as a transitional device (1.12 ἀδελφοί = Philippians) or in order to bring the participant back into the foreground of the discourse (2.12 ἀδελφοί = Philippians; 3.1; 3.17 [specifying a smaller group, following first-person plural grammar]; 4.1 [specifying a smaller group, following first-person plural grammar]; 4.8; 4.15). (2) Most peripheral participants only appear individually a few times and thus are encoded with a full noun phrase, indefinite pronoun, or (more infrequently) an inferable—examples of these appear throughout the letter. An exception to this general pattern occurs with participle clauses, in which a participle functions as the verb (without a separate subject) as well as indicates the

[2×]; 1.23 [2×]; 1.25 [2×]; 1.27 [4×]; 1.28; 1.30 [3×]; 2.2 [4×]; 2.3; 2.4; 2.5; 2.12; 2.14; 2.15; 2.16 [3×]; 2.17 [3×]; 2.18; 2.19 [2×]; 2.20; 2.22; 2.23 [2×]; 2.24; 2.25; 2.26; 2.27; 2.28 [3×]; 2.29 [2×]; 3.2 [3×]; 3.3 [3×]; 3.6; 3.6; 3.7; 3.8 [4×]; 3.9 [2×]; 3.10; 3.11; 3.12 [5×]; 3.15 [2×]; 3.16; 3.17 [2×]; 3.18 [3×]; 3.20; 4.2 [2×]; 4.3 [2×]; 4.4 [3×]; 4.6; 4.8; 4.9 [5×]; 4.10 [4×]; 4.11 [2×]; 4.12 [3×]; 4.13; 4.14 [2×]; 4.15; 4.16; 4.17 [2×]; 4.18 [4×]. Verbal suffixes include here indicators of person and number (finite verbs) and of number alone (participles).

86. 1.21 [2×]; 1.22; 1.23 [2×]; 1.24; 1.25; 1.29 [2×]; 2.23; 2.25; 3.1; 3.10; 3.13 [3×]; 3.14; 3.16; 4.10; 4.11 [2×]; 4.12 [5×]. Note, however, that in the case of the 'zero-anaphora infinitives' in 1.21-22 the dative pronoun μοι is added for clarity; cf. ὑμῖν prior to the infinitives in 1.29.

87. Notice here how pronouns are used to distinguish between various implied readers ('yourselves', 'each one') and an indefinite class of 'others'. If the *UBSGNT* text is correct, then the author, after using the singular ἕκαστος, moves back to the plural ἕκαστοι in alignment with the plural implied reader.

88. Adverbial use of καί is often an indicator of comparison when a pronoun encodes a main participant.

89. The term 'focus' is understood here in the Hallidayan and Prague School sense of communicative dynamism, i.e. the focal element is the main (or central) point (or element) of the information unit; see Halliday, *Functional Grammar*, pp. 315-16. This term is preferred to 'emphasis' since it more precisely explains the function of frontshifting. For example, the positioning of εἰς κενόν at the front of the two clauses in 2.16 does not seem to indicate emphasis but rather suggests that Paul's *main* point concerns the Philippians' *successful* Christian progress (i.e. their Christianity is not in vain).

subject by means of grammatical number; for example, the clause ὁ ἐναρξάμενος ἐν ὑμῖν ἔργον ἀγαθόν in 1.6 most likely has God as its unexpressed subject (cf. 1.14; 1.16; 1.28; 2.3; 2.6; 2.7 [3×]; 2.8; 2.13; 2.30). However, the overall iconicity principle does apply to *peripheral participants* when they play a more prominent role in a certain section of discourse, that is, when they have *referential persistence*. For example, references to Jesus Christ follow the iconicity principle in 1.29, in 2.6-9 (but notice how a full noun phrase is used again in 2.10-11 probably to distinguish 'Jesus' from 'God'), and in 3.20-21. The same principle applies once in a reference to God (2.13) and is also true of discussions of Timothy (2.19-23) and of Epaphroditus (2.25-30).[90]

These observations are useful for interpreting certain clauses in the discourse. For example, in 3.13 (ἀδελφοί, ἐγὼ ἐμαυτὸν οὐ λογίζομαι...) the main participants receive additional coding three times (more than any other clause in the discourse), viz. vocative ἀδελφοί, pronoun ἐγώ (subject), and pronoun ἐμαυτόν (complement). Here is a clear case in which Paul draws particular attention to his subsequent point (...κατειληφέναι)—a theme central to the immediate section but one which is especially related to himself and the Philippians. That is, Paul marks his grammar so as to set it apart from the surrounding text.

Information status is not only reflected in the use of full noun phrases, various pronominals, and verbal suffixes, but, as is true for many languages, informational requirements of discourse also influence choices of word order. I am interested here in the functions of word order variations in terms of the information flow of *participants*.[91] Generally speaking, in New Testament Greek a grammaticalized subject typically occurs before a complement—SO[92] word order occurs

---

90. Compare also how the unidentified 'proclaimers of Christ' in 1.15 are first identified with an indefinite pronoun and then subsequently with an article (1.16-17) and zero-anaphora (1.17 [2×])—more coding to less coding.

91. Cf. S.E. Porter, 'Word Order and Clause Structure in New Testament Greek: An Unexplored Area of Greek Linguistics Using Philippians as a Test Case', *FN* 6 (1993), pp. 177-206, and M.E. Davison, 'New Testament Greek Word Order', *Literary and Linguistic Computing* 4 (1989), pp. 19-28. My own study of the formal structures of word order in the letter confirms Porter's quantitative analysis, while developing it along the lines of information flow theory.

92. S = subject; V = verb; and O = object/complement (direct or indirect object and predicate adjective/nominative).

approximately 84% of the time in Philippians.[93] In 22 clauses SR (subject–predicate nominative/adjective) is the pattern, with only one case in which the predicate nominative/adjective (R) precedes the subject (1.8a). In 19 clauses the subject (S) precedes the complement (O), but in 7 instances the complement (O) precedes the subject (S). This SO pattern is significant for interpreting especially one clause in the letter, viz. 1.7 διὰ τὸ ἔχειν με ἐν τῇ καρδίᾳ ὑμᾶς.[94] Not only does the general SO regularity suggest that this clause is to be understood as 'I have you in my heart' instead of 'You have me in your heart', but such a reading is also substantiated by the same SO pattern in an infinitive clause in Phil. 1.10 εἰς τὸ δοκιμάζειν ὑμᾶς τὰ διαφέροντα.

When the verb is considered in the word order scheme, there is some dispute whether New Testament Greek has an unmarked SVO or VSO word order.[95] The issue centres around the placement of the verb. In response, SVO (as well as SOV) and VSO seem to be fair characterizations depending on the nature of the grammatical subject. (1) If the subject's information status is new then its unmarked position is prior to the verb, typically the first major word in the clause. In the case of *main participants*, the first referential use follows this word order (1.1). (2) Because *peripheral participants* are typically new in status, they too are generally initial in the clause.[96] A prime example of this is the use of 'God' Θεός as subject, which almost always appears before the verb and usually at the beginning of the sentence (1.6 ὁ ἐναρξάμενος is an

93. For other studies in support of this pattern, see Porter, 'Word Order', pp. 188-89. There is enough variation in other Greek authors to suggest that while the pattern of SO is generally true, various other factors (e.g. idiolect, situation, genre) may result in other dominant patterns.

94. This pattern has already been demonstrated as a general feature of New Testament Greek, with specific mention of its relevance for Phil. 1.7 debate (J.T. Reed, 'The Infinitive with Two Substantival Accusatives: An Ambiguous Construction?', *NovT* 33 [1991], pp. 1-27); yet B. Witherington III, *Friendship and Finances in Philippi: The Letter of Paul to the Philippians* (Valley Forge, PA: Trinity Press International, 1994), p. 38, can still claim: 'Verse 7 is ambiguous, but in view of what follows in v. 8, I take it to mean that Paul is saying, "you have me in your heart"'.

95. VSO is the view of several standard grammars; see Porter, 'Word Order', pp. 186-87, for discussion.

96. 1.6; 1.9; 1.12; 1.13; 1.14; 1.15; 1.16; 1.17; 1.19-20; 1.22; 1.23; 1.24; 1.26; 1.28 [2×]; 2.1 [4×]; 2.5; 2.6; 2.9; 2.10; 2.11 [2×]; 2.13; 2.20; 2.21; 2.27; 3.4; 3.7; 3.8; 3.15; 3.18; 3.21; 4.3; 4.5; 4.6; 4.7; 4.8; 4.9; 4.19; cf. 1.2; 4.23 (verbless clauses).

inferable of 'God'; 2.9, 13, 27; 3.15; 4.9, 19). The one exception is 1.8a where μάρτυς (ὁ Θεός is the subject in view of the attached article)[97] perhaps plays a focal role in the clause, indicating that Paul's point here is to establish a witness for his personal feelings.[98] With respect to peripheral participants, another exception occurs in 1.20c μεγαλυνθήσεται Χριστός. The post-verb position of 'Christ' here is perhaps due to the initial positioning of prepositional phrases and adverbs ('always') so as to contrast (ἀλλά) with the initial ἐν οὐδενί in the previous clause. (See below for a possible explanation of the VOS word order in 4.21b, 22.) (3) If the subject is evoked or inferable, then there *is* a difference between main participants and peripheral participants with respect to word order. Whereas peripheral participants are typically clause-initial, *main participants*, if they are expressed apart from the verbal suffix (e.g. pronoun), appear either after the verb (1.7; 1.10; 1.12; 4.15) or prior to the verb but after some other major linguistic item such as a prepositional phrase or complement (1.7; 2.18). This order may be changed for the sake of comparison/contrast with another participant in the co-text (2.18; 2.19; 2.24; 2.28; 3.3; 3.4)[99] or for the purpose of focus (4.11). That is, the unmarked position is after the verb and the marked position (indicating comparison/contrast or focus) is before the verb.

The previous regularities relate to the grammatical subject, but the majority of participants in clauses play other grammatical roles: for example, complement (e.g. direct and indirect objects), modifier (genitives), head-term in a prepositional phrase. When considering the information flow of complements, which tend to have more word order independence in the clause than modifiers and prepositional phrases, it is again advantageous to differentiate between main participants and peripheral participants. (1) In complement functions (direct and indirect objects; predicate nominatives and adjectives), *main participants* typically appear somewhere after an initial participant(s) (1.2; 3.13; 3.15; cf. 4.15; 4.16), usually after the verb (1.3-5; 1.7; 1.8; 1.25; 1.27; 2.3;

97. See L.C. McGaughy, *Toward a Descriptive Analysis of ᵉEINAI as a Linking Verb in New Testament Greek* (SBLDS, 6; Missoula, MT: Society of Biblical Literature, 1972).

98. In 3.15, Θεός is still functionally initial, since it follows a demonstrative pronoun which, if it has anaphoric reference, always appears first in the clause. In other words, there is a hierarchy to the regularities of word order, with some patterns having precedence over others.

99. καί is often used as an indicator of comparison with a participant or event in the previous discourse.

2.19; 2.26; 3.1; 3.7; 3.17; 3.18; 4.3; 4.13; 4.21; 4.22) except in the case of comparison or contrast with a previous participant (1.29). (2) *Peripheral participants*, when serving as complements,[100] fall before[101] or after[102] the verb—OV, VO, SOV, SVO. In all variations, they typically respect the SO word order. It is worth noting that named participants (e.g. Timothy, Epaphroditus, Euodia, Syntyche) are always introduced as the first word of their clause (2.19; 2.25; 4.2 [2×]), most likely because they are being introduced as participants which have some referential persistence. (3) Lastly, if two evoked (or inferable) participants are in the same clause, the one considered the focal participant (which includes peripheral participants with referential persistence) tends to appear prior to a less prominent participant, even if this means breaking the typical SO word order. This may explain (a) the appearance of the datives in 1.18 before the subject 'Christ', viz. the focus of Paul's immediate discussion concerns the different ways in which Christ is proclaimed (the topic of vv. 15-17), and (b) the somewhat anomalous word order in 4.21, 22 ἀσπάζονται ὑμᾶς οἱ σὺν ἐμοὶ ἀδελφοί, ἀσπάξονται ὑμᾶς πάντες οἱ ἅγιοι, viz. greeting is the topic of the clauses and it is the greeting of the Philippians which is in view.

Lastly, there are two grammatical expressions in Greek which regularly follow a given–new (or anaphoric–non-anaphoric) information flow, regardless of word order, viz. relative pronouns (1.30; 2.5; 2.6; 2.20; 3.7; 3.15; 3.18; 3.21; 4.3; 4.8; 4.9) and demonstrative pronouns (1.7; 1.9; 1.18; 1.19-20; 1.22; 1.25; 1.28; 2.5; 2.23; 3.7;[103] 3.15 [2×]; 4.8; 4.9). When the pronoun represents already 'given' information (anaphoric reference) it appears as the first major word in the clause, whether it is a subject, complement, or in a prepositional phrase. The rest of the clause

100. This includes infinitive clauses that complete other clauses in which they are embedded (e.g. 1.14).

101. 1.4; 1.7; 1.9; 1.12; 1.13; 1.14; 1.15; 1.17; 1.17; 1.22 [2×]; 1.23; 1.25; 1.30; 1.30; 2.2 [3×]; 2.3; 2.4 [2×]; 2.5; 2.6; 2.7 [2×]; 2.14; 2.16; 2.18; 2.19; 2.20 [2×]; 2.21; 2.22; 2.23 [2×]; 2.25; 2.27; 2.29; 3.1; 3.7; 3.8; 3.8; 3.13 [2×]; 3.15 [3×]; 3.17; 3.18; 3.19; 3.20; 4.2 [3×]; 4.6; 4.8; 4.9 [2×]; 4.13.

102. 1.6 [2×]; 1.7; 1.10 [2×]; 1.11; 1.14 [2×]; 1.17; 1.27; 1.28; 2.2; 2.6 [2×]; 2.8 [2×]; 2.9 [2×]; 2.12; 2.15; 2.19 [2x]; 2.23; 2.25; 2.27; 2.28 [2×]; 2.29; 2.30; 3.2 [3×]; 3.4; 3.6; 3.7; 3.8; 3.8; 3.9; 3.10; 3.13; 3.18; 3.20; 3.21 [3×]; 4.3; 4.5; 4.7 [2×]; 4.8; 4.11; 4.12 [3×]; 4.17 [2×]; 4.18 [2×]; 4.19; 4.21.

103. This is a particularly revealing example since the demonstrative, referring to the preceding discourse, precedes the verb but the other complement appears after the verb: **ταῦτα** ἥγημαι διὰ τὸν Χριστὸν **ζημίαν**.

typically involves new information. This would suggest, for example, that the content of Paul's prayer in 1.9 τοῦτο προσεύχομαι is to be found in the preceding discourse,[104] most likely referring to his desire for the Philippians (i.e. his desire to visit them). In contrast, if a demonstrative refers to upcoming information (cataphoric reference)—that is, it does not represent given information—then it appears towards the end of the clause (1.6). In other words, the word order of discourse referentials such as relative pronouns and demonstratives depends upon their anaphoric or cataphoric function. This is particularly evident in 3.15 in which a peripheral participant, 'God', comes after the demonstrative (τοῦτο ὁ Θεὸς ὑμῖν ἀποκαλύψει), even though the expected location of a peripheral participant as subject is at the beginning of the clause.

The following chart attempts to summarize the above observations. The principles supplied are only intended as *regularities* of discourse, not absolute rules of language. Nevertheless, they provide a basis for the analysis of information flow in other New Testament discourse.

Main Participants

Iconicity Principle:

1.   Grammatical subjects: Initial references are expressed with full noun phrases. Subsequent references are expressed with verbal suffixes, zero-anaphora (infinitive or verbless clause), or pronouns (first and second person)—in that order of relative frequency.
2.   Complements (direct and indirect objects; predicate adjectives and nominatives): Evoked references are almost always expressed with pronouns (first and second person) or, less frequently, with zero-anaphora.

Word Order:

1.   The subject typically precedes the complement.
2.   Grammatical subjects: If the subject's information status is new then its unmarked position is before the verb, and it is typically the first major word in the clause. If the subject's information status is evoked or inferable, then its unmarked position is

---

104.   Against P.T. O'Brien, *Philippians* (Grand Rapids: Eerdmans, 1991), p. 73, who takes it with the following ἵνα clause.

either after the verb or prior to the verb but after some other major linguistic item such as a prepositional phrase or complement (i.e. it is not clause-initial).

3. Complements (direct and indirect objects; predicate adjectives and nominatives): Main participants, in their unmarked position, appear after an initial participant(s) and usually after the verb.

4. The above three patterns may be altered (i.e. marked) for the sake of comparing or contrasting a participant with another one in the immediate discourse or, more rarely, for the sake of focus.

Peripheral Participants

Iconicity Principle:

1. Subjects and complements: Full noun phrases (or more rarely indefinite pronouns) are generally used to express peripheral participants, unless a participant has referential persistence beyond one clause in which case subsequent references are typically made with third-person pronouns. However, once a peripheral participant loses its referential persistence then it requires a full noun phrase when it is reintroduced into the discourse.

Word Order:

1. The subject typically precedes the complement.

2. Grammatical subjects: Peripheral participants typically appear as the first major word in the clause.

3. Complements: Complements appear almost with equal frequency before and after the verb. However, several pre-verb placements are due to (a) the use of a pronoun or demonstrative (which appear at the beginning of a clause when anaphoric reference applies) and (b) the first reference to a peripheral participant which subsequently has some referential persistence.

Of course, the study of information flow in other texts needs to be compared with this one. Nevertheless, in the canonical letter to the Philippians there are recognizable patterns of information flow which not only follow Givón's iconicity principle and can be explained in functional terms but also prove useful in the task of interpretation.

6. *Conclusion*

In closing, linguistics is not a panacea for all of the hermeneutical difficulties faced by New Testament interpreters, nor should it be proposed as such. It has much to contribute to New Testament studies, nonetheless, by way of methodological clarity and quantitative analysis. Although linguists have been rightly criticized at times for mere fact-gathering with no clear methodology, the growing trend of cultural and ideological interpretations of biblical texts may often be criticized for lack of an 'adequate linguistic basis'.[105] As Halliday puts it, 'the study of discourse...cannot be separated from the study of the grammar that lies behind it'.[106] Discourse analysis, the object of Halliday's inquiry, may provide one avenue through which modern linguistics may be presented in a somewhat coherent hermeneutic, accessible and usable to the New Testament scholar. The results of such research, of course, will not go without challenge. When linguistic analysis supports common belief, many respond that 'everyone knows that'. When it provides an unexpected finding, the response is that 'you can prove anything with linguistics'.[107] Rather than respond in isolationism, those who are convinced that New Testament interpretation necessitates an analysis of a text's lexico-grammatical structure must be explicit about their linguistic method and apply it to actual texts (preferably whole texts or text corpora) so that it may be critiqued and improved upon or discarded.

If one thing is clear about the present status of linguistics and biblical studies it is that there is much to be done if the wealth of information in general linguistics is to have an impact on New Testament hermeneutics. This will become even more accentuated in the future according to W. Chafe's prophecy about the future of linguistic studies:

> My guess is that much of what passes for syntax today will be explained in functional-discourse terms tomorrow... I have a vision of language structure in which the relevance of syntax as currently conceived will decline, while morphology at one end, discourse at the other, will share between them most of what is necessary to understand what has traditionally been called grammar.[108]

105. See Stubbs, 'Grammar', p. 202, who directs this criticism at modern literary and cultural studies of discourse.
106. Halliday, *Functional Grammar*, p. 345.
107. Cf. J.F. Burrows, 'Computers and the Study of Literature', in *Computers and Written Texts* (ed. C.S. Butler; Oxford: Basil Blackwell, 1992), p. 183.
108. W. Chafe, 'Looking Ahead', *Text* 10 (1990), p. 21.

If Chafe's prophecy comes true, and there are signs that it is already so, then much is left to do with respect to our understanding of the Greek language of the New Testament and its functional use in actual discourse. On the one hand, traditional notions of morphology are being challenged (e.g. tense); on the other hand, little headway has been made regarding the influence of discourse on New Testament syntax. It is hoped that the present essay, noticeably indebted to other New Testament linguists, will further provoke a renewed interest in Greek grammar and linguistics.

SOCIAL-SCIENTIFIC CRITICISM OF THE NEW TESTAMENT:
AN APPRAISAL AND EXTENDED EXAMPLE

Philip Richter

1. *Introduction*

John Gager once spoke of the relationship between biblical studies and
sociology as akin to that between two warring tribes: 'Shall we marry
our enemies?', he asked, provocatively.[1] By now, we can report that the
marriage has taken place and social-scientific approaches have become a
more or less acceptable member of the biblical studies household,[2] but
the relationship is still uneasy. Since many of the founding figures of
sociology were profoundly anti-religious and reductionistic it is not
surprising that biblical critics have been slow to forge an alliance with
sociology. A more mature assessment of sociology reveals that it is not
intrinsically antipathetic to religious belief: it merely treats human belief
and behaviour *as if* they were largely socially patterned; this does not
rule out the possibility that there are other important dimensions to
human experience that lie outside the sociological frame.

The relationship between sociology and biblical studies is not
altogether new. Its earliest stages lie at the end of the nineteenth century,
with, for instance, the work of W. Robertson Smith on the Old
Testament.[3] The work of the Chicago School of New Testament studies
in the early decades of this century gave a particular, although short-
lived, boost to the relationship.[4] The current blossoming of the relation-

1.   J.G. Gager, 'Shall we Marry our Enemies?: Sociology and the New
Testament', *Int* 36 (1982), pp. 256-65.
2.   For example, J.H. Elliott, *What is Social-Scientific Criticism?* (Minneapolis:
Fortress Press, 1993); B. Holmberg, *Sociology and the New Testament: An
Appraisal* (Minneapolis: Fortress Press, 1990).
3.   *Lectures on the Religion of the Semites* (London: A. & C. Black, 1894).
4.   See, for example, S.J. Case, *The Evolution of Early Christianity* (Chicago:
University of Chicago Press, 1923); also R.W. Funk, 'The Watershed of the

ship owes much to two key factors: *conducive currents within biblical scholarship itself* and *contemporary liberation movements*. The social-scientific approach to biblical studies is a logical extension of both form criticism and redaction criticism. It offers additional tools with which to analyse the *Sitz im Leben* of oral and written traditions, focusing increasingly on the readers as much as the writers. At the same time, the concerns of liberation theology have encouraged research into the concrete experience of the early Christian movement, itself, it is presupposed, an oppressed and marginalized community.[5] It is assumed that 'it is especially the voices of the exodus, prophetic, and Jesus traditions in their original context that speak of the oppressed and the liberating power of God to free them'.[6]

The growing relationship between the two disciplines has taken a variety of forms. It is best expressed in terms of the following continuum of sociological approaches (Table 1). There is no attempt here to generate a hierarchy of approaches. Some biblical sociologists would want to claim that their approaches are more solidly sociological than others, making use of the latest explanatory theories, models and hypotheses. However, even John Gager, after he has made such a claim, has to backtrack and admit that *sociological interpretation* cannot take place apart from *social description* and vice versa.[7] Social description has a proper place in the domain of sociology, for instance, in the field of Community Studies. Some biblical scholars would prefer to limit themselves to social description, since this appears to be a more objective, less theory-driven, approach. In fact the researcher will always be influenced, consciously or unconsciously, by theoretical models: social description 'is no safe haven for exegetes and historians leary of theory or murky about models'.[8]

American Biblical Tradition: The Chicago School, First Phase 1892–1920', *JBL* 95 (1976), pp. 15-17.

5.   In fact, this stereotype of 'socio-economic underdog' does not completely fit the early Christian movement: see Holmberg's discussion, *Sociology and the New Testament*, pp. 21-76.

6.   C. Osiek, 'The New Handmaid: The Bible and the Social Sciences', *TS* 50 (1989), pp. 260-78 (274); see also C. Rowland and M. Corner, *Liberating Exegesis: The Challenge of Liberation Theology to Biblical Studies* (London: SPCK, 1990).

7.   'Shall we Marry our Enemies?', pp. 258-59.

8.   J.H. Elliott, 'Social-Scientific Criticism of the New Testament: More on Methods and Models', *Semeia* 35 (1986), pp. 1-33 (9).

Description of social facts	Social history	Using a sociological concept analytically	Using sociological theories and models
E.g., J. Jeremias (1969) *Jerusalem in the Time of Jesus* (London: SCM Press)	E.g., A. Malherbe (1977) *Social Aspects of Early Christianity* (Baton Rouge: Louisiana State University Press)	E.g., G. Theissen (1978) *The First Followers of Jesus* (London: SCM Press)[9]	E.g., W.A. Meeks (1983) *The First Urban Christians* (New Haven: Yale University Press)

SOCIAL DESCRIPTION   SOCIAL SCIENCE METHOD

Table 1[10]

2. *Concerns and Benefits of Social-Scientific Analysis*

a. *Concerns*

Whilst biblical studies may have decided to wed its erstwhile enemy there are good reasons for it to handle its new partner with care and with some critical distance. I propose now to summarize briefly some of the key areas of concern.

1. *Eclecticism*. There has been a rather cavalier tendency to select from the world of sociology whatever concepts and models look as if they might be useful. As Carolyn Osiek puts it, 'we are still at the "adopt a sociologist" stage'.[11] Sometimes there is little awareness that there may be significant theoretical differences between the sociologists adopted. Too little attention has been paid to John Elliott's identification of six main types of sociological theorizing: structural functionalism, conflict theory, exchange theory, symbolic interactionism, phenomenology and

---

9. See Holmberg's comment on Theissen's use of the church-sect categorization: 'a few scholars do not use it to explain anything at all (Theissen, Rowland)' (*Sociology and the New Testament*, p. 113).

10. For reasons of brevity I have given just one example of each category. For a recent survey, see Osiek, 'The New Handmaid', also C. Osiek, *What are they Saying about the Social Setting of the New Testament?* (New York: Paulist Press, 1992). The continuum is based on my mapping of the field in 1984: 'Recent Sociological Approaches to the Study of the New Testament', *Rel* 14 (1984), pp. 77-90; see Holmberg's appraisal, *Sociology and the New Testament*, pp. 4-6.

11. 'The New Handmaid', p. 277.

ethnomethodology.[12] A welcome exception is Osiek who gives a very helpful example of the different ways in which structural functionalist, conflict, and symbolic 'models' would interpret the household codes in Eph. 5.21–6.9 and Col. 3.18–4.1.[13] Biblical scholars need to know how the concepts and models they select relate to sociological theory and ongoing critical discussion within the discipline: it is unsatisfactory merely to 'borrow' sociological bits and pieces as an outsider.

2. *Crude functionalism.* Biblical sociologists have tended to assume that texts reflect the needs and interests of particular communities. D.L. Mealand, for instance, treats the theme of *the dangers of wealth* in the teaching of Jesus as a reflection of the socio-economic conditions of the early Christian movement: the earliest layers of Gospel tradition (substantially reflected in Mark's Gospel), he concludes, must derive from economically precarious communities.[14] This is far too simplistic an approach and may well fail to do justice to the literary dynamics of the text. It is perfectly possible for writings from a prosperous background to criticize wealth and idealize poverty. As Jonathan Z. Smith remarks, 'I can think of no more aristocratic theme in Hellenistic literature than the idealization of the naked sage (Diogenes versus Alexander and the like)'.[15]

The functionalist argument often runs along these lines: the researcher looks at the characteristic make-up of early Christian communities and identifies a number of typical needs or forms of deprivation amongst their membership and then concludes that the early Christian movement was successful in attracting its followers because it offered means of resolving these needs. For example, Wayne Meeks suggests that Pauline

12. Elliott, 'Social-Scientific Criticism of the New Testament', p. 7.

13. Osiek, 'The New Handmaid', pp. 271-73; however it would be more accurate if she spoke of the structural functionalist, conflict, and symbolic *theoretical perspectives*, rather than *models*: see further Elliott, 'Social-Scientific Criticism of the New Testament', p. 7.

14. D.L. Mealand, *Poverty and Expectation in the Gospels* (London: SPCK, 1980); cf. T.E. Schmidt, *Hostility to Wealth in the Synoptic Gospels* (Sheffield: JSOT Press, 1987).

15. J.Z. Smith, 'Too Much Kingdom, too Little Community', *Zygon* 13.2 (1978), pp. 123-30 (128); see also Richard Fenn's reminder that the language of religion may 'romanticize, distort, conceal, or ignore various aspects of social life' (*The Death of Herod: An Essay in the Sociology of Religion* [Cambridge: Cambridge University Press, 1992], p. 28).

Christianity had a particular appeal for people suffering from 'status inconsistency', whose achieved status was higher than their ascribed status. The functionalist argument leaps ahead far too rapidly, however. It does not explain why people turned to the early Christian movement, rather than other means of resolving their needs—for example, excessive drinking! John Milbank has suggested that Stoicism would have been a much better solution for status inconsistency.[16] Equally, it does not provide evidence that people became Christian *because* they recognized a solution to their needs; there is, of course, no possibility of ever asking them! It is certainly dangerous to argue that Christianity was in some way a uniquely functional solution; as Milbank warns, 'it has to be suspected that this is just a baptizing with necessity of what we now know to have occurred'.[17]

3. *Translation.* It is deceptively easy for biblical sociologists simply to translate biblical terminology into sociological terms and believe that they have thus advanced our understanding. John Milbank concludes that the sociology of the New Testament merely *redefines* and *redescribes* Christian origins in terms of 'the "human", "social" plot which we consciously live out today'.[18] As James Dunn pointed out in his 'theological surveyor's report': 'the fact that the apostle Paul and Max Weber both use the word "charisma" creatively should provide an opportunity for dialogue between the usages, not for the latter to swamp the former'.[19] The translation process often involves some massaging of data and also the danger of tautological reasoning. The argument proceeds something like this: early Christianity can be interpreted as a millenarian sect; millenarian sects are characterized by X, Y, & Z (for instance, an egalitarian social ethic, alienation from the surrounding society etc.); early Christianity must have had these features, even if some have been obliterated in the records we have now.[20] One should

16. J. Milbank, *Theology and Social Theory* (Oxford: Basil Blackwell, 1990), p. 118.

17. *Theology and Social Theory*, p. 118; for a general critique of deprivation theories, see P. Heelas and A.M. Haglund-Heelas, 'The Inadequacy of "Deprivation" as a Theory of Conversion', in W. James and D.H. Johnson (eds.), *Vernacular Christianity* (Oxford: JASO, 1988), pp. 112-19.

18. Milbank, *Theology and Social Theory*, p. 121.

19. J.D.G. Dunn, 'Testing the Foundations', *THES*, 7 September 1984, p. 13.

20. For instance, Francis Watson's depiction of the Pauline communities as sectarian suffers from the tendency to manipulate and homogenize the Pauline data:

not lose sight of the fact that the sociological concept of the 'sect' was partly modelled on the early Christians, and on later Christian groups trying to recapture the 'purity' of the early days of the faith. It is easy here to fall into the trap of circular reasoning.

4. *Problems of historical distance.* It is not possible for New Testament sociologists to directly observe their subject matter. This means that they will, unlike contemporary sociologists, not be able to control the collection of data and will have to work with inadequate and biased texts. The historical sociologist must, of necessity, deal with 'fossilized evidence that has been preserved by chance or for purposes very different'.[21] In addition, most of the theoretical tools will be of modern derivation: it may not always be legitimate to apply modern tools to ancient cultures. New Testament sociologists can easily fall into the trap of *sociocentrism*, 'the tendency to see things the other side of the industrial revolution as if that revolution changed nothing in our patterns of social perception'.[22]

5. *Relationship to the text.* On the one hand, it is sometimes suggested that social-scientific criticism, used in isolation from other approaches, can tend to create too great a gulf between the text and the interpreter, stressing differences rather than similarities between ancient culture and our own.[23] On the other hand, critics have suggested that sociology instead *reduces* the proper gulf between text and interpreter, by redescribing New Testament history according to modern sociological theories and models. This may, John Milbank surmises, 'merely reflect our desire to reassure ourselves that the past was really like the present'.[24] There is some truth in both criticisms, depending on which particular New Testament sociologist one is dealing with.

F. Watson, *Paul, Judaism and the Gentiles: A Sociological Approach* (Cambridge: Cambridge University Press, 1986); cf. W.S. Campbell, 'Did Paul Advocate Separation from the Synagogue? A Reaction to Francis Watson: Paul, Judaism and the Gentiles: A Sociological Approach', *SJT* 42 (1989), pp. 457-67.

    21. C.S. Rodd, 'On Applying a Sociological Theory to Biblical Studies', *JSOT* 19 (1981), pp. 95-106 (105).

    22. R.L. Rohrbaugh, '"Social Location of Thought" as a Heuristic Construct in New Testament Study', *JSNT* 30 (1987), pp. 103-19 (113).

    23. For example, depictions of early Christianity as a millenarian sect; see T.F. Best, 'The Sociological Study of the New Testament: Promise and Peril of a New Discipline', *SJT* 36 (1983), pp. 181-94 (184).

    24. Milbank, *Theology and Social Theory*, p. 121; cf. n. 30 below.

6. *Neglect of relevant areas of sociology*. As I have already hinted in 1. above, New Testament sociologists have been somewhat selective and limited in their exploration of sociological theories and models. In particular, it is remarkable that the sociology of criminality and deviance has hardly ever been applied to New Testament data. Given that the founder of the early Christian movement was himself convicted and executed as a criminal, and subjected to crucifixion—an especially degrading and demeaning form of punishment—it is, to say the least, surprising that these relevant sub-disciplines of sociology have been neglected. Later in this chapter I propose to offer an extended example of how the *labelling approach* to deviancy, itself derived from the theoretical perspective of *symbolic interactionism*, may help to throw light on the ways in which the early Christians were able to confront, neutralize, and even reverse, the various stigmas attaching to them.

b. *Benefits*
If there are, as I have suggested, grounds to respond with caution to the partnership between biblical studies and sociology, there are also grounds for welcoming this closer relationship. I propose now to identify some of the benefits social-scientific approaches can bring to the biblical studies household.

1. *Incarnational approach*. It is not surprising, given the subject matter of early Christian faith—'the Word made flesh'—and given that Christianity has been described as 'the most material of all religions', that biblical scholars have increasingly begun to take sociological factors into account. As Howard Clark Kee puts it, 'both the divine speaking in Jesus of Nazareth and the human hearing in various contexts call for analysis of specific contexts'.[25] The human person is inevitably part and parcel of a particular society, and it is within the fabric of that society that the Kingdom of God is experienced, discerned and expressed. Treatments of early Christianity omitting the sociological dimension are in danger of being docetic and unduly abstract. 'As with any human being or reality, the soul is not to be had without the body, i.e., we are not going to see the meaning of early Christianity unless we see the social embodiment of this meaning and the dialectic process between belief and social structure this entails.'[26]

25. H.C. Kee, *Knowing the Truth* (Philadelphia: Fortress Press, 1989), p. 105.
26. Holmberg, *Sociology and the New Testament*, p. 3; cf. T.F. Best, who help-

2. *Anti-idealist approach.* Ironically, New Testament studies have sometimes focused almost exclusively on theological ideas and the conflicts surrounding them. Even form criticism tended in this direction. Social-scientific approaches to the New Testament offer an improved opportunity to discern a more accurate *Sitz im Leben*. They are a helpful antidote to the fallacy of idealism: the notion that 'the determining factors of the historical process are ideas and nothing else, and that all developments, conflicts and influences are at bottom developments of, and conflicts and influences between ideas'.[27]

3. *Balance between individual and collective understandings of Christianity.* The fruits of social-scientific approaches to the New Testament constitute a useful corrective over against any interpretations of Christianity which are too privatized and over-focused on the individual's spirituality. As Stephen Barton notes, 'from the very beginning, following Jesus was a thoroughly social commitment, which involved the shaping of a corporate life engaged in an all-pervasive (if sometimes implicit) way with questions of morality, politics, economics, law, and culture'.[28] Hence, social-scientific approaches may help to overcome false dichotomies between, for instance, the *social* and *personal* gospel.

4. *Rediscovery of the past as 'a strange country'.* There has sometimes been a tendency in New Testament studies to depict the past in terms of modern concerns or in terms of theological conflicts dating from the time of the Reformation.[29] Social-scientific approaches to the early Christian movement have the welcome capacity to be less subjective and less ethnocentric, taking us beyond received stereotypes. Paradoxically, the better the early Christian movement is known, the stranger and more distant from the modern world it may seem.[30]

fully warns against New Testament sociology's own tendency to abstraction 'drawing us away from the real world of experience to that of intellectual constructs describing that experience' ('The Sociological Study of the New Testament', p. 193).

27. B. Holmberg, *Paul and Power* (Lund: Gleerup, 1978), p. 205.

28. S.C. Barton, 'The Communal Dimension of Earliest Christianity: A Critical Survey of the Field', *JTS* 43 (1992), pp. 399-427 (426-27).

29. See J.H. Neyrey, 'Witchcraft Accusations in 2 Cor. 10–13: Paul in Social Science Perspective', *Listening* 21.2 (1986), pp. 160-70, esp. 160-61.

30. See, for instance, B.J. Malina's work, based on models derived from Mediterranean cultural anthropology: *The New Testament World* (Atlanta: John

5. *New questions eliciting new answers.* Social-scientific approaches to the New Testament place the biblical scholar in an excitingly new relationship with the text. New questions[31] are likely to elicit valuable new answers from familiar data:

> It is now possible to speak of something fundamentally new in biblical studies, not in the sense that older and more traditional approaches have been rendered obsolete, but that a new set of assumptions has made it possible to understand early Christianity in significantly new ways.[32]

Bengt Holmberg, for example, concludes that John H. Elliott's sociological exegesis of 1 Peter[33] throws important new light on the letter's ambivalence towards the outside world and 'helps to explain certain properties of the letter's content, rather better than conventional perspectives'.[34]

3. *Stigmatization and Destigmatization*

My intention here is to examine the usefulness of certain theories and models from a sub-discipline within sociology—the Sociology of Deviance—which up to now has been largely neglected by New Testament scholars. The term 'deviance' in sociology has a more general use than in normal parlance and refers to 'non-conformity to a given norm, or set of norms, which are accepted by a significant number of people in a community or society', which may or may not be subject to criminal sanctions.[35]

a. *Symbolic Interactionism and Social Reaction Theory*
Given that the early Christians were subject to a variety of stigmas, as I shall demonstrate shortly, I propose to examine some of the ways in

Knox Press, 1981); also J.H. Neyrey (ed.), *The Social World of Luke–Acts: Models for Interpretation* (Peabody, MA: Hendrickson, 1991); also P.F. Esler, *The First Christians in their Social Worlds: Social-Scientific Approaches to New Testament Interpretation* (London: Routledge, 1994), pp. 19-36.

31. See, for example, the extensive sets of questions itemized by Kee, *Knowing the Truth*, pp. 65-69.

32. Gager, 'Shall we Marry our Enemies?', p. 256.

33. *A Home for the Homeless: A Sociological Exegesis of 1 Peter, Its Situation and Strategy* (London: SCM Press, 1981).

34. Holmberg, *Sociology and the New Testament*, p. 94.

35. A. Giddens, *Sociology* (Cambridge: Polity Press, 1993), p. 116; see also N. Abercrombie *et al.*, *Contemporary British Society* (Cambridge: Polity Press, 1994), pp. 472-82.

which those stigmas could have been resisted. Here I will be drawing on models from sociology, from within the *symbolic interactionist* perspective and, more particularly, *social reaction* theory.

Symbolic interactionism understands human identity as something that is not a static entity, but instead is a continuously shaped and reshaped *outcome* of processes of social interaction. According to symbolic interactionists most interaction between human beings involves the exchange of symbols: 'we constantly look for "clues" about what type of behaviour is appropriate in the context and about how to interpret what others intend'.[36] 'Social symbolic interactions are the loci where values, motivations, tensions, desires and interests find expression; there, symbols are exchanged and negotiated'.[37] Symbolic interactionists have paid particular attention to the processes whereby someone *becomes* a deviant.

Social reaction theory is sometimes loosely known as *labelling theory*. It has been described recently as: 'perhaps the most widely useful approach to understanding aspects of crime and deviant behaviour'.[38] Social reaction theory focuses on the interaction between 'rule violators' and 'rule enforcers'. Deviance is understood not so much as a property *inherent in* certain ways of behaviour, but instead as a property *conferred upon* the behaviour in question by a given social audience.[39] As Howard Becker, one of the best known social reaction theorists, puts it in a well-known paragraph:

> Social groups create deviance by making the rules whose infraction constitutes deviance, and by applying those rules to particular people and labelling them as outsiders. From this point of view, deviance is not a quality of the act the person commits, but rather a consequence of the application by others of rules and sanctions to an 'offender'. The deviant is one to whom that label has been successfully applied; deviant behaviour is behaviour that people so label.[40]

36. Giddens, *Sociology*, p. 716: he gives the example of a couple going out on their first date, trying to read each other's 'signals'; see also D. Downes and P. Rock, *Understanding Deviance* (Oxford: Clarendon Press, 1988), pp. 166-91.

37. N. Ben-Yehuda, *The Politics and Morality of Deviance: Moral Panics, Drug Abuse, Deviant Science, and Reversed Stigmatization* (Albany: State University of New York Press, 1990), p. 15.

38. Giddens, *Sociology*, p. 132.

39. See further K.T. Erikson, 'Notes on the Sociology of Deviance', *Social Problems* 9 (1962), pp. 307-14 (308).

40. H. Becker, *Outsiders* (New York: Free Press, 1963), p. 9.

It is law makers and law interpreters and enforcers who define what and who is criminal. Hence the labelling of deviance tends to reflect the power structure of society. Once a person is labelled as a 'criminal', that individual is stigmatized; the degree of stigma will depend on the type of crime and the extent to which society sees it as discrediting. Labelling theorists distinguish between *primary deviation*, when a person is labelled as a criminal, and *secondary deviation*, when the person lapses into further deviance and comes to accept the deviant label as applying to him or herself.

The sociologist Erving Goffman defines stigma as a deeply discrediting attribute or behavioural characteristic that (in certain social contexts) reduces the possessor 'from a whole and usual person to a tainted, discounted one'.[41] The stigmatized person is disqualified from full acceptance by society. The term 'stigma' originally derived from the Greek στίγμα, meaning bodily signs cut or branded into the body to denote that a person was a criminal, slave or traitor. As well as criminal stigma—for instance, of having a criminal conviction or having been in prison—there are also stigmas associated with mental or physical handicap, race, nationality, or religion. Sometimes whole groups can be stigmatized: for example, a new religious movement or 'cult' like 'The Family'.

As well as analysing how it is that some people are labelled with and (passively) assume deviant identity, labelling theory has also tried to account for the ways in which individuals give meaning to their acts and to take account of the exercise of choice on the part of the person labelled as deviant.[42] Symbolic interactionist theory presupposes that acceptance or rejection of a deviant label can always be subject to negotiation, even after stigmatization has occurred.[43] In particular, it is possible that a person labelled deviant will fight back against that stigma, sometimes successfully.

I have selected two typologies of destigmatization from the labelling

---

41. E. Goffman, *Stigma: Notes on the Management of Spoiled Identity* (Harmondsworth: Pelican, 1968), p. 12.

42. See further P.G. Schervish, 'The Labelling Perspective: Its Bias and Potential in the Study of Political Deviance', *The American Sociologist* 8 (1973), pp. 47-57.

43. For example, in the course of the interaction between juvenile offenders and their Probation Officer they may be labelled as 'sick' rather than 'bad': see E.M. Schur, *Labelling Deviant Behavior: Its Sociological Implications* (London: Harper & Row, 1971), pp. 59-60.

theory perspective as of particular interest for the New Testament scholar: those of Rogers and Buffalo, and Warren.

b. *Rogers and Buffalo*
This is a most helpful typology, which can, to some extent, be developed as a predictive model. It is a dynamic taxonomy of fighting-back techniques (movement is possible across modes), recognizing that people 'are in constant reflective dialogue with reality rather than simply determined by it'.[44]

COLLECTIVE RESPONSE

INDIVIDUAL'S STRATEGY	*Magnification*: the tendency for the deviant label to take on salience or primacy	*Manipulation*: the tendency for the label to undergo change via influences resulting from persuasion, deception, skill, etc.	*Obliteration*: the tendency for the label to be erased, cancelled, or made obsolete
Assent: agreement with or acceptance of the deviant label	1. Acquiescence	4. Channelling	7. Reinterpretation
Rejection: disagreement with or denial of the deviant label	2. Repudiation	5. Evasion	8. Redefinition
Exchange: an attempt to substitute or switch labels	3. Flight	6. Modification	9. Alteration

(based on Rogers and Buffalo, *'Fighting Back'*, p. 106)

Table 2

In *Table 2* Rogers and Buffalo offer a typology of nine possible adaptations to a deviant label. I will analyse each of these separately below. Each of these modes of 'fighting back' against stigma involves

44. J.W. Rogers and M.D. Buffalo, 'Fighting Back: Nine Modes of Adaptation to a Deviant Label', *Social Problems* 22 (1974), pp. 101-18; Rogers cites examples of movement between modes in J.W. Rogers and G.L. Mays, *Juvenile Delinquency and Juvenile Justice* (New York: John Wiley & Sons, 1987), p. 120.

different combinations of individual strategies and likely societal responses to the individual's tactics.

Rogers and Buffalo make a number of predictions based on their typology. They note that socio-economic factors are likely to play some part in the choice of adaptations: the severely disadvantaged are less likely or able to *repudiate*, *evade*, or *modify* the stigma and are more likely to espouse *acquiescence* or *flight*. They also suggest that *acquiescence* and *flight* are more likely to be found where the unit analysed is an individual person, and for *reinterpretation* and *redefinition* to be more often found where a group is concerned. Adaptations will vary according to the method by which labels were applied: understanding, insight, support and firmness are most likely to result in *alteration*; on the other hand, cruelty, humiliation, and revenge will more likely inspire a life-long stance of *repudiation* and conflict. Adaptations will also vary according to the types of behaviour labelled deviant: if political actions are labelled deviant then the most palatable adaptations are likely to be *repudiation*, *reinterpretation* or *redefinition*, **not** *flight*, for instance. It can further be predicted that adaptation (8) may be facilitated where the deviant challenge is based on values implicit in the cultural heritage of the dominant group.[45] There is also evidence that destigmatization processes are most likely to be effective if they are associated with political or religious world views, 'crystallizing and generating an independent power base'.[46]

c. *Warren*

Underlying the typology of Rogers and Buffalo is the presupposition that the obliteration of a stigma involves the attainment of 'normalcy', by change of behaviour on the part of the deviant, by change of societal norms or by change of society's perception of the deviant. Their typology accounts for some, but not all, instances of destigmatization. There is no *a priori* reason why the obverse of deviance should always be normalcy. Some deviants seem to obliterate their stigma by becoming supra-normal or heroic and achieving (an equally all embracing) positive charisma. For this reason it is valuable to supplement and augment Rogers and Buffalo's typology by considering Carrol A.B. Warren's

45. See H.E. Gross, 'Draft Protestors', *Sociological Quarterly* 18 (1977), pp. 319-39, esp. his proposition H4.

46. Ben-Yehuda, *The Politics and Morality of Deviance*, p. 248.

complementary analysis of modes of destigmatization.[47]

Warren offers a three-fold typology of 'charismatic destigmatization' (to be analysed in more detail below), involving:

i) individual purification;
ii) transcendence; *or*
iii) collective aristocratization.

Warren chooses to focus on *charismatic* destigmatization because deviance and charisma are 'inversely related concepts'.[48] Deviance involves the imputation of a negative, sub-human ontological 'essence' or 'nature' to a human being; charisma, on the other hand, amounts to a 'mirror image' of this—the imputing of positive, 'super-human' nature. Warren comments: 'the charismatic and the deviant are more closely related to each other than either is related to the normal'.[49] She concludes that charisma is an apt choice of route for stigmatized people to choose as their escape route from stigma, because 'the identity of normal may be further in moral distance for the stigmatized than that of charismatic'.[50]

I intend now to apply these two typologies of dealing with stigma from labelling theory to New Testament data in order to further illuminate and categorize the strategies of dealing with stigma at work in Luke–Acts and the Pauline writings. As far as can be ascertained this is a substantially novel approach to the data in question. Previous treatments[51] have drawn on, for instance, cognitive dissonance theory (from the sub-discipline of social psychology) but have rarely drawn directly on the sociology of deviance in reference to dealing with stigma.

Bruce J. Malina and Jerome H. Neyrey have drawn on labelling and

47. C.A.B. Warren, 'Destigmatization of Identity: From Deviant to Charismatic', *Qualitative Sociology* 3.1 (1980), pp. 59-72.

48. J. Katz, 'Deviance, Charisma and Rule-Defined Behavior', *Social Problems* 20 (1972), pp. 186-202 (194).

49. Warren, 'Destigmatization of Identity', p. 70.

50. Warren, 'Destigmatization of Identity', p. 70.

51. Previous treatments of destigmatization in the New Testament include: M. Harris (*Cows, Pigs, Wars and Witches* [New York: Vintage Books, 1978]), who builds on the work of S.G.F. Brandon; J. Gager (*Kingdom and Community* [Englewood Cliffs, NJ: Prentice-Hall, 1975]), who draws on social-psychological *cognitive dissonance* theory; a more systematic application of cognitive dissonance theory is represented by U. Wernik, 'Frustrated Beliefs and Early Christianity', *Numen* 22 (1975), pp. 96-130.

280   *Approaches to New Testament Study*

deviance theory in their analysis of conflict in Luke–Acts.[52] They conclude that 'the whole Christian tradition describes the usual neutralization ploys whereby Jesus escapes the negative labelling process'.[53] Although they offer a helpful treatment of the (in this instance, Jewish) legal processes involved in the deviantization and stigmatization of Jesus—for instance, the part played by status degradation rituals[54]—and they address ways in which the labelling process can be interrupted, they fail to analyse ways in which stigmatization might be *reversed*. There is an implicit dismissive reference to Rogers and Buffalo's article on p. 118 (and the article is listed in the 'works consulted'). However, it is by no means evident that Malina and Neyrey have fully assimilated Rogers and Buffalo's arguments: for instance, they misleadingly claim that the strategy of *flight* does not apply to Jesus or his disciples because Jesus 'did not *flee* from his enemies';[55] this is a simplistic understanding of Rogers and Buffalo's category.

It is puzzling that Malina and Neyrey try to apply a model based on techniques of *neutralization* to New Testament data. According to their definition, neutralization is a technique whereby people can 'overcome the unfathomable chasm between saying one thing and doing another',[56] simultaneously upholding (internalized) institutional values, yet violating them behaviourally. It is unclear how this fits the New Testament material, if at all: surely in the eyes of Jesus and his followers his behaviour and beliefs were mutually consistent and no such 'unfathomable gulf' existed.

Their treatment of status degradation rituals as *rites of passage* resulting in the ascribing of stigma is helpful, but again somewhat flawed. They are right to draw attention to the ways in which Jesus' status is 'publicly and ritually changed to that of a dishonourable and impotent person'.[57] However, they do not appear to be able to agree on where to place the Cross in the rites of passage sequence: on p. 107 it belongs to the *liminal* stage, whereas on p. 116 it belongs to the stage of *reaggregation*!

52. B.J. Malina and J.H. Neyrey, 'Conflict in Luke–Acts: Labelling and Deviance Theory', in Neyrey (ed.), *The Social World of Luke–Acts*, pp. 97-122.
53. Malina and Neyrey, 'Conflict in Luke–Acts', p. 108.
54. See Malina and Neyrey, 'Conflict in Luke–Acts', pp. 107, 115-17. See also their imaginary reconstruction of the priest's 'case record' relating to Jesus.
55. Malina and Neyrey, 'Conflict in Luke–Acts', p. 118.
56. Malina and Neyrey, 'Conflict in Luke–Acts', p. 108.
57. Malina and Neyrey, 'Conflict in Luke–Acts', p. 116.

My own study, unlike that of Malina and Neyrey, focuses on destigmatization, rather than neutralization, techniques and takes account of wider forms of stigma, not restricted to that resulting from a legal process.[58]

The two typologies used in my study—Rogers and Buffalo, and Warren—were selected because of their capacity to analyse deviance on the part of social movements, as well as individuals, within a symbolic interactionist frame of reference. The nature of the New Testament data itself seems to confirm the appropriateness of using models drawn from labelling theory (as opposed to other sociological theoretical frameworks): there would appear to be nothing *inherently* stigmatizing about the behaviour of Jesus and the early Christians or about Jesus' mode of death; crucifixion, for instance, might be interpreted as degrading punishment or heroic martyrdom. Equally if, as we will see, there is evidence within the New Testament data of attempts to resist the imputation of stigma, this would appear to call for the application of a theory of deviance that treats the imputation of deviance and equally the adoption (or otherwise) of a deviant identity as *outcomes of a process of social interaction* (rather than automatically arising from the violation of certain given societal norms).

The two destigmatization typologies selected represent a coherent and wide-ranging account of the available repertoire of individual and collective responses to a deviant label. Each of the modes of destigmatization identified by Rogers and Buffalo, and Warren involves (if it is to be a successful strategy) one or more of the following: alteration in the deviant's behaviour, alteration in societal norms, and/or alteration in the way society perceives the deviant's behaviour.

I now propose to establish that Jesus and, both by association and independently, his followers were stigmatized as 'deviant' by significant audiences in their social world and then to examine ways in which the early Christian movement resisted the stigmas imputed to them.

4. *Stigmatization of the Early Christian Movement*

a. *The Trial, Conviction and Crucifixion of Jesus*
One of the best attested facts about Jesus is that he was convicted and crucified as a lawbreaker. We can be less certain, however, about the charges on which he was indicted, the nature of the legal process, which

---

58. As does Goffman's treatment: see Goffman, *Stigma*, p. 14.

legal authority (Roman or Jewish) found Jesus guilty of a capital charge and who exactly carried out the penalty.

All the Gospels imply that the final verdict rested with the Roman authorities and that the Jewish authorities at this time either could not or would not carry out a capital sentence; indeed the Fourth Gospel reports that the Jews had no authority to carry out such a sentence (Jn 18.31). Even if, as is disputed, the Jews had the capacity to carry out a sentence of crucifixion, there may have been other reasons why they would not have done so. If, for instance, the mission of Jesus was liable to be (mis)understood in seditious terms as some of the charges against him imply (e.g. Lk. 23.1-2; Jn 19.12) then it may well have been important for the priestly group to hand Jesus over to the Romans in order to demonstrate their own pro-Roman loyalties.[59]

It is likely that the sentence ultimately carried out on Jesus was principally a Roman, rather than a Jewish, one. It is true that we can presuppose a good deal of autonomy on the part of the Jewish judicial system at this time.[60] However it is not plausible that the Roman authorities were merely enacting a verdict of the Sanhedrin. If this were so, a Jewish mode of execution would surely have been used.[61] Jewish involvement in the death of Jesus should nevertheless not be minimized, if only because Jewish sources that mention Jesus themselves generally specify that Jesus was condemned by the Jews and that he justly deserved execution.[62]

It is not possible to be certain about all the details of Jesus' conviction and execution, largely because our primary sources in the New Testament are not independent historians.[63] We can however safely assume that Jesus was stigmatized as 'deviant' by being condemned as a lawbreaker on a capital charge, and that both Jewish and Roman

---

59. See further C. Rowland, *Christian Origins* (London: SPCK, 1985), p. 173.

60. As Bammel notes ('The Trial before Pilate', in E. Bammel and C.F.D. Moule [eds.], *Jesus and the Politics of his Day* [Cambridge: Cambridge University Press, 1984], pp. 415-51), the Jewish judicial system was 'left intact by the Romans as far as possible' (p. 435).

61. See P. Winter, *On the Trial of Jesus* (Berlin: de Gruyter, 1961), p. 62.

62. See D.R. Catchpole, *The Trial of Jesus* (Leiden: Brill, 1971), pp. 1-11; also W. Horbury, 'The Trial of Jesus in Jewish Tradition', in E. Bammel (ed.), *The Trial of Jesus* (London: SCM Press, 1970), pp. 103-21.

63. See Winter, *On the Trial of Jesus*, pp. 1-8; indeed Winter suggests that Jn 18.31 (see above) has its basis in the 'theological scheme' of the Fourth Gospel (p. 88); this is refuted by Catchpole, *The Trial of Jesus*, pp. 247-48.

legal processes were involved to varying degrees.

Stigma would have attached to Jesus not merely by virtue of being branded a criminal and executed, but also because of the manner of his death—crucifixion—and the nature of the charges against him. Crucifixion, as a specific form of capital punishment, was regarded in the Roman world as a humiliating and demeaning mode of execution. It was seen as a barbaric penalty, as utterly offensive and even 'obscene'.[64] There is hardly any evidence in the ancient Roman world of a death by crucifixion being interpreted in a positive sense.[65] Crucifixion was a 'most cruel and disgusting penalty' (Cicero, *In Verrem* 2.5.165) and was almost always inflicted on the lower classes and slaves or on those convicted of crimes against the state.[66]

In the Jewish world crucifixion would not necessarily have been viewed in such negative terms. It is true that it is often asserted that victims of crucifixion would have automatically fallen under the curse and stigma of Deut. 21.23 and therefore have caused profound religious offence; Gal. 3.13 is usually cited in support of this claim.[67] However there is no evidence, except for Gal. 3.13, that Deut. 21.23 was ever previously understood as referring to crucifixion. It is in any case unlikely that Jews would have regarded crucifixion per se as a religiously offensive mode of death. Surely the eight hundred Pharisees killed under Alexander Jannaeus (Josephus, *Ant.* 13.14.2), Judah the Galilaean and family (*Ant.* 18.1) and every other Jew crucified during rebellions against the Roman occupation would not have been considered to have died 'accursed by God'. There is no evidence that this was so: they would have been heroes, not victims of a curse. Hence, as far as the Jewish audience was concerned, the stigma attaching to Jesus derived not so much from the mode of execution as the *grounds* of execution.

The early Christians understood the charges against Jesus as falling into two main categories: (a) religious (e.g., blasphemy: Mk 14.64; Mt. 26.65) and (b) political (e.g., sedition: Lk. 23.1-2; Jn 19.12). Both

---

64. M. Hengel, *Crucifixion* (London: SCM Press, 1977), p. 22.

65. Hengel in his extensive study (*Crucifixion*, p. 64) finds just one legendary instance.

66. See G.E.M. de St Croix, 'Why Were the Early Christians Persecuted?', *Past and Present* 26 (1963), pp. 6-38.

67. See B. Lindars, *New Testament Apologetic* (London: SCM Press, 1961), p. 233.

sets of charges would have branded Jesus with stigma: in the *first* case, particularly to Jewish eyes, as a 'blasphemer' and in the *second* case, particularly to Roman eyes, as a 'traitor' or 'political subversive'. Presumably the ultimate charge on which Jesus was executed was that of sedition against the Roman state, in view of the fact that the mode of execution—crucifixion—particularly fitted that crime. However, the Gospel traditions suggest that the other, religious, charges featured strongly, at least as far as the Jewish legal process was concerned. Sociologically speaking, questions as to the historicity and applicability[68] of these charges are unnecessary: as symbolic interactionists are fond of quoting, 'if men[69] (*sic*) define situations as real, they are real in their consequences'.[70]

Jesus was therefore stigmatized, in various ways and for various audiences, by virtue of being branded a criminal, a threat to the state, and a religious deviant, and by being executed in a particularly demeaning and discrediting manner.[71] His followers, by association, will also have attracted stigma. The variety of deviance imputed to Jesus by Jewish and Roman audiences is bound to have rubbed off to some degree on his followers who would have been tainted, in the eyes of the wider world, by their association with a crucified lawbreaker. In addition, the early Christian movement independently attracted other forms of stigma, to which we now turn.

68. For instance, it is uncertain whether Jesus would have been accused of blasphemy, at least as it is defined by *m. Sanh.* 7.5 (uttering the name of YHWH); we cannot be sure that the Mishnah necessarily reflects legal procedures at the time of Jesus, since it only attained its present form in the second century CE: see Catchpole, *The Trial of Jesus*, pp. 154, 258-60; also A.E. Harvey, *Jesus and the Constraints of History* (London: Gerald Duckworth, 1982), who suggests that 'the offence consisted, fundamentally, of diminishing God's honour by usurping some privilege or prerogative due to him alone' (p. 170).

69. In this case the early Christians.

70. W. Thomas and D.S. Thomas, *The Child in America* (New York: Alfred A. Knopf, 1928), pp. 571-75.

71. There were other stigmas attaching to Jesus—for example, his home town (Jn 1.46); Jesus was thought to be mad (Mk 3.21), although, as J.P. Hes and S. Wollstein ('The Attitude of Ancient Jewish Sources to Mental Patients', *Israel Annals of Psychiatry and Related Disciplines* 2.1 [1964], pp. 103-16) point out, mental illness would have attracted a different and lesser stigma then than now—but these will not be addressed here.

b. *Early Christian Experiences of Stigmatization*
1. *The Jewish world.* The available evidence suggests that whilst Christians were not necessarily 'excommunicated' from the synagogue[72] they would have been perceived as heretics and cursed (at least implicitly) thrice-daily in the synagogue service,[73] subject to a certain amount of counter-propaganda[74] and probably not have been allowed to mix completely freely with Jews.[75]

The stigma of belonging to a heretical group will have been reinforced by official Jewish harassment of Christians (Acts 4.5-18; 5.27-42; 9.1-2; 1 Thess. 2.14-16) which could involve punishment (2 Cor. 11.24-25; Acts 5.40) and even persecution to death (Acts 6.12–7.60). Mob violence against Christians is also mentioned (Acts 17.5-9; 21.27-28; 23.20-22).

2. *The Graeco-Roman World.* Christians were undoubtedly stigmatized to varying degrees by the Roman world. Tacitus, for instance, denounced them as *odium humani generis* ('the enemy of mankind': *Ann.* 15.44). There is evidence that the early Christian movement would have attracted a variety of stigmas, including that of being a new and alien *superstitio* and being a (potentially) subversive movement. The Christian *superstitio* would have been perceived as threatening to disrupt the *pax deorum* and to alienate the gods' goodwill, because of its exclusive monotheism and refusal to recognize the gods. Moreover it was a novel as well as an alien cult; this would (unlike Judaism) have offended against the innate conservatism and respect for ancestral traditions of the

72. See, for example, Acts 13.42-43; 18.4; 19.8; cf. Jn 9.22; 12.42; 16.2; there is no independent evidence of anyone being permanently banned or excommunicated from the synagogue before at least 200 CE; see S.T. Katz, 'Issues in the Separation of Judaism and Christianity after 70 CE: A Reconsideration', *JBL* 103 (1984), pp. 43-76 (48-53).

73. Dating from the inclusion of the *birkat ha-minim* in the Eighteen Benedictions at Yavneh (c. 80–90 CE).

74. According to Justin, Jews had circulated accounts of Christ as a Galilean deceiver whose disciples stole his body and then claimed he was risen (*Dialogue with Trypho* 17.108).

75. Justin claims that Jews were prohibited from conversation (presumably about religious matters) with Christians (*Dialogue with Trypho* 38.112); however it is unlikely that a legal ban on social intercourse was in effect, not least because the Mishnah does not mention any such ban.

Roman world.[76] The early Christians would probably have attracted stigma not totally unlike that attaching to certain new religious movements or 'cults' today. Equally, the early Christian movement would tend to be seen as secret clandestine 'voluntary associations' or clubs (*hetaeriae*).[77] *Hetaeriae* were often regarded as potential seedbeds of both immorality and political conspiracy, and, consequently, frequent attempts were made to ban them.[78] Tertullian, even as late as the early third century CE, sees fit to defend Christianity against the charge that the Christian *collegium* is in some way politically subversive (*Apol.* 39) or open to charges of treason (e.g., *Apol.* 10.1; 28.3ff.). Periodically the Christians were subject to harassment and persecution by the Roman authorities—for instance, the scapegoating of Christians by Nero for the great fire of Rome in 64 CE—and this will have reflected and amplified their stigmatization as deviant. After the Neronian persecution being a Christian would henceforth have necessarily involved 'by definition, membership of an anti-social and potentially criminal conspiracy'.[79]

We may conclude, therefore, that the early Christian movement will have had to contend with multiple stigmatization, both in its own right and because of its association with the condemned and crucified lawbreaker, Jesus.

5. *Fighting Back: Processes of Dealing with Stigma in Luke–Acts and Paul*

As we shall see below, examination of Luke–Acts and the Pauline writings confirms that the early Christians reflected in these writings perceived Jesus and, by association, themselves as subject to stigmatization. According to Paul the cross of Jesus was labelled as mere 'folly' by the Graeco-Roman world (1 Cor. 1.23). The vehemence with which Luke protests Jesus' innocence (and that of his apostles) suggests that

76. See, for example, Plutarch (writing at the end of the first century CE): no one should 'distort and sully one's own tongue with strange names and barbarous phrases to disgrace and transgress the god-given ancestral dignity of our religion' (*On Superstition* 166b [LCL]); also, R.L. Wilken, *The Christians as the Romans Saw Them* (New Haven: Yale University Press, 1984), pp. 32, 48-67.

77. See Pliny, *Ep.* 10.96.7.

78. See Wilken, *The Christians as the Romans Saw Them*, pp. 31-47; also W.A. Meeks, *The First Urban Christians* (New Haven and London: Yale University Press, 1983), pp. 77-80.

79. De St Croix, 'Why Were the Early Christians Persecuted?', p. 8.

the stigma of his alleged guilt was deeply felt. Furthermore there is evidence that the early Christians in question were concerned about how wider society viewed them. Even for Paul (who apparently did not expect the present age to last very long, 1 Cor. 7.29) it was important that the Christian community presented itself in positive terms to outsiders. Both Paul and especially Luke interpreted Christian ethics in terms of virtues already highly prized and approved by pagan society, with a view to receiving its approbation. It is very likely that these writings reflect an interest in overcoming perceived stigma. The most straightforward explanation of the stress on the innocence of Jesus in Luke–Acts is that Luke is here attempting to reduce or obliterate stigma. Beneath the predominantly *positive* thrust of early Christian belief and evangelization there runs a *defensive* undercurrent concerned with the all-too-human problem of finding oneself stigmatized.

I propose now to apply the two destigmatization typologies mentioned above of Rogers and Buffalo and of Warren from the sociology of deviance to New Testament data and to contrast and compare some examples of destigmatization techniques used (consciously or unconsciously) by Paul and Luke–Acts in order to better understand responses in these sources to the stigma attaching to the crucified and condemned Jesus and his followers. I begin by examining the usefulness of Rogers and Buffalo's typology in relation to evidence from these two New Testament sources:

a. *Rogers and Buffalo Typology*
1. *Acquiescence*. In acquiescence 'the person acknowledges the face validity of (the) deviant label'.[80] Label imposition is not contested and (at least temporarily) the label is accepted. In some cases acquiescence will involve the deviants' own self perception as well as their behaviour and they will agree that the deviant label fits them and rightly applies to them. Sometimes, however, acquiescence will merely constitute the adoption of an expedient and compliant (fictive) facade.

This mode of adaptation is found in neither Paul nor Luke–Acts. It has, one supposes, too many overtones of duplicity and/or prevarication, if acquiescence were for the sake of expediency. If, on the other hand, acquiescence were genuine then this would amount to complete acceptance of the stigmas attaching to Jesus and his followers; it is not surprising that this strategy fails to be reflected in these writings.

---

80. Rogers and Buffalo, 'Fighting Back', p. 105.

2. *Repudiation*. With repudiation the stigmatized individuals reject the deviant label imposed on them and claim that they are in fact innocent or normal (depending on the nature of the stigma). 'It's all lies...it isn't so!' claims the stigmatized person. Successful resistance to stigmatization using this mode usually requires considerable determination on the part of the deviants and skilful advocacy on their behalf; equally some degree of resources and power on the part of the deviants and/or their advocates are frequently necessary for this strategy to succeed. The use of this destigmatization tactic to 'fight back' against the imposition of stigma will tend to evoke a response on the part of society whereby the deviant label is magnified and becomes increasingly prominent. It is likely that deviants who use this tactic unless and until they are successful will suffer an increased sense of frustration and will tend to evoke scorn in others, thereby magnifying the deviant label.

Repudiation of stigma is a strong feature in Luke–Acts. Whilst the assertion of Christ's innocence is not entirely absent from Paul (e.g., 2 Cor. 5.21) it is emphasized in Luke–Acts. The innocence of Jesus in relation to Jewish law and especially Roman law is strongly emphasized by Luke: Pilate states 'I have myself examined (Jesus) and found nothing in him to support your charges...no more did Herod' (Lk. 23.14, 15). In his account of the Sanhedrin hearing Luke omits any mention of a verdict (Lk. 22.71; cf. Mk 14.64); in Acts 13.27-28 Paul explicitly states that the Jews 'found no cause of death in him'. There seem to be deliberate parallels drawn by Luke between the legal appearances described in Acts and Jesus' own trial. The apostles and their colleagues are made to present their case before the same Jewish court responsible for convicting and crucifying Jesus (Acts 4.15; 5.21, 27, 34, 41; 6.12, 15; 22.30; 23.1, 6, 15, 20, 28; 24.20).[81] The hearings of Jesus before Pilate and Herod Antipas (Lk. 23.1-25) seem to have a similar structure and content to Paul's appearances before Festus and Agrippa II (Acts 25–26).[82] The proven innocence of Paul (Acts 23.29; 25.18-20, 25; 26.31-32) functions to demonstrate Jesus' own innocence. Acts underlines the innocence of Paul (and, by association, Jesus) by virtue of tests even more conclusive than those of the law court: by surviving

---

81. See A.A. Trites, 'The Importance of Legal Scenes and Language in the Book of Acts', *NovT* 16 (1974), pp. 278-84.

82. See R.F. O'Toole, 'Luke's Notion of "Be Imitators of Me as I Am of Christ" in Acts 25–26', *BTB* 8.4 (1978), pp. 155-61 (156).

shipwreck and snake bite Paul is found guiltless.[83] Luke's interest in proving the innocence of Jesus centres on the Roman legal verdict of Jesus' guiltlessness (Lk. 23.14, 15; cf. Acts 26.31). A Christian audience is in all likelihood predominantly in view, to whom Luke is seeking to show the Roman Empire in a relatively good light:[84] Christians can safely trust in Roman magistrates and their just verdicts[85] and rest content that Jesus was righteous[86] and innocent.

The deviant labels imputed to Jesus are thus rejected and a determined and sustained attempt is made to establish Jesus' innocence. The evidence adduced lends considerable weight to the probability that the early Christians both perceived Jesus (and themselves) as stigmatized and explored ways of reducing or eliminating the stigmas. This is by far the most straightforward explanation of this material.

By comparison, repudiation is a very much less significant feature of the Pauline writings; clearly Paul is likely to be using alternative strategies for dealing with stigma instead.

3. *Flight*. Flight as a 'mode of adaptation' represents an effort to exchange labels by, for instance, 'change of name, school, neighbourhood, or hometown'[87] or 'passing' as normal. Some forms of flight will tend to accentuate societal focus on the deviant label and fail to reduce the imputation of stigma, especially where emotional withdrawal or aberrant behaviour is involved. Changes in name or locale are more

---

83. See G. Miles and G. Trompf, 'Luke and Antiphon: The Theology of Acts 27–28 in the Light of Pagan Beliefs about Divine Retribution, Pollution and Shipwreck', *HTR* 69 (1977), pp. 259-67 (265-66).

84. See P. Walaskay, *And so We Came to Rome* (Cambridge: Cambridge University Press, 1983); this does not exclude the possibility that Luke also has in mind a Roman audience and may, for instance, be trying to capitalize on Roman respect for ancestral religious traditions: see P.F. Esler, *Community and Gospel in Luke–Acts* (Cambridge: Cambridge University Press, 1987), pp. 214-17.

85. Although individual Roman officials are sometimes portrayed in a poor light, the Roman legal system is not portrayed as anti-Christianity per se: see Esler, *Community and Gospel in Luke–Acts*, pp. 209, 217.

86. Lk. 23.47: the translation 'righteous' is to be preferred to 'innocent'—why otherwise should the centurion 'praise God' for the execution of an innocent person?; 'righteous' includes the notion of innocence but implies something more: see B. Beck, 'Imitatio Christi and the Lucan Passion Narrative', in W. Horbury and B. McNeil (eds.), *Suffering and Martyrdom in the New Testament* (Cambridge: Cambridge University Press, 1981), pp. 30-40, 42-47.

87. Rogers and Buffalo, 'Fighting Back', p. 108.

likely to constitute a successful strategy. Deviants who try to 'pass' as conventional members of the community may well live in fear that one day their former identity may become evident.[88] However if they successfully establish themselves in their new identity this will tend to mitigate the scale and significance of any subsequent disclosure of their former label.

The flight mode of destigmatization is regarded by both Paul and Luke as illegitimate. Rather than choosing this strategy themselves they castigate it as inappropriate. Luke, for instance, makes clear that when Peter attempts to pass off[89] his involvement with Jesus, when he denies Jesus in the courtyard of the high priest's house after Jesus' arrest, Peter is disowning him (Lk. 22.61) and this, as Luke makes clear elsewhere (9.26; 12.9), means Peter is himself in danger of being disowned by the Son of Man. In Paul there is evidence of more subtle forms of 'flight' on the part of Paul's opponents. At Corinth his opponents try to pass as 'normal', eschewing a stigmatized lifestyle of humiliation and suffering such as might be expected were they to properly acknowledge Jesus. They 'stress the belief that Christ's death was a substitute for ours to the exclusion of the Pauline conviction that Christians must participate in the suffering of Christ'.[90] The Corinthians want 'instant glory' and to leave behind the way of the cross. Paul is at pains to counter this tendency: 'wherever we go we carry death with us in our body, the death that Jesus dies, that in this body also life may reveal itself' (2 Cor. 4.10). Doubtless one reason why 'flight' is deprecated by Paul and Luke–Acts is the inherent secrecy involved in this mode of adaptation. Early Christianity was always, although to varying degrees, mission-minded and never content to become merely a conventicle.

4. *Channelling*. Channelling is the next form of adaptation. Here, using Rogers and Buffalo's typology, we are looking for evidence in Luke–Acts and Paul of a label being 'used as a source of identity',[91] a negative

---

88. See Goffman, *Stigma*, pp. 92-113.

89. It is interesting that there is one stigma Peter cannot escape: 'he is a Galilean!' (Lk. 22.59).

90. M.D. Hooker, 'Interchange and Suffering', in Horbury and McNeil (eds.), *Suffering and Martyrdom in the New Testament*, pp. 70-83 (82); see also D. Georgi, *The Opponents of Paul in Second Corinthians* (Edinburgh: T. & T. Clark, 1987), pp. 280 and *passim*.

91. Rogers and Buffalo, 'Fighting Back', p. 110.

label being transformed into 'a fulfilling means of self-expression, personal identity, and social effectiveness'.[92] In some cases the deviant label may lose all undesirable connotations, at least as far as the deviants' own perceptions of themselves are concerned. For example, ethnic minority groups who have suffered negative labelling may express what they see as proper pride in their colour, identity and cultural heritage rather than agreeing to their assimilation to the dominant culture.

There is evidence in Luke–Acts and Paul of negative labels being used as a source of identity and being regarded as reasons for pride rather than shame. Channelling is however much more characteristic of Paul than of Luke.

Acts 5.41 encourages the early Christian communities to take pride in their identity: '[the apostles] went...rejoicing that they had been found worthy to suffer indignity for the sake of the Name'. Channelling is, however, a theme more characteristic of Paul where it is explicitly linked with the death of Jesus (Gal. 6.14). The family of words in the New Testament relating to 'boasting' or 'glorying' is used almost exclusively by Paul.[93] Paul 'boasts in the Lord' (e.g., Gal. 6.14; 1 Cor. 1.31; 2 Cor. 10.17; 2 Cor. 11.31) and boasts of the faithful service and dedication of fellow Christians working to glorify God (e.g., Rom. 15.17; 1 Thess. 2.19, 20; 2 Cor. 9.2). Nevertheless Paul does not appear to have complete freedom of choice when it comes to selecting this mode of destigmatization. Because boasting for Paul can have negative connotations this strategy is not as prominent as it might be in his writings. Paul deprecates boasting in the wrong path of salvation—the law, not Christ—and boasting in the Jews' alleged special and exclusive standing with God (Rom. 10.3). There is some overlap between this category and the notion of 'collective aristocratization', which we shall examine below. I will leave consideration of possible pride in one's identity as a 'chosen people' until then.

5. *Evasion*. In evasion, deviants seek to reject the negative label imputed to them, by resorting to verbal manipulations intended to neutralize public (and self) disapproval of their deviancy.[94] The forms evasion may take include:

92. Rogers and Buffalo, 'Fighting Back', p.109.
93. See F. Pack, 'Boasting in the Lord', *ResQ* 19.2 (1976), pp. 65-71.
94. Here Rogers and Buffalo build on, but go beyond, G.M. Sykes and D. Matza's analysis of stigma-neutralization tactics on the part of deviants:

a.   Denial of responsibility: this is essentially a defence plea on the part of deviants that 'I was forced into it...something/someone made me/us do it!' Explanations include 'broken homes, parental rejection, sibling rivalry, bad companions, etc.'.[95] In the New Testament this might be a defence plea based on the claim that Jesus' sufferings and death were 'necessary' and part of the divine purpose.

b.   Condemnation of the condemners themselves, as equally 'deviant' and with no proper claim to the moral high ground.

c.   Invoking of a higher law or a differing view of reality: this often involves appeal to religious beliefs and principles, or, alternatively, the claim that the long term welfare of society will be better served by (this particular form of) deviance—for instance, civil disobedience.[96]

Evasion, as a technique of stigma reversal, is more characteristic of Luke–Acts than Paul.[97] I turn now to the motif of *denial of responsibility*, as an example of this strategy.[98] Luke repeatedly uses the verb *dei*, 'it is necessary', to represent God's control of events 'so firmly imbedded is the presupposition of God as Supreme Powerbroker'[99] (e.g., Lk. 2.49; 4.43; 9.22; 13.33; 17.25; 19.5; 21.9; 22.37; 24.7, 26, 44; Acts 1.16, 21; 3.21; 4.12; 5.29; 9.6, 16; 14.22; 15.5; 16.30; 17.3; 19.21;

'Techniques of Neutralization: A Theory of Delinquency', *ASR* 22 (1957), pp. 664-70. Stigmatization can not only be neutralized but also *reversed* in certain circumstances.

95. Rogers and Buffalo, 'Fighting Back', p. 111.

96. Another, extended, example is given by Ben-Yehuda, *The Politics and Morality of Deviance*, pp. 221-50, who cites the case of Abu-hatzira, an Israeli government minister who had some success in 'attributing (his) assumed deviance to accusations made by inhabitants of another and opposing symbolic-moral universe' (p. 246).

97. Each of these three types is present in both Luke–Acts and Paul. The first two types are however more characteristic of Luke–Acts and the final type is more dominant in the Pauline writings.

98. For examples of categories (b) and (c) in Luke–Acts, see Malina and Neyrey, 'Conflict in Luke–Acts', pp. 119-20.

99. F.W. Danker, 'Theological Presuppositions of St Luke', *Currents in Theology and Mission* 4 (1977), pp. 98-103 (98); see also D. Juel, *Luke–Acts: The Promise of History* (Atlanta: John Knox Press, 1983), who goes as far as to suggest that 'argument for scriptural necessity (was) one of the major purposes in writing the two volumes' (p. 56).

20.35; 23.11; 24.19; 25.10; 27.24; cf. Mk 8.31; Mt. 16.21). This is related to the notion that Christ's sufferings are foretold and required by Scripture (Lk. 18.31; 22.37; 24.26, 44; Acts 10.43; 13.29; 17.3) and hence Jesus' conviction and execution were God's responsibility. Luke refers to a divine plan being realized in the life, death and resurrection of Jesus (Lk. 7.30; Acts 2.23; 4.28; 20.27). Consequently the trial and death of Jesus were acts of obedience towards God (cf. Heb. 3.2, 6). When Jesus is told that Herod 'had a contract out on his life' (Lk. 13.31) he meets this with the forthright declaration that the course of his ministry, including his death, is in God's hands alone. Divine necessity does not, however, mean divine determinism. The danger of this 'did he fall or was he pushed?' argument as part of deviance disavowal is that it could equally well be brought into play by the 'true deviants' of the piece: that is, those who actually betrayed and condemned Jesus. Hence Luke also puts stress on the element of individual moral responsibility: for example, according to Lk. 22.22 the Son of Man is going his *appointed* way, but Judas must bear full responsibility for the part he plays (Acts 1.18, 19).

There is less sense in Paul of the divine necessity of Jesus' career and death, although traces exist (e.g., 1 Cor. 15.3). There is however evidence that the unbelief and rejection on the part of the Jews is seen as part of the divine purpose. Romans 9–11 in particular explores the tension between divine predestination, which includes the fall of Israel, and human freedom. The blame is laid squarely on Israel's shoulders, excepting a small remnant (Rom. 9.27; 11.5): 'all day long I have held out my hands to a disobedient and contrary people' (Rom. 10.21). Paul brings out, to a greater extent than Luke (Lk. 13.6-9), the paradox that 'God has consigned all to disobedience, that he may have mercy upon all' (Rom. 11.32): Israel's predestinarian fall is also a reflection of the divine 'predestinating grace that determines the ungodly to righteousness and life'.[100] Paul, therefore, does not over-stress the element of predestination to fall on Israel's part because this is always held in creative tension with his desire for (and apparent belief in the practicability of) Israel's salvation.

Once again however it has become apparent that Paul and Luke do not have complete freedom of manoeuvre and are not able to fully espouse this mode of destigmatization without qualification. This is because they are constrained by other theological factors. For example, condemnation of the (Jewish) condemners cannot be thoroughgoing and

100. C.K. Barrett, *Essays on Paul* (London: SPCK, 1982), p. 168.

comprehensive, if the continuing possibility of repentance on the part of Jews is also presupposed.

6. *Modification.* With modification, in Rogers and Buffalo's typology, an attempt is made by the stigmatized to 'exchange the negative label for a "better" one' through 'manipulation of name, adjective, image or form'.[101] The feasibility of this strategy depends on the inherent ambiguity of people's motives and the possibility that varying interpretations can be made of their actions. For example, a fearful person who might attract such deviant labels as 'coward' or 'chicken' may attempt to substitute the labels 'sick' or 'hurt' in their place. Such ambiguity of motives allows for the possibility of room for compromise and flexibility and hence modification on the part of those imputing deviance.[102] Here we need to look for evidence in Paul and Luke–Acts of tendencies to exchange earlier perceptions of the crucified Messiah for 'labels' likely to be more acceptable to the wider society (or to the population that matters in the wider society).

Modification is more characteristic of Luke–Acts than the Pauline writings. There appears to be an attempt being made to exchange the negative label of 'political subversive' for the more acceptable label 'religious dissident' and he subtly shifts the burden of responsibility for Jesus' death from the Romans to the Jews. Pilate's affirmation of Jesus' innocence in regard to the charge of sedition is emphasized in Luke's Gospel: no sooner has Jesus answered Pilate's question, 'Are you the king of the Jews?', than Pilate pronounces Jesus' innocence (23.4). Earlier, Jesus' answers to the Sanhedrin are probably intended to show Luke's readership that any charge brought before Pilate should properly have had only a religious content.[103] This reinforces the impression that a Graeco-Roman rather than a Jewish audience is primarily in view here in Luke–Acts.

Paul seems to reject this strategy, at least in the form it takes amongst his 'docetic' opponents. Paul's opponents in 1 Corinthians may well be seeking to substitute a path of 'instant glory' (e.g., 1 Cor. 4.8ff.) for the way of the cross, in place of all the humiliation, suffering and stigma the latter involves. They are in danger of obliterating the sufferings and the

101. Rogers and Buffalo, 'Fighting Back', pp. 111-12.
102. See, for example, the song 'Gee, Officer Krupke!' from the musical, 'West Side Story' (Stephen Sondheim).
103. Walaskay, *And so We Came to Rome*, p. 39.

crucifixion that make Christ the way of salvation and, in turn, are part of the Christian's experience.[104] In contrast to this 'docetic' tendency Paul reemphasizes the gospel of a crucified Christ (1 Cor. 1.23) and the necessity of believers to continue to suffer with Christ (1 Cor. 4.9-13; see also 2 Cor. 4.8-10; 6.4-10; Rom. 8.17; Phil. 3.10). Elsewhere Paul describes those whose way of life does not conform to Christ's sufferings and death as 'enemies of the cross of Christ' (Phil. 3.18).

7. *Reinterpretation.* When reinterpretation occurs the deviants accept the negative label imputed to them but subsequently, through the process of reinterpretation, the label is successfully erased. The deviants do not necessarily change their behaviour, instead either societal norms or society's perception of the deviants' actions change.[105] The crucial difference between this category and redefinition is that here the stigma is accepted (unlike in redefinition—see below) and only later through successful reinterpretation is it obliterated. As with redefinition our interest within the scope of the present study lies not in whether the strategy was ultimately successful (evidence for this lies in the subsequent history of the church, particularly under the Emperor Constantine) but in the (conscious or unconscious) tactics of the early Christians directed towards ultimate obliteration of the deviant label.

Reinterpretation as a mode of destigmatization is more characteristic of the Pauline writings. The stigma attaching to Jesus because of the nature and grounds of his execution (cf. Deut. 21.23 LXX)[106] is accepted by Paul, as is the deviant label 'accursed'. Gal. 3.13 may well be a reflection of (Jewish) anti-Christian polemic, objecting that Jesus' conviction and death on a cross rendered him accursed.[107] The acceptance of this stigma does not in any way diminish the salvific significance of Jesus and his cross. Paul speaks of Jesus becoming a curse for our salvation (Gal. 3.13), perhaps in the sense of being an (innocent) scape-

104. See also Hengel, *Crucifixion*, pp. 18, 90.

105. This mode of response to stigma has been highlighted recently by H. Mödritzer (*Stigma und Charisma im NT und seiner Umwelt* [Freiburg: Universitätsverlag; Göttingen: Vandenhoeck & Ruprecht, 1994]), who suggests that the early Christians sometimes embraced stigma as part of their deviant/charismatic role.

106. Traditionally the proven offence was that of blasphemy or idolatry; see P. Fredriksen, 'Paul and Augustine: Conversion Narratives, Orthodox Traditions, and the Retrospective Self', *JTS* 37 (1986) pp. 3-34 (11-12).

107. See Lindars, *New Testament Apologetic*, p. 233.

goat (cf. Gal. 4.4-5),[108] who could bear his people's sins.[109] Far from papering over the scandal and stigma of the crucified Messiah Paul actually accepts that this is an accursed death. Moreover he seems to be happy to accentuate the scandal elsewhere: Paul describes his message in 1 Cor. 1.17, with polemical accentuation, as λόγος τοῦ σταυροῦ; he will proclaim none other than the crucified Messiah (1.23; 2.2; Gal. 3.1). It is Jesus 'nailed to a cross', 'a stumbling block to Jews and folly to the Greeks' (1 Cor. 1.23) who is 'the power and the wisdom of God' (v. 24). The emphasis is on the stigma and weakness and strange folly of the cross, to be joyfully embraced by Christian believers: the stigma of crucifixion openly demonstrates the power of God.

Luke, by comparison, seems to regard the stigma of the crucifixion as something to be rejected rather than accepted. We find a toning down of references to Deut. 21.23 (e.g., Acts 5.30; 10.39). The contrast is made between the utmost disgrace of being 'hanged on the tree' and the subsequent exaltation of Jesus by God (Acts 5.30-31). Here we may have a hint that a person who died in this way was accursed but, if so, this is a stigma that must be instantly rejected. There is, it is true, implicit acknowledgment of the 'scandal of the cross' in Luke—'this child is destined to be a sign which men reject...'[110] (Lk. 2.34)—but, unlike Paul, Luke shows no intention to accentuate this scandal.

8. *Redefinition.* The crucial difference between redefinition and reinterpretation is that with redefinition the stigma is rejected by the stigmatized, and then later this definition of their identity is accepted by a wider public. This category bears some notable similarities with reinterpretation. The deviants do not necessarily change their behaviour; instead society redefines what is normative and the hitherto 'deviant' behaviour elicits a new and positive social response. An example of this is found in the varying social responses to alcohol consumption in the USA at the times of prohibition and post-prohibition. The time span

108. See D.R. Schwartz, 'Two Pauline Allusions to the Redemptive Mechanism of the Crucifixion', *JBL* 102 (1983), pp. 259-68.

109. The death of Jesus is understood by Paul to redeem from the curse of the law; i.e., the curse of an erroneous, too narrow, exclusivist understanding of the law (cf. Gal. 3.14); see J.D.G. Dunn, 'Works of the Law and the Curse of the Law', *NTS* 31 (1985), pp. 523-42.

110. See J.A. Fitzmyer, *The Gospel according to Luke I–IX* (New York: Doubleday, 1981), p. 23.

involved in achieving redefinition may well be considerable and even beyond the lifetime of the deviant. Joan of Arc, for instance, was executed as an heretical deviant in 1431, but canonized 489 years later. By contrast, Menachem Begin, erstwhile commander-in-chief of the ETZEL 'terrorist group' in Palestine in the 1940s, was later lauded as 'freedom fighter' and became Israeli prime minister.

Both Paul and Luke, whatever their different emphases, are evidently engaged in strategies of 'redefinition'.[111] They are clearly interested in promoting redefinition of the (stigmatized) identity of Jesus (and, by association, the identities of the early Christians), such that the various stigmas that have been imputed will tend to be obliterated. Jesus has been vindicated and made both Lord and Christ (Acts 2.36).

For Paul, the crucifixion is not merely a stigma to be overcome, it is a means of salvation to be embraced (e.g., Rom. 3.21-26; 5.10-11; 6.3-11; 8.32; 1 Cor. 15.3; 2 Cor. 5.14-15, 18-21; Gal. 2.21; 3.13; 1 Thess. 5.10). In 1 Cor. 2.6-16 Paul relates the cross of Jesus to God's 'secret and hidden wisdom' which none of the 'rulers of the age' understood: only those who 'possess the spirit' (v. 13) can begin to understand the true meaning. It is likely that here he refers to the human rulers who crucified Jesus, just as he is referring to human practitioners of the wisdom of the world earlier (1 Cor. 1.20).[112] Hence we find here an implicit attack on the authority of the powers who stigmatize and the belief that sooner or later those possessing the gift of true understanding will discern Jesus as 'the Lord of glory' (v. 8).[113]

Turning now to Luke–Acts, we find a similar attempt to reinterpret the stigma of the crucifixion. Jesus has been vindicated and made both 'Lord and Christ' (Acts 2.36). His innocence has been demonstrated by

111. See also Richard Fenn, who notes that, given that Jesus could be construed as seditious or foolhardy, the synoptic Gospels are 'attempts at reconstruction of his actions into acts of redemption, salvation...' (*The Death of Herod*, p. 63).

112. It is unlikely that ἄρχοντες refers to demonic or supernatural beings: in the New Testament it never occurs in that sense when it occurs in the plural (e.g., Lk. 23.14, 35; 24.20; Acts 3.17; 4.8, 25; 13.27; Jn 7.26, 48; 12.42; Rom. 13.3). See W. Carr, 'The Rulers of this Age—1 Cor. 11.6-8', *NTS* 23 (1976), pp. 20-35.

113. There is a creative tension in Paul's writings between the 'sequence' (glory–humiliation–exaltation as 'Lord of glory') language of 1 Cor. 2.6-16 and the 'dialectic' ('crucified Messiah') language of 1.18–2.5: see R.S. Barbour, 'Wisdom and the Cross in 1 Cor. 1 & 2', in C. Andresen and G. Klein (eds.), *Theologia Crucis—Signum Crucis: Festschrift für Erich Dinkler zum 70 Geburtstag* (Tübingen: J.C.B. Mohr, 1979).

the reversal of events represented by the resurrection (3.14ff.). There is, also, the claim that the stigmatizers are using erroneous criteria of judgment. In Lk. 9.26 the *Son of Man* is presented as the decisive arbiter of human destiny. The followers of Jesus are urged not to accept worldly standards and hence be 'ashamed of [Jesus]'. In Acts 10.42 *Jesus* is described as the designated 'judge of the living and the dead': 'of this [God] has given assurance to all by raising him from the dead' (Acts 17.31). In Acts 4.5-12, in the context of an appearance before a court comprising representatives of those who had condemned Jesus, Peter's (to his Jewish hearers, astonishing) pesher-exegesis of Ps. 118 (117 LXX) asserts that Jesus, far from being rejected and stigmatized, is rightfully elevated to be the corner stone (v. 11). Thus the contrast between God's estimate of Jesus and human estimates, especially the estimate of the Jewish hierarchy, is highlighted.[114] As in Paul, salvific significance is attached to the death of Jesus (Lk. 22.19, 20;[115] 24.43; Acts 20.28; Lk. 24.46-47; Acts 5.30-31; 10.43; 13.38-39), which is not merely an ignominious prelude to exaltation.

9. *Alteration*. The last mode of adaptation to stigma identified in Rogers and Buffalo's typology is that of alteration. Here the deviants exchange their former (stigmatized) behaviour for that which is socially demanded and approved. The deviants alter their behaviour to coincide with societal expectations in an attempt to substitute a positive label for the deviant label. There is no guarantee that the strategy will be completely successful. In some instances the deviant label is exchanged for a new yet still relatively negative label, such as 'ex-con'.

This is not part of the repertoire of responses that characterize either Paul or Luke–Acts. By definition, this could not be a Christian strategy if it were adopted; it would amount to apostasy (e.g. Jn 6.66; 2 Pet. 2.21). Alteration would involve renouncing Christian belief and practice altogether.

b. *Warren's Typology*
I turn now to examine the usefulness of Warren's complementary destigmatization typology, which, because it specifically deals with

114. See F.F. Bruce, 'New Wine in Old Wine Skins: III. The Corner Stone', *ExpTim* 84 (1972), pp. 231-35.
115. The longer text is to be preferred because of the overwhelming number of Greek MSS which support it and also the principle of *lectio difficilior*.

charisma as the obverse of deviance, appears to be particularly appropriate to our data.

1. *Individual purification*. Individual purification denotes 'the movement, through transformation of acts and identity, into a new moral self'.[116] This may happen by:

(a) Sacred mode, in which a person claims to be 'reborn' by divine agency and to be given a 'new pure being, whose prior essences and arenas of immoral action have been erased'.[117] Warren cites Charles Colson who moved from being a 'crooked, power-hungry politician' (of Watergate fame) to being a 'humble and repentant Christian'. *Or*

(b) Secular mode, in which, through the heroic striving of the actor, one is transformed from, in the eyes of others, 'wicked' to 'good'; although, as Warren notes, 'those moral deeds which provide evidence for purification must...be of a dramatic rather than a mundane nature',[118] the farther the person originally falls from grace, the more grace they need to achieve charismatic identity. *Secular* individual purification can be seen at work within a newspaper account of Ian Botham's 1988 European walk in aid of charity which was given the headline 'Walking back to godliness': it cited Malcolm Muggeridge's statement that 'a man ultimately has to decide to be either a saint or a sod' and concluded that 'Ian Botham has not quite made up his mind yet. He is, however, not mucking about with the messy grey areas in between.'[119]

The stigma of being a follower of the crucified Messiah may have led to attempts to use (either mode of) individual purification as a strategy of destigmatization. In particular, there is evidence of moral actions being enjoined upon the early Christians, not merely for their inherent rightness in the sight of God, but also with an eye to the approbation of the wider society.

The sort of ethics enjoined upon Christians in Luke–Acts are simple human (though in this case divinely inspired) virtues likely to commend themselves to non-Christians (e.g., 'self control' [Acts 24.25]; humility [20.19]; self-sufficiency [20.34]). The approval, or otherwise, of outside society is clearly significant for Luke (e.g., Acts 2.47). What impresses

116. Warren, 'Destigmatization of Identity', p. 62.
117. Warren, 'Destigmatization of Identity', p. 63.
118. Warren, 'Destigmatization of Identity', p. 63.
119. *The Guardian*, 4 April 1988. Another instance is the 'Redemption of... fallen hero', Washington Mayor, Marion Barry (*The Observer*, 18 September 1994).

the pagan centurion in Lk. 23.47 is the righteousness of Jesus, his 'consistency of character'.[120] A number of the least context-dependent speeches in Acts (e.g., 2.14-41; 3.12-26; 7.1-60; 10.34-47; 13.17-41; 13.46-47; 20.18-35; 24.10-21, (-25); 26.2-29) portray Christian teaching 'as a creditable variant of the kind of ethical providential monotheism that educated pagans might be expected to attend to respectfully'.[121]

The ethics of the Pauline churches are also developed 'not in complete isolation, but with an eye toward the way outsiders will perceive them'.[122] Paul is clearly interested in the effect Christians' beliefs and behaviour will have on non-Christians (1 Thess. 4.12; 1 Cor. 14.23). He frequently makes use of conventional catalogues of vices and virtues, commonly found in Graeco-Roman and Hellenistic Jewish moral philosophy of that period (e.g., lists of vices: Rom. 13.13; 1 Cor. 5.10-11; 6.9-10; Gal. 5.19-21; lists of virtues: 2 Cor. 6.6-7; Phil. 4.8)[123] and likely to be appreciated as indicators of moral rectitude by the wider world (whether pagan or Jewish).

However, Paul places his appeals to conventional ethics within a radically new context: the purpose of good behaviour is to 'please God' (1 Thess. 4.2), not merely to win the approval of other human beings (cf. 1 Thess. 2.4, 6). The God who is to be pleased has raised Jesus from the dead (1 Thess. 1.10), 'tests our hearts' (2.4), and will finally judge (1.10; 5.8). The impending time of ultimate judgment will also be the parousia of Jesus (1 Thess. 1.10; 2.19; 5.9, 23), who will also have a forensic function (4.6). It is with the coming judgment in mind that Paul presents moral life in terms of conventional virtues and vices. An even more fundamental presupposition underlying Pauline ethics, however, is the death of Christ which brings about not primarily a new moral imperative but rather a new state of life: reconciliation with God (Rom. 5.1-11; 2 Cor. 5.16-21). It is 'those who belong to Christ Jesus [who] have crucified the flesh with its passions and desires' (Gal. 5.24). The cross

120. Beck, 'Imitatio Christi and the Lucan Passion Narrative', pp. 28-47.

121. F.G. Downing, 'Ethical Pagan Theism and the Speeches in Acts', *NTS* 27 (1981), pp. 544-62 (544).

122. See W.A. Meeks, 'Since Then You Would Need to Go out of the World', in T. Ryan (ed.), *Critical History and Biblical Faith: New Testament Perspectives* (Villanova, PA: Villanova University Press, 1979), pp. 1-23 (16).

123. See further W.A. Meeks, *The Moral World of the First Christians*, p. 127; see also A.J. Malherbe, *Moral Exhortation: A Greco-Roman Source Book* (Philadelphia: Westminster Press, 1986).

contradicts any notion that human achievement can lead to a righteous life (1 Cor. 1.30, 31). Baptism 'into Christ' overcomes the believer's orientation to sin. Evidently this extra theological baggage would not have been so likely to win Christians approval in the outside world, especially when the new life 'in Christ' was associated with a tendency towards equality and intimacy within the Christian community, features which would have seemed unusual and disturbing, rather than commendable, to the outside observer.[124]

For theological reasons the strategy of individual purification is a more minor theme in Paul but clearly evident in Luke–Acts. Clearly, there are attendant risks to the use of this strategy. The ethics enjoined may be pictured so much in terms of conventional pagan virtues that the divine initiative is obscured and the sacred mode of individual purification becomes increasingly indistinguishable from the secular mode. Luke seems to be more in danger of falling into this trap than Paul. Both Luke and Paul however make significant use of this strategy of destigmatization.

This, it should be noted, reinforces our previous assumption that the early Christians reflected in these writings were interested in the labels imputed to them by society at large. It was not only a matter of convincing Christian converts that they had ground for pride rather than shame in their new identity; the approbation of the wider society was also sought.

2. *Transcendence*. Warren notes that 'destigmatization by transcendence is a matter of practical rather than moral performance'.[125] 'Transcendence involves superior performance in areas seen as normally closed to those of the given category of person.'[126] Where such prowess is within a socially valued frame of action these 'superior performances' then become a source of charismatic self, transcending the previous negative identity. One example of this mode of charismatic destigmatization is that of Helen Keller who was able to transcend the stigma of multiple handicap (complete blindness, deafness and dumbness) by her educational achievements. Another example is that of the so-called 'Bird Man of Alcatraz', a convicted murderer who, because he developed substantial

---

124. Meeks, *The Moral World of the First Christians*, pp. 110-13.
125. Warren, 'Destigmatization of Identity', p. 64.
126. Warren, 'Destigmatization of Identity', p. 65.

ornithological knowledge and expertise whilst in prison, received much public support in his fight against receiving the death penalty.

One way of translating this into New Testament terms is to concentrate on the miracles of Jesus and those of the early Christians as examples of socially valued 'superior (practical) performances' likely to facilitate transcendence of erstwhile negative identity. Given this frame of reference, the transcendence mode of destigmatization appears to be found to a greater degree in Luke–Acts where the miracles of Jesus and those of his followers are given a relatively high profile and significance.

Luke attempts to demonstrate the validity of Jesus' claims to Messiahship and Lordship by 'many convincing proofs' (Acts 1.3). There is a special interest in and stress on the miraculous, both in the Gospel and Acts. 'Signs and wonders' characterize the ministry of Jesus (Lk. 7.1-17, 22; 13.32; Acts 2.22) and the lives of his disciples (Acts 2.43; 4.30; 5.12; 6.8; 8.6; 14.3; 15.12). The fame of Jesus, according to Luke, is based predominantly on his mighty works more so than on his teaching (e.g., Lk. 4.37; cf. Mk 1.28; 5.15; 7.17; 23.8). Miracles authenticate both Jesus (7.22-23; 8.39; cf. Mk 5.19) and his followers (Acts 13.9-12; 14.3). Miracle-working is a key feature of the literary genre Luke draws on and himself adapts: the Hellenistic-Roman romance, which tended to function as 'propaganda in connection with a cult'.[127]

Paul also takes for granted that miracles can be the basis of belief in God (1 Cor. 2.4; Rom. 15.18-20) and that they authenticate his own ministry (2 Cor. 12.12; Rom. 15.19; Gal. 3.5). However, because of his underlying apocalyptic world view Paul plays down his own charismatic gifts and his ability to work miracles. His weaknesses and sufferings (2 Cor. 12.10) are ultimately more important to him than his miracle working: 'he regards them as trials through which the righteous must pass as God prepares them for the final struggle against the powers of evil'.[128]

However both Luke and Paul are aware of the dangers attending this strategy (even if they are not necessarily consciously aware that they are using such a strategy!); not least there is no guarantee that miracles will be attributed by the audience to *divine* empowerment and legitimation (see Lk. 11.15; Acts 26.24).

127. H.C. Kee, *Miracle in the Early Christian World* (New Haven: Yale University Press, 1983), p. 193.

128. Kee, *Miracle in the Early Christian World*, p. 172.

3. *Collective aristocratization.* A common tactic of deviant collectivities, Warren notes, is to 'define themselves as better than normals' and to 'frame themselves as a chosen people'.[129] In this way they project a new and 'supra-normal' group image into the world. Collective aristocratization represents an attempt to destigmatize an entire category of deviants. Where collective aristocratization tactics are used by social movements the ultimate end in view is redefinition of the entire category by society. For example, this mode of charismatic destigmatization may be used by gay groups wanting to assert pride in their sexual identity.

There is in Luke–Acts and Paul some evidence that the Early Church began to see itself as a new 'people of God' with a novel and special place in God's purposes, but this emerges to a greater extent in Paul.

In Luke–Acts there are no clear-cut claims that Christians are the (replacement) chosen people. Except for Acts 15.14 and 18.10 λαός refers to Israel; where it does refer to the Church it is indefinite and does not imply that the Church has supplanted empirical Israel. The earliest Jerusalem Christians are depicted as pious Jews, attending the Temple daily (Acts 2.46; 3.1) and religiously orthodox (Acts 10.9; 15.1-5; 21.20). However, Luke's orientation towards Judaism is ultimately negative: the climax and final focus of Acts, Acts 28.17-28, indicates that God's judgment is pronounced on Judaism; Jews as a whole (vv. 25, 26) had rejected the Christian message, although there were always exceptions in the case of individuals (v. 24). The parable of the vineyard stresses the violent destruction awaiting the (Jewish) opponents of Jesus (Lk. 20.9-19; cf. Mt. 21.33-46). Christianity is a separate religion: converts, gentile and Jewish, must each 'put [their] trust in the Lord Jesus Christ' (Acts 11.17). Luke–Acts seems to reflect a church which is a distinct entity, separate from empirical Israel, beginning, at least, to question her very claim to be the chosen people.

Paul seems to have gone further in explicitly understanding the Christian movement as a new People of God (Gal. 6.16),[130] which Jews would have to enter on a same basis as Gentiles: the basis of faith in Jesus Christ (Gal. 3.29). In addition there was a separate entry rite, baptism, and separate worship, on the first day of the week (1 Cor. 16.1). The defining mark of the new People of God was not to be circumcision, but rather the cross of Christ (Gal. 6.12, 14). The relationship to

129. Warren, 'Destigmatization of Identity', p. 67.

130. This probably refers to Christians, rather than those who do not walk by 'this rule' who would be less likely to be wished 'peace and mercy': cf. Gal. 1.8-9.

the People of God as formerly understood is one of equality however, not superiority (Rom. 11.17-18). The new People of God is a divine creation, giving no ground for human boasting (Gal. 6.14). Paul tells his readers 'not to boast over the branches that have broken off' (Rom. 11.18) and which the Christians have supplanted. Although the Pauline churches seem to set themselves apart from (and morally superior to) outsiders (1 Cor. 6.4), they are probably still closer to the category 'Jewish reform-movement' rather than 'sect'.[131] It is evident that this self-perception of the church as the new People of God is restrained (leading some biblical commentators to quite different conclusions).[132] Other theological factors are at work here, precluding complete adoption of this destigmatization strategy.

There are, therefore, limits to how far Paul and Luke can encourage their readers to project a group image of themselves as a 'chosen people', if they are to still allow for the possibility of conversion on the part of individual Jews.

In terms of Warren's typology, 'collective aristocratization' is therefore in evidence in both Paul and Luke–Acts, but could not be described as a dominant feature in Luke–Acts. It is more characteristic of Paul's churches.

6. *Conclusion*

The intention of this study has been to attempt a systematic categorization of the destigmatization techniques evident in Luke–Acts and the Pauline writings, with the help of two typologies from the sociology of deviance.

131. See Holmberg, *Sociology and the New Testament,* p. 106; cf. Watson, *Paul, Judaism and the Gentiles,* who claims that early Christianity developed from a reform-movement into a sect; see Campbell's critique ('Did Paul Advocate Separation from the Synagogue?'); if Pauline Christianity was sectarian it was as a *conversionist sect,* unable to segregate itself from those it also hoped to convert (see 1 Cor. 5.10) and 'thus not a very sectarian sect' (Holmberg, p. 96).

132. For example, W.D. Davies concludes that 'within God's purpose the Jewish people always remain the chosen people', in 'Paul and the People of Israel', *NTS* 24 (1977), pp. 4-39 (17).

Summary of findings (** = stressed; * = present, but not stressed;
– = not in evidence; X = castigated):

COLLECTIVE RESPONSE

INDIVIDUAL'S STRATEGY	*Magnification*: the tendency for the deviant label to take on salience or primacy	*Manipulation*: the tendency for the label to undergo change via influences resulting from persuasion, deception, skill, etc.	*Obliteration*: the tendency for the label to be erased, cancelled, or made obsolete
Assent: agreement with or acceptance of the deviant label	1. Acquiescence Luke–Acts: – Paul: –	4. Channelling Luke–Acts: * Paul: **	7. Reinterpretation Luke–Acts: * Paul: **
Rejection: disagreement with or denial of the deviant label	2. Repudiation Luke–Acts: ** Paul: *	5. Evasion Luke–Acts:** Paul: *	8. Redefinition Luke–Acts: ** Paul: **
Exchange: an attempt to substitute or switch labels	3. Flight Luke–Acts: X Paul: X	6. Modification Luke–Acts: * Paul: X	9. Alteration Luke–Acts: X Paul: X

Rogers and Buffalo

Table 3

1. Individual Purification Luke–Acts: ** Paul: *	2. Transcendence Luke–Acts: ** Paul: *	3. Collective Aristocratization Luke–Acts: * Paul: **

Warren

Table 4

The study has discovered that the modes of destigmatization identified in the two typologies are not distributed in a uniform manner throughout Luke–Acts and the Pauline writings. There are important differences between Paul and Luke–Acts in the areas highlighted by the typologies. 'Repudiation', 'evasion', 'individual purification' and 'transcendence' are more characteristic of Luke–Acts. On the other hand, 'channelling', 'reinterpretation' and 'collective aristocratization' are more typical of Paul. According to Rogers and Buffalo's schema (see table 3), it will be noted, the Pauline emphases are more characteristic of a 'tactical relationship' of 'assent' on the part of the deviants vis-à-vis those who label them. The Luke–Acts emphases, by contrast, cluster in the 'rejection' tactical relationship column in table 3.

The differences between Luke–Acts and Paul in relation to the 'tactical relationships' axis of Rogers and Buffalo's typology are also reflected in Warren's schema. Warren's category of 'collective aristocratization' would presumably be classified according to the tactical relationship of 'assent' in Rogers and Buffalo's typology. As might be expected, this category is more characteristic of Paul than Luke–Acts. The categories of 'individual purification' and 'transcendence' would, in all likelihood, be classified according to the tactical relationship of 'exchange'. Again, as might be expected, these two categories are more characteristic of Luke–Acts than Paul (only Luke–Acts fits in the 'exchange' column on Rogers and Buffalo's table). So 'assent' is more typical of Paul, and 'rejection' and 'exchange' more characteristic of Luke–Acts in their 'manouevering vis-à-vis their labellers in terms of attitude and action' (tactical relationship). This bears out earlier impressions that Paul has a much more positive attitude to the stigma of the crucified Messiah and that the very objections to Jesus' Messiahship are made elements of 'a much deeper positive doctrine'[133] in the Pauline writings.

It is noteworthy that certain predictions made in connection with Rogers and Buffalo's model are borne out in this study. One was the prediction that 'acquiescence and flight might be found more often at the individual level; reinterpretation and redefinition at a group level'. We have confirmed that the early Christian groups reflected in Luke–Acts and the Pauline writings were more likely to espouse reinterpretation and redefinition rather than acquiescence and flight; indeed the strategy of flight that Peter is represented as toying with (as an individual) is regarded as an illegitimate response by Luke.

Another prediction, according to Rogers and Buffalo's model, was that Luke–Acts' espousal of mode of adaptation (2. repudiation) would mean that in the interaction between deviant and social context there would be 'the tendency for the deviant label to take on salience or primacy'. Magnification occurs partly because of the actions or claims of the persons labelled and partly through societal magnification. If the writing of Luke–Acts coincides with the inclusion of the curse against the *minim* in the Eighteen Benedictions at Yavneh (80–90 CE)—a curse that would probably have been understood by Christians as meant to

133. Lindars, *New Testament Apologetic*, p. 135.

include themselves, amongst others—this would lend support to the proposal that one outcome of the modes Luke used to 'fight back' against stigmatization was magnification of the deviant label. This is not to assume that Luke–Acts' repudiation is 'cause' and exclusion as heretics is 'effect', or vice versa; the process is viewed from 'an interaction frame'.[134] There are however, it should be noted, countervailing modes of social response in Luke–Acts—manipulation and obliteration—as in Paul.

It would seem from this study that neither Paul nor Luke had complete freedom of manoeuvre when they came to select (albeit probably unconsciously) from the repertoire of destigmatization strategies open to them; they were, we have noted, constrained by theological factors. The destigmatization tactics of 'denial of responsibility' (e.g., 'condemnation of the condemners') and 'collective aristocratization', for instance, could not be applied in a thoroughgoing manner by Luke and Paul to the Jewish condemners at least, because of the continuing possibility of repentance on the part of Jews. The constraining influence of such theological factors helps to explain why the modes of destigmatization identified in the typologies of Rogers and Buffalo, and Warren were not found to be distributed in a uniform manner throughout Luke–Acts and the Pauline writings.

Rogers and Buffalo point out that their typology is dynamic and allows for the likelihood of movement across and between modes. Our findings in Paul and Luke–Acts would suggest that movement has occurred between Paul (50–60 CE) and the time of writing Luke–Acts (80–90 CE). This may perhaps be partly due to the perceived ineffectiveness in practice of the earlier strategies or may represent a response to a change in audience. Luke often seems ultimately to have in mind a Hellenistic Roman context, although the writings are clearly addressed primarily to a Christian audience. The Pauline writings are, on the other hand, typically addressed to a form of Christian community with closer boundaries over against the outside world, although the wider Graeco-Roman world is not totally eclipsed from view. Given these different contexts 'collective aristocratization', as the (new) 'Israel of God' (Gal. 6.16), was a strategy more likely to be associated with the Pauline writings.

---

134. Rogers and Buffalo, 'Fighting Back', p. 107; although, as was noted above, *repudiation* is made more likely if the deviant label is applied in a humiliating or vengeful way.

Both Luke–Acts and Paul, however, still have, to some degree, a Jewish (or Judaizing) audience also in mind; indeed some of the material alluded to was unlikely to have been properly understood except by those with a Jewish background (e.g., Gal. 3.10). This is consistent with the prediction made earlier on the basis of H.E. Gross's theory, that 'redefinition' may be facilitated where the deviant challenge is based on values implicit in the cultural heritage of the stigmatizing group. The allusions by Paul and Luke to the Hebrew Bible and Jewish hermeneutics—for example, the use of pesher exegesis of Psalm 118 (117 LXX)—is likely to have facilitated the use of the 'redefinition' strategy.

The use of these two typologies has helped to cast new light on particular aspects of the New Testament data. For instance, it has helped to account for the stress on divine destiny and the fulfilment of Scripture in Luke–Acts. The conventional biblical scholar would tend to interpret this distinctive feature of Luke–Acts in terms of Luke's theology. G.B. Caird, for example, notes how this fits with Luke's core belief that in Jesus the drama of world redemption is being played out, according to a plot determined by God and involving God as an actor who makes a personal appearance on stage.[135] That kind of interpretation is not far short of the mark, but it is not completely satisfying. Is not Luke–Acts also a response to audiences who claim that the crucified Messiah is not part of the plan of world redemption? The New Testament scholar has much to gain from taking into account sociological as well as theological motives.

My purpose has not been to suggest that either Paul or Luke was acquainted with the sort of insights we have derived from the social sciences, but that simply, unconsciously, they have selected only certain of the possible modes of response to stigma from the available repertoire.

There are inevitably attendant difficulties involved in applying sociological analyses to historical data. It is inherently impossible to test our conclusions using the normal empirical techniques of, for instance, interview, questionnaire or field work because of the problem of historical distance. However, within the sociological analysis I have undertaken of the New Testament data it has become evident that there exists a degree of 'fit' between these typologies and the New Testament data, such that new light is thrown on a broad range of (at first sight unconnected) data. This has helped to explain particular problems and

---

135. G.B. Caird, *St Luke* (Harmondsworth: Penguin Books, 1963), p. 34.

suggested new questions for New Testament scholars to ask of their sources.

Labelling theory predicts that destigmatization processes are most likely to be effective if they are associated with political or religious world views. This suggests that the stigma-reversal strategies adopted by the early Christians had a good chance of success. It is difficult to gauge how successful these strategies were in practice: it depends on the measuring point. Success in fighting back against stigma will be differently gauged, depending on whether the first century, the Constantine era, or the twentieth century is taken as a yardstick. The Christian faith will always be 'folly' and a 'stumbling block' to some. In the meantime the strategies identified in this study have helped Christians bear the 'marks of Jesus' (στίγματα—Gal. 6.17).

THE HERMENEUTICS OF LIBERATION*

David Tombs

> The liberation theologian goes to the scriptures bearing the whole weight
> of the problems, sorrows and hopes of the poor, seeking light and inspira-
> tion from the divine word. This is a new way of reading the Bible: the
> hermeneutics of liberation.[1]

1. *Introduction: In the Parish of the Poor*

There can be no understanding of the hermeneutics of liberation without
an appreciation of the life and death struggles of the communities in
which they emerged. The countries of Latin America, alongside those of
Africa and Asia, the other continents of the so called 'Third World', are
typified by almost overwhelming levels of poverty.[2] Jean-Bertrand
Aristide, Haitian priest, politician and theologian, refers to Latin America

---

*   I am particularly indebted to Rebecca Dudley, of Christian Aid, for providing
valuable material on the Latin American context and its significance for the way the
Bible is read by liberation theologians.
    1.   L. Boff and C. Boff, *Introducing Liberation Theology* (trans. P. Burns; TLS,
1; Maryknoll, NY: Orbis Books; Tunbridge Wells: Burns & Oates, 1987), p. 32,
Portuguese orig. *Como fazer Teología da Libertação* (Petrópolis: Editora Vozes,
1986).
    2.   In 1986, L. and C. Boff (*Introducing Liberation Theology*, pp. 2-3) offered as
'conservative estimates' of this global scandal:

> —five hundred million persons starving;
> —one billion six-hundred million people whose life expectancy is less than sixty
> years;
> —one billion living in absolute poverty;
> —one billion, five-hundred million persons with no access to the most basic medical
> care;
> —five hundred million with no work or only occasional work and a per capita income
> of less than $150 a year.

and the Caribbean as 'the parish of the poor'.[3] Its history is the history
of suffering and struggle for the majority of its people. Uruguayan
historian Eduardo Galeano describes it as a continent of 'open veins'.[4]
Since the conquest of the region, five centuries ago, its wealth has been
exploited for the benefit of Europe and, more recently, the United
States. Industrialization and trade have brought high living standards to
Europe and North America but have done little to solve the problems
facing the vast majority of people in Latin America. The gap between
the rich countries of the north and the poor countries of the south has
grown ever wider. At the same time the distance in Latin America
between the wealthy minority and the impoverished majority has also
been growing.[5]

In 1492 the Bible arrived in Latin America hand in hand with the
sword of Spanish conquistadors.[6] The alliance between Catholic church
and Spanish crown was a disaster for the indigenous people. War, dis-
ease and the inhuman conditions of slavery took a terrible toll on the
Indians. Church authorities colluded with the genocide of native
American nations and the enslavement and transportation of millions of
Africans. Throughout its history in the Americas the Church has been
more concerned with preserving its privileges than protesting the suffering of the common people.[7] The Church has given religious support to

3.   J. Aristide, *In the Parish of the Poor: Writings from Haiti* (trans. and ed.
A. Wilentz; Maryknoll, NY: Orbis Books, 1990).

4.   E. Galeano, *Open Veins of Latin America: Five Centuries of the Pillage of a
Continent* (trans. C. Belfrage; New York: Monthly Review Press, 1973), p. 12,
Spanish orig. *Las venas abiertas de América Latina* (Mexico: Siglo Veintiuno
Editores, 1971).

5.   Galeano (*Open Veins of Latin America*, p. 13) argues that the glaring
inequality between rich and poor countries continues to grow dramatically: 'The
United States citizen's average income is seven times that of a Latin American and
grows ten times faster. And averages are deceptive in view of the abyss that yawns
between the many poor and the rich few south of the Rio Grande. According to the
United Nations, the amount shared by 6 million Latin Americans at the top of the
social pyramid is the same as the amount shared by 140 million at the bottom'.

6.   See esp. H.M. Goodpasture (ed.), *Cross and Sword: An Eyewitness History
of Christianity in Latin America* (Maryknoll, NY: Orbis Books, 1989).

7.   See E. Dussel, *A History of the Church in Latin America: Colonialism to
Liberation (1492–1979)* (trans. and rev. A. Neely; Grand Rapids: Eerdmans, 1976),
Spanish orig. *Historia de la iglesia en América Latina: Coloniaje y liberación*
(Barcelona: Nova Terra, 3rd edn, 1974). An extensive collection of papers and an
excellent bibliography are offered in *idem* (ed.), *The Church in Latin America: 1492–*

the civil authorities in return for civil support for the Church's religious authority.

Standing at either end of Latin America's five hundred years of suffering, the Dominican Friar Bartolomé de las Casas,[8] a sixteenth-century dissident appalled at the inhuman treatment of the Indians, and Oscar Romero, the twentieth-century archbishop murdered for his outspoken views against the injustices of Salvadoran society,[9] are powerful archetypes of Christian commitment to the oppressed. As such they can be seen as representative of a much wider process in the contemporary Latin American church. The theological challenges posed by the oppressed led both Las Casas and Romero to a deep rethinking of faith. Since the 1960s hundreds of thousands of others within the Church have undergone a similar conversion when faced by the social scandals of Latin America.[10] For thousands of Christians the cost has been arrest, imprisonment, torture and sometimes, as in Romero's case, death.[11] Reflecting on and expressing the implications of commitment to the Latin American poor has given rise to 'liberation theology' as a new approach to theology and 'the hermeneutics of liberation' as a new way of reading the Bible.

Liberation theology involves a radical reorientation of theological

---

1992 (Maryknoll, NY: Orbis Books; Tunbridge Wells: Burns & Oates, 1987).

8.   See B. Casas, *The Devastation of the Indies: A Brief Account* (New York: Seabury, 1974). See also G. Gutiérrez, *Las Casas: In Search of the Poor of Jesus Christ* (Maryknoll, NY: Orbis Books, 1993), Spanish orig. *En busca de los pobres de Jesucristo* (Lima: Centro de Estudios y Publicaciones, 1992).

9.   O. Romero, *Voice of the Voiceless: The Four Pastoral Letters and Other Statements* (trans. M. Walsh; Maryknoll, NY: Orbis Books, 1985); *idem, The Violence of Love: The Words of Oscar Romero* (trans. J. Brockman; New York: Harper & Row, 1988; London: Collins, 1989). On the life of Romero, see J.R. Brockman, *Romero: A Life* (Maryknoll, NY: Orbis Books, 1989); J. Sobrino, *Archbishop Romero: Memories and Reflections* (trans. R. Barr; Maryknoll, NY: Orbis Books, 1990 [Spanish originals 1980–1989]).

10.   See S. Mainwaring and A. Wilde (eds.), *The Progressive Church in Latin America* (Notre Dame, IN: University of Notre Dame Press, 1989). It should be noted that although liberation theology is predominantly a Catholic phenomenon it has found parallels in progressive circles of Protestantism in Latin America.

11.   See esp. the statistical tables for the period 1964–1978 in P. Lernoux, *Cry of the People: The Struggle for Human Rights in Latin America—The Catholic Church in Conflict with U.S. Policy* (New York: Penguin Books, 1982 [1980]), pp. 463-70. The figures for the 1980s are equally stark. For example, in 1989 six Jesuits and their housekeeper were murdered at the Universidad Centroamericana, San Salvadoor.

methods and scholarly values that has provoked sharp controversy inside and outside Latin America. Advocates of liberation theology see it as a vibrant and challenging manifestation of Christian faith, an authentic response to the social reality of Latin America and a credible profession of the God of life in the face of a crucified people. Critics claim that liberation theology is based on a simplistic and reductionist reading of the gospel. They question its legitimacy as an interpretation of the word of God and argue that it is based on superficial analysis and unscholarly foundations. This chapter is concerned with assessing the crucial issues in this vitally important debate. In particular, the aim is to discuss whether any contemporary approach to reading the New Testament can afford to ignore the fundamental questions posed by the hermeneutics of liberation.

2. *Theology from the Underside of History*

The first task in assessing the significance of liberation theology for New Testament studies is to outline the fundamental principles and methodological foundations that are associated with the liberationist approach.

a. *Fundamental Principles of Latin American Liberation Theology*
Although liberation theology cannot be reduced to the thought of any single individual, the Peruvian Priest Gustavo Gutiérrez provides the most authoritative starting point for a consideration of its fundamental principles.[12] Gutiérrez played a crucial role in the emergence of Latin American liberation theology and continues to be one of its most influential proponents.[13] Gutiérrez's contributions in the formative years of the movement (1968–1975) were decisive in winning official support for liberation theology from the Latin American bishops and setting its theological agenda.[14] Two particular contributions by Gutiérrez during this time deserve special mention.

12. For an excellent bibliography on liberation theology, see P. Richard, 'The Theological Literature of Latin America', in L. Boff and V. Elizondo (eds.), *Theologies of the Third World: Convergences and Differences* (Edinburgh: T. & T. Clark, 1988), pp. 76-79. Also very helpful is the collection of translated primary documents in A. Hennelly (ed.), *Liberation Theology: A Documentary History* (Maryknoll, NY: Orbis Books, 1990).

13. See R.M. Brown, *Gustavo Gutiérrez: An Introduction to Liberation Theology* (Maryknoll, NY: Orbis Books, 1990); C. Cadorette, *From the Heart of the People: The Theology of Gustavo Gutiérrez* (Oak Park, IL: Meyer-Stone, 1988).

14. For a concise history of the development of liberation theology in Latin

First, Gutiérrez was a theological adviser at the second Latin American Episcopal Conference (CELAM II, Medellín 1968). The Conference was organized to allow the bishops to work together in relating the findings of Vatican II to their own situation.[15] As it turned out, a relatively small number of progressive bishops, guided by Gutiérrez and other radical advisers, persuaded the Conference to make the needs of the Latin American poor a critical element in their theological thinking. The Medellín documents offered considerable official support for those, like Gutiérrez, who were developing a radical reorientation of theological priorities. The Conference's final statement took a crucial step in this direction by emphasizing the theological importance of engagement with the Latin American social context. As the conclusion to the Medellín documents put it:

> In the light of faith that we profess as believers, we have undertaken to discover the plan of God in the 'signs of the times'. We interpret the aspirations and clamors of Latin America as signs that reveal the direction of the divine plan.[16]

Gutiérrez's second vital contribution to the development of liberation theology was his seminal work, *The Theology of Liberation*.[17] This remarkable work was the first, and remains one of the most powerful, systematic account of the new theological agenda. Looking back at *The Theology of Liberation* in his later work, Gutiérrez identifies two key insights that shaped the book and which have served as fundamental

America, see R. Gibellini, *The Liberation Theology Debate* (trans. J. Bowden; London: SCM Press, 1987), pp. 1-8, Italian orig. *Il Dibattito sulla Teologia della Liberazione* (Brescia: Editrice Queriniana, 1986). A more extensive treatment is offered by C. Smith, *The Emergence of Liberation Theology: Radical Religion and Social Movement Theory* (Chicago: University of Chicago Press, 1991). For primary documents, see Hennelly (ed.), *Liberation Theology*, pp. 43-121.

15. Medellín is therefore seen by most commentators as a decisive factor in the subsequent crystallization of liberation theology. For the significance of Vatican II and Medellín on the origins of liberation theology, see Smith, *The Emergence of Liberation Theology*, pp. 94-164.

16. *Documents of the Medellín Conference, the Church in the Present-Day Transformation of Latin America in the Light of the Council*, II (Washington, DC: Latin American Division, United States Catholic Conference, 1970), p. 38.

17. G. Gutiérrez, *A Theology of Liberation: History, Politics and Salvation* (trans. and ed. C. Inda and J. Eagleson; Maryknoll, NY: Orbis Books, 1973; London: SCM Press, 1974), Spanish orig. *Teologiá de la liberación: Perspectivas* (Lima: Centro de Estudios y Publicaciones [CEP], 1971).

principles in liberation theology ever since: first, a theological method in which theology is always a 'second act' after a commitment to liberation; and secondly, the need to make an 'option for the poor' and articulate theology from the perspective of the oppressed.[18]

These two principles are shared in the work of all the major thinkers in the movement.[19] Together they characterize what Gutiérrez sees as the new approach to theology from the 'underside of history'. Understanding the thinking behind these principles is therefore crucial to understanding liberation theology's hermeneutical method.

1. *The commitment to liberation and theology as a second act.* Theology does not take place in a social vacuum but always arises in relation to particular historical contexts and social situations.[20] In *A Theology of Liberation* Gutiérrez challenges traditional theological approaches that distance theology from everyday concerns and real life conflicts. He rejects the idea that theology is an abstract subject concerned with pre-existent and timeless truths concerning an other-worldly spiritual realm. Instead Gutiérrez presents the primary task of theology as the struggle with issues firmly located in human history. Theologians cannot escape their social context nor should they treat it as a distraction and try to ignore it. The social issues that are present in the social context should be central to theological endeavours; authentic theology comes from positive engagement with social situations. Gutiérrez's theology therefore emphasizes historical concerns as an essential starting point for theology. Authentic theology cannot be developed without reference to the social situation. Doctrinal debate and theological thought should not set the theologian's agenda but should arise as part of the response to engagement with history. Theology is both *reflection on* and *response to* the social situation confronting the theologian. Gutiérrez's widely quoted understanding of theology describes it as 'a critical

18. Gutiérrez (*The Power of the Poor in History*, p. 200) writes: 'From the beginning, the theology of liberation had two fundamental insights. Not only did they come first chronologically, but they have continued to form the very backbone of this theology. I am referring to its theological method and its perspective of the poor'.

19. L. and C. Boff (*Introducing Liberation Theology*, pp. 4-9) refer to the first step as 'Liberating action or Liber-a(c)tion' and the second step as 'faith reflecting on liberating practice'.

20. For a clear and forceful argument along these lines, see Gutiérrez, *The Power of the Poor in History*, p. 212.

reflection on Christian praxis in the light of the Word'.[21] In a particularly memorable passage he comments:

> Theology is reflection, a critical attitude. *Theology follows; it is the second step.* What Hegel used to say about philosophy can likewise be applied to theology: *it rises only at sundown.*[22] [emphasis added]

In a later work, Gutiérrez repeats the same principle in a slightly different way:

> The theological moment is one of critical reflection from within, and upon, concrete historical praxis, in confrontation with the word of the Lord as lived and accepted in faith…[23]

Other liberation theologians have followed Gutiérrez in making this central to their understanding of theology. For example, the Brazilian theologian Clodovis Boff describes theology as 'reading of the praxis of Christians in the light of God's word'.[24]

Liberation theology takes as its starting point the social reality of Latin American history. Liberation theologians argue that their work should recognize and respond to the inhuman suffering of the Latin American people. José Míguez Bonino, an Argentinean theologian, describes the liberation approach as theology 'after the fact'.[25]

Reflection on social injustice should not just involve detached observation and abstract reflection followed by a purely academic exercise in theological thought. The Boffs argue that in view of the social injustices of Latin America the only response a Christian can make is wholehearted commitment to the liberation of the oppressed:

21. Gutiérrez, *Theology of Liberation*, pp. 3-15 (13). This fundamental insight was first elaborated by Gutiérrez at a meeting of theologians in Petrópolis, Brazil, in March 1964; see Hennelly (ed.), *Liberation Theology*, pp. 43-61.

22. Gutiérrez, *Theology of Liberation*, p. 11.

23. Gutiérrez, *The Power of the Poor in History*, p. 200. Gibellini (*The Liberation Theology Debate*, pp. 4-5) summarizes alternative expressions of the formula in Gutiérrez's works.

24. C. Boff, *Theology and Praxis: Epistemological Foundations* (trans. R. Barr; Maryknoll, NY: Orbis Books, 1987), p. 139, Portuguese orig. *Teología e practica* (Petrópolis: Editora Vozes, 1978).

25. According to Míguez Bonino (*Doing Theology in a Revolutionary Situation* [Philadelphia: Fortress Press, 1975; UK edn *Revolutionary Theology Comes of Age*, London: SPCK, 1975], p. 61): 'Latin American theology of liberation is beginning to emerge (as all theology?) *after the fact*, as the reflection about facts and experiences which have already evoked a response from Christians'.

> How are we to be Christians in a world of destitution and injustice? There
> can be only one answer: we can be followers of Jesus and true Christians
> only by making common cause with the poor and working out the gospel
> of liberation.[26]

The term 'liberation' as used in this sense originated with Gutiérrez's earliest work. By focusing attention on liberation Gutiérrez sought to emphasize the integral relationship between salvation and history. The full title of Gutiérrez's first book, *A Theology of Liberation: History, Politics and Salvation*, reflects Gutiérrez's perception that salvation and the temporal realms of history and politics are inseparable.

Some critics have alleged that liberation theology wishes to *fully equate* salvation with political liberation. However, it is hard to support this claim from Gutiérrez's published work. On the contrary, in his writing Gutiérrez distinguishes between three different levels of liberation and stresses that together they form a *single complex process*: first, at an economic and political level, liberation applies to oppressed peoples and social classes; secondly, at the existential level of human freedom, liberation applies to people taking conscious responsibility for their own historical destiny; finally, at the theological level, liberation is understood as liberation from sin.

Gutiérrez does not see himself as deliberately reducing or marginalizing this third level and he states unequivocally that it is of fundamental importance.[27] He explains that in using the term 'liberation' he is trying to do justice to all three levels of the one process and avoid 'idealist or spiritualist approaches, which are nothing but ways of evading a harsh and demanding reality'.[28] In theological circles at the time, attempts were being made to formulate a 'Theology of Development' in accordance with the dominant notions of 'development' and 'progress'. When invited to make a presentation at the Consultation on Theology and Development in Cartigny, Switzerland, November 1969, Gutiérrez argued that it was *liberation* not *development* that would provide the right way forward.[29]

---

26. L. and C. Boff, *Introducing Liberation Theology*, p. 7.

27. Gutiérrez (*Theology of Liberation*, p. 37) emphasizes that 'Christ the Savior liberates man from sin, which is the ultimate root of all disruption of friendship and of all injustice and oppression'.

28. Gutiérrez, *Theology of Liberation*, p. 37.

29. Gutiérrez's paper ('Notes on a Theology of Liberation', in *In Search of a Theology of Development: A Sodepax Report* [Lausanne: SODEPAX, 1969]) was an

Gutiérrez's advocacy of 'liberation' was influenced by other progressive thinkers in Latin America during the 1960s. New ways of thinking in other academic disciplines had created an 'atmosphere of liberation' amongst intellectuals across the continent.[30] In left-wing circles 'liberation' had come to be understood as implying an overturning (revolution) of existing procedures.[31] The terminology of liberation had gained particularly strong currency in social sciences and educational theory.

In the social sciences the rise of 'dependency theory', a Latin American critique of the commonly accepted development models, was particularly important. The accepted development theory at the time was that Latin America, and other Third World countries, would gradually progress to being developed economies. Latin American countries were expected to continue their traditional role as exporters of primary goods and providers of cheap labour.[32] Further development along these lines was encouraged by development loans and aid packages from the rich countries. Against this prevailing wisdom, dependency theorists argued that such 'development' would deepen, rather than alleviate, Latin America's problems. They argued that a far more radical change was needed because the root of the problem lay in Latin America's continuing dependency on the rich nations. This dependency allowed the rich countries to ensure that economic trade relations always worked to their advantage. The western models of 'progress' and 'development' were seen by dependency theorists as reinforcing this dependency. Real progress could only come by rejecting this unfair relationship and ending the state of dependency. According to dependency theorists what Latin

updated version of a previous paper given in Chimbote, Peru, in July 1968 (*Hacia uno teología de la liberacíon* [Montevideo: MIEC Documentation Service, 1969]). *A Theology of Liberation* is a direct development of these two papers. Hennelly offers a translation of the Chimbote paper, 'Toward a Theology of Liberation', in Hennelly (ed.), *Liberation Theology*, pp. 62-76.

30. L. Boff and C. Boff, *Salvation and Liberation: In Search of a Balance between Faith and Politics* (trans. R. Barr; Maryknoll, NY: Orbis Books, 1984), pp. 14-17, Portuguese orig. *Da libertação: O sentido teológico liberaçãoes das sócio-historicas* (Petrópolis: Editora Vozes, 1979).

31. See H. Assmann, *Theology of a Nomad Church* (Maryknoll, NY: Orbis Books, 1976) pp. 49-51, Spanish orig. *Teología desde la praxis de la liberación* (Salamanca: Sígueme, 1973), Part 1.

32. W.W. Rostow, *The Stages of Economic Growth: A Non-Communist Manifesto* (Cambridge: Cambridge University Press, 1960).

America really needed was liberation from its position in the world economy.[33]

In the field of education the work of Paulo Freire in Brazil had a dramatic impact on educational thought throughout the continent. Freire's approach to popular education aimed at empowering marginalized people through a process of 'conscientization'. Freire's thinking developed the idea that as human subjects people must be the agents of their own liberation. He was highly critical of educational approaches that failed to respect this principle and offered a radical pedagogic approach that was intended to break down rather than reinforce the usual power relationships between the authority of the educator and the dependency of those being educated.[34]

Taking his lead from these developments, Gutiérrez wished to show that a similarly new approach was needed in theology.[35] Gutiérrez did not create the understanding of liberation *ex nihilo*. He was conscious of its implications in both dependency theory and radical pedagogy and sought to adopt it and adapt it for theology. Gutiérrez argued that 'liberation' is a better term for understanding the three levels of salvation (political, existential and theological) that he had distinguished in the single complex process mentioned above.

At the political and economic level 'liberation' contrasts with political development and economic growth. Gutiérrez was influenced by the claims of dependency theorists that at the political and economic level the dominant models of development were part of the problem, rather than part of the solution. The economic and political well-being of Latin America rested on rejection of such 'developmentalism'. The way forward was to be found in freedom from such development not reforms to it.[36]

33. See, for example, F.H. Cardoso and E. Faletto, *Dependency and Development in Latin America* (trans. M. Uruqudi; Berkeley: University of California Press, 1979), Spanish orig. *Dependencia y desarollo* (Mexico City: Siglo Veintiuno Editores, rev. edn, 1969).

34. P. Freire, *Pedagogy of the Oppressed* (trans. M. Ramos; New York: Continuum, 1970; London: Sheed and Ward, 1972; Portuguese orig. 1968).

35. See Gutiérrez, *Theology of Liberation*, pp. 21-36, 91-92.

36. The influence of dependency theory on the early work of Gutiérrez and other liberation theologians needs to be emphasized. However, dependency theory has come in for considerable criticism and later works in liberation theology have been much more tentative about its adequacy as an analysis of development at the economic and political level. Compared with *A Theology of Liberation*, Gutiérrez's more recent

At the second, existential level, 'liberation' contrasts with personal growth. It seems that Gutiérrez's rejection of personal 'growth' was very similar to his rejection of social 'development'. In both cases the more fundamental question is the framework in which development or growth take place. In both cases the term 'liberation' can serve to draw attention to more basic questions. For example, Freire claimed that instead of promoting personal growth the dominant models of education disempowered people and undermined their personal freedom.[37] Viewed from one perspective such education might be seen as evidence of personal growth but Freire argued that it might also be seen at an existential level as a dehumanizing process in which human subjects are transformed into less than human objects. At the existential level, Gutiérrez's preference for 'liberation' appears to reflect the fundamental importance of existential freedom. The theologian is therefore to be critical of any understanding of personal growth which covertly reduces rather than increases the real liberties that an individual may enjoy.

At the third, theological level, it is possible to speak of liberation from sin but inappropriate to speak of this in terms of 'development'. The term 'liberation' captures the Christian understanding of sin as bondage requiring release. Christian orthodoxy rejects the belief that humanity can save itself from its sinful situation. Thinking of salvation in terms of development or reform runs the risk of underemphasizing the theological conviction that salvation is dependent on God's grace as well as human response.

Gutiérrez has been criticized for oversimplifying the theological nature of salvation by representing it purely in terms of human liberation struggles and equating theology with politics. Two features of *A Theology of Liberation* might be used to support such claims. First, Gutiérrez primarily deals with liberation at the first level (political and economic) and even his understanding of the third level emphasizes its relation to the first. Secondly, Gutiérrez explicitly describes his theology as a 'political hermeneutics of the Gospel'. However, this is to ignore Gutiérrez's analysis of salvation in which all three levels are *essential to*

works give dependency analysis much less prominence. For an extended discussion of current evaluations of dependency theory, see A.F. McGovern, *Liberation Theology and its Critics: Towards an Assessment* (Maryknoll, NY: Orbis Books, 1990), pp. 125-29, 156-76.

37. See especially the discussion of 'Banking Education' in Freire, *Pedagogy of the Oppressed*, pp. 57-61.

and *inseparable from* each other. His emphasis on politics is a corrective rather than a denial of the other concerns of theology.[38] Gutiérrez insists that 'To talk about the political dimension is not to disregard the multi-dimensional nature of human beings but rather to take it into account'.[39]

An alternative subject of criticism has been liberation theology's alleged commitment to violence as an essential component of its theology.[40] Critics have pointed to the active participation of Christians in social movements in Central America, especially the involvement of Nicaraguan Christians in the overthrow of Somoza in 1979.[41] Elsewhere in Latin America there have been other highly publicized instances of priests joining guerilla groups. Camilo Torres, who was a friend of Gutiérrez, is perhaps the best known example. He resigned his priest-hood in 1965 and joined a guerilla group only to be shot a few weeks afterwards in the Colombian jungle.[42]

However, Torres is very much the exception and not the rule. To equate liberation theology with guerilla priests reduces the movement to extreme and untypical examples.[43] Most liberation theologians follow orthodox Catholic teaching on the use of violence. However, critics who are unaware of the original meaning of their terminology may misunder-stand their views. For example, Gutiérrez's understanding of liberation theology as part of a move from developmentalism to social revolution was not a call to armed insurrection.[44] It was a rejection of token reforms that did not address the real issues and an indication, in the

38. See further G. Gutiérrez, 'Liberation Praxis and Christian Faith', in R. Gibellini (ed.), *Frontiers of Theology in Latin America* (Maryknoll, NY: Orbis Books, 1979), pp. 1-33 (9-12, 20-21), Italian orig. *La nuova frontiera della teologia in America Latina* (Brescia: Editrice Queriniana, 1975).

39. Gutiérrez, 'Liberation Praxis and Christian Faith', p. 10.

40. E. Lynch, *Religion and Politics in Latin America: Liberation Theology and Christian Democracy* (New York: Praeger, 1991), p. 91.

41. See Berryman, *The Religious Roots of Rebellion*, pp. 51-89.

42. See C. Torres, *Revolutionary Priest: The Complete Writings and Messages of Camilo Torres* (ed. J. Gerassi; trans. J. de Cipriano *et al.*; London: Cape, 1971).

43. On Nicaragua, see A. Bradstock, *Saints and Sandinistas: The Catholic Church in Nicaragua and its Response to the Revolution* (London: Epworth Press, 1987); T. Caberstreo, *Revolutionaries for the Gospel: Testimonies of Fifteen Christians in the Nicaraguan Government* (Maryknoll, NY: Orbis Books, 1986).

44. Gutiérrez, *Theology of Liberation*, p. 25. On Gutiérrez and violence, see Brown, *Gustavo Gutiérrez*, p. 214; see further R.M. Brown, *Religion and Violence* (Philadelphia: Westminster Press, 2nd edn, 1987).

terminology of the time, of the dramatic extent to which society had to change.[45]

2. *The preferential option for the poor.* Gutiérrez's second insight stems from the perceived failure of the churches, academic theologians and biblical scholars in Europe and North America to successfully address the pressing issues of justice. Liberation theologians argue that because theology and biblical scholarship are usually conceived in comfortable affluence they have failed to concern themselves with the real needs of the majority of humanity. Liberation theology argues that to be effective the commitment to liberation needs to be guided by a shift in social perspective. Theology must take on the viewpoint of the poor and re-read the world and the word from their position. As the Bishops expressed it at Puebla in Mexico, during the third meeting of CELAM (1979), 'We affirm the need for conversion on the part of the whole Church to a preferential option for the poor, an option aimed at their integral liberation'.[46]

This conversion to the poor goes alongside a fundamental shift in how poverty itself is seen. Liberation theologians challenge the fatalistic acceptances of poverty as inevitable and reject any suggestion that poverty should be accepted as part of God's ordained plan for the poor. Liberation theologians do not put responsibility on the poor for bringing the situation on themselves through individual laziness or personal misfortune. Instead poverty is identified as a structural issue affecting the poor as a social class. Its causes are seen to be sinful social structures that result in exploitation and oppression.[47] To talk of the poor in terms of the 'oppressed' highlights the social relations that cause poverty.[48]

45. On the relationship between liberation theologies and European theologies of revolution, see Gibellini, *The Liberation Theology Debate*, p. 16.

46. See *Puebla: Evangelization at Present and in the Future of Latin America: Conclusions* (Official English Edition of the Third General Conference of Latin American Bishops, Puebla, Mexico, 1979; Slough: St Paul Publications, 1980), §1134.

47. For the categories of the oppressed recognized at CELAM II, see *Puebla*, §§32-39; cf. Gutiérrez, *The Power of the Poor in History*, pp. 133-34. The groups identified are: young children, juveniles, indigenous peoples, peasants, labourers, the underemployed, the unemployed, the marginalized, the urban slum dwellers, the elderly. The Boffs (*Introducing Liberation Theology*, pp. 25-29) extend the list to include those oppressed due to race, ethnicity or sex.

48. For discussion of 'Who are the Poor Today, and Why?', see J. Pixley and

Throughout history there have been those motivated by Christian concern who have acted for the poor or on their behalf but liberation theologians demand more than this.[49] For liberation theologians true compassion—'suffering with'—the poor cannot remain as a theoretical principle proclaimed from a position of privilege. Taking on the viewpoint of the poor is not just an intellectual exercise, it requires a genuine solidarity at the level of experience. Liberation theology holds that joining in the struggles of the poor requires, and subsequently promotes, a change in social location on the part of the theologian. In order to be genuinely open to the perspective of the poor a theologian must share in their real experience. The Boffs put the matter bluntly: 'Without a minimum of "suffering with" this suffering that affects the great majority of the human race, liberation theology can neither exist nor be understood'.[50]

To sum up, the commitment to liberation and the preferential option for the poor provide the fundamental principles for both *a new starting point* and *a new set of criteria* for theology. These two issues—engagement with social issues and solidarity with the poor—are so fundamental that they raise a further question about whether those who do not share the same perspective can expect to have an adequate understanding of liberation theology. A realistic evaluation of liberation theology and its approach to the New Testament must start by recognizing that its fundamental orientation is very different to the usual concerns of academia. As the Boffs put it,

> Underlying liberation theology is a prophetic and comradely commitment
> to the life, cause and struggle of these debased and marginalized human
> beings, a commitment to ending this historical-social iniquity.[51]

C. Boff, *The Bible, the Church and the Poor* (trans. P. Burns; TLS, 6; Maryknoll, NY: Orbis Books; Tunbridge Wells: Burns & Oates, 1989), pp. 17-52, Portuguese orig. *Opção pelos pobres* (Petrópolis: Editora Vozes, 1987).

49. Leonardo Boff (*Salvation and Liberation*, p. 3) describes the change in the Church's approach: 'the strategy whereby the church comes to the aid of the poor has undergone a change. In times gone by, the church was bound to the dominant classes, and it was through their mediation that the church reached out to the poor, to whom the dominant classes were giving "assistance". The presence of the church was "assistentialistic", paternalistic. The church came to the aid of the poor, it is true, but made no use of the resources of the poor in instituting a process of change. Now the church goes directly to the poor, joining them in their struggles...'

50. L. and C. Boff, *Introducing Liberation Theology*, p. 3.

51. L. and C. Boff, *Introducing Liberation Theology*, p. 3. See also C. Boff, *Feet-*

This is in sharp contrast to the traditional expectation that theologians should seek peaceful seclusion, in the Church or academia, away from the distractions of worldly affairs. This may alarm those who are more used to approaching the subject as an academic discipline in which the agenda is set by scholarly debate. However, for liberation theologians the scholarly debates that have traditionally characterized theology have often missed the true significance of the Christian gospel. Traditional theological approaches have failed the Latin American people because they have failed to start in the right way (by understanding theology as critical reflection on Christian praxis) and failed to start from the right place (the commitment to the poor and oppressed).

b. *A New Way of Doing Theology*

Liberation theologians emphasize that in following the two fundamental insights discussed above they are not just concerned to highlight neglected topics of traditional Christian concern. It would not be enough for theologians to give themes like oppression and liberation more attention in their study of the Bible. Liberation theology claims that what is needed is a whole new direction in theology. For the biblical themes of poverty, oppression and liberation to be properly understood and responded to authentically a new theological *method* is required.[52] Gutiérrez makes this clear when he says, '...the theology of liberation offers us not so much a new theme for reflection as a *new way* to do theology'.[53]

For Gutiérrez the proper understanding of the gospel is inseparable from an active response to it. The Christian is called to make true their faith in action.[54] Gutiérrez argues that in the Bible the knowledge of God

---

on-the-Ground-Theology: A Brazilian Journey (trans. P. Berryman; Maryknoll, NY: Orbis Books, 1987), Portuguese orig. *Teología-Pé-No-Chão* (Petrópolis: Editora Vozes, 1984).

52. The most detailed study of the biblical notion of the oppressed has been carried out by E. Tamez, *Bible of the Oppressed* (trans. M. O'Connell; Maryknoll, NY: Orbis Books, 1982). Chs. 1–5 are the Spanish orig. *La Biblia de los oprimidos: La opresión en la teología bíblica* (San José: DEI, 1979) and chs. 6–7 are from *La hora de la vida* (San José: DEI, 1978).

53. Gutiérrez, *Theology of Liberation*, p. 15.

54. Gutiérrez (*Theology of Liberation*, p. 10) claims '...only by doing this truth will our faith be "veri-fied", in the etymological sense of the word'; cf. Gutiérrez, *The Power of the Poor in History*, p. 201.

is inseparable from action for justice, knowing God involves unity with God through action.[55]

The Mexican scholar, José Porfirio Miranda, offers support for this in his comments on Jer. 22.16:

> Here we have an explicit definition of what it is to know Yahweh. To know Yahweh is to achieve justice for the poor. Nothing authorises us to introduce a cause-effect relationship between 'to know Yahweh' and 'to practice justice'.[56]

The commitment to action that is distinctive of the liberationist approach marks the basic reorientation of the theological agenda. José Míguez Bonino, an Argentinean Protestant liberation theologian, calls this 'a new way of "doing theology"'.[57] The idea of 'doing theology' serves as an effective reminder that in the liberationist view theological thinking can never be separated from practice and action. Consciously echoing Marx's eleventh thesis on Feuerbach Gutiérrez writes: 'This is a theology which does not stop with reflecting on the world, but rather tries to be part of the process through which the world is transformed'.[58]

1. *Orthodoxy and orthopraxis.* The term 'praxis', derived from Marxist thought, is used to emphasize the dialectic of action and practice guided by reflection and thought. *Orthodoxy*, understood as the 'proclamation of and reflection on statements understood to be true', makes way for *orthopraxis* as the true criterion for liberation theology.[59] The Uruguayan theologian Juan Luis Segundo argues that orthopraxis should be seen as transcending orthodoxy:

55. See Gutiérrez, *The Power of the Poor in History*, pp. 7-8.

56. J.P. Miranda, *Marx and the Bible: A Critique of the Philosophy of Oppression* (trans. J. Eagleson; Maryknoll, NY: Orbis Books, 1984; London: SCM Press, 1977), p. 44, Spanish orig. *Marx y la biblia: Critica a la filosofia de la opresión* (Salamanca: Ediciones Sígueme, 1971).

57. Míguez Bonino, *Doing Theology in a Revolutionary Situation*, p. 82.

58. Gutiérrez, *Theology of Liberation*, p. 15.

59. Gutiérrez, *Theology of Liberation*, p. 10. Cf. Míguez Bonino (*Doing Theology in a Revolutionary Situation*, p. 81) who argues: 'Theology, as here conceived, is not an effort to give a correct understanding of God's attributes or actions but an effort to articulate the action of faith, the shape of praxis conceived and realized in obedience. As philosophy in Marx's famous *dictum*, theology has to stop explaining the world and start transforming it. *Orthopraxis*, rather than *orthodoxy*, becomes the criterion for theology' [emphasis original].

...orthodoxy possesses no ultimate criterion in itself because being orthodox does not mean possessing the final truth. We only arrive at the latter
by orthopraxis. It is the latter that is the ultimate criterion of the former,
both in theology and in biblical interpretation. The truth is truth only when
it serves as the basis for truly human attitudes.[60]

Understood in this way the shift from orthodoxy to orthopraxis is not a
denial of orthodoxy's importance. Orthopraxis can be understood as the
attempt to develop and enlarge orthodoxy rather than replace it. In
other words, it comes not to abolish but to fulfil orthodoxy.[61]

However, whether the legitimate concerns of orthodoxy are respected
and reinvigorated (as liberation theologians claim) or whether they are
compromised and subjected to theological reductionism (as the critics
allege) is a fiercely disputed issue. The controversy is not helped by *a
priori* judgments, from one side or the other, on the basis of terminology alone. This point needs to be recognized when assessing liberation theology against the academic orthodoxy of theological and biblical
scholarship, as well as the confessional orthodoxy of the Church. An
unhelpful polarization of positions can result that puts orthodoxy and
scholarship on one side in opposition to orthopraxis and social activism
on the other. If a fair assessment is to be made the debate needs to be
shifted away from sweeping and dogmatic generalizations. On the one
hand there needs to be a clear willingness to take specific criticisms
raised against liberation theology seriously; on the other hand critics
must try to appreciate the full context in which such views are held.

2. *The non-believer and the non-person.* For Gutiérrez the shift in theological criteria in Latin America can be understood as a change in focus
away from the 'non-believer' and towards the 'non-person'. This

60. J.L. Segundo, *The Liberation of Theology* (trans. J. Drury; Maryknoll, NY:
Orbis Books; 1976), p. 32, Spanish orig. *Liberatión de la teología* (Buenos Aires:
Ediciones Carlos Lohlé, 1975).
61. In introducing the distinction between orthopraxis and orthodoxy in his early
work Gutiérrez (*Theology of Liberation*, p. 10) was careful to state that the intention
was not to deny the meaning of orthodoxy but 'to balance and even to reject the primacy and almost exclusiveness which doctrine has enjoyed in Christian life and above
all to modify the emphasis, often obsessive, upon the attainment of an orthodoxy
which is often no more than fidelity to an obsolete tradition or a debatable interpretation. In a more positive vein, the intention is to recognize the work and importance of
concrete behaviour, of deeds, of action, of praxis in the Christian life'.

provides the overall context for the challenges presented by liberation theology.[62]

The fundamental problem that has influenced theology in developed western nations has been the secular challenge to religious belief. The Christian gospel has been forced to demonstrate its credibility in the increasingly secularized culture which Bonhoeffer referred to as 'a world come of age'. Since Schleiermacher the non-believer has increasingly set the agenda for theology in Europe and North America.[63] However, as liberation theologians see it the problems for theology in the Third World are not so much the problems of the non-believer but the non-person: the millions who are deprived of basic physical necessities and elementary human rights.[64] According to the Boffs,

> The gospel is not aimed chiefly at modern men and women with their critical spirit, but first and foremost at 'nonpersons', those whose basic dignity and rights are refused them.[65]

For the Salvadoran theologian, Jon Sobrino, all modern Christian theology has developed within the boundaries set by the Enlightenment. However, the differences between European and Latin American theology reflect a responsiveness to the two different phases of the Enlightenment. Sobrino sees the two phases as represented in two key figures: the first in Immanuel Kant; the second in Karl Marx.[66] According to Sobrino the first phase looked to 'the liberation of reason from all authority' whereas the second looked to 'not just a liberation of

62. Gutiérrez, *The Power of the Poor in History,* pp. 169-221; see also L. and C. Boff, *Introducing Liberation Theology,* p. 8.

63. See F.D. Schleiermacher, *On Religion: Speeches to its Cultured Despisers* (trans. J. Oman; New York: Harper & Row, 1958 [ET 1894]).

64. Gutiérrez (*The Power of the Poor in History,* p. 193) says: 'This is why our question is not how to speak of God in an adult world. That was the old question asked by progressivist theology. No, the interlocutor of the theology of liberation is the 'nonperson', the human being who is not considered human by the present social order—the exploited social classes, marginalized ethnic groups, and despised cultures. Our question is how to tell the nonperson, the nonhuman, that God is love, and that this love makes us all brothers and sisters'.

65. L. and C. Boff, *Introducing Liberation Theology,* p. 8.

66. J. Sobrino, *The True Church and the Poor* (trans. M. O'Connell; Maryknoll, NY: Orbis Books; 1984), p. 10, Spanish orig. *Resurrección de la verdadera iglesia: Los pobres, lugar teológico de la eclesiología* (Santander: Editorial Sal Terrae, 1981).

the mind, but a liberation from the misery of the real world'.[67]

The differences between European and Latin American approaches relate to the different phases taking priority in theological thought. Thus, whilst some theologians in Europe and North America have grappled with the 'death of God' in Latin America it is the 'death of the oppressed' that sets the agenda for liberation theology. The 'death of God' debate focused largely on how belief was to be understood philosophically in the secularized cultures of developed societies. The proponents of the death of God theology were involved with the apologetics of Christian belief. By contrast concern for the 'death of the oppressed' in liberation theology is first and foremost Christian apologetics for life.

A similar contrast can be identified in approaches to biblical studies. Much of the biblical scholarship in Europe and North America aims to free the reading of the New Testament from literalism and naive historicism. The scholarly successes in this regard have certainly been one of the great achievements of biblical criticism in the last century. However, Latin American theologians now ask whether biblical scholars have responded to only part of the Enlightenment challenge. The challenge raised by Sobrino is that the biblical scholarship that is really needed, at least in Latin America, is scholarship that frees the text to work for the integral liberation of a crucified people: putting the demands of the nonperson to the forefront.

3. *Reading the Word and the World*

The new way of doing theology with a commitment to liberating action and the preferential option for the poor provides a new approach to the study of the Bible. Liberation theology has developed a distinctive hermeneutical method for reading both the word and the world.

a. *Liberating Hermeneutics*
Liberating hermeneutics is not intended to be a scholarly exercise undertaken by professional theologians and then offered to the poor. The active participation of a faith community is necessary from the outset.

1. *Rooting theology in the people.* Liberation theology is distinctive in its approach to *who* does theology. The common split between the academic theologian and the people is rejected; instead the theologian is

67. Sobrino, *The True Church and the Poor*, p. 11.

challenged to forge an organic solidarity with the people.[68] Liberation theology takes place at different levels—the professional, the pastoral and the popular. At each level there is a different emphasis in the theological forms even though each level is interdependent on the others.[69] The Boffs refer to the different parts of a tree to explain the different parts of this single process:

> Liberation theology could be compared to a tree. Those who see only professional theologians at work in it see only the branches of the tree. They fail to see the trunk which is the thinking of priests and other pastoral ministers, let alone the roots beneath the soil that hold the whole tree—trunk and branches—in place. The roots are the practical living and thinking—though submerged and anonymous—going on in tens of thousands of base communities living out their faith and thinking it in a liberating key.[70]

The popular base of liberation theology is institutionally rooted in the *comunidades eclesiales de base* (CEBs) or Base Christian Communities.[71] Usually the groups have someone who acts as a facilitator but this need not be a priest.[72] The intention of the facilitator is not to instruct but to provoke the discussion and dialogue. Base communities can be found throughout Latin America and are particularly strong in Brazil.[73]

68. On the practical ways that such solidarity might be shown at different levels of commitment, see L. and C. Boff, *Introducing Liberation Theology*, p. 24.

69. See the chart in L. and C. Boff, *Introducing Liberation Theology*, p. 13.

70. L. and C. Boff, *Introducing Liberation Theology*, p. 12.

71. For a brief summary, see P. Berryman, *Liberation Theology: The Essential Facts about the Revolutionary Movement in Latin America and Beyond* (New York: Pantheon, 1987), pp. 64-68. For an accessible introductory survey, see J. Marins, T.M. Trevisan and C. Chanona, *The Church from the Roots: Basic Ecclesial Communities* (London: Catholic Fund for Overseas Development, 1989 [ET 1983]). For an excellent collection of papers on a wide variety of issues related to the Base Christian Communities, see S. Torres and J. Eagleson (eds.), *The Challenge of Basic Christian Communities* (Papers from the International Ecumenical Congress of Theology, 1980, Sao Paulo, Brazil; trans. J. Drury; Maryknoll, NY: Orbis Books, 1981). For a Protestant perspective, see G. Cook, *The Expectation of the Poor: Latin American Basic Ecclesial Communities in Protestant Perspective* (Maryknoll, NY: Orbis Books, 1985).

72. For the ecclesiological vision underlying the CEBs, see L. Boff, *Church: Charism and Power: Liberation Theology and the Institutional Church* (trans. J. Diercksmeier; New York: Crossroad; London: SCM Press, 1985), Portuguese orig. *Igreja: Carisma e poder* (Petrópolis: Editora Vozes, 1981).

73. Edward Cleary (*The Church in Latin America Today: Crisis and Change*

2. *The three mediations of the hermeneutical circle.* The second distinctive feature of liberating hermeneutics is how the Bible is read. Reading
the Bible is seen as a hermeneutical circle involving three different stages
or 'mediations'.[74]

The first stage is the socio-analytic mediation. Liberating exegesis
looks beyond traditional Christian concerns to investigate much broader
social issues. It attempts to link micro and personal concerns to macro
and structural issues. For example, it moves from individual issues of
violence in Central American countries like Nicaragua and El Salvador
to the structural reasons (political and economic) for the region's civil
wars. In Brazil discussion of hunger and personal poverty might eventually lead on to the consideration of the foreign debt and the systems of
world trade. For a deeper analysis of the social situation the group's
discussion might draw upon models and theories from social science.
This is seen as necessary if the group's social understanding is to go
beyond superficial symptoms to understanding the real causes at the
root of social issues. Marxist concepts and ideas might be drawn upon at
this stage, if they are seen as contributing something valuable, but are
not the only type of social analysis used.

The second stage is the hermeneutical mediation. Liberating exegesis
seeks to read the Bible and Christian tradition in accordance with the
commitment to liberation and the preferential option for the poor
described above. Some of the most important biblical material for this is
the Exodus, but liberation theologians also emphasize Genesis and the
Prophets in the Old Testament, and the Gospels and Revelation in the
New Testament. By contrast Proverbs and the Pauline epistles usually
receive relatively little attention, although this is not a hard and fast rule.
As the Boffs comment, 'The hermeneutics of liberation stresses these
veins, but not to the exclusion of everything else'.[75] Furthermore, the
perspectives brought to the texts by the community may open up fresh
perspectives on what seem to be less relevant texts. As Gutiérrez says,

---

[Maryknoll, NY: Orbis Books, 1985], p. 104) gives an estimated 100,000 CEBs in
Latin America with approximately one million members in Brazil and at least as many
in other Latin American countries.

74. See L. and C. Boff, *Introducing Liberation Theology*, pp. 22-42; cf. L. and
C. Boff, *Salvation and Liberation*, pp. 1-13. The theoretical foundations of the
approach and the methodological issues that they raise are discussed in much more
depth in C. Boff, *Theology and Practice*.

75. L. and C. Boff, *Introducing Liberation Theology*, pp. 32-33.

'When the reading of the Bible is done as a community, as a church, it is always an unexpected experience'.[76]

Inevitably any such reading is 'selective'. However, liberation theologians claim that selectivity is inevitable and their reading of the Bible is a legitimate consequence of their professed bias in favour of the poor. Furthermore, the fact that the Bible is interpreted by the community discussing the text together, rather than the individual extracting a meaning on their own, means that any interpretation has to be publicly justified.[77] Each interpretation is measured against the community's experience as well as the individual's.

Nonetheless, some critics argue that this involves an unwarranted manipulation of biblical material and that the option for the poor derives from non-biblical sources. Even scholars who accept that the Bible often speaks with more than one voice, and therefore agree that some hermeneutical selectivity is inevitable, may still disagree with the reading proposed by liberation theologians. The fact that the liberationist reading of the Bible is selective may not be problematic in principle but what is actually selected still has to be justified.

After social analysis and hermeneutical mediation, the third stage is practical mediation. Liberating exegesis commits itself to practical action to incarnate its vision and judgment. The 'action element' in liberation theology covers a wide variety of options from very small scale practical projects at a local level to national movements on social issues. The practical mediation completes the hermeneutical circle but does not end the process. The theologian is ready to start the circle with renewed commitment to the poor.[78]

Invariably there is a 'political' dimension to involvement with many of these practical actions. The practical outworking of faith in the political

76. G. Gutiérrez, *The God of Life* (trans. M. O'Connell; Maryknoll, NY: Orbis Books; London: SCM Press, 1991), p. xvii, Spanish orig. *El Dios de la vida* (Lima: Centro de Estudios y Publicaciones, rev. edn, 1989).

77. See E. Cardenal, *The Gospel in Solentiname* (trans. D.D. Walsh; 4 vols.; Maryknoll, NY: Orbis Books, 1976–1982), Spanish orig. *El evangelio en Solentiname* (2 vols.; Salamanca: Ediciones Sígueme, 1975–1977).

78. Thus L. and C. Boff (*Introducing Liberation Theology*, p. 39) conclude: 'Liberation theology is far from being an inconclusive theology. It starts from action and leads to action, a journey wholly impregnated by and bound up with the atmosphere of faith. From analysis of the reality of the oppressed, it passes through the word of God to arrive finally at specific action. "Back to action" is a characteristic call of this theology. It seeks to be a militant, committed and liberating theology'.

arena is not just defensible in the Latin American context but essential. The Boffs describe political action as a 'true form of faith' even though they recognize that 'faith cannot be reduced to action'.[79]

An important model for this hermeneutical process was provided by Catholic action experiments that originated in France in the 1950s. Under Catholic Action Christian biblical teaching was applied to issues arising in everyday life through a process involving three stages: see– judge–act. The idea was to encourage the reading of the Bible and the application of scriptural principles to issues arising in the home or workplace.

Liberation theology develops the pastoral circle of see–judge–act and radicalizes its conservative tendencies at each stage: extending its field of concerns to the social and political; emphasizing the importance of social analysis; and including active participation in the struggle against social injustice as an essential part of the process. Each mediation reflects the exegete's preliminary commitment to solidarity with the poor.

b. *The Gospel according to Liberation Theology*

The theological foundations and hermeneutical principles outlined above provide the framework for a closer look at the gospel message as it is interpreted in liberation theology. A crucial question is whether the gospel of liberation is a legitimate, indeed essential, liberation of the gospel for Latin America or whether it sacrifices the integrity of the text by adopting alien ideologies in an uncritical way.[80] To examine this further, three key elements in liberationist readings of Luke's Gospel will be considered. As Pixley and Boff point out, Luke's Gospel has a particular emphasis on liberation themes. Jesus is presented as one of the poor and committed to the poor in his words and actions.[81] Three aspects of this commitment deserve particular attention: the proclamation of the kingdom of God; the promise to the poor; the role of Christ as Liberator.

79. See L. and C. Boff, *Introducing Liberation Theology*, p. 39.

80. For example, the International Theological Commission, an advisory body to the Pope that reported on liberation theology in 1976, claimed that liberation theology oversimplified biblical themes; see 'Human Development and Christian Salvation', *Origins* 7 (November 3, 1977), orig. published as an appendix in *Comisión teológica internacional: Teología de la liberación* (ed. K. Lehmann; Madrid: BAC, 1978).

81. Pixley and Boff, *The Bible, the Church and the Poor*, p. 59.

1. *The proclamation of the kingdom of God.* Luke's presentation of Jesus reading from Isa. 61.1-2 in the synagogue at Nazareth (Lk. 4.16-21) identifies the origins of Jesus' ministry as the proclamation of the kingdom of God and the Lord's year of favour:

> The Spirit of the Lord is upon me because he has anointed me to bring good news to the poor.
>
> He has sent me to proclaim release to the captives and recovery of sight to the blind, to let the oppressed go free, to proclaim the year of the Lord's favour (NRSV).

According to the Boffs,

> The kingdom or reign of God means the full and total liberation of all creation, in the end, purified of all that oppresses it, transfigured by the full presence of God. No other theological or biblical concept is as close to the ideal of integral liberation as this concept of the kingdom of God.[82]

The proclamation of the kingdom is therefore of central importance to liberation readings of the Gospels.[83] Jesus is seen as proclaiming the kingdom not only in his preaching but also in his actions.[84] Particular acts of liberation (for example, healings and exorcisms) are to be understood as making the kingdom concrete in the present.[85]

> The kingdom of God is something more than historical liberations, which are always limited and open to further perfectioning [*sic*], but it is anticipated and incarnated in them in time, in preparation for its full realization with the coming of the new heaven and the new earth.[86]

---

82. L. and C. Boff, *Introducing Liberation Theology*, p. 52; cf. L. Boff, *Jesus Christ Liberator: A Critical Christology of our Time* (trans. P. Hughes; Maryknoll, NY: Orbis Books, 1978; London: SPCK, 1980), pp. 63-64, Portuguese orig. *Jesus Cristo libertador: Ensaio de cristologia crítica para o nosso tempo* (Petrópolis: Editora Vozes, 1972).

83. See, for example, J. Pixley, *God's Kingdom: A Guide for Biblical Study* (Maryknoll, NY: Orbis Books; London: SCM Press, 1981).

84. On Lk. 11.20, see Boff, *Jesus Christ Liberator*, p. 283.

85. L. and C. Boff (*Introducing Liberation Theology*, p. 54) claim: 'The kingdom is not presented simply as something to be hoped for in the future; it is already being made concrete in Jesus' actions. His miracles and healings, besides demonstrating his divinity, are designed to show that his liberating proclamation is already being made history among the oppressed, the special recipients of his teaching and first beneficiaries of his actions'.

86. L. and C. Boff, *Introducing Liberation Theology*, p. 53.

Thus when Jesus is questioned by the followers of John the Baptist (Lk. 7.18-23) he cites in reply his actions towards the poor and oppressed. Leonardo Boff takes this as demonstrating that Jesus is not only proclaiming the kingdom but actually bringing it about by his presence (cf. Lk. 11.20; Lk. 17.21).[87] He notes that the term 'the kingdom of God' occurs '122 times in the Gospels and 90 times on the lips of Jesus'.[88]

Recognizing the centrality of the kingdom and debates over its future or realized fulfilment are hardly new in New Testament studies. In these terms there is relatively little, apart perhaps from emphasis, that distinguishes the liberationist reading of Luke from other approaches. However, liberation theologians wish to do more than engage in academic debates as to what constituted the original gospel message. Rather they want to take seriously the revolutionary *nature* of the kingdom and the radical changes in social, political and economic relationships that it entails.

2. *Blessed are the poor.* According to liberationist readings of Luke, the solidarity that existed between Jesus and the poor is an example to be followed and a justification of the option for the poor. In this reading, the birth narratives stress Jesus' own poverty and situate him amongst the most humble.

> ...[Luke] stresses the fact of Jesus' poverty, and the meaning of his life as a sign of hope for the poor. Jesus was born in a stable because his parents could provide nothing better, and those who celebrate the event to the accompaniment of a heavenly chorus are humble shepherds looking after their flocks in the fields.[89]

The proclamation of the kingdom is a special blessing for the poor. However, liberation readings of Luke emphasize that the kingdom is not good news for everyone.[90] Luke's account draws attention to the revolutionary challenge of the kingdom and its reversal of social roles so that the least is the greatest (Lk. 9.46-48; 22.25-26).

87. On Lk. 17.21, see Boff, *Jesus Christ Liberator*, p. 280.
88. Boff, *Jesus Christ Liberator*, p. 52.
89. Pixley and Boff, *The Bible, the Church and the Poor*, p. 59.
90. For a good case study of liberating exegesis applied to Matthew's understanding of judgment, see F. Watson, 'Liberating the Reader: A Theological-Exegetical Study of the Parable of the Sheep and the Goats (Matthew 25.31-46)', in F. Watson (ed.), *The Open Text: New Directions for Biblical Studies* (London: SCM Press, 1993), pp. 57-84.

Mary's Magnificat (Lk. 1.46-53) is seen as pointing to 'the struggle to establish a world of egalitarian relationships, of deep respect for each individual, in whom god-head dwells'.[91] The Sermon on the Plain (Lk. 6.20-49; cf. Mt. 5.1-12) gives particular prominence to the different fates awaiting the rich and the poor: thus Lk. 6.20 'Blessed are you who are poor, for yours is the kingdom of God' is contrasted with Lk. 6.24 'But woe to you who are rich, for you have received your consolation'.[92] Liberation readings tend to highlight the warnings to the rich in the parable of Dives and Lazarus (Lk. 16.19-31), Jesus' command to the rich young aristocrat who sought to follow him (Lk. 18.18-23), and the emphatic teaching on the dangers of wealth (Lk. 18.24-27).[93]

Luke's condemnation of respectable society which presents an outer appearance of piety while bearing responsibility for the blood of the prophets (Lk. 11.47-51; cf. Isa. 1.15) points to the same hypocrisy in Latin American society. Likewise, the description (Lk. 23.12) of the alliance of convenience between Herod and Pilate is seen as having a contemporary parallel in the way that the rich and powerful in Latin America unite to preserve their interests. According to the liberationist reading, the kingdom of God will sweep away the oppression of the poor and weak by the rich and strong. The promises to the poor of the judgment that is to come (Lk. 18.1-8a) take on great significance when read by the oppressed people in today's Latin America. They give a concrete meaning to the 'Good News' that Jesus proclaimed.

3. *Jesus Christ liberator.* In *Jesus Christ Liberator* Leonardo Boff introduced the term 'liberator' as liberation theology's distinctive Christological title: 'In Luke...Jesus is presented as the liberator of the poor, the sick, sinners, the socially and religiously marginalized'.[94] Boff's

91. See I. Gebara and M.C. Bingemer, *Mary, Mother of God, Mother of the Poor* (trans. P. Burns; TLS, 7; Maryknoll, NY: Orbis Books; Tunbridge Wells: Burns & Oates, 1989), pp. 72-73, Portuguese orig. *Maria, mãe de Deus e mãe do pobres* (Petrópolis: Editora Vozes, 1987).

92. See J.L. Segundo (*The Historical Jesus of the Synoptics* [trans. J. Drury; Maryknoll, NY: Orbis Books, 1985], p. 8, Spanish orig. first part [pp. 1-284] of *El hombre de hoy ante Jesus de Nazareth* [Madrid: Ediciones Christiandad, 1982]) on the differences between Luke and Matthew.

93. E. Hoornaert, *The Memory of the Christian People* (trans. R. Barr; TLS, 5; Maryknoll, NY: Orbis Books, 1988; Tunbridge Wells: Burns & Oates, 1989), p. 221, Portuguese orig. *A memória do povo cristão* (Petrópolis: Editora Vozes, 1986).

94. Boff, *Jesus Christ Liberator*, p.6.

book applied to Christology the fundamental insights that Gutiérrez had already pioneered in *A Theology of Liberation*.[95] Both works emphasize the importance of the historical realm and its social and political dimensions in any understanding of Christian faith and doctrine.[96]

The term 'liberator' has particular resonance in Latin America. Simon Bolívar, who is honoured as national hero in many South American countries, led independence movements throughout the continent and is widely referred to as 'el liberador' or 'the liberator'. In applying the term 'liberator' to Christ, Boff was consciously trying to redress the distorted picture of Christ that has been created by ignoring his political significance. In this Boff is as emphatic as Gutiérrez that political liberation does not exhaust the Christian message. In fact, the original version of the book was quite tentative about the political and economic dimensions of liberation although perhaps Boff would have wished to say more on these if his own situation had been different.[97] However, Boff rejects any suggestion that Jesus is to be seen as liberator only in terms of promising deliverance from foreign domination and economic oppression. Such oversimplification fails to do justice to the Christian gospel in both first-century Palestine and twentieth-century Latin America. Boff emphasizes that it is the human person, the society and

95. For other contributions to Latin American Christology, see the collection in J. Míguez Bonino (ed.), *Faces of Jesus: Latin American Christologies* (trans. J. Drury; Maryknoll, NY: Orbis Books, 1984), Spanish orig. *Jesús: Ni vencido ni monarca celestial* (Buenos Aires: Tierra Nueva, 1977). See also C. Bussmann, *Who Do You Say? Jesus Christ in Latin American Theology* (Maryknoll, NY: Orbis Books, 1985), German orig. *Befreiung durch Jesus? Die Christologie der lateinamerikanischen Befreiungstheologie* (Munich: Kösel, 1980).

96. A similar emphasis is to be found in the Christology of Jon Sobrino. See J. Sobrino, *Christology at the Crossroads: A Latin American View* (trans. J. Drury; Maryknoll, NY: Orbis Books; London: SCM Press, 1978), Spanish orig. *Cristología desde América Latina* (Mexico City: Centro de Reflexión Teológica, 1976); *idem, Jesus in Latin America* (Maryknoll, NY: Orbis Books, 1987), Spanish orig. *Jesús en América Latina: Su significado para la fe y la cristología* (San Salvador: Universidad Centroamericana; Santander: Sal Terrae, 1982).

97. As Boff notes in his Preface to the English translation (p. xii), the work was originally published in Brazil in 1972 when the repression of the Church was particularly severe and the word 'liberation' was forbidden in all communications media. The Epilogue (pp. 264-95) added to the English translation includes much more explicit attention to the political significance of liberation and its implications for Latin America.

the totality of reality that all undergo God's transformation.[98]

Considerable attention is given to the second level of liberation identified by Gutiérrez, the freedom of the whole person. Jesus is described as the liberator of consciences and the inaugurator of a new humanity.[99] Boff presents Jesus as challenging the oppressive aspects of the Jewish religion and enslavement to its laws. His death is the responsibility of the religious authorities as well as the political powers because in his commitment to total liberation he set all the authorities of the day against him.[100]

4. *Liberating Hermeneutics*

In an early assessment of liberation theology Alfredo Fierro described liberation theology as 'profession of faith' rather than 'critical reflection on faith'.[101] The implication is that liberation theologians are not concerned with the intellectual disciplines required by academic theology. Other critics have similarly questioned its intellectual rigour and the strength of its scholarly foundations. Segundo acknowledges that in its early days liberation theology 'clearly evoked a certain amount of academic disdain from the great centres of theological thought around the world...as a well-intentioned but rather naive and uncritical effort...'[102]

In partial response to the general criticism that liberation theology neglects academic scholarship it might be observed that many liberation theologians received their training in the academic theological disciplines from major European centres of theology. Gutiérrez, for example, studied at Louvain, Lyons and Rome. If there is a question mark against liberation theology on the basis of its scholarly standards it is not because its theologians do not have the appropriate qualifications; rather, the issue is whether the option for the poor detracts from their commitment to scholarship. As far as the New Testament is concerned the crucial question is whether the commitment to put academic theology at

98. Boff, *Jesus Christ Liberator*, p. 55; cf. p. 105.

99. Boff, *Jesus Christ Liberator*, pp. 63-79.

100. Boff, *Jesus Christ Liberator*, pp. 100-120 (120).

101. A. Fierro, *The Militant Gospel: An Analysis of Contemporary Political Theologies* (trans. J. Drury; London: SCM Press, 1977), p. 328, Spanish orig. *El evangelio beligerante* (Estella, Navarra: Editorial Verbo Divino, 1974).

102. Segundo, *The Liberation of Theology*, p. 5.

the service of the poor leads to theological priorities that compromise the scholarly integrity of their interpretation of the Bible.

This question will be discussed below but before doing so it is important to question which level of liberation theology such criticism is aimed at. It is easier to criticize the contribution of scholarship to liberation theology *if the criticism is directed at the popular level.* However, the critic should recognize that the same can be said of any theological method or application of scholarship that moves away from specialist academic circles to a wider audience. Even if such criticisms could be substantiated, and the discussion below will suggest that matters are not always as straightforward as they seem, it can hardly be right to make this the basis for rejecting liberation hermeneutics in its entirety. The whole notion of the three levels to liberating hermeneutics—professional, pastoral and popular—rests on different degrees of specialist and scholarly training at each level. Therefore, in addition to considering the popular level, some attention will also have to be given to the work of Clodovis Boff who has clarified the theoretical foundations at the professional level.[103] However, although concentrating on the popular and professional levels focuses the hermeneutical issues most clearly, this should not be taken as suggesting that the pastoral level is less important. The popular and professional readings are held together by the pastoral dimension and the different levels should not be assessed in isolation.

It should also be remembered that the main proponents of liberation theology being referred to here are general theologians not biblical experts. Gutiérrez, Leonardo and Clodovis Boff, Sobrino and Segundo are at the 'professional' level but they are not specialists in New Testament studies.[104] For example, Gutiérrez makes extensive use of the New Testament but his purpose is always theological and there is rela-

---

103. This point is extensively elaborated in D. Regan, *Church for Liberation: A Pastoral Portrait of the Church in Brazil* (Leominster, Herefordshire: Fowler Wright Books, 1987). For an excellent example of Bible readings and discussion resources produced at the pastoral level, see the pastoral team of Bambamarca, *Vamos Caminando: A Peruvian Catechism* (trans J. Medcalf; London: SCM Press, 1985), Spanish orig. *Vamos caminando* (Lima: Centro de Estudios y Publicaciones, 1977). See also the Bible readings and mediations of the Brazilian Bishop Dom Hélder Câmara, *Through the Gospel with Dom Helder Camara* (trans. A. Neame; Maryknoll, NY: Orbis Books; London: Darton, Longman & Todd, 1986).

104. This point is well made by Watson, 'Liberating the Reader', p. 58.

tively little sustained and detailed exegesis in his main works.[105] Professional biblical exegetes committed to liberation theology do exist in Latin America, and include J. Severino Croatto, Jorge Pixley and Elsa Tamez; however, much of their work focuses on the Old Testament.[106]

a. *The Popular Level: Reading the Gospel in Base Communities*

The differences in theological priorities between liberation theologians and other academic approaches to the Bible emerge clearly from the work of Carlos Mesters, a Dutch Carmelite, who has worked extensively with base communities in Brazil. Mesters makes explicit the theological priorities when the Bible is read in the base communities:

> The Bible is read and studied in order to know better the present situation and the calls from God that exist in it. The ultimate aim of the people's use of the Bible *is not so much to interpret the Bible, but to interpret their lives.*[107] [emphasis original]

For Mesters the role of the Bible in the communities is as a 'Mirror of Life'. When the people discuss a text they also discuss their own situation. The story of the people of God in the Bible is a mirror for looking at their story in history.[108] Mesters argues that the people's approach is justified because the Bible's importance to life should take precedence over academic studies that are not orientated to application:

> Finally, the common people are putting the Bible in its proper place, the place where God intended it to be. They are putting it in second place. Life

---

105. Even Gutiérrez's treatment of Job, his most sustained treatment of a biblical book, gives priority to theological questions over textual issues. See G. Gutiérrez, *On Job: God-Talk and the Suffering of the Innocent* (trans. M. O'Connell; Maryknoll, NY: Orbis Books, 1987), Spanish orig. *Hablar de Dios desde el sufrimiento del inocente* (Lima: Centro de Estudios y Publicaciones, 1986).

106. For example, E. Tamez, *Bible of the Oppressed*; J.S. Croatto, *Exodus: A Hermeneutics of Freedom* (Maryknoll, NY: Orbis Books, 1981); J. Pixley, *On Exodus: A Liberation Perspective* (Maryknoll, NY: Orbis Books, 1987).

107. C. Mesters, *Defenseless Flower: A New Reading of the Bible* (Maryknoll, NY: Orbis Books, 1989), p. 71, Portuguese orig. *Flor sem defesa: Uma expliçcaão da biblia a partir do povo* (Petrópolis: Editora Vozes, 1983).

108. Mesters, *Defenseless Flower*, p. 2; cf. p. 70: 'In the people's eyes the Bible and life are connected. When they open the Bible they want to find in it things directly related to their lives, and in their lives they want to find events and meanings that parallel those in the Bible. Spontaneously they use the Bible as an image, symbol, or mirror of what is happening to them here and now'.

takes first place! In so doing, the people are showing us the enormous
importance of the Bible and, at the same time, its relative value—relative to
life.[109]

For Mesters the relative value given to traditional biblical scholarship is
something to rejoice at rather than regret. He does not see this as a
negation of the academic disciplines in biblical study but a recognition
that biblical interpretation demands more than academic study.
Authentic interpretation of the Bible primarily means engaging with the
people in interpreting the real life issues they are facing and not studying
the text solely for scholarly interest.

Mesters argues that the exegete needs to do more than study the text
if they are to read the Bible properly in Brazil. Mesters identifies three
forces which come into operation when the Bible is read in the base
communities:

> Life, science, and faith. People, exegesis, and church. Three forces in con-
> stant tension, each with its defenders, attempting in its own way to make its
> contribution to the correct use of the Bible in the church. [110]

These three forces are mixed together for mutual interference and
illumination.[111] The people are not expected to accept the specialist contributions of academic exegesis as passive recipients of a higher learning.
The contribution of expertise is in both directions. The community contribute expertise and insights derived from their experiences to challenge
the way in which the professional theologian interprets the Bible. Rather
than being a threat to the academic integrity of biblical study, this two-
way process is a valuable balance and guide for it.

Applying the Bible to life in this way can open the door to popular
misinterpretation. Specialists in biblical studies have an essential role in
using their knowledge to guide the community's discussion. Mesters
recognizes that the people's contribution is far from infallible. For
example, there is a danger in oversimplifying historical issues if historical
criticism is entirely ignored. The connections that the people make
between the Bible and their own community may be arbitrary, and have
no real basis in either the Bible or in their own lives, or oversimplify
deep and complex dynamics.

---

109. C. Mesters in Torres and Eagleson (eds.), *The Challenge of Basic Christian
Communities*, p. 209; cf. Mesters, *Defenseless Flower*, pp. 5-10.
110. Mesters, *Defenseless Flower*, p. 107.
111. Mesters, *Defenseless Flower*, pp. 106-11.

Mesters argues that when used properly biblical criticism can free the reader from the fundamentalist 'prison of the letter'. However, concern for historicity does not and should not come first for the people of the communities. Mesters turns the tables on the critics and argues that it is they who are in danger of oversimplifying the complexity of the issues. Although historical questions are important in freeing the Bible from the chains of fundamentalist literalism there is a danger that giving too much weight to historical enquiries will create a new prison of 'historicism'.

Mesters claims that at the popular level the community intuitively take a way between these opposite dangers by interpreting the text in a symbolic way that is neither fundamentalist nor historicist. In defence of their approach he argues that 'a symbolic explanation of the facts is not always the product of a naive, uncritical, or prescientific under-standing'.[112] The people follow their own priorities: 'They try to be faithful, not primarily to the meaning the text has in itself (the historical and literal meaning), but to the meaning they discover in the text for their own lives'.[113] Historical concerns for the original meaning of the text develop as the people reflect on and examine what they understand the Bible is saying for their lives and struggles.[114] The people's reading is therefore always an unfinished interpretation. Understanding is provisional on further experiences and remains open to revision in response to theological scholarship. Thus for all its imperfections and potential dangers Mesters insists on the legitimacy of the people's reading.[115]

Despite the undoubted achievements of the scholarly tradition the religiously learned have never had a monopoly on religious truth. Mesters points to the conflicts that were provoked when Jesus took the Scriptures away from the experts of his day and started to interpret them in a new way.[116] Jesus did not conduct theology or biblical studies in an academic institution but through a passionate engagement with the real life issues of first-century Palestine. Liberation theologians would

112.   Mesters, *Defenseless Flower*, p. 6.
113.   Mesters, *Defenseless Flower*, p. 9.
114.   Mesters, *Defenseless Flower*, p. 9.
115.   Mesters, *Defenseless Flower*, p. 71.
116.   Mesters, *Defenseless Flower*, pp. 8-9; cf. Segundo's claim (*The Liberation of Theology*, p. 82) that in the New Testament: 'It is an historical fact that the people who were *best informed about God's revelation in the Old Testament* let Jesus pass by and failed to see in him the new and definitive divine revelation. The Christian message has come down to us through the *amaretz* of Israel, that is, the people who were less knowledgeable about the law and its interpretation' [emphasis original].

argue that detachment from worldly concerns is a more serious error than involvement with social issues and political struggles.[117]

Mesters criticizes academic exegesis for losing its sense of serving those who strive to live in faith. Whereas academic scholarship was once a radical challenge to the dogmatic use of the Bible he argues that it has now lost its radical edge:

> Academic exegesis no longer has the courage it had in the first half of this century, when, with excellent results, it criticized the overly dogmatic use of the Bible in the church. Today it no longer has the same courage to see and criticize the overly dogmatic use of the Bible, both inside and outside the church.[118]

For Mesters, the scholarly work of the exegete is not determined by the norms of academia but is guided by the concerns of the communities and the contributions of the people. If liberation hermeneutics fails according to traditional academic standards then conversely these traditional academic standards fail according to the basic principles of liberation theology. Liberation theologians press those who interpret the Bible to choose the values that are most important in Latin America.

b. *The Professional Level: Theory and Practice*
Liberation theology certainly poses important questions as to what is most important in the study of the Bible. However, traditional biblical scholars might still insist that the traditional biblical disciplines remain a necessary element in any hermeneutical approach. If liberation theology does pay inadequate attention to historical scholarship it runs the danger of constructing interpretations of the New Testament with little basis in the text or in history. As indicated above, it is the role of the professional theologian or exegete to provide scholarly guidance and correct misinterpretations which are likely to arise at the popular level. For criticisms of liberation theology to have real force they would need to demonstrate that this professional guidance is either flawed or ineffectual. Criticisms would carry much more weight if they could show that even at the professional level its theological method is historically naive and fails to appreciate the historical challenges required in New Testament study.

---

117. Segundo (*The Liberation of Theology*, p. 81) puts it bluntly: 'Indeed Jesus seems to go so far as to suggest that one cannot recognize Christ, and therefore come to know God, unless he or she is willing to start with a personal commitment to the oppressed'.

118. Mesters, *Defenseless Flower*, p. 158.

There have certainly been criticisms of how the historical method has been applied in some treatments of the gospel by liberation theologians.[119] However, although such criticisms of imperfect practice are noteworthy they do not settle the more important question of whether the methodological approach is flawed in principle. On this more fundamental point, Clodovis Boff, in his book *Theology and Praxis: Epistemological Foundations*, seeks to articulate and defend the methodological foundations on which the hermeneutics of liberation rest.[120]

Boff cautions against simplistic attempts to equate a direct 'correspondence of terms' between the situation of oppressed people in biblical times and the oppressed people of Latin America today. For example, he challenges the claim that the relationship between the contemporary Christian community and the current political context is identical to the relationship between Jesus and his political context. Boff describes as 'problematic and vulnerable in the extreme' any simple links between: Roman power and imperialism; the Sadducees' power and the power of the dependent bourgeoisies; the Zealots and revolutionaries; the Jewish people and oppressed peoples; Jesus and Christians.[121] The contemporary community cannot simplistically read off easy answers from what Jesus said and did in his context and transfer them directly to current situations. The potential differences in context must be recognized and their significance appreciated.

Since there can be no straightforward equations between now and then Boff argues instead for an indirect link through a 'correspondence of relationships'. The Jesus of the Gospels has to be understood with reference to the political context of the time, just as the contemporary community must understand itself with reference to its current context. Links between the text and community's situation should only be attempted after both the text and the community have been related to their own respective contexts. Boff calls this a 'relationship of relationships' because it is concerned first with how each relates to its own context and then with the relationship of these relationships. In

119. For discussion of Boff, Sobrino and Segundo in these terms, see McGovern, *Liberation Theology and its Critics*, pp. 73-82.

120. Boff, *Theology and Praxis*, esp. pp. 132-53.

121. Boff, *Theology and Praxis*, p. 145. See esp. the dramatic art work in P. Scharper and S. Scharper (eds.), *The Gospel in Art by the Peasants of Solentiname* (Maryknoll, NY: Orbis Books; Dublin: Gill and Macmillan, 1984).

some cases the relationships might be quite similar; on other matters there may be important differences. However, the closeness of the relationship cannot be settled *a priori* and the contemporary community cannot just assume that it shares the same context as the Jesus of the Gospels. The crucial challenge is not to try to do as Jesus did (since this rests on the contexts being the same) but to try to relate to the contemporary context as Jesus related to his (since this allows the contexts to be different).[122] Boff explains the significance of this change of focus:

> We need not, then look for formulas to 'copy', or techniques to 'apply', from scripture. What scripture will offer us are rather something like orientations, models, types, directives, principles, inspirations—elements permitting us to acquire, on our own initiative, a 'hermeneutic competency', and thus the capacity to judge—on our own initiative, in our own right— 'according to the mind of Christ', or 'according to the Spirit', the new, unpredictable situations with which we are continually confronted. The Christian writings offer us not a *what*, but a *how*—a manner, a style, a spirit.[123]

Boff suggests that following this course will provide a middle way between 'hermeneutic positivism' in which the meaning is too narrowly defined and 'improvisation *ad libitum*' in which there is a surfeit of meanings.[124]

The role of the exegete is to develop prowess and skill to guide this process during the hermeneutical mediation just as the social analyst should contribute expertise during the socio-analytic mediation. This is the place for the other hermeneutical approaches discussed in the chapters of this volume. The exegete draws upon them to open up the original meaning of the text in the past and its current meaning in the present. However, these different disciplines are not primarily valued in their own right, but for their contribution to the hermeneutics of liberation.

5. *Challenging Bias*

The relevance of liberation theology for New Testament studies has been the subject of fierce debate.[125] In support, some welcome it as a forceful

---

122. Boff (*Theology and Praxis*, p. 146) suggests that this more sophisticated model is also suggested by the hermeneutic practice of the primitive church.
123. Boff, *Theology and Praxis*, p. 149.
124. Boff, *Theology and Praxis*, pp. 149-53.
125. For an overview discussion on the use of the Bible in liberation theology,

and relevant restatement of the gospel and warmly acknowledge the new perspectives that the hermeneutics of liberation open up on biblical texts.[126] In opposition, others argue that its presentation of the gospel manipulates the biblical material for its own ends and presents a distorted and inappropriately politicized Christ. A particular focus of critics' concern is whether liberation theologians derive their fundamental themes from the Gospels themselves or whether they are taken from secular thought, political ideologies or social activism.

Assessing this criticism is particularly difficult because liberation theology demands understanding on its own terms. Liberation theology raises the whole question of how any theological judgments should be made and which criteria should be used. Liberation theologians argue that theology needs to be liberated from many of the traditional values and attitudes which have constrained it. Judgments on liberation theology's contribution to New Testament studies may ultimately rest on judgments on alternative visions of what New Testament study is intended to achieve. At the heart of the disagreement is the fact that liberation theologians commit themselves to the bias involved in the preferential option for the poor. Critics of liberation theology wish to challenge liberation theology's bias whereas for liberation theologians the bias is essential and intended to be challenging.

In this section two aspects of this debate will be explored: first, that in its reading of the Bible liberation theology in effect reduces Christianity to Marxism; and secondly, that liberation theology offers a selective and subjective reading in contrast to the objective approach that is expected to distinguish scholarly enquiry.

a. *Gospel and Ideology*
The political nature of the liberation approach has provoked considerable criticism from different quarters.[127] Since its early success in enlisting official support at Medellín liberation theology has been subjected to

---

see McGovern, *Liberation Theology and its Critics*, pp. 62-82; cf. *idem*, 'The Bible in Liberation Theology', in N.K. Gottwald (ed.), *The Bible and Liberation: Political and Social Hermeneutics* (Maryknoll, NY: Orbis Books, 1989).

126. An excellent example is C. Rowland and M. Corner, *Liberating Exegesis: The Challenge of Liberation Theology to Biblical Studies* (Biblical Foundations in Theology; London: SPCK, 1990).

127. For a sustained critique at a political level, see M. Novak, *Will it Liberate?* (Mahwah, NJ: Paulist Press, 1986).

hostile reactions from powerful sectors in the Latin American church hierarchy.[128] The Vatican has also shown a keen interest in the work of some of the leading liberation theologians and their alleged Marxist sympathies.[129] John Paul II's experience of the Church's opposition to state socialism in Poland is a powerful factor in his suspicions about Latin America. The Pope's visit to Nicaragua in 1983 and his clash with the four priests who had taken government posts under the Sandinistas contributed to an increasingly hostile attitude to liberation theology from within the Vatican.[130] As a result of this hardening in official attitude Cardinal Ratzinger, Prefect of the Congregation for the Doctrine of Faith, prepared an 'Instruction on Certain Aspects of the "Theology of Liberation"' intended to bring liberation theologians into line with ecclesial authority.[131]

It is noticeable that some passages in the 'Instruction' read as if they might have been written by liberation theologians themselves, for example:

> The Gospel of Jesus Christ is a message of freedom and a force for liberation. In recent years this essential truth has become the object of reflection for theologians, with a new kind of attention which is itself full of promise.[132]

128.   In the Latin American Church the conservative opponent of liberation theology, Alfonso López Trujillo, was elected secretary-general of CELAM in November 1972, at a meeting in Sucre, Bolivia. Together with the Belgian Jesuit, Roger Vekemans, he set up a new conservative periodical, *Tierra Nueva* (Bogota), which has maintained a steady stream of fiercely critical articles. Gutiérrez (*The Power of the Poor in History*, p. 214 n. 1) claims that 'the periodical reshuffles its arguments with dogged tenacity'.

129.   For discussion of the tensions between the Vatican and Latin American Church over liberation theology, see P. Lernoux, *People of God: The Struggle for World Catholicism* (New York: Viking, 1989).

130.   See Hennelly (ed.), *Liberation Theology*, pp. 318-47; Bradstock, *Saints and Sandinistas*, pp. 59-69.

131.   See McGovern, *Liberation Theology and its Critics*, pp. 15-19.

132.   Congregation for the Doctrine of Faith (Cardinal J. Ratzinger), 'Instruction on Certain Aspects of the Theology of Liberation' (Vatican City: 1984), § Introduction; republished in *Origins* 14 (13 September 1984) and Hennelly (ed.), *Liberation Theology*, pp. 393-414. The full text and a detailed response are given in J.L. Segundo, *Theology and the Church: A Response to Cardinal Ratzinger and a Warning to the Whole Church* (trans. J. Diercksmeier; Minneapolis, MN: Winston Press; London: Geoffrey Chapman, 1985).

However, despite taking over the language of liberation in some regards the 'Instruction' is a fierce attack on liberation theology.[133] Thus the 'Instruction' moves quickly from commendation to condemnation on the issue of Marxism:

> But the 'theologies of liberation', which deserve credit for restoring to a place of honour the great texts of the prophets and of the Gospel in the defence of the poor, go on to make a disastrous confusion between the poor of the scripture and the proletariat of Marx.[134]

Essentially liberation theology stands accused on two grounds. First, that it is wrongly committed to the idea of class conflict and the necessity of violence as presented in Marxist social analysis.[135] Secondly, that in accepting ideas from Marxist social analysis liberation theology mistakenly commits itself to an atheistic philosophy and 'a reductionist reading of the Bible'.[136]

One figure in liberation theology for whom the second criticism might have some basis is the Mexican José Porfirio Miranda. In his early and influential work *Marx and the Bible*, Miranda argued strongly that 'to a great degree Marx coincides with the Bible'.[137] Equally provocatively he wrote in *The Bible and Communism*:

> for a Christian to claim to be anticommunist... without doubt constitutes the greatest scandal of our century... The notion of communism is in the New Testament, right down to the letter—and so well put that in the twenty centuries since it was written no one has come up with a better definition of communism than Luke in Acts 2.44-45 and 4.32-35.[138]

133. Segundo (*The Liberation of Theology*, p. 4) warned of this danger back in the early 1970s: 'ecclesiastical authorities themselves have adopted the terminology of liberation. Gradually this has led to a watering down of its content, so that language of liberation is emptied of all real meaning'.

134. 'Instruction' (§9.10). This criticism had already been made by Ratzinger in an article in the Italian magazine *30 Giorno* reprinted as J. Ratzinger, 'Liberation Theology', in Hennelly (ed.), *Liberation Theology*, pp. 367-74.

135. In particular it is claimed ('Instruction', §10.1) that liberation theology has adopted *a priori* a classist viewpoint 'which has come to function as a determining principle.

136. 'Instruction', §10.5.

137. Miranda, *Marx and the Bible*, p. xvii.

138. J.P. Miranda, *Communism in the Bible* (trans. R. Barr; Maryknoll, NY: Orbis Books, 1982), pp. 1-2, Spanish orig. *Comunismo en la Biblia* (Mexico City: Siglo Veintiuno Editores, 1981).

Such claims are clearly designed to be startling and it is hardly surprising that they have stirred opposition. However, it has been pointed out that Miranda's main point in *Marx and the Bible* is to emphasize the biblical concern for justice. His highly individualistic use of Marxist concepts and a Marxist framework for this task can hardly be described as 'uncritical' Marxism. His subsequent work *Marx against the Marxists*, a sustained attack on common Marxist beliefs, makes clear that he is anything but an orthodox Marxist. Quite apart from this, Miranda's position is far from typical amongst liberation theologians.[139]

The 'Instruction' does not name any particular theologian but there is little doubt that it does not restrict itself to Miranda, and that both Gustavo Gutiérrez and Leonardo Boff were included in its intended target. However, in contrast to Miranda's work, the attitude to Marxism in the works of Gutiérrez and Boff is much more complex.[140] For example, Gutiérrez's early writings make extensive reference to Marxist thought, particularly the French Marxist Althusser and the Peruvian José Mariátegui, but he sees them at the service of liberation theology rather than vice-versa. Marxism is not used because of an uncritical allegiance to its philosophy. It is only drawn upon when its analysis serves the cause of the poor by illuminating the real causes of their oppression.[141] Míguez Bonino describes the social analysis of Gutiérrez's *A Theology of Liberation* as 'avowedly Marxist' but makes clear that this is by no

139. See J.P. Miranda, *Marx against the Marxists: The Christian Humanism of Karl Marx* (trans. J. Drury; Maryknoll, NY: Orbis Books; London: SCM Press, 1980), Spanish orig. El cristianismo de Marx (Mexico City: Siglo Veintiuno Editores, 1978). One commentator has argued that the relative absence of Marxist influence is actually liberation theology's greatest failing! See A. Kee, *Marxism and the Failure of Liberation Theology* (London: SCM Press, 1990).

140. For Boff's response, originally printed in the Brazilian newspaper *Folha de São Paulo*, see 'Vatican Instruction Reflects European Mind-Set' in LADOC 15 (January–February 1985); reprinted in Hennelly (ed.), *Liberation Theology*, pp. 415-18. Gutiérrez's response, in an interview with the Peruvian newspaper *La República*, is also translated in LADOC 15 (January–February 1985) and reprinted in Hennelly (ed.), *Liberation Theology*, pp. 419-24. Gutiérrez responds further to the 'Instruction' in 'The Truth Shall Make You Free', in Gutiérrez, *The Truth Shall Make You Free: Confrontations* (trans. M. O'Connell; Maryknoll, NY: Orbis, 1990), pp. 85-200, Spanish orig. *La verdad los hará libres: Confrontationes* (Lima: Centro de Estudios y Publicaciones, 1986).

141. Gutiérrez's essay 'Theology and the Social Sciences', in his *The Truth Shall Make You Free* (pp. 53-84), offers an extensive discussion of the role of social analysis in general and Marxism in particular.

means an uncritical acceptance of a dogmatic Marxist worldview but a selective use of certain Marxist ideas.[142] Likewise, it is true that the Marxist model of dialectical social science is given an important place in the social science perspectives that are referred to by the Boffs.[143] Nonetheless references to Marx or Marxist ideas are virtually non-existent in Boff's work.

This chapter cannot be the place for a systematic assessment of the relationship between liberation theology and Marxism.[144] However, it is at least possible to summarize the differences of opinion. For critics, liberation theology's sympathy for at least some aspects of Marxist social analysis is a serious flaw in its approach. For supporters of liberation theology, the commitment to Marxist analysis is not in itself a flaw although particular uses of it might be. They deny that liberation theology reduces the gospel to Marxism and claim that the gospel takes clear priority over any Marxist elements in their theology. Perhaps the most crucial issue of dispute is whether Marxist ideas can help theologians in the task of social analysis (as liberation theology claims) without entailing determinism, atheism and other aspects of Marxist philosophy (as the Vatican fear).

It should be said that the influence of Marxism is strongest in the earlier works of liberation theologians, published in the early 1970s, and it has been given much less attention in subsequent works. This is partly because other concerns of liberation theology, in particular new perspectives on Latin America's spirituality and cultural heritage, have received more attention.[145] Nevertheless a clear resolution to the controversy between the Vatican and the liberation theologians remains some way off and the role of Marxism remains a highly sensitive issue. The silencing of Leonardo Boff (May 1985–March 1986) created considerable tension between the Vatican and the Brazilian Church and although there have since been signs of movement to greater understanding on both sides there is also evidence of ongoing and deep-seated

142. Míguez Bonino, *Doing Theology in a Revolutionary Situation*, p. 71.

143. L. and C. Boff, *Introducing Liberation Theology*, p. 28.

144. See A.F. McGovern, *Marxism: An American Christian Perspective* (Maryknoll, NY: Orbis Books, 1980).

145. G. Gutiérrez, *We Drink from our Own Wells: The Spiritual Journey of a People* (trans. M. O'Connell; Maryknoll, NY: Orbis Books; London: SCM Press, 1984), Spanish orig. *Beber en su propio pozo: En el itinerario de un pueblo* (Lima: Centro de Estudios y Publicaciones, 1983).

mutual suspicion.[146] A second 'Instruction' dealing with the more positive aspects of liberation theology was published in 1986 and at the same time the Pope sent a warm letter to the Brazilian Bishops.[147] However, relations with the Vatican continued to be difficult for both Boff and Gutiérrez and eventually Boff left his Religious Order, the Franciscans, and resigned his priesthood in June 1992.[148]

b. *Commitment and Neutrality*

Liberation theologians have been accused of subjectively 'reading into the Gospels' the prior convictions that they hold. However, the notions of objectivity and subjectivity are notoriously difficult and nowhere more so than in issues relating to religious faith and politics. In their reading of the Bible God is not seen as being neutral but as opting to take the side of the poor.[149] Liberation theologians claim that God took on the cause of the poor and oppressed in Jesus. Those who wish to read the New Testament in an authentic theological way are called upon to make the same commitment themselves.

When criticized for the self-confessed bias in the preferential option for the poor, liberation theologians are quick to reply that neutrality is a spurious ideal for a Christian theologian or biblical scholar.[150] Any suggestion that other approaches to the New Testament do not have their own biases is highly contentious. Liberation theologians argue that traditionally Christianity has furthered the interests of the ruling powers. In some instances this support has been direct and deliberate, for example the religious sanction that the Church gave to the conquistadors. In many other instances the influence may be unintentional and

---

146. See H. Cox, *The Silencing of Leonardo Boff: The Vatican and the Future of World Christianity* (Oak Park, IL: Meyer-Stone Books, 1988; London: Collins, 1989).

147. Congregation for the Doctrine of the Faith (J. Ratzinger), *Instruction on Christian Freedom and Liberation* (Vatican City: Libreria Editrice Vaticana, 1986); John Paul II, 'Letter to the Brazilian Bishops, 1986', published in part in *National Catholic Reporter*, 9 May 1986.

148. Boff's letter explaining his decision was printed in *The Tablet* (11 July 1992), pp. 882-83.

149. See Pixley and Boff, *The Bible, the Church and the Poor*, p. 237.

150. Segundo (*Historical Jesus of the Synoptics*, p. 40) points out that interpretation is unavoidable in any use of the Bible: 'we are indulging in sheer illusion if we pretend that we can go to the canonical Gospels and find an uninterpreted Jesus there'.

indirect. For example, one of the reasons that the authenticity of liberationist readings is not always discerned by readers of the New Testament is that translations have not always been helpful in making them clear. Pixley and Boff describe the legitimation of the *status quo* given by the choice of words used in translations of biblical texts. They claim that modern translations have nullified harsh meanings. For example, in Isa. 57.15 the word *dakka'* is rendered as 'contrite/humbled', when its meaning is 'downtrodden/oppressed'.[151]

For liberation theologians it is not so much a matter of theology *taking sides* as theology *changing sides*. They argue that theology has never been neutral and that approaches that try to separate themselves from political issues fail to challenge the *status quo*. Far from being neutral such approaches serve the established powers and mitigate against change. At a political level they are therefore conservative. Liberation theologians charge that in the face of the overwhelming injustices of Latin America such 'neutral' disengagement cannot be a choice for Christian theologians who are committed to proclaiming the Good News and contributing towards the kingdom of God. Hugo Assmann writes:

> If the historical situation of dependence and domination of two-thirds of humanity, with its thirty million deaths per year from hunger and malnutrition, does not now become the starting point for any Christian theology, in the rich and dominant countries as well, theology will no longer be able to locate and give specific historical expression to its basic themes... For this reason 'it is necessary to save the church from its cynicism'.[152]

As was suggested above the challenge of liberation theology is not just its message but its method. It is no coincidence that Gutiérrez's *A Theology of Liberation* was soon followed by Segundo's *The Liberation of Theology*. The gospel of liberation (relating to *message*) goes

---

151. Pixley and Boff (*The Bible, the Church and the Poor*, p. 249 n. 5) comment: 'The version [of Isa. 57.15] given here is an adaptation of the NEB, whose version of the last two lines—"to revive the spirit of the humble, to revive the courage of the broken"—is an example of what the author is complaining of, but not as bad as the JB's: "to give the humbled spirit new life, to revive contrite hearts". The problem of modern translations dodging references to oppression in this way is very general. The *Biblia Latinoamericana*, of which an English version, *The Christian Community Bible*, is now available, redresses this tendency, more positively in the Spanish than in the English'.

152. Assmann, *Theology for a Nomad Church*, pp. 37-38, cited in Gibellini, *The Liberation Theology Debate*, p. 4.

hand in hand with the liberation of the gospel (relating to *method*). If the methodological challenges of liberation theology are taken seriously they raise great difficulties for anyone trying to assess liberation theology from an uncommitted standpoint.[153] For Gutiérrez, the commitment to liberation is essential to understanding the gospel.[154] For many western scholars this is precisely the problem. Gutiérrez sets out the precondition for an informed understanding of liberation theology when he says 'Apart from this relationship to practice, the theology of liberation is incomprehensible'.[155] However, it is the commitment to liberation and the circular reasoning based upon it that is the contentious issue.

The importance of the gap that exists between the liberation theologians and their critics should not be underestimated. For the Boffs a new type of theological 'training' is required.[156] On the one side liberation theologians might agree with the Boffs that:

> From all this, it follows that if we are to understand the theology of libera-
> tion, we must first understand and take an active part in the real and
> historical process of liberating the oppressed. In this field, more than in
> others, it is vital to move beyond a merely intellectual approach that is
> content with comprehending a theology through its purely theoretical
> aspects, by reading articles, attending conferences, and skimming through
> books. We have to work our way into a more biblical framework of refer-
> ence, where 'knowing' implies loving, letting oneself become involved
> body and soul, communing wholly—being committed, in a word— as the
> prophet Jeremiah says: 'He used to examine the cases of the poor and
> needy, then all went well. Is not that what it means to know me?—it is
> Yahweh who speaks' (Jer. 22.16). So the criticisms made of liberation
> theology by those who judge it at a purely conceptual level, devoid of any
> real commitment to the oppressed, must be seen as radically irrelevant.[157]

153. As Segundo (*The Liberation of Theology*, p. 81) writes: 'we must ask the same question that has been asked by various Latin American theologians in recent days: Is it possible to know and recognize the liberation message of the Gospel at all without a prior commitment to liberation?'

154. Gutiérrez (*Theology of Liberation*, p. 269) writes: 'Only by participating in their [the people's] struggles can we understand the implications of the Gospel message…'

155. Gutiérrez, *The Power of the Poor in History*, p. 169.

156. The Boffs (*Introducing Liberation Theology*, p. 24) write: 'Anyone who wants to elaborate relevant liberation theology must be prepared to go into the "examination hall" of the poor. Only after sitting on the benches of the humble will he or she be entitled to enter a school of "higher learning"'.

157. L. and C. Boff, *Introducing Liberation Theology*, p. 9.

For critics this simply confirms the fundamentally flawed basis of liberationist claims to offer an authentic interpretation of the gospel. The commitment to the oppressed colours all other conclusions. According to the critics this highlights the weaknesses that they see in liberation theology's approach. But for liberation theologians it is an essential way forward in view of the situation in Latin America.

5. *Conclusion*

In the ongoing debate the commitment to liberation will remain a central issue of contention. It is significant that other perspectives on liberation have given rise to criticisms of Latin American liberation theology from a rather different direction. Black theologians from North America and South Africa have challenged the Latin Americans to take seriously issues of race and ethnicity, especially in countries like Brazil. Theologians from elsewhere in the Third World have raised the distinctive concerns of Africa or Asia to challenge theologians in Latin America to extend their theological awareness. Debates over the relationship of Christianity with other religions in Asia and the relationship with indigenous cultures in Africa have stimulated similar discussion amongst Latin Americans on the issues in general and their implications for indigenous American traditions in particular.[158] Feminist theologians have challenged the largely male-dominated proponents of Latin American liberation theology to enlarge their vision of liberation.[159]

Recognizing the wider understanding of oppression and liberation in these ways has contributed new dimensions to the hermeneutics of liberation.[160] Drawing the new challenges together has created many of the most creative developments in Latin American liberation theology. Elsa Tamez, the Costa Rican biblical scholar, has been foremost in this

158. See L. Boff, *Good News to the Poor: A New Evangelization* (trans. R. Barr; Maryknoll, NY: Orbis Books; Tunbridge Wells: Burns & Oates, 1992), pp. 95-114, Portuguese orig. *Nova evangelização: Perspectiva dos oprimidos* (Petrópolis: Editora Vozes, 1990).

159. See E. Tamez (ed.), *Through her Eyes: Women's Theology from Latin America* (Maryknoll, NY: Orbis Books, 1989), Spanish orig. *El rostro femenino de la teología* (San Jose: Editorial DEI, 1986).

160. Excellent collections are provided in R.S. Sugirtharajah (ed.), *Voices from the Margin: Interpreting the Bible in the Third World* (London: SPCK, 1991); U. King (ed.), *Feminist Theology from the Third World: A Reader* (London: SPCK, 1994), esp. pp. 183-242.

field. Tamez combines liberation theology with a feminist outlook and sensitivity to native Amerindian traditions.[161] She particularly criticizes the influence on Latin American society of 'machismo' and explores its significance for liberation theologians.[162]

Liberation theology offers a powerful challenge to traditional scholarly approaches to New Testament study. Its hermeneutical principles have been the subject of lively debate and particular questions have been put as to whether it can be taken seriously as an academic discipline, whether it can claim scholarly objectivity and whether it is historically naive in its treatment of the New Testament world. The purpose of this chapter has been to introduce the key elements in the controversy and to suggest that at the heart of the matter is liberation theology's commitment to the poor and oppressed. At one level the criticisms raised in this chapter have considerable force but at a different, and perhaps deeper, level liberation theologians can argue that this is because they do not share with their critics the same theological priorities.

Liberation theologians claim that their approach did not arise in response to intellectual questions or scholarly debates on hermeneutical method in western academia but 'was born when faith confronted the injustice done to the poor'.[163] The self-proclaimed bias of liberating hermeneutics is at the root of much of the debate. Liberation theologians insist that any assessment of their position must recognize and do justice to their bias to the poor; critics see the presupposed bias to the poor as responsible for many of the problems.

In arguing their case liberation theologians like the Boffs take care to restrict their claims about liberation theology *to the Latin American context*. They accept that the liberation approach 'is not the only possible and legitimate reading of the Bible' and that the themes that speak to the poor 'may not be the most important themes in the Bible (in themselves), but they are the most relevant (to the poor in their situation of oppression)'.[164] However, this should not serve to minimize liberation theology's wider significance. Although nobody should expect

---

161. See esp. E. Tamez, 'The Power of the Naked', in *idem*, *Through her Eyes*, pp. 1-14.

162. E. Tamez, *Against Machismo: Interviews by Elsa Tamez* (trans. and ed. J. Eagleson; Oak Park, IL: Meyer-Stone Books, 1987), Spanish orig. *Teólogos de la liberación hablan sobre la mujer* (San Jose: Editorial DEI, 1986).

163. L. and C. Boff, *Introducing Liberation Theology*, p. 3.

164. L. and C. Boff, *Introducing Liberation Theology*, pp. 32-33.

hermeneutics of liberation to be directly transferable to situations elsewhere there can be no doubt that the issues raised by contemporary Latin American liberation theologies have a potentially universal relevance. For example, there is ongoing debate as to its validity and discussion of what such an approach would look like if it developed at grass roots level in countries like Britain.

During this century the centre of Christianity has moved inexorably south as the numbers of Christians in Africa, Asia and Latin America have continued to rise and the numbers in Europe and North America have fallen. The coming millennium is likely to dramatically increase the theological influence of the southern hemisphere. In future the contextual theologies developed in Lima and São Paulo may rival the traditional centres of theology in Europe and North America. Viewed from this perspective the current rise of third world liberation theologies may only be a taste of what is to come.

SURVIVING SCRIPTURE : DEVELOPING A FEMINIST HERMENEUTIC OF THE NEW TESTAMENT

Beverley Clack

1. *Introduction: Feminist Critical Interpretation and the Problem of the Bible*

'Caution! Could be dangerous to your health and survival.'[1]

So writes Elisabeth Schüssler Fiorenza when advising feminists of the dangers of reading the Bible. The Bible has been used by some readers to justify the suppression of women. For feminists who wish to express their spirituality through the Christian tradition, this presents a problem. How are the writings which form the source material of the Christian tradition to be interpreted? Christianity defines its boundaries by reference to the normative scriptural tradition. So, any feminist attempting to argue theologically must ground her position and ideas in the New Testament Scriptures which form the basis for the Christian faith.

When one considers the nature of these Scriptures, the acute problem facing feminists becomes clear. Scripture has been shaped by males in a patriarchal context. The canon has been established to support the concerns of the men who decided what was and what was not to be included. A scriptural religion views certain texts as the authoritative source for theological ideas. If new theological ideas are to be accepted as authoritative, they have to have some connection with the kind of ideas expressed by the biblical writers. Scripture is thus normative for theology. And the Christian Scriptures have been shaped and defined in a patriarchal context.

Feminists are committed to challenging and destroying patriarchy. Patriarchy literally means 'the rule of the fathers', but it is more

---

1.   E. Schüssler Fiorenza, 'The Will to Choose or to Reject: Continuing our Critical Work', in L. Russell (ed.), *Feminist Interpretation of the Bible* (Oxford: Basil Blackwell, 1985), pp. 125-36 (130).

specifically understood as the system which supports the idea that men represent the totality of what it is to be human. This is most obviously expressed in the claim that using the male generic pronoun is appropriate when talking of humanity as a whole. An account of theological language which uses exclusively male language for God accepts and legitimates this claim. The assumption seems to be that it is 'more natural' to use male pronouns and images when one talks of God, just as it is 'more natural' to use male gender language when talking of humanity. This connection between the male and God is viewed by feminists as no less than blasphemous, for the male is idolized to the point of being equated with God.[2] When feminists reject this account of human being, they are expressing their ethical commitment to liberation. All areas of human life and endeavour, including religious belief, are to be judged according to this *a priori* commitment. If a religious tradition or religious belief fails to concur with this fundamental commitment, that belief or tradition must be rejected.

So how have feminists approached the Scriptures? Not only have the Scriptures been formed within a patriarchal society, but these writings have also served to support a patriarchal view of human relationships. Mary Daly writes that 'The Judaic-Christian tradition has served to legitimate sexually imbalanced patriarchal society'.[3] If this is the case, there appear to be only two alternatives for feminists. The first requires the rejection of the Christian tradition as irredeemably patriarchal, a position advocated by writers such as Daphne Hampson.[4] Alternatively, some liberating feature of the Bible needs to be found which allows the biblical tradition to be viewed as offering a critique of all systems of oppression, including patriarchy.

The role played by the Bible in establishing and perpetuating patriarchy is at the heart of the issue for feminists. To what extent can a feminist be a Christian, *and* retain her integrity? This becomes more pressing when one considers two issues intimately connected to this question. First, if the Bible is in some sense normative for Christian belief, yet is itself the product of a patriarchal age, can a feminist who is also Christian use this document? Can Christianity be interpreted in such

---

2.   Cf. R. Ruether, *Sexism and God-Talk* (London: SCM Press, 1983), p. 23.

3.   'After the Death of God the Father: Women's Liberation and the Transformation of Christian Consciousness', in C. Christ and J. Plaskow (eds.), *Womanspirit Rising* (San Francisco: Harper & Row, 1979), p. 54.

4.   Cf. D. Hampson, *Theology and Feminism* (Oxford: Basil Blackwell, 1990).

a way that the impact of patriarchal forms and ideas is defused? Mary Daly shows the difficulty with attempting to 'de-patriarchalize' the text in an imaginary discussion that she has with her earlier Christian self in the 'post-Christian' introduction to *The Church and the Second Sex*:

> 'Professor Daly', I would say, 'don't you realise that the medium *is* the message? Don't you see that efforts of biblical scholars to re-interpret texts, even though they may be correct within a certain restricted perspective, cannot change the overwhelmingly patriarchal character of the biblical tradition? Moreover, this "modern" historical accuracy about details has often been associated with an apologetic zeal that overlooks patriarchal religion's function of legitimising patriarchy.'[5]

This issue of how texts inform and are informed by cultural presuppositions is vital. Can the Bible ever escape its patriarchal roots? Much depends upon an understanding of how texts are read; notably, how texts inform ideas. This issue will be addressed in the conclusion to this chapter.

The second point arises from this first concern. The Gospel accounts are written from a male perspective. This results in the silence (possibly the absence?) of women from the tradition as derived from the Bible. Schüssler Fiorenza illustrates this trend to great effect when she comments on the account of Christ's passion in Matthew's Gospel. Three people figure prominently in this account. Two—Judas and Peter—betray and deny Jesus. One—an unnamed woman—anoints him, thus showing that she has understood the significance of his ministry. Schüssler Fiorenza comments: 'The name of the betrayer is remembered, but the name of the faithful disciple is forgotten because she was a woman'.[6] Women are silent in Scripture or absent from the text. In many instances, women are defined purely in terms of their relationship to the men of the Christian story. Alternatively, they are defined in relation to male-defined models of femininity (so, virgin or whore). To what extent can a different understanding of woman be found in the biblical texts? In recent years, some feminists have turned to non-scriptural spiritual movements, such as Wicca or Goddess spirituality, feeling that the Bible cannot be reinterpreted to give full weight to the life and experience of women. One of the main issues to be considered in this

5. M. Daly, *The Church and the Second Sex* (New York: Harper & Row, 1975), pp. 21-22.

6. E. Schüssler Fiorenza, *In Memory of Her* (New York: Crossroad, 1983), p. xiii.

chapter concerns the extent to which a feminist interpretation of New Testament writings is possible or, moreover, adequate.

These, then, are the problems confronting a feminist as she approaches the Bible. How are the biblical sources to be used? In this chapter, I wish to offer an account of feminist hermeneutics which will focus upon the extent to which Daly's objection to such a methodology can be overcome. In order to do this, the exegetical approaches of two leading feminist scholars, Rosemary Radford Ruether and Elisabeth Schüssler Fiorenza, will be examined. Having considered the principles on which their approaches are based, their methods will be applied to specific New Testament texts. It will then be possible to determine the extent to which feminist exegesis can challenge those who, like Daly, deny that the biblical sources can be saved from sexism.

2. *Schüssler Fiorenza and Ruether: Developing a Feminist Hermeneutic*

a. *Elisabeth Schüssler Fiorenza*

At the heart of Schüssler Fiorenza's approach to the New Testament texts is an attempt to reclaim the Bible for women. Central to this attempt is her concern to give a voice to the women who are the silent witnesses of the Gospel story. Unlike Daly, she does not believe that women are absent from the Gospels and the development of the church as outlined in the New Testament. Rather, she believes that we can discern the shadowy presence of our foresisters in the New Testament texts. These women have been silenced by the writers of the tradition, but not erased. Schüssler Fiorenza's task is, in part, to give voice to their silence. This involves showing the connection between the androcentrism of the New Testament accounts of the ministry of Christ and the context in which these texts arose. Thus much of her work attempts to expose the way in which the patriarchal context of the early church influenced the formation of the Christian tradition. If biblical texts are to be understood correctly, they must be considered within the cultural context which shaped the ethos of the New Testament. Hence she writes of her task as moving 'from androcentric texts to their socio-historical context'.[7] It is not enough to consider biblical texts purely in terms of their content. The content must be placed within the context of the time at which these texts were written. And that involves confronting the

---

7. Schüssler Fiorenza, *In Memory of Her*, p. 29.

patriarchal bias of that particular time in history.

Schüssler Fiorenza does not attempt to deny the extent to which the biblical texts have been influenced and in many ways determined by patriarchy. However, she feels that the Bible can be read in such a way that, rather than legitimate and perpetuate ideals of male-domination, it actually provides a challenge to a hierarchical account of human relations. The Bible need not be read as a historical archetype for human relations, which is itself normative for any theological discussion. So, for example, when discussing the ordination of women, it is often stated that biblical evidence has to be provided to support the claim that women should be priests. Those opposed to such a move may argue that the Bible offers a picture of human relations which sees men and women as having different, divinely ordained roles. Schüssler Fiorenza sees such an application of Scripture as inappropriate. In contrast, she suggests that although the Bible offers a picture of the oppressive reality which is patriarchy, it also presents a critical review of the hierarchical ordering of human relations which is patriarchy. By considering the key position of the women around Christ, she believes that the biblical sources offer a radical 'prototype' for human relations. Women are affirmed, just as Christ affirmed these women.

Thus Schüssler Fiorenza's hermeneutic has a dual function. Initially, she is exposing the way in which Scripture has been used by the Church to support patriarchy. Once this connection has been revealed, she seeks to show how a different reading of Scripture, which places women at the centre of Christian life and theology, can be achieved. Intimately connected to this concern is the place that she believes any feminist hermeneutic must start from; and that is 'the advocacy stance for the oppressed'.[8] As Bonhoeffer exhorted his reader to see history from the standpoint of 'the outcast, the suspects, the maltreated, the powerless, the oppressed, the reviled',[9] so Schüssler Fiorenza applies this concern for the oppressed and marginalized in society to women. This principle forms the bedrock for her hermeneutic.

At the outset of her development of a hermeneutic, Schüssler Fiorenza is extremely critical of accepting unquestioningly the idea of 'biblical authority'. Indeed, she gives her feminist beliefs *a priori* status. Thus the touchstone for assessing any biblical passage lies with ascertaining the

8. Schüssler Fiorenza, *In Memory of Her*, p. 29.
9. D. Bonhoeffer, *Letters and Papers from Prison* (ed. E. Bethge; trans. R. Fuller, F. Clarke and J. Bowden; London: SCM Press, 1974), p. 17.

extent to which a text can be shown to support or undermine patriarchy.

In this way, Schüssler Fiorenza stresses the importance of placing texts in their wider context. How do the biblical texts relate to contemporary ideas? To what extent do readings of the Bible continue to legitimate patriarchy? Schüssler Fiorenza is radical in her solution to the way in which patriarchal biblical texts inform current theological ideas. She writes that 'patriarchal texts should not be allowed to remain in the lectionary but should be replaced by texts affirming the discipleship of equals'.[10] It is at this point that Schüssler Fiorenza is open to challenge by feminists such as Hampson and Daly who adopt a 'post-Christian' position. It could be claimed that by using Scripture in this way Schüssler Fiorenza is merely evading the real issue. A selective approach to Scripture may make the Bible more palatable for feminists who wish to remain Christian, but it ignores the problem of the way in which the Bible is used and interpreted within a scripturally defined religion. It could be claimed that the whole ethos offered by the Bible undermines the belief in the fundamental humanity of women.

Having established the critical nature of a feminist hermeneutic, Schüssler Fiorenza goes on to offer her ideas on how feminists can interpret the Christian message. She places great emphasis on the role of celebration and ritual as found in the context of 'Women-Church'. In such gatherings, women rewrite and reflect upon the biblical narrative, a process Schüssler Fiorenza calls 'celebrating our foresisters'.[11] While this element of Schüssler Fiorenza's thinking is clearly important, it is not altogether clear what she has in mind here. Her concern is to show how ideas of sisterhood and a sense of self-awareness are not negated or rejected in the New Testament.[12] But the extent to which this goal is attainable is debatable. Bearing in mind the 'silence' of women in the New Testament writings, some kind of reconstruction will be necessary, perhaps along the lines of Michéle Roberts's retelling of the story of Mary Magdalene.[13] But would this creative rewriting of a biblical narrative be compatible with New Testament exegesis? It could be argued that Schüssler Fiorenza has moved some way from what would normally be understood as the task of the biblical exegete.

10. Schüssler Fiorenza, 'The Will to Choose or to Reject', p. 132.
11. Schüssler Fiorenza, 'The Will to Choose or to Reject', p. 135.
12. Schüssler Fiorenza, 'The Will to Choose or to Reject', pp. 130-35.
13. M. Roberts, *The Wild Girl* (London: Minerva, 1991).

This somewhat selective approach to Scripture might lead to the objection that Schüssler Fiorenza is reading into the Bible elements which suit her own political agenda; in other words, she is shaping Scripture to suit her feminist concerns. In order to address this objection, it may prove valuable to consider ideas on the way in which texts are read. This issue will be considered in the conclusion to this chapter. At this stage, Schüssler Fiorenza's own response to this charge will suffice. She suggests that all approaches to the Bible will be limited to personal and individual responses to the material which is present in the disparate collection of writings known as Scripture. So she writes:

> Historical biblical studies, like historical studies in general, are a selective view of the past whose scope and meaning is limited not only by the extant sources and materials, but also by the interests and perspectives of the present.[14]

This is important. Schüssler Fiorenza is drawing the reader's attention to the way in which *all* readings of Scripture will to some degree be selective. Feminists are often accused of a selective approach to Scripture, but this fails to appreciate the extent to which all scholars speak out of the context in which they find themselves. The originality of feminists lies in the tacit acceptance that all scholarship reflects basic *a priori* concerns.

Schüssler Fiorenza is clearly concerned to develop a biblical hermeneutic which enables feminists to use the Bible as an appropriate source for authentic Christian theology, a source which does not itself undermine or compromise feminist ideals for justice. Her solution is to focus on critical analysis of the biblical text—in terms of its internal coherence and its relation to the wider social context of the time.

b. *Rosemary Radford Ruether*

A rather different approach is offered by Rosemary Radford Ruether. Ruether, like Schüssler Fiorenza, is a Christian as well as a feminist. However, Ruether's key concern when dealing with the Bible is not that of a biblical scholar. Her primary concern is with developing a feminist hermeneutic appropriate to the development and exposition of feminist theology. Thus her method is less concerned with reworking the biblical material and more concerned with identifying and applying biblical

---

14. Schüssler Fiorenza, *In Memory of Her*, p. xxii.

principles which can then be employed in the development of a feminist theology.

Ruether's theology reflects her primary feminist concern with social justice. As such, she identifies the key principle of *feminist* theology as the concern to affirm the full humanity of women. This has implications for the way in which she will approach the biblical material:

> The critical principle of feminist theology is the promotion of the full humanity of women. Whatever denies, diminishes, or distorts the full humanity of women is, therefore, appraised as not redemptive. Theologically speaking, whatever diminishes or denies the full humanity of women must be presumed not to reflect the authentic nature of things, or to be the message or work of an authentic redeemer or a community of redemption.[15]

Like Schüssler Fiorenza, Ruether recognizes the need to assess Scripture in the light of her *a priori* feminist ideals. She admits to a selective approach to Scripture—and with good cause. As with other theologians[16] she accepts the primacy of moral beliefs. Thus Ruether begins with an *a priori* notion of what constitutes the good—in this case, that which affirms the full humanity of women. She will then judge the biblical texts according to whether they cohere with this core feminist concern.

Ruether's idea of what constitutes the good is closely connected to the feminist concern to establish the full humanity of women, and her epistemology reflects this central belief. According to Ruether, women's experience forms both the content and the criteria for truth. Her hermeneutic reflects a woman-centred focus.

It is important at this stage to explore what Ruether means when she writes of 'experience'. Experience, used in this context, is a notoriously difficult concept to define. Ruether could be referring to individual experience, collective experience, the experiences of life or the experience of a particular social setting. In practice, Ruether defines experience in its widest possible sense: she sees religious experience, personal experience and our experience of the world and community as all interrelated. All these elements constitute the total experience of life. Experience viewed from a feminist perspective can be given an additional meaning. Any feminist interpretation of Scripture must bear in mind the way in which *women* experience the world. Although Ruether does not explore

15. Ruether, *Sexism and God-Talk*, p. 19.
16. Cf. S. Sutherland, *God, Jesus and Belief* (Oxford: Basil Blackwell, 1984), ch. 1.

explicitly the difference between talking generally of experience and specifically of women's experience, it is possible to suggest a way of defining women's experience of the world. The experience of oppression which forms the overarching context for women in a patriarchal society will influence the way in which women view the world. At the same time, the possibility of sisterhood, of connection with other women, is also present. When this phenomenon occurs, a way of breaking free from the oppression which is patriarchy becomes possible.

It could be argued that Ruether is offering a radical approach to biblical exegesis when she makes experience—and women's experience at that—the criterion for establishing truth. She denies that this is the case. Indeed, she exposes as false and misleading the idea that there could be a theology or a Scripture which did not reflect human experiences of life: 'What have been called the objective sources of theology, scripture and tradition, are themselves codified collective human experience'.[17] No attempt to talk of God, or religion, or human life can ever be purely objective. Feminist theology exposes as false the idea that theology could ever be objective in this way. The feminist approach is unique not in the sense that it starts with experience, but that it starts with *women's* experience. Ruether, in drawing our attention to an inappropriate view of theological praxis, is particularly helpful. Objectified truth is never that; rather it tends to reflect the concerns of those who interpret the texts and establish the normative beliefs of a tradition.

This observation leads Ruether to write of the 'hermeneutical circle'. Human experience, she claims, is both the beginning and the end for any attempt to reflect upon Scriptures. In other words, just as human experience itself gives rise to religious ideas, so human experience is used to reflect on these ideas with a view to making relevant previous religious insight for a new generation. Tradition stays alive when reflection on the key texts can speak to an individual's experience of life from generation to generation.[18]

Of course, this positive approach may also identify a potential problem. What if a tradition is so moulded in a patriarchal past that this circle merely succeeds in perpetuating patriarchy? This is the point that both

17. Ruether, *Sexism and God-Talk*, p. 12.

18. It might be interesting to explore the idea that this is one implication of an incarnational approach. Theology does not then deal with metaphysical speculations, but with the idea that humanity, thisworldliness, bodiliness have been affirmed in the person of Christ, proclaimed as the God in human flesh.

Daly and Hampson make in their critiques of Christianity. Any attempt to restate Christian doctrine will merely recommunicate the patriarchal context which defined first-century Christianity.[19] Ruether believes that such a pessimistic approach to the scriptural tradition is unjustified. Indeed, one of the implications of taking seriously the notion of 'experience' is that our own experience of contemporary life and values allows us to reflect upon and criticize biblical ideas which are out of step with modern moral sensitivities. So: 'Codified tradition both reaches back to roots in experience and is constantly renewed or discarded through the rest of experience'.[20] Ruether is not merely applying contemporary ethical ideals to the Bible. Within Scripture, she claims, it is possible to discern a 'biblical critical principle'.[21] The Bible contains passages which are critical of hierarchy, patriarchy and oppression. This self-critical approach she grounds in the prophetic writings and also the teachings of Christ. Thus Ruether believes that 'feminist readings of the Bible can discern a norm within Biblical faith by which the Biblical texts themselves can be criticized'.[22] It is not simply a case of submitting the Bible to the standards of our time; the Bible itself offers a critique of hierarchical trends still prevalent in our society.

Central to Ruether's approach is the application of texts which show this principle at work. A good example of this application is her exegesis of Isaiah 61. The first two verses of this chapter, according to Ruether, offer a challenge to nationalism. God is not viewed in purely tribal terms. Rather, God is described as liberator, the One who stands alongside the oppressed:

> He has sent me to bring good news to the oppressed,
> to bind up the brokenhearted,
> to proclaim liberty to the captives,
> and release to the prisoners... (Isa. 61.1 NRSV)

Such sentiments are juxtaposed with vv. 5-7. Here, Ruether discerns a strident nationalism which views foreigners as potential slaves. Their wealth is to be confiscated, and God is revealed as truly and totally the

19. Hampson's account (*Theology and Feminism*, ch. 1) sees Christianity as a historical faith, which must always appeal to its roots in the historical beginnings of the Christian faith, that is, in a patriarchal society.

20. Ruether, *Sexism and God-Talk*, p. 12.

21. R. Ruether, 'Feminist Interpretation: A Method of Correlation', in Russell (ed.), *Feminist Interpretation of the Bible*, pp. 111-24 (117).

22. Ruether, *Sexism and God-Talk*, p. 23.

Approaches to New Testament Study

God of Israel. Ruether sees vv. 1-2 as offering a critique of such nationalism and offering a new way of seeing God.

These words from Isaiah are given further import in Luke 4. At this point in the Gospel, Christ declares these words to have been fulfilled in his ministry. When considering this passage, Ruether directs the reader's attention to the way in which Christ's ministry is directed at Gentiles as well as Jews, thus fulfilling the promise of Isaiah's words. Reading those words today, she says, a further dynamic can be explored. We live in a post-Holocaust world. This means that it is important to apply this message of God's love for all—Jew and Gentile—in a way that combats all oppressive views of human beings; and that includes anti-semitism. Her concern to offer a contemporary theology is thus very much to the fore. It is not just a case of analysing biblical texts. The implications of this analysis must be applied to contemporary theological discourse.

Ultimately, Ruether's concern is to discern those elements within Scripture which support her account of Christianity as liberating, as fundamentally concerned with social justice. For Ruether, there is a correlation between the texts, how they have been experienced and how we experience them now. And this way of considering the Bible is, she believes, present within certain parts of Scripture. In this sense she is saying that feminist theology is not doing something unprecedented. Rather, its adoption of a 'prophetic critique' can be traced to the biblical texts themselves. Indeed, feminist theology can be seen as rediscovering a lost part of the tradition: the prophetic critique.

A critic might ask to what extent the biblical writings can be separated from the way in which these texts have traditionally been read. As Ruether points out, Scripture has been used throughout the history of the Christian tradition to support patriarchy. One gets the feeling, however, that she has failed to address the question of the extent to which the hermeneutical circle merely perpetuates patriarchy.

Like Schüssler Fiorenza, Ruether explicitly applies an ethical *a priori* stance to the biblical material. She believes that critical consideration of the biblical texts reveals a 'golden thread' running through the Scripture. This 'golden thread' expresses the message of the prophetic critique—that God is liberator, not oppressor and that belief in the full humanity of women is a logical conclusion from this understanding of God. At the same time, Ruether's approach to Scripture is somewhat different from Schüssler Fiorenza's. Ruether approaches the Bible as a resource for developing a feminist theology. She is not, first and foremost, a biblical scholar. Her concern is with the living Christian tradition, and the development of a theology which takes account of feminist concerns.

3. *Feminist Exegesis in Practice: Galatians 3.28*

a. *Schüssler Fiorenza: Textual Analysis of Scripture*
Schüssler Fiorenza's hermeneutic concentrates on textual analysis. This involves not only consideration of the content of a text (i.e. what it says) but also an appreciation of how that text coheres with the historical context which gave rise to those ideas in the first place.

In Gal. 3.28, Paul describes the radical new state of human relations brought about by the redemptive work of Christ: 'There is no longer Jew or Greek, there is no longer slave or free, there is no longer male and female; for all of you are one in Christ Jesus (NRSV)'. When working on the meaning and interpretation of this text, Schüssler Fiorenza adopts what could be called a 'two-pronged' approach. She considers this text alongside other documents from the same period, whilst also observing its connection with other Pauline passages. The aim of feminist exegesis is to establish the meaning of this passage. Is Paul offering a radical political reappraisal of human relationships which rejects the hierarchical structure inherent in patriarchy? Alternatively, is he talking of spiritual liberation? In other words, he is claiming that all are free and equal in a spiritual sense. This 'spiritual' interpretation of the freedom of Christ is not, however, to be applied to the hierarchies which structure human life and society—including the structures of the Church.

Schüssler Fiorenza begins by considering how these words relate to the wider historical context of the early Christian world. She believes that the content of the verse can be paralleled with actual events of the time. By approaching the passage in this way, a radical interpretation of this text can be admitted. Citing a letter from Pliny to the Emperor Trajan in the early second century CE, she notes that women 'servants' (or slaves?) were ministers in the church of Bithynia.[23] This suggests that Christians of the time truly believed that they had been 'set free' by Christ—and that this freedom affected the social structures which ordered human relations. Being set free had concrete implications; it was not primarily understood in some ethereal, otherworldly sense. Rather,

23. Schüssler Fiorenza, *In Memory of Her*, p. 204.

the freedom of Christ challenged the hierarchical structuring of human relationships.

Schüssler Fiorenza begins, then, by setting these words from Galatians in their historical context. These ideas, she believes, arose from first-century debates surrounding the effect of Christ's salvific act on human relations. Such debates arose in a culture where biological assumptions were made concerning the nature of cultural, racial and social differences. For the early Christians, these assumptions were challenged by the liberating act of Christ. To first-century Christians, all such distinctions were considered insignificant, an idea which is supported by contemporary reports of the way in which those Christians behaved.

Likewise, the meaning of these words can be clarified by considering them in relation to other Pauline texts. Paul's discussion of what made one a Christian reveals a similar sense of the way in which Christ's message liberated men and women from hierarchical social roles. Paul's discussion of circumcision mirrors the kind of ideas which can be discerned in Gal. 3.28. Paul states that baptism is the mark of the believer. As such, circumcision is no longer necessary for expressing the belief that one is a 'son of God'.[24] This, obviously, has direct implications for the status of women within Christianity. Women, unlike men, cannot be circumcised.[25] But women, like men, can be baptized. The freedom offered by Christ means that all—regardless of gender, nationality or social standing—can be sons and daughters of God.

In terms of a feminist approach to Scripture, this could be seen as the positive side of the coin. Less positive might be an exploration of Pauline texts that leave the door open for a patriarchal interpretation. Indeed, Schüssler Fiorenza does not shrink from recognizing this. In particular, she considers the kind of passages within the Pauline epistles which seek to restrict the freedoms enjoyed by Christian women of the time. 1 Cor. 11.2-16 addresses the question of how women should wear their hair. The attempt to control women by dictating how they should behave and in particular how they should dress seems much in evidence here. The attempt to control women by dictating modes of dress is traceable throughout the history of the Christian tradition. Tertullian, in particular, wrote a long treatise on the apparel of women.[26] Schüssler Fiorenza

24. See Paul's discussion of 'spiritual circumcision' in Rom. 2.25-29.
25. It is important to recognize that female circumcision is not the same as male circumcision, involving as it does mutilation of the sexual organs.
26. Tertullian, 'On Female Dress', in *The Writings of Tertullian*, I (trans.

seeks to show that this Pauline passage has to be understood in its socio-cultural context. To wear one's hair loose at the time was suggestive of two lifestyles. One might be identified as a member of one of the ecstasy cults common at the time. Alternatively, loose hair was associated with uncleanness. Thus, Schüssler Fiorenza argues, Paul's concern here is not with restricting women's freedom, but with avoiding any misunderstanding about the kind of religion and lifestyle practised by the Christians.

But does such an interpretation ultimately escape the problems identified by feminists when approaching the Bible? At heart, the problem seems to be the way in which the biblical sources have been read—and particularly the way in which cultural attitudes to women have been both read into the text and formed by its contents. It is by no means clear that Schüssler Fiorenza's approach escapes these fundamental difficulties.

Summary. Schüssler Fiorenza's approach focuses on analysis of the text. To do this effectively, she considers the content of the text, its relation to other biblical texts, and how it relates to the general historical context. But to what extent does her method enable Christian feminists to challenge the post-Christian stance of radical feminists like Daly?

Schüssler Fiorenza does attempt to give a voice to the silenced women of the Christian tradition. In her attempt to do this, she places the Christian message in its historical context. She accepts that this context was defined by patriarchy, and this leads her to recognize the ambiguous nature of Scripture. Scripture can be used either to support patriarchy or to attack it. Much, however, is dependent upon the ideas that one brings to the text, and which one subsequently reads out of the text. In other words, one's initial ethical stance will influence one's reading of Scripture. Schüssler Fiorenza seems to accept that this is the case. Her method is, of necessity, dictated by her feminist concern for liberation. Thus she writes that 'a feminist critical theology of liberation must...be particular and concrete'.[27] This is fine for Schüssler Fiorenza—she wants to say that no hermeneutical method is ever objective. However, does this evade the real issue—that is, the way in which the Christian Scriptures have been used and still are used to oppress women? If I approach the text with a belief that male supremacy is

S. Thelwall; Edinburgh: T. & T. Clark, 1869).
    27. Schüssler Fiorenza, 'The Will to Choose or to Reject', p. 128.

divinely ordained, will I be challenged by the passages within Scripture that Schüssler Fiorenza would claim reject such a view?

Schüssler Fiorenza is critical of the methods of theologians such as Letty Russell, Rosemary Radford Ruether and Phyllis Trible—yet does her own work escape the criticisms she makes of these writers? She claims that these theologians fail to face up to the patriarchal nature of the Christian texts by concentrating on finding universal, timeless truths which then provide a critique of patriarchy.[28] Whilst Schüssler Fiorenza does not approach the text with a view to finding some kind of universal truth within it, it is not self-evident that her method addresses any more definitively the criticisms of the post-Christians. Remember, Daly claims that 'the medium is the message'. In other words, the patriarchal formulation of the Bible means that ideas of male domination will be communicated through the text. No amount of feminist reconstruction of the Christian story will change this. Schüssler Fiorenza offers a convincing account of how a feminist might survive her encounter with Scripture, but it is not clear that the central issue of the way in which the text both supports and is shaped by patriarchy is adequately addressed in her writings.

b. *Ruether: Scripture as a Resource for Feminist Theology*
Ruether's approach to Scripture, while mirroring Schüssler Fiorenza's concern with the primacy of one's feminist commitment, is less concerned with providing an analysis of the text which also places it within its historical context. Her concern is to show how Scripture can be used as a resource for Christian theology. It is this concern with the living Christian religion which forms the focus for her hermeneutic. It is particularly important that she should be able to show how Scripture can be used as a resource for feminist theology, as she wishes to combat the anti-Christian sentiments of writers like Daly and Hampson. At the same time, she wants to question the validity of alternative feminist spiritualities which suggest that women should return to the Goddess.[29] Ruether feels that adopting these pre-Christian religious traditions does not help feminists combat male domination. All religions are to some extent shaped by patriarchy—and that includes ideas of the Goddess.[30]

28. Schüssler Fiorenza, *In Memory of Her*, p. 27.
29. Cf. C. Christ, 'Why Women Need the Goddess', in Christ and Plaskow (eds.), *Womanspirit Rising*, pp. 273-87.
30. Ruether could be challenged here. Her criticism is only valid if one needs to

Ruether goes on to claim that the New Testament can be shown to offer an understanding of God which radically challenges hierarchical notions of divinity and humanity. By applying Ruether's hermeneutic to Gal. 3.28, it is possible to see how her theological approach attempts to show this, whilst also differing from Schüssler Fiorenza's biblical analysis.

Initially, Ruether claims that any verse must be read alongside those elements of New Testament theology which reflect the biblical critique of hierarchy. Thus, when approached in this way, Gal. 3.28 offers a liberating vision of human relations. The radical reappraisal of human structures offered in this verse is necessary if one is to take seriously the incarnation as the process by which God becomes flesh. This reading coheres with her development of a radically non-hierarchical God, which she grounds in the revelation of Christ. She reads Gal. 3.28 as offering 'a vision of a new social order in which all the relations of sex, race, and class of divisiveness will be overcome in Christ'.[31] These words offer an alternative vision of the future, a future where human relations are not formed according to the dictates of patriarchy. And it is commitment to this future which ties the Christian message to the feminist commitment to social justice. There is common ground between the biblical tradition and feminist theology.

Thus, when Ruether turns her attention to Gal. 3.28 her method of correlation is illustrated to clear effect. Her reading of Galatians is such that there is a direct correlation between her feminist critical principle and the 'biblical critical principle'. It is here that the main difference between Ruether and Schüssler Fiorenza should be noted. Ruether's approach to biblical exegesis is less analytical than Schüssler Fiorenza's. Schüssler Fiorenza considers the placing of the text, different possible meanings, and the overall context, whilst Ruether's reading is more directly linked to showing that Scripture can and does support a feminist concern with social justice. In this sense, Ruether, to a greater extent than Schüssler Fiorenza, could be accused of selectivity in her use of Scripture. Yes, Galatians 3 fits well with her feminist concerns, but would 1 Tim. 2.11 where Paul writes that women should be silent in church?

Ruether does not accept this criticism. Indeed, like Schüssler Fiorenza, she accepts that the Bible must be judged according to certain ethical *a priori* concerns. We need to decide which elements of the Bible speak to

ground one's ideas in tradition and Scripture. Carol Christ's work suggests that this need not be the case.

31. Ruether, *Sexism and God-Talk*, p. 26.

our contemporary experience and which do not. We need to show discernment in our use of Scripture. So when she writes of the way in which symbols cease to have meaning, she could also be commenting on her own hermeneutic. Just as any religious symbol must be judged according to its relevance for contemporary people, so any biblical passage must be held alongside women's experience: 'If the symbol does not speak authentically to experience, it becomes dead and is discarded or altered to provide new meaning'.[32] If some biblical passages no longer speak to the current situation, they are to be discarded. When approaching Scripture, Ruether is going to have first and foremost in her mind her yardstick of what is good—that which affirms the full humanity of women. It is for this reason that her approach has been termed a 'golden thread' approach. Ruether identifies a central ethical concern and seeks to show the way in which this concern can be discerned in key biblical texts. In effect, she is deciding which biblical passages are to be given priority. For example, Galatians, a text which affirms the full humanity of woman, is deemed 'good', whilst 1 Corinthians 11, with its restrictive ideas on woman's appearance, is not.

Summary. Ruether's concern with the biblical text is to provide a tool for feminist theology. As such, she is confident with a reductionist approach to Scripture—after all, don't all theologians to some extent pick and choose from the biblical material? Her 'golden thread' approach enables her to discern a strand in the Bible which supports her fundamental concern with advocating the equality and freedom of women. Yet has she, any more than Schüssler Fiorenza, addressed the problems raised by post-Christian feminists? Can the Bible ever escape the consequences of the patriarchal context against which it was formed?

4. *Conclusion*

a. *How Texts are Read*
Both Schüssler Fiorenza and Ruether draw attention to the way in which the Bible has been used to oppress women. In order to show how feminists can survive an encounter with Scripture, they offer an alternative reading of the Bible which supports the feminist concern with liberation. Feminists are often challenged precisely on this point. Should

---

32. Ruether, 'Feminist Interpretation: A Method of Correlation', p. 111.

alternative readings of biblical texts be offered? Non-feminist critics often accuse feminist exegetes of undermining the intrinsic authority of the text. By challenging the authority of certain (patriarchal) passages, the authority of the whole Scripture appears to be challenged. Feminist critics, on the other hand, attack the kind of hermeneutic offered by Ruether and Schüssler Fiorenza by claiming that the Bible cannot be read other than as a history of patriarchal oppression. As such, it should be rejected.

It may be appropriate at this point to consider the process by which texts are read.[33] Reading a text is never a simple matter. All readers bring their own baggage to the text that they are reading. Consequently, reading involves something like a 'snowball' effect. Not only do the ideas encountered in a text influence the reader's ideas, but the reader's own ideas shape the way in which the ideas put forward in the text are interpreted. The reader's ideas are not only influenced by the text; they also influence an understanding of the text. So, if I envisage God as a warrior, oppressive and judgmental, the Bible may well help to construct that image, but it will also be read with that image in my mind. As a consequence, the text not only informs my concept of God. The initial ideas I have of God mean that the text is interpreted in the light of those ideas.

When the Bible is read, a further element is discernible. Commentators and their readings of the text will also influence the way in which the biblical material is interpreted. This is particularly the case when one considers the way in which different translations offer different perspectives on the original text. So, the New Revised Standard Version of the Bible with its emphasis on inclusive language will tend towards a 'liberal' reading of the text. The Good News Bible, by way of contrast, will offer a reading of the original sources which is consistent with its 'evangelical' stance.

When one considers the way in which texts are read, it becomes evident that the primary criticism of selectivity against the feminist hermeneutic is without force. Feminists are not alone in bringing their own ideas and beliefs to the biblical material. All reading is like this.

Yet the patriarchal nature of the biblical texts still needs to be addressed. Not only do readers bring their own ideas to bear on the reading of texts, but our ideas are also influenced by the text. Schüssler

33. I wish to acknowledge the help and guidance of Robert Lindsey, Oriel College Oxford, in clarifying my ideas on this matter.

Fiorenza and Ruether offer convincing accounts of how a feminist might survive an encounter with Scripture. Yet it could be claimed that their hermeneutics still fail to address the issue of the way in which the Bible has been used historically to support patriarchy. Would feminists be better advised to escape the dangers of scriptural religion altogether?

b. *Feminist Spirituality*
Ruether herself considers the extent to which religion supports patriarchal notions of the supremacy of the male. At one point, she suggests that the influence of patriarchy is all-pervasive:

> In fact, the more one studies different religious traditions and their early roots, the more one is tempted to suggest that religion itself is essentially a male creation. Could it be that the male, marginalized from direct participation in the great mysteries of gestation and birth, asserted his superior physical strength to monopolize leisure and culture and that he did so by creating ritual expressions that duplicated female gestating and birthing roles so as to transfer power of these primary mysteries to the male?[34]

Religion, according to Ruether, can be viewed as something constructed by men, for men. Men, marginalized from the creative process of reproduction, needed a substitute, and found it in the creation of religious rituals of birth, rebirth and death. Ruether's comments challenge not only scriptural religion, but also non-scriptural religions, including those surrounding the Goddess. But it should be remembered that there is an added difficulty for the biblical tradition. The texts as we have them were written in a patriarchal period. These texts have been used historically to support the suppression of women, and still to this day can be used in this way. Yet Ruether is saying that *all* religious traditions as we understand them have to be questioned. If all religious expression is influenced by patriarchy, what are women to do? It might be argued that feminists need to take on board this idea and explore their spirituality in a totally different way, a way which is independent of established religious traditions. But is this way just as fraught with difficulties as attempting to interpret the Bible in a 'feminist-friendly' way? Will free spiritual expression merely descend into wishy-washy sentimentality? Ruether and Schüssler Fiorenza offer their own accounts of how feminists might survive Scripture. It is up to individual women, as they come into contact with the biblical texts, to decide the extent to which their

---

34. R. Ruether, 'Renewal or New Creation?', in S. Gunew (ed.), *Reader in Feminist Knowledge* (London: Routledge, 1991), p. 278.

hermeneutics offer a living possibility of feminist Christianity. Survival or escape? This is the issue facing women when they consider the adequacy of biblical hermeneutics.

INDEXES

INDEX OF REFERENCES

OLD TESTAMENT

NEW TESTAMENT